Y. BAR-HILLEL / ASPECTS OF LANGUAGE

ASPECTS OF LANGUAGE

ESSAYS AND LECTURES ON PHILOSOPHY OF LANGUAGE,
LINGUISTIC PHILOSOPHY AND METHODOLOGY
OF LINGUISTICS

BY

YEHOSHUA BAR-HILLEL

*Professor of Logic and Philosophy of Science
in the Hebrew University of Jerusalem*

1970

THE MAGNES PRESS · THE HEBREW UNIVERSITY · JERUSALEM
NORTH-HOLLAND PUBLISHING COMPANY – AMSTERDAM

Distributed (all countries outside Israel) by
North-Holland Publishing Company
P.O. Box 3489, Amsterdam, The Netherlands

Library of Congress Catalog Card Number 73-97195
ISBN 0 7204 6033 6

©

The Magnes Press, The Hebrew University
Jerusalem 1970

Printed in Israel
at Central Press, Jerusalem

To Rudolf Carnap

CONTENTS

INTRODUCTION

I. PHILOSOPHY OF LANGUAGE

1. Bolzano's Definition of Analytic Propositions — 3
2. Comments on Logical Form — 25
3. Mr. Geach on Rigour in Semantics — 29
4. Bolzano's Propositional Logic — 33
5. Indexical Expressions — 69
6. Husserl's Conception of a Purely Logical Grammar — 89
7. On Lalic Implication and the *Cogito* — 98
8. On Mr. Sørensen's Analysis of "To Be" and "To Be True" — 100
9. Critical Comments on the Introductory Papers on Logic, Language and Communication — 104
10. Can Indexical Sentences Stand in Logical Relations? — 112
11. Remarks on Carnap's *Logical Syntax of Language* — 116
12. Et Tu, Diodorus Cronus? — 143
13. Imperative Inference — 146
14. Review of *The Structure of Language* — 150
15. Universal Semantics and Philosophy of Language: Quandaries and Prospects — 182
16. Argumentation in Natural Languages — 202
17. Argumentation in Pragmatic Languages — 206
18. Review of Theodore Drange's *Type Crossings* — 222

II. LINGUISTIC PHILOSOPHY

19. Analysis of "Correct" Language — 231
20. The Revival of "The Liar" — 244
21. New Light on The Liar — 253
22. A Prerequisite for Rational Philosophical Discussion — 258
23. Neorealism *vs.* Neopositivism: A Neo-Pseudo Issue — 263
24. Do Natural Languages Contain Paradoxes? — 273

III. METHODOLOGY OF LINGUISTICS

25.	Cybernetics and Linguistics	289
26.	On Recursive Definitions in Empirical Sciences	302
27.	Some Linguistic Problems Connected with Machine Translation	308
28.	Three Methodological Remarks on *Fundamentals of Language*	317
29.	Decision Procedures for Structure in Natural Languages	329
30.	On a Misapprehension of the Status of Theories in Linguistics	340
31.	Dictionaries and Meaning Rules	347
32.	A Neglected Recent Trend in Logic	354
33.	The Outlook for Computational Semantics	357
34.	Review of John Lyons' *Introduction to Theoretical Linguistics*	364

Notes on the Publicational History of the Different Essays   375

INTRODUCTION

This collection of essays and lectures covers similar though not just the same ground as a previous collection, *Language and Information* (Addison–Wesley Publishing Company, Reading/Palo Alto/London, 1964). While language is the main theme of both books, the earlier collection took a technical approach, treating on the one hand the highly theoretical subjects of algebraic linguistics and semantic information, and on the other hand applications to machine translation and mechanized information retrieval.

Most of the essays and lectures collected in the present volume were written in a more "philosophical" vein. Some deal with various topics from the *philosophy of language*; others take up issues from what should perhaps be called the *logic of natural languages*, including contributions made to this field by philosophers such as Bolzano and Husserl, whose importance for some of today's burning questions has not been sufficiently realized. Other topics discussed are better classified under *linguistic philosophy*, i.e., those recent brands of philosophy which for the first time in history ceased to take it for granted that philosophy, like science, politics, ethics or aesthetics, is usually formulated in natural language. Critical scrutiny of this fundamental fact has led different linguistic philosophers to diverse and even opposing conclusions. The *linguistic naturalists* regard ordinary speech as by and large sacrosanct, in order as it is, and see in often unnoticed deviations from it the perhaps most potent source of philosophical pseudo-problems. The *linguistic constructionists*, on the other hand, tend to believe that natural languages have so many faults that it is rather the adherence to ordinary speech which creates these pseudo-problems. The most promising way of avoiding them is seen in the construction of artificial language systems in which science can be expressed. It is a recurrent theme of some of my later essays to point out that these views are complementary rather than incompatible. Both views suffer from a myopia stemming from the underdeveloped state of linguistic theory. The resulting gap almost by necessity encouraged a speculative rather than a scientific treatment of the philosophy of language. I regard myself as being engaged in a kind of crusade to persuade anybody who is ready to listen that an adequate understanding of the nature of natural language, that all-pervasive tool of human culture, demands a synthesis of the various brands of linguistic philosophy, based on a scientifically adequate conception of language. A better understanding of language should help us in achieving not only a better grasp of our physical environment but also a better comprehension of the human world and, last but not least, of ourselves.

I think I owe the reader an apology. He will doubtless quickly realize, perhaps already from the titles of the essays, that a number of topics have been treated over and over again. From a careful reading of the essays themselves, he will, in addition also, perhaps to his annoyance, realize that the treatment of the topics has sometimes undergone serious changes from essay to essay, up to a total of four or five. I can only hope that he will agree with me that the changes in my conceptions were not wanton but express a developing understanding of the issues concerned and perhaps he will forgive my obtuseness in not having been able to see the light at once. In fact, it might help if I confess right off that I am not at all sure that I shall stick to my latest attempt in each case. For instance, I am by no means certain that my latest treatment of the Liar Paradox in Chapter 24, after three previous attempts in Chapters 5, 19, and 20, will be my last and, in this connection, that I shall remain satisfied with my latest terminological proposals as to the sentence — statement — utterance (— proposition — judgment — assertion) muddle. I would not, of course, have dared to tax the reader's patience to such a degree, had it not been my serious feeling that my failures were not a purely personal affair and that they might therefore yield some more generally useful lessons.

In the Introduction to *Language and Information*, I told enough of my intellectual autobiography to cover the present book, too. Let me only quote here a part of one sentence close to the end of that Introduction: "... equally strong was his [Chomsky's] influence on my philosophy of language, in particular as a kind of counterbalance to that of Carnap, though this might not show in the present volume." Well, in the present volume, it shows.

As a token of my gratitude to Rudolf Carnap for the boundless inspiration I received from reading his publications and from talking to him in person, alas, on far too rare occasions, an inspiration without which probably not a single essay in this collection could have been written at all, and certainly not in the form it was written — I dedicate this book to him.

PHILOSOPHY OF LANGUAGE

BOLZANO'S DEFINITION OF ANALYTIC PROPOSITIONS

In view of recent discussions on the nature of analytic truth, it should be interesting to inquire into the treatment which this subject received by the most outstanding logician of the first half of the 19th century, the Czech philosopher, theologian, and physicist Bernard *Bolzano*.

Our investigation will turn upon section 148 of Bolzano's four-volume masterwork, *Wissenschaftslehre* (1837). Only occasionally shall we need to refer to other parts of this work. This section, headed "Analytic or Synthetic Propositions", comprises pages 83–89 of the second volume and is divided into three subsections of less than two pages altogether, followed by four annotations, filling the next five pages. I dwell so long upon these bibliographical particulars only to bring into full light the wealth of systematic and historic material contained in these few pages.

1. *Pre-History*

Bolzano's aim, in §148, was to define a concept which could serve as an adequate explication for what is now commonly termed 'logical truth'. Though this aim is nowhere explicitly stated, there can be no doubt about it, just as *Kant* before him and many logicians after him doubtless aimed at the same target when they proposed their respective definitions.

Bolzano devotes the greater part of his fourth annotation to the discussion of many such attempts made by his predecessors and contemporaries. He mentions *Aristotle*, *Locke*, *Crusius* (the German logician of the first half of the 18th century who was probably the first to use the terms 'analytic' and 'synthetic' in their Kantian senses), *Kant* and many other minor philosophers. He easily succeeds in proving the inadequacy of Kant's two definitions for 'analytic', the one given in his *Logik* and equating, in effect, Analytic[1] with Identical, the other

---

[1] Whenever suitable, I shall follow Carnap in using the method of *capitalizing* to avoid, as far as possible, collisions with customary English grammar without relying on the palliative of double quotation marks. Sometimes, however, the latter method will be used, especially after 'proposition' — in this case the quotes will not quote at all. In our case, I write 'Analytic' instead of 'the property of being analytic'. Compare R. CARNAP, *Meaning and Necessity*, 1947, p. 17 note 10 and p. 27 note 15. This book will in future be referred to as 'MN'.

much better known in the introduction to the Critique of Pure Reason, where he proposes to call propositions 'analytic', whose predicate-concept is contained (perhaps in a hidden manner) in the subject-notion. Bolzano points out (p. 87) the vagueness of the term 'contained' and argues that, according to a quite natural interpretation of this term, the proposition "The father of Alexander, King of Macedonia, was King of Macedonia" ought to be analytic, a consequence which Kant certainly did not intend to be drawn.

But to even more refined versions of Kant's definition, given by some of his followers, replacing the vague 'contained' by more precise terms, such as those making use of 'essential characteristics', Bolzano objects that only one type of proposition conforms to them, namely 'A (which is B) is B'. But should not, continues Bolzano, also propositions of the type 'Every object is either B or non-B' be counted among the analytic propositions?

Having thus convinced himself of the inadequacy of all prior approaches he started to attack the subject along a new and highly original line.

2. *Terminological Remarks*

We must, first of all, acquaint ourselves with Bolzano's terminology to a degree sufficient for our purpose. Incidentally, these preliminary steps are of more than historical importance, as we shall see immediately.

Let it therefore be noted that Bolzano uses the term *'proposition'* ['Satz an sich'] as that which is expressed by a sentence, which is merely a linguistic expression [ein sprachlicher Ausdruck] of a proposition. This distinction, now familiar to everyone, was probably drawn, in such concise and explicit terms, for the first time by Bolzano himself. (For those interested in ontological aspects, let it be added that Bolzano denies often and strongly any kind of existence, being, or actuality to propositions — in contradistinction to sentences and judgments.)

Propositions are composed of *concepts* [Vorstellungen an sich] which are as objective as the propositions themselves and must be distinguished (a) from their linguistic expressions, (b) from the thoughts of them, and (c) from their objects [Gegenstände], if they have such objects at all. Every constituent of a simple proposition is a concept; in the proposition "Titus is idle", the *singular concept*[2] [Einzelvorstellung] Titus is the

---

[2] It seems to me that this term corresponds almost exactly to the term 'individual concept', invented by either *Church* or *Carnap* or both of them independently. W. V. QUINE in "The Problem of Interpreting Modal Logic" (PIML), The Journal of Symbolic Logic, vol. 12 (1947), pp. 41–48, refers to 'individual concepts' as "Church's

subject-concept, Idle the predicate-concept, and Is the Copula (concept). (Incidentally, Bolzano develops at length a curious theory that not forms of 'to be' but of 'to have' are to be regarded as the copulas of the standard forms of propositions. Happily enough, this theory plays almost no part in our restricted domain of interest, so that we may disregard it, without thereby distorting Bolzano's intentions.)

Let us coin the word 'objectal' to render Bolzano's 'gegenständlich' ('objective' is obviously not suited). Some concepts are objectal, some, such as Round Square or Golden Mountain, are not.

3. *Universally Valid*

In his search for an adequate explication of 'logically true', Bolzano was led by the old idea of the formality of logic, its independence of content. It is one of Bolzano's greatest achievements that he succeeded in giving this vague idea an exact and testable formulation.

He started with the improved version of Kant's definition. Sure enough, he had exhibited the inadequacy of this definition, but as far as it went, it worked. "A which is B is B" was a logical truth, though not the only form of it. But why was it a logical truth? Because, said Bolzano, the concept B ('B' is a constant of undetermined meaning; there are no variables in Bolzano's logic, probably because there are no variables in ordinary language, but with the help of his specially invented method

---

phrase" (p. 47). Carnap, on the other hand, in MN, p. 39 and p. 41, speaks of 'individual concept' as a term coined by himself for a concept of a new kind.

It is perhaps interesting, in this connection, to note that in Bolzano's theory there is indeed "corresponding to each concrete object, a multitude of distinguishable entities" (PIML, p. 47), namely, interchangeable concepts of equal extension [Wechselvorstellungen von einerlei Umfang], though Bolzano does not accept, of course, the other side of the "queer ontological consequences" to deny the existence of material objects.

But these entities are not "objects". The distinctions which made *Meinong*, the *Russell* of *The Principles of Mathematics*, and C. I. *Lewis* populate the universe with different kinds of objects, actual, possible, and impossible ones, are made by Bolzano without recourse to such dubious modes of speech, which would considerably complicate ordinary language (to leave alone ontological considerations) by distinguishing between concepts which are objectal (compare the end of this section) and those which are not, a distinction drawn by Carnap for exactly the same purpose in his lengthy discussion of this subject in MN, §36. Carnap's terms are 'not empty' for 'objectal' and 'empty' for 'not objectal'. Carnap draws furthermore the important distinction between 'F-empty' and 'L-empty', whereas Bolzano does not distinguish between the corresponding two kinds of non-objectality, exemplified by Golden Mountain and Round Square.

of Variation of Concepts, Bolzano successfully overcomes this handicap) occurred in it *vacuously*. He did not use these words, of course. But in this convenient form, due to *Quine*, we may render what Bolzano formulated as "because the concept B may be varied at will without thereby disturbing the truth of the proposition" (p. 83). This vacuous occurrence of a concept embodies the content-independence of the proposition, ensures its formal character, so that if the proposition is true at all, it is so formally, logically.

Generalizing, Bolzano defines 'universally valid' and 'universally contravalid' as follows (in a slightly modernized and rigorized form):

The proposition p is called *universally valid (universally contravalid) with respect to the class of concepts A* if and only if the propositions which may be developed from p by varying at will every occurrence of the elements of A in p (provided that all the occurrences of the same concept are replaced by occurrences of the same other concept and provided that the resulting propositions are objectal) are all of them true (false) (§147, p. 82).

If p is universally valid with respect to A, then every element of A occurs in p vacuously, and the truth of p is therefore independent of the content of these concepts. Were it not for the fact that Universally Valid was a relative concept, so that one and the same proposition might at the same time be universally valid with respect to A but not with respect to some different B, this concept would already have been Bolzano's choice for an explication of Logically True, and Universally Contravalid analogously for Logically False.

4. *Bolzano's Definition of 'Analytic'*

To remove the relativity of Universally Valid and thereby reach the desired aim, two natural ways lay open to Bolzano: He could have used either what we could call today general or existential quantification, that is, he could have defined a proposition as *analytic* — though rejecting Kant's definition of this term, he still stuck to it as the term which should serve as the explicator[3] of 'logically true' — either as a proposition *all* of whose concepts occurred vacuously in it, or as a proposition *at least one* of whose concepts occurred vacuously in it. The first possibility seems to us more promising and so it must have appeared to Bolzano. But — it did not work, "because, were we allowed

---

[3] Coined along the line of Carnap's 'designator' and 'predicator'. See MN, p. 6 note 6.

to vary at will all constituent concepts of a proposition, we could change it into any other proposition whatever, hence obtain from it true as well as false propositions" (p. 83). This argument contains a curious error, of which I know no explanation, considering Bolzano's exceptional logical skill and insight; we can *not* obtain any proposition whatever from any other proposition, even if we are allowed to vary *all* its concepts — we cannot, e.g., obtain from the proposition "2 = 2" the proposition "2 = 3", as the reader will easily verify. In spite of this error, Bolzano's argument remains substantially in force, since we can still obtain from clearly logical truths equally clearly logical falsehoods by this method — we might obtain from "2 = 2" the proposition "2 ≠ 2".

Bolzano is therefore obliged to choose the other way. His definition, in effect:

> p is *analytic* = $_{Df}$ at least one[4] constituent concept of p occurs in p vacuously.

Before going on to discuss this definition, let us note that Bolzano uses 'analytic' as a generic term comprising both 'analytically true' and 'analytically false'. It is well known that a term corresponding to Bolzano's 'analytically false' was lacking in Kant's terminology, and that therefore Kant's classification of propositions into analytic and synthetic ones was by no means exhaustive. This failure was avoided by Bolzano. *Dubislav* returned, some 90 years later, to Bolzano's proposal[5] and it has been accepted, in effect, in Carnap's recent terminology, where 'analytic' and 'contradictory' have been replaced by 'L-true' and 'L-false'.

'Synthetic' is defined then as 'not analytic', and these two terms, in Bolzano's usage, therefore exhaust the possibilities.

---

[4] *Smart*, in his otherwise well-written paper on "Bolzano's Logic" (*The Philosophical Review*, vol. 53 (1944), pp. 513-533) makes a mistake in the translation of the relevant passage which completely distorts its meaning. He translates Bolzano's "...auch nur eine einzige..." by "...only one..." instead of "...at least one...", apparently overlooking the word "auch".

[5] In *Über die sogenannten analytischen und synthetischen Urteile*, 1926. This book is not at my disposal, and I am referring to it through Carnap's terminological remarks at the end of § 14 of *The Logical Syntax of Language*, 1937. I do not know, therefore, whether Dubislav reached this proposal independently or under the influence of Bolzano. Since Dubislav knew the works of Bolzano well, I guess that the second alternative is the correct one.

5. *Quasi-Analytic Sentences*

Is now everything in order? Bolzano himself is not yet satisfied. In his first annotation (p. 84), he remarks that there are sentences which express analytic propositions without seeming to do so. "One would not recognize at once that the proposition 'Every effect has its cause' is... analytic, which it really is." This can be readily seen as soon as we replace in its given linguistic expression the word 'effect' by the synonymous (L-equivalent)[6] expression 'thing which has a cause', thereby transforming the sentence 'Every effect has its cause' into 'Every thing which has a cause has its cause', which exhibits the analyticity of the proposition expressed by both sentences.

With Bolzano, Analytic is a characteristic of propositions, hence a non-semiotical[7] concept, but Bolzano is not fully consistent, and we were already obliged, in the preceding passage, to change his own wording somewhat so as to avoid open inconsistencies. For the same purpose, we shall now introduce a semantic predicate applying to sentences and corresponding to the "objective" predicate 'analytic' which applies to propositions. Let us therefore call a sentence *analytic* if it expresses an analytic proposition and renders all occurrences of the same concept in the proposition by occurrences of the same expression in the sentence, but let us call a sentence *quasi-analytic* if it expresses an analytic proposition but does not render all occurrences of the same concept by occurrences of the same expression — where two concepts are "the same concept" if their expressions are L-equivalent, though not necessarily *intensionally isomorphic*,[8] and two expressions are "the same expression", if every occurrence of the one is an occurrence of the other, and vice versa.

We can now say that the purpose of Bolzano's remark mentioned at the head of this section was to draw attention to the occurrence of quasi-analytic sentences, surely an important point; as a matter of fact, in Quine's usage, the class of analytic sentences is broader than that

---

[6] 'synonymous' is Quine's term and meant here in the sense used by him in the third passage of p. 44 in PIML; 'L-equivalent' is Carnap's term, extended by him in MN, p. 14 to hold for all kinds of designators.

[7] Analytic, as a characteristic of propositions, belongs to the non-semiotical, objective part of the metalanguage in question, it is an "absolute" concept in the terminology of CARNAP's *Introduction to Semantics* (IS), 1942, which has been abandoned in MN, since it was likely to arouse metaphysical associations; see MN, p. 25 note 12. Bolzano, of course, uses 'analytic' in this objective sense quite naively.

[8] I.e., built up out of an equal number of L-equivalent smallest sub-designators, cf. MN, §14.

of what he calls logical truths — the equivalent of *our* analytic sentences (the equivalence is not exact, see later, §7) — by containing, in addition, what we termed just now quasi-analytic sentences.[9]

Quine considers the possibility of assimilating the quasi-analytic sentences to properly analytic sentences — I am now returning to Bolzano's implemented terminology — by reducing all terms to primitive ones. But he rejects this possibility, and rightly so, since the assumption of the existence of a standard set of extra-logical primitives in a *real* (which I take to be synonymous with 'natural') language is wholly fictitious. Bolzano, on the other hand, makes exactly this assumption, and we might therefore ask why he did not choose this way of taking account of the quasi-analytic sentences, instead of the more complicated one with the help of L-equivalent expressions, and this the more so as the method of elimination of defined expressions is superior to the method of replacement by synonyms in being *effective*, since the "reduced" form of every sentence can be reached in a finite and definite number of steps. The answer is probably that Bolzano was well aware of the theoretical character of his assumption of the existence of primitive concepts — necessitated by certain philosophical considerations — and did not wish to bind his theory of analytic propositions to this impractical assumption.

One should, in addition, realize that not only is the method of elimination inferior to that of replacement, with respect to real languages, but it is so also for most kinds of artificial language systems, a fact overlooked, or at least not sufficiently stressed, by Quine. Let us suppose, following an example given by Carnap,[10] that the rules of designation of a certain semantic system state that both the primitive symbols 'a' and 'b' designate Chicago. Then the sentence 'a = b' is quasi-analytic, but the method of elimination is not forceful enough to show this. More generally, whenever logical relations hold between the designata of the primitive descriptive signs of a semantic system, the method of elimination is not sufficient to reveal the quasi-analyticity of many sentences. With respect to such a system, quasi-analyticity has to be defined with the help of replacement by synonyms, in spite of the non-effective character of this method.

This non-effectiveness is strikingly illustrated by Bolzano himself. Though he stresses that "the recognition whether a proposition given

---

[9] See PIML, pp. 43-44.
[10] IS, p. 87.

in its linguistic expression is analytic or synthetic, often requires somewhat more than a superficial look at its words", he himself falls prey to the indefiniteness of the method involved. The proposition "The angle sum of a triangle is equal to two right angles" is considered by him as synthetic, though the sentence expressing it is really quasi-analytic, since it can be transformed, putting synonyms for synonyms, into 'The angle sum of a polygon with 3 sides is equal to (3–2) times two right angles', in which '3' occurs vacuously, according to a well known theorem of elementary geometry.

6. *Logically Analytic*

I am afraid that the last passage of the preceding section must have brought the reader's patience to an end. He must have become convinced of the almost ridiculous inadequacy of Bolzano's definition of 'analytic'. If it follows from this definition that the proposition expressed by 'The angle sum of a polygon with 3 sides is equal to (3–2) times two right angles' is analytic, well, then that settles it. And it *does* follow. Bolzano himself gives immediately after his definition as an example of an analytic proposition "A morally bad man deserves no respect", the concept Man occurring vacuously in it!

A short passage in his fourth remark shows that Bolzano was aware of the deviation from current philosophical usage involved in his definition. He says: "...I allowed myself the previous definition, though I know that it makes the concept of analytic propositions somewhat broader than it is usually thought of; one does not normally count propositions like those cited in subsection 1 [the above-mentioned "moral" proposition and another similar one] among the analytic ones" (p. 88). We can only wonder about the lack of perspective which caused him to believe that his definition is only "somewhat broader", but even in this case, we must ask, what prevented him from looking for a more adequate definition?

Well, the answer to this question has already been given. Bolzano simply saw no other way. He strongly — and rightly — felt that analyticity has something to do with vacuous occurrence, but in view of the fact that the demand for vacuous occurrence of *all* constituent concepts of a proposition for its being analytic would be self-defeating, he just had no other choice.

It is hard to believe that Bolzano could acquiesce in this state of affairs. He must have thought about this subject over and over again and tried many ways to narrow down his definition to make it a reasonable explication of 'logically true'. But then it came over him, and in the short subsection 3, he embodied what is surely one of the most important and ingenious single logical achievements of all times. Let me add immediately that, for reasons which I shall explain in detail later on, I simply cannot believe that this subsection was composed at the same time as subsection 1 and the mentioned annotations. Let us therefore take for granted, for the time being, that this subsection was introduced by Bolzano at the very last moment, perhaps during the printing, so that he was no longer able to rewrite this section or perhaps the whole book.

Before reproducing this subsection in full, it has to be said that subsection 2 contains four examples of analytically true propositions, namely: A is A; A, which is B, is A; A, which is B, is B; Every object is either B or non-B.

Now we are ready:

The examples of analytic propositions, given just now in subsection 2, differ from those of subsection 1 in that for the recognition of the analytic nature of the former no other than logical knowledge is necessary, since the concepts, which form the invariable part of these propositions, belong all of them to logic; whereas for the recognition of the truth or falsity of the propositions of the kind of subsection 1 wholly different knowledge is required, since, in this case, extra-logical [der Logik fremde] concepts intrude. This distinction is rather unstable, as the domain of concepts which belong to logic is not determined so sharply that no controversies should ever arise about it. Nevertheless, it should sometimes prove to be profitable to take account of this distinction; and one might, therefore, call propositions of the kind mentioned in subsection 2 *logically* analytic or analytic in the *narrower* sense, those of subsection 1, on the other hand, analytic in the *broader* sense.

Bolzano has found the way out of his dilemma. Not all concepts must occur vacuously, this is too much. Neither at least one of them, this is far too little. For a proposition to be "logically analytic" — what an expression! — it is sufficient that *all extra-logical concepts* occur vacuously. Bolzano must have hesitated very much on the subject of delimitation between logical and extra-logical concepts (by the way, *Popper's* proposal to use 'formative'[11] instead of 'logical' has much to be said for it) — and which good logician in our times has not felt

---

[11] This proposal which coincides, incidentally, with that made by MORRIS in *Signs, Language, and Behaviour*, 1946 — Morris' term is 'formator' for 'formative sign' — appears in "New Foundations for Logic", Mind, vol. 56 (1947), pp. 193-235, especially p. 209 note 1.

the same?¹² —, but though he was not very happy about it, he finally saw that this was the only means to come to an adequate explication of 'logically true', and so he made, reluctantly and carefully, this last step.

Whether he was not so sure about the soundness of this distinction or whether, according to the hypothesis which we shall envisage immediately, he had not the time or opportunity, anyhow, he did not change his terminology in accordance with his new insight and preferred to coin the pleonastic term 'logically analytic' instead of renaming his old 'analytic' by, say, 'universally valid' (absolutely, not with respect to some class of concepts) and using 'analytic' in place of his unfortunate innovation.

Disregarding these terminological issues, important as they may be for the history of logic and the psychology of Bolzano, I think that we are fully entitled — and, I should say, morally obliged — to call the following definition of 'analytic'

Bolzano's definition of 'analytic proposition':

A proposition p is *analytic* $=_{df}$ all the descriptive constituent concepts of p occur in p vacuously.¹³

Let us add the corresponding definition of 'analytic sentence' which I personally would not hesitate to call once again

Bolzano's definition of 'analytic sentence':

A sentence s_1 is analytic $=_{df}$ there is a sentence s_2 which results from s_1 by replacing some (or all) descriptive expressions which form part of s_1 by L-equivalent expressions, such that all descriptive expressions which form part of s_2 occur in s_2 vacuously.

(This definition is, of course, relative to some language-system.¹⁴)

---

¹² POPPER, *ibid.*, p. 203 note 1, declares that he has removed the difficulties of distinguishing between these two kinds of signs, but refers for particulars to a paper which I have not yet seen.

¹³ QUINE, *Mathematical Logic* (ML), 1940, p. 2, writes "The logical truths, then, are describable as those truths in which only the basic particles alluded to earlier [the logical particles] occur essentially."

¹⁴ Quine's definition, PIML, p. 44, is: "...a statement is *analytic* if by putting synonyms for synonyms it can be turned into a logical truth", where 'logical truth' is defined on the preceding page in a different way from that in ML (cf. the preceding note), but the formulations may be easily shown to be L-equivalent, under certain suitable and obvious assumptions.

7. *A Conjecture on the Composition of the* Wissenschaftslehre

Even a superficial study of Bolzano's *Wissenschaftslehre* reveals that this book is full of misprints, mistakes, inconsistencies, etc., all obvious signs of insufficient revision. I have no way to inform myself of the history of its composition and printing and shall be grateful to anybody who will point out to me facts which will either confirm or disconfirm the conjecture I am going to make.

My conjecture is that the *Wissenschaftslehre* did not receive a final reading, for reasons unknown to me, so that several parts, written at different times, probably years apart, were embodied side by side, without the necessary adjustments. I conjecture, in particular, that subsection 3 of §148 was composed much later than the other parts of this section, so late indeed that its far-reaching consequences for the whole section, even for the whole Bolzanian logic, were not worked out. My reasons for this conjecture are:

1. It seems incredible to me that Bolzano could have written the annotation with "somewhat broader", mentioned above, *at the same time* at which he envisaged so clearly the difference between 'analytic in the wider sense' and 'analytic in the narrower sense'.

2. It seems hardly believable that Bolzano should have made use of such an inadequate terminology if the relevant concepts stood, *at the same time*, at his disposal. (The only other reasonable explanation, in the case of simultaneity, would be — as already mentioned — an extremely strong feeling of hesitation and uncertainty with regard to the distinctions drawn in subsection 3.)

3. Only once in the long annotations to §148 are the concepts defined in subsection 3 mentioned again, and — so far as I could find out — never at some other place.

Add to all this the general remarks made above on the bad revision of the whole book, the fact that the book had been edited by "some of his friends",[15] according to the title-page, and my conjecture gains some plausibility. It is quite possible that the existing literature on Bolzano's biography — which does not stand at my disposal — settles this question, but in case that not, I should think it a worthy task for somebody who has the necessary equipment to inquire into the composition of one of the most outstanding books in the history of logic, Bolzano's *Wissenschaftslehre*.

---

[15] It is known that Bolzano was the victim of persecutions by the Austrian government. It is quite possible that this fact had a certain influence on our issue.

8. *Frege's and Husserl's Definition of 'Analytic'*

Bolzano's definition made apparently no impression on his contemporaries and shared, thus, the fate of his other achievements in logic and mathematics. Even *Frege*, born in the very same year in which Bolzano died, who continued and brought to new life the Leibnizian attitude to logic, of which Bolzano was the only major exponent in the two centuries between *Leibniz* and Frege, did not rely on Bolzano when he framed his own definition of 'analytic' as 'what can be proved with the help of the universal laws of logic and definitions', a definition which is both vaguer and less general than that of Bolzano, since it makes essential use of the method of elimination, the shortcomings of which have already (§5) been discussed.

The definition given by Bolzano was much more congenial to *Husserl*. It is well known that interest in Bolzano was revived primarily by Husserl who estimated him highly and claimed him as a companion in his anti-psychologistic fight. Husserl used to quote Bolzano quite often, and it is therefore the more astonishing that he does not mention Bolzano explicity when he presents his own definition of 'analytic'.

I shall quote the relevant passage[16] rather freely and discontinuously, since I am utterly unable to understand certain parts of it or to translate others which I believe to have understood:

> *Analytically necessary propositions*, so we may define, are propositions the truth of which is completely independent of the specific descriptive nature of their Gegenständlichkeiten [!]...; hence propositions which may be *completely "formalized"* and described as special instances or empirical applications of the ... formal or analytic laws obtained by such a formalization. In an analytic proposition, it must be possible to replace every descriptive [sachhaltig] matter by the empty form *something*, keeping fully intact the logical form of the proposition ...

If we take the last quoted sentence as a definition, instead of having it as a consequence from the much more obscure original definition, we have an almost complete counterpart of what we called Bolzano's definition and an almost explicit mentioning of the "vacuous occurrence" playing the central role in it. The two occurrences of the word 'almost' in the previous sentence refer to the following shortcomings of Husserl's formulation: There is, normally, not *one* empty form *something* but several, one for each logical type, so that the replacement of descriptive terms by variables — this is most probably the meaning of Husserl's words — must keep the type and indicate, in addition,

---

[16] *Logische Untersuchungen*, II, 2nd ed., 1913, p. 255.

the connections existing between the replaced terms. It would evidently not do to replace 'Every white horse is a horse' by 'Every something something is a something' but only by something like 'Every something$_2$ something$_1$ is a something$_1$'. The second failure of Husserl is his disregard of what we called quasi-analytic sentences and the necessity of transforming a given sentence, prior to its "formalization", by the method of replacement by synonyms, at least in certain cases.

9. *Pseudo-Analytic Sentences*

We shall now deal with some points which, though not lying in the line of development of Bolzano's main idea, are still of sufficient interest for themselves.

As a kind of counterpart to what we called quasi-analytic sentences, Bolzano mentions the fact that there are sentences which look externally as if they expressed analytic propositions but, in fact, do not so. As an example of such "*pseudo-analytic*" sentences, as we might call them, Bolzano quotes a sentence which had already been characterized by Leibniz as "an identical sentence which is not without use", namely: 'Every learned man is a man'. Bolzano remarks that in so far as this sentence is not without use, it is not identical (analytic), since its real meaning is something like "Even a learned man is fallible", which is certainly not analytic. (Indeed? The last proposition *is* analytic, according to Bolzano's original definition, since the concept Learned appears in it vacuously! This is perhaps the reason why Bolzano omitted the word 'Mensch' in the transformed sentence and wrote the adjective 'gelehrter' with a capital 'G', thereby turning it into a substantive ['scholar']. The German original sentence is 'Auch ein gelehrter Mensch ist ein Mensch', the transformed sentence 'Auch ein Gelehrter ist noch fehlbar'. But even if Bolzano should have used this rather unfair trick to cover an obvious failure of his original definition, it would still be extremely unsatisfactory that "Auch ein Gelehrter ist fehlbar" should be synthetic and the proposition "Auch ein gelehrter Mensch ist fehlbar" analytic. But we have dealt enough with this question.)

Bolzano does not mention any method how to recognize the pseudo character of an apparently analytic sentence. He probably believed that this question did not belong to logic proper, which was for him — to repeat once more this well known fact — a strictly non-pragmatic affair, but to the pragmatic dimension of semiotic, and if he believed so, he was certainly right. We, anyhow, shall now leave this subject for this very reason.

10. *Is Analytic an Objective Concept?*

There must have been in Bolzano's time a rather vivid discussion of the question whether the classification of propositions into analytic and synthethic ones is objective and rigid, or subjective and flexible, such that the same proposition might be analytic for some people, synthetic for others. This discussion continued for a long time afterwards and is probably not outdated even today. It should therefore be of some interest to hear Bolzano's opinion on this subject. Let it be reminded that the object-language dealt with is a natural one with no rigid semantic rules.

Bolzano cites (p. 89) a characteristic statement of a contemporary logician, *Maass*, whom he quotes often with approval and admiration. Maass said: "One can define a triangle as a figure, whose angle sum is two right angles; in this case, the proposition that the angle sum of a triangle is two right angles, regarded as synthetic in accordance with the normal definition, becomes analytic". Bolzano continues: "I think otherwise. Since I do not regard a proposition as a mere connection of words which state something, but as the *sense* of this statement, I cannot admit that the proposition: The angle sum etc., remains the same whether one connects the word 'triangle' with this concept or the other". The same sentence — two occurrences of the same word-sequence-design — expresses two different propositions. The propositions are different, for "to recognize that propositions are different from one another, it is enough that they consist of different concepts, though referring to the same object" (p. 89).

Though Bolzano's reasoning strongly appeals to recent attitudes, its uncritical acceptance may lead to strange, even contradictory formulations. It is but natural to say that the two occurrences of the word 'triangle' in the mentioned two occurrences of the word-sequence-design 'The angle sum of a triangle is two right angles', though differently defined, express both the property Triangle, have the property Triangle as their intension, so that we come to the consequence that the property Triangle is different from the property Triangle. And it is indeed not difficult to see how similar formulations arise in Bolzano's writings and how he struggles to find appropriate expressions for his sound logical insights.

The source of Bolzano's difficulties is, in the main, his lack of discrimination between object-language and metalanguage — this is not an accusation, of course, but only a historically understandable statement of fact. Let us try to see what the introduction of this discrimination will lead us to.

Suppose we have two semantic systems, S_1 and S_2, which differ from each other only in that in S_1 'triangle' is defined as 'polygon with three sides', in S_2 as 'polygon with an angle sum of two right angles'; we need not, for our purposes, specify any further the properties of these systems, except in stating that their vocabularies are typographically identical. The metalanguage M, in which we discuss both S_1 and S_2, contains once again a vocabulary, part of which is typographically identical with those of S_1 and S_2, such that to each word of the two object-languages there corresponds as its translation the typographically identical word of M.

The rules of designation of S_1 and S_2 are given by the mentioned translation into M. But we cannot, of course, simply formulate the two rules with which we are concerned here as

DR-1   'triangle' is a translation of 'triangle',

DR-2   'triangle' is a translation of 'triangle'.

We must formulate them, so as to avoid ambiguities, somewhat like

DR-1A 'triangle$_M$' is a translation of 'triangle' (in S_1).

DR-2A 'triangle$_M$' is a translation of 'triangle' (in S_2).

But from the L-equivalence (in S_1) of 'The angle sum of a triangle is two right angles' with 'The angle sum of a polygon with three sides is two right angles' follows the L-equivalence (in M) of 'The angle sum of a triangle...' with 'The angle sum of a polygon with three sides...' (omitting the subscripts wherever irrelevant); and from the L-equivalence (in S_2) of 'The angle sum of a triangle...' with 'The angle sum of a polygon with an angle sum of two right angles...' follows the L-equivalence (in M) of 'The angle sum of a triangle...' with 'The angle sum of a polygon with an angle sum of two right angles...'; hence the L-equivalence (in M) of 'The angle sum of a polygon with three sides is two right angles', an obviously factual sentence, with 'The angle sum of a polygon with an angle sum of two right angles is two right angles', an equally obviously L-true sentence.

The source of this contradiction lies, of course, in the rules DR-1A and DR-2A. Stipulating 'triangle$_M$' as a translation of both 'triangle' (in S_1) and 'triangle' (in S_2), we thereby implied the L-equivalence of 'triangle' (in S_1) with 'triangle' (in S_2), to which we were not entitled. We should have somehow indicated which term in M serves as a translation of a term of S_1 and which of a typographically identical term of S_2, perhaps by using 'triangle$_M^1$' and 'triangle$_M^2$' — we assumed that M contained translations of 'triangle' (in S_1) and 'triangle' (in S_2), but made the mistake to believe that the same term in M could serve for both purposes. We may identify, under the conditions laid down for S_1 and S_2, 'polygon$_M^1$' with 'polygon$_M^2$' but we cannot do this for 'triangle$_M^1$' and 'triangle$_M^2$'.

The correct formulation of the designation rules should therefore have been:

DR-1B 'triangle$_M^1$' is a translation of 'triangle (in S_1)',

DR-2B 'triangle$_M^2$' is a translation of 'triangle' (in S_2)

from which no contradictions can be deduced.

'Triangle$_M^1$' and 'triangle$_M^2$' are equivalent but not L-equivalent, and Bolzano is therefore right, when he says that the sentence 'The angle sum of a triangle...' (in S_2) expresses an analytic proposition, and the sentence 'The angle sum of a triangle...' (in S_1) expresses a synthetic proposition, in other words, that the proposition expressed by 'The angle sum of a triangle...' (in S_2) is analytic, but the proposition expressed by a typographically identical word-sequence (in S_1) is synthetic; these propositions are therefore different, though expressed by typographically identical sentences which are moreover equivalent and even *extensionally isomorphous*,[17] in so far as corresponding expressions in these sentences refer to the same objects.

For a clear exhibition of the decisive improvement introduced into the discussion of such questions by the discrimination of object-language and metalanguage, let us listen to an imaginary discussion started by Bolzano's criticism of Maass' subjective conception of 'analytic'. Maass could have given Bolzano the following reply: "My dear Bolzano, what you have so admirably explained to me is, of course, perfectly right. One must distinguish between a proposition and its various linguistic expressions. But still, tell me, the proposition that the angle sum of a triangle is two right angles, is it objectively analytic or objectively synthetic?" To which Bolzano answers: "Well, that depends upon what you understand by 'triangle'. If...". But here Maass interrupts impatiently: "But this very moment you have said that the characteristic of any proposition is objectively determined; how can it depend upon my understanding of one of the terms used to express it?" Bolzano breaks into a long silence, struggling for words to explain to his partner what seems so obviously true to himself. But he does not find them; he can't find them, since a vital discrimination is lacking. And here we come to his aid. With the help of some four-dimensional

---

[17] Coined in analogy to Carnap's 'intensionally isomorphous' and defined in the same way, with 'L-equivalent' replaced by 'equivalent'.

trick, we intrude into the discussion and say: "Excuse our interruption, but the point is simple. In which language, Professor Maass, have you asked your question?" And after having explained him, and Bolzano, the necessary distinctions, we continue: "Now, the expression you used 'the proposition that the angle sum of a triangle is two right angles' was meant to belong to (the non-semiotical, objective part of the metalanguage) M, but — triumphantly smiling — there is no such expression as 'triangle' in M, but only 'triangle$_M^1$' and 'triangle$_M^2$'. Now either what you asked is senseless, as out of accord with the grammatical rules of M, or else you meant by 'triangle' either 'triangle$_M^1$' or 'triangle$_M^2$'. As soon as you will tell us which of the two you intended to, our friend, the excellent mathematician Bolzano, will give you an immediate reply, or perhaps do you mean to renounce your question altogether?" And then we vanish again, leaving Bolzano and Maass to recover from their miraculous adventure and finish their argument by themselves.

After this journey into the past, let us return to dry logic. A proposition p expressed by a sentence s in a language-system S, properly interpreted by translation into a uniquely understood metalanguage M, is "objectively" either analytic or synthetic. Since ordinary languages are not systems, the expression '*the* proposition p expressed by the sentence s in some ordinary language' is objectionable and misleading. So long as the respective language, or a sufficient part of it, is not systematized, there is no unique proposition corresponding to the sentence s, and we may, if we like, express this state of affairs, by saying that the character of p is "subjective", i.e., depending upon the silent systematizations of the different users of s.

11. *Identity of Propositions*

It is worthwhile, in this connection, to see how Bolzano understood 'identity of propositions'. We shall not deal here with Bolzano's theory of the material and formal equivalence of propositions, though its knowledge is necessary for a full understanding of his opinion concerning identity of propositions. Owing to lack of space, we shall content ourselves with as much as can be grasped without that.

His various remarks concerning this subject are not all of them completely consistent, which is perfectly understandable in view of the lack of an appropriate terminology. We shall therefore make use only of those passages which seem to us to express his main intentions. I would not hesitate to formulate Bolzano's criterion for the identity of two propositions expressed by two different sentences as *intensional isomorphism*, provided we could have persuaded him to overcome his reluctance to use such a phrase as '*two identical* propositions' — a reluctance which he expresses for instance when he says that "there are no two completely equal propositions" (p. 2) or "propositions of identical meaning are not many, but One proposition" (p. 140).[18]

In any case, less than that would certainly not have done. He explicitly denies the identity of the propositions expressed by 'Cajus is the father of Titus' and 'Titus is the son of Cajus' on the ground that, in spite of their L-equivalence, their subjects and predicates are different (p. 140-141).[19] On the other hand, he denies the identity, and even the

---

[18] And which is shared by *G. E. Moore*, who, more than a century later, asks "how could it be correct to say that" certain *two* propositions "are the same proposition, unless it were correct to say that" the first "is *one* proposition" and the second "is *another?*" ("Russell's 'Theory of Descriptions'", *The Philosophy of Bertrand Russell*, 1944, p. 207). Moore's struggles continue over several pages and are quite understandable, as well as those of Bolzano, from the point of view of ordinary usage, where 'two' is used, almost without exception, as synonymous with 'two different' — what would you think of a man who orders two fried eggs and having got them starts arguing that he meant *two identical eggs*? But since acceptance of common usage in this point would mean to introduce terrible complications in mathematics and logic alike, it is hardly conceivable that the now accepted usage of 'two' as not excluding 'two identical' will be abandoned.

[19] Moore, *ibid.*, p. 210 f., deals with a completely analogously constructed pair of propositions, namely "The sun is larger than the moon" and "The moon is smaller than the sun". He apparently tends to look upon these propositions as two different logically equivalent propositions and not as One proposition, though the sentences expressing them do not fulfil a condition which Moore regards as sufficient for their being considered as expressions of different propositions, namely that the one sentence brings before the mind of those who understand it ideas which the other will not do. Though Moore apparently regards the mentioned sentences as not only L-equivalent but even as *pragmatically equivalent* — I believe that we may thus paraphrase his 'bringing ideas before the mind'-clause —, he still tends to look upon them as different propositions. It is almost certain that what makes him think so is the fact that his criterion of identity is "intensional isomorphism plus pragmatic equivalence". He is of course entitled to choose his criterion as he likes, and it might be that this is even the criterion which is unconsciously applied in many cases of ordinary usage, but one must bear in mind that so long as no pragmatic systems have been constructed, the pragmatic component in it will seriously hamper its workability.

I now see that my criticism of Moore in "Analysis of 'Correct' Language", Mind, vol. 55 (1946), pp. 338-339 [reprinted here as Ch. 19] was not justified. I stated there that "I can therefore by no means see what should prevent the mentioned sentences... from expressing the *same* proposition, in *every* "correct" usage of the word 'same'", since the expressed propositions were simultaneously L-equivalent and pragmatically

(L-) equivalence of the propositions expressed by 'An equilateral triangle is equiangular' and 'An equiangular triangle is equiangular', though they are *extensionally isomorphous*, in his words, "composed in the same manner out of equivalent but not L-equivalent parts" (p. 138). This example shows, incidentally, that Bolzano envisages here a concept somewhat weaker than Extensionally Isomorphous, which might perhaps be called *Extensionally Homomorphous* (and analogously *Intensionally Homomorphous*),[20] which holds between sentences (and between propositions, in Bolzano's usage) if they may be broken up into an equal number (at least two) of equivalent (L-equivalent) parts which need not be the smallest subdesignators.

As already remarked at the beginning of this section, I could not possibly exhaust all that Bolzano has to say on this subject, lacking some vital terms, but I hope to have shown that everybody who is interested in the clarification of concepts such as Identity Of Proposi-

---

equivalent. There *is* one "correct" usage of 'same' in which the mentioned propositions are not the same proposition.

[20] This concept is probably referred to, though not specially named, by Carnap when he speaks about "at least similar intensional structures" in MN, p. 60.

It seems to me that Intensional Isomorphism is too strong a demand for the analysis of certain cases of belief-sentences (see MN, § 13) and that in these cases Intensional Homomorphism will do.

The sentences 'The diagonals of every square are congruent and perpendicular upon each other' and 'The diagonals of a rectangle with equal sides are congruent and perpendicular upon each other' are not intensionally isomorphous, since no expression in the first is L-equivalent to 'rectangle' in the second, but they are *equivalent in analytic meaning*, according to Lewis' terminology in "The Modes of Meaning", Philosophy and Phenomenological Research, vol. 4 (1943), pp. 236-249, since his condition (1) is fulfilled, 'square' being elementary and equal in intension with 'rectangle with equal sides'; they are also intensionally homomorphous, according to our definition. Whether they are pragmatically equivalent, depends, of course, upon the definition of this term; but it seems that for certain "natural" definitions of this term, they will not be pragmatically equivalent for everybody who understands English. And finally, I do not know whether they bring different ideas before the minds of those who understand them. I hope that this synopsis will have aided somewhat to a future final explication of the various meanings of 'synonymous'.

One more point: Lewis states *ibid.*, p. 246, that 'equilateral triangle' and 'equiangular triangle' have the same intension. This seems to me such an obvious mistake, that I am completely at a loss what to do about it. Lewis defines Intension as something "delimited by any correct definition", and accordingly, 'equilateral triangle' and 'equiangular triangle' have most certainly not the same intension. I am the more embarrassed, since Carnap, who cites this passage, does not react at all to the blunder involved.

tions will draw much profit from a close study of Bolzano's relevant remarks which contain, as usual, illuminating discussions of quotations from (then) contemporary logicians.

12. *'Analytic Proposition'* — *Contradictio in Adjecto?*

Bolzano quotes (p. 86) Solomon *Maimon*, a contemporary of Kant and one of his most acute critics, as denying the attribute Proposition from the meanings of expressions like 'A = A'. Maimon's reason is that such expressions cannot serve as antecedents in inferences, an argument to which Bolzano readily assents — in fact, he himself has a theorem which states that analytic propositions may be omitted from the premises of a derivation — without, however, recognizing it as sufficient to prove its point. Bolzano says no more on this subject, but it is probable that he thought Maimon's proposal to be inconvenient, since it would have greatly complicated the rules of formation. "John is wise" as well as "John is not wise" would have been propositions but not their disjunction "John is wise or not wise", assuming that Maimon would have extended his rejection to any analytic proposition.

I mention this particular point, since its analogue with regard to contradictory propositions has been ardently discussed in recent publications.

13. *Tautological and Identical Propositions*

Propositions of the form 'A is A' form a subclass of the class of analytic propositions. Bolzano uses for them, and only for them, the terms 'tautological' and 'identical', indiscriminately (p. 84). He sharply opposes the definition of other logicians who applied the term 'identical' to propositions of the form 'A is B' where A and B were "interchangeable concepts (**Wechselvorstellungen**), i.e., concepts of identical extension", since in accordance with this definition the proposition "A triangle is a figure the angle sum of which is two right angles" would be identical, "which is surely not intended to" (p. 86).

We may formulate Bolzano's terminological proposal in Carnap's terms in the following form: Sentences of the form 'A = B' will be called 'identical' if 'A' and 'B' have equal intensions, but not if they have equal extensions only. It seems to me that this proposal indeed stands in closer connection with ordinary usage than that of his opponents.

Though Bolzano explicitly decides to call only propositions of the form 'A is A' identical, it seems that he intended to characterize, or at least hesitated whether not to characterize, by the same attribute also propositions of the form 'If p then p'. He states immediately after the passage quoted at the beginning of §5: "The same (i.e., that a proposition is identical, or at least analytic, though its expression does not look so) holds of the propositions: If A is greater than B, then B is smaller than A, etc.". Now this proposition can be transformed, putting synonyms for synonyms, into "If A is greater than B, then A is greater then B", which is a clearly analytic proposition, but by no means an identical one, according to Bolzano's own definition. Since the exact meaning of the decisive phrase 'identical, or at least analytic' is not clear, we must leave it open whether Bolzano intended to characterize also compound propositions of the form 'If p then p' as identical.

14. *Terminological Proposals*

I should like to end this paper with some proposals concerning the use of the main terms discussed in it. Two procedures are now common in this regard: the one works haphazardly with them, hoping for the best — the dismal fact being however that this pious hope is almost never fulfilled and misunderstandings arise without any possibility to control them; the other is to define in every paper anew the sense in which these terms are going to be used.

To escape between the horns of this inconvenient dilemma, there is only one way open: to determine, by explicit convention, the exact senses ("exact", *cum grano salis*, of course) of these terms once and for all.

The following terminology is proposed for consideration. Its leading ideas are (a) minimization of synonyms, hence full exploitation of existing terms, (b) maximum adherence to etymology; it is a well known fact that, in spite of explicit formulations, many people seek, for instance, the "analysis" in analytic sentences and are disappointed, and as a consequence hostilely biassed, if they do not find it.

1. For discussions of natural languages, let us use 'logically true' and 'logically false' in their customary senses, which are, in my opinion, broader than those given them by Quine ('logically true' is rather to correspond to his 'analytic'). As a common generic term, let us use '(logically) *determinate*', corresponding approximately to Bolzano's 'logically analytic'.

2. Let us use 'factually true' for 'true but not logically true', and, correspondingly, 'factually false' and 'factual'.

3. For technical discourse on (interpreted) language-systems, let us use the terms '*L-true*', '*L-false*', '*L-determinate*', '*F-true*', '*F-false*', and '*F-determinate*', respectively.

4. Let us call sentences whose truth follows from the logic of truth-functions, characterized by Carnap successively as "L-true by NTT" and "L-true by PL"[21] — '*tautologically true*' or '*tautological*', when referring to natural languages, '*T-true*', when referring to systems.

5. Let us call sentences whose falsity follows from the logic of truth-functions '*contradictorily false*', '*contradictory*' and '*T-false*', respectively.

6. Let us call any sentence, whether in natural languages or in systems, of the form '$a = b$' '*an identity-sentence*'. The use of the terms 'identically true' and 'identical' as semantic predicates will be avoided.

7. In non-technical discourse on natural languages only, let us call sentences of the forms 'A-B is B' and 'A-B is not non-B', '*analytically true*', sentences of the forms 'A-B is not B' and 'A-B is non-B' '*analytically false*', sentences of either forms '*analytic*'. Only by explicit convention should it be allowed to use 'analytic' instead of 'analytically true' and 'contradictory' instead of 'analytically false', and this only if no collisions with the proposed standard usages of these words are expected.

The reader will have noticed that most proposed technical terms are in accord with Carnap's terminology.

---

[21] For a discussion of these terms, see CARNAP, "Modalities and Quantification", The Journal of Symbolic Logic, vol. 11 (1946), pp. 33-64, especially p. 38 note 4.

COMMENTS ON LOGICAL FORM

Logical Form is one of the central concepts of modern analytic philosophy. Far-reaching conclusions have been drawn from the fact that two sentences (or propositions, or facts) have the same logical form, are *equiform*. Even a superficial investigation of Bertrand Russell's philosophical writings will show the decisive importance he assigns to this concept.

In this note I shall try to prove that Logical Form, as used by Russell, is a highly ambiguous concept and that, as a result, any philosophical thesis which appeals to it will have to be regarded with suspicion. Whether, and to what extent, such a thesis can hope to survive a critical analysis of its underlying conception of logical form is a matter to be decided in each individual case.

Let us consider the following seven sentences:
1. Socrates loves Plato.
2. Othello hates Desdemona.
3. Socrates is human.
4. 5 is prime.
5. 5 divides 15.
6. Humanness is a property.
7. Socrates loves wine.

Out of these seven sentences, 1, 2, 5, and 7 have on various occasions[1] been declared by Russell — explicitly or by implication — to be equiform, and for various reasons: sentences 1 and 2, because 2 can be obtained from 1 by three *step-by-step replacements* of its constituents by others, such that each intermediate sentence is significant — the intermediate sentences might be, for example, "Socrates loves Desdemona", and "Socrates hates Desdemona"; sentences 1 and 5, because

---

[1] I mention only "The Philosophy of Logical Atomism", *Monist*, 28:495–527 (1918); *ibid.*, 29:32–63, 190–222, 345–80 (1919), especially pp. 60 and 202ff.; *Introduction to Mathematical Philosophy* (London: George Allen and Unwin, 1919); *Our Knowledge of the External World* (New York: Norton, 1914); "Reply to Criticisms", in *The Philosophy of Bertrand Russell*, P. A. Schilpp, editor (Evanston, Ill.: Library of Living Philosophers, 1946), p. 698. Since Russell, in the last mentioned book, deals with the *form of sentences*, as far as I know for the first time, having dealt in previous publications only with the forms of propositions and facts, I presume he has recognized that the difficulties connected with the "constituents" of propositions and facts are insurmountable. The following discussion will therefore deal with sentential equiformity only.

5 can be obtained from 1 by a *simultaneous replacement* of its three constituents by the corresponding three constituents of 5, viz., "Socrates" by "5", "loves" by "divides", and "Plato" by "15"; sentences 1 and 7, because 7 can be obtained from 1 by a *single replacement* of one constituent.

None of these four sentences is equiform with any of the remaining sentences, 3, 4, or 6, since these three are all of the subject-predicate form, whereas the former express two-termed relations. On the other hand, 3, 4, and 6 are equiform among themselves by virtue of simultaneous replaceability.

The use of different criteria for the applicability of the same concept is a legitimate procedure only if these criteria can be proved to be equivalent, or, at least, if it can be shown that no contradiction will arise from their simultaneous employment. However, no such proof has been given for the criteria listed above, nor can one be given. It is easy to show that, as they stand, they lead to contradictory conclusions:

a. Sentences 1 and 5 are equiform by the second criterion of simultaneous replaceability. On the other hand, they are nonequiform by the first criterion of step-by-step replaceability, as the reader will readily verify.

b. Sentences 1 and 3 are equiform by simultaneous replaceability. On the other hand, they are nonequiform by the third criterion (single replacement), since 1 expresses a two-termed relation, while 3 has the subject-predicate form. If we count every occurrence of "is" in these sentences as an occurrence of the *same* word (and there are well-known reasons for not doing so), then 1 and 3 are equiform by the criterion of step-by-step replaceability, the intermediate sentence being "Socrates is Plato".

It is not difficult to appreciate the reasons which led Russell to use three different and partly inconsistent criteria for establishing the equiformity of sentences. The first is too weak (in one respect; in another it will prove too strong, as we shall see later) and not sufficient to establish the equiformity of 1 and 5 which, according to the intuitions of Russell, must be declared equiform by any adequate criterion. The second is too strong, since by its use every pair of sentences with the same number of words would be equiform, certainly a most undesirable result. (It is probably also too weak, since it would also require that every pair of sentences with an unequal number of words be nonequiform, whereas "5 divides 15" and "15 is divisible by 5" should be equiform.) The third criterion, finally, amounts to no more than an appeal to the aforementioned intuitions.

Let us now proceed to show the respect in which even the first criterion is too strong. According to it, 1 and 7 are equiform. But also according to it, "Socrates drinks wine" and "Socrates drinks heavily" would be equiform, once again an intuitively most unsatisfactory result. If, to avoid this disaster, one requires that the replacing word be *isogenous*[2] with the replaced word, then 1 and 7 will not be equiform, since "Plato" and "wine" are not isogenous.

Having proved my point negatively, I shall now outline a series of terms which should inherit the place of "equiform". Let us first recall the definitions of two concepts from General Syntax: Two expressions are *isogenous* if each may replace the other significantly in *every* sentence. Two expressions are *related* if one may replace the other in *some* sentences.[3] "Socrates" and "Plato", for example, will probably be isogenous in any formalized counterpart of ordinary language, whereas "Plato" and "wine" will only be related. We are now in a position to develop the following series of terms:

a. Two expressions (and especially sentences) will be called *sign-isomorphous* if both are sequences of an equal number of words which are isogenous by pairs in their given order.

b. Two expressions will be called *expression-isomorphous* if both are sentences of an equal number (at least two) of expressions which are isogenous by pairs in their given order.

c. Two expressions will be called *sign-equistructural* if both are sequences of an equal number of words such that the genus-difference of all corresponding words is constant. (Constant genus-difference is exemplified by sentences 1 and 5 or by 6 and "Socrates is a Greek", where "is a" is systematically ambiguous.)

d. The definition of "expression-equistructural" is obvious.

e. Two expressions will be called *sign-homomorphous* if both are sequences of an equal number of words which are identical by pairs with the exception of one pair which consists of related words.

f. The definition of "expression-homomorphous" is obvious.

Let us now have a last look at our seven guinea-pig sentences, this time through the spectacles of the terminology we have just introduced.

---

[2] Cf. the next paragraph.

[3] These definitions, as well as the concluding paragraphs of this paper are of moderate accuracy only. Stricter definitions are given by R. Carnap in his *Logical Syntax of Language* (London: Kegan Paul, Trench, Trubner & Co., 1937), pp. 169–70. See also my elaboration of these definitions in "On Syntactical Categories", *Journal of Symbolic Logic*, 15:1–16 (1950) [reprinted in LI as Ch. 1].

If we suppose them to belong to a formalized counterpart of ordinary language about which we shall assume only that it stands in rather close connection to common English, we can characterize them as follows:

a. Sentences 1 and 2 are sign-isomorphous and no two other sentences in our list are sign-isomorphous.

b. Sentences 1, 3, and 7 are expression-isomorphous — that is, if we assume that in our system the two occurrences of the ordinary expression "is human" in the two ordinary sentences "Socrates is human" and "Erring is human" are rendered by different and nonisogenous expressions. (On a contrary assumption, 1 and 3 will be only expression-homomorphous.) Sentences 4 and 5 are also expression-isomorphous.

c. Sentences 1 and 5 are sign-equistructural.

d. All seven sentences are expression-equistructural (but, of course, not *all* sentences are expression-equistructural with one of our seven sentences; "All Greeks are human" is not expression-equistructural with any of them).

e. Sentences 1 and 7 are sign-homomorphous.

Let it finally be noticed that whereas the first four defined relations (the *iso-* and *equi-* ones) are all of them equality relations, so that their abstractive classes may be introduced, the last two (the *homo-* ones) are not. "Socrates loves Plato" and "Socrates drinks wine" are not sign-homomorphous with one another, though both are sign-homomorphous with "Socrates loves wine".

MR. GEACH ON RIGOUR IN SEMANTICS

In a recent note,[1] Mr. P. T. Geach offers a series of criticisms of Carnap's treatment of semantics. He aims to prove that this discipline can be no good since one of its leading exponents makes so many blunders. His conclusion is that it may perhaps after all not be so foolish to undertake 'direct analysis' in language everybody can read.

I must confess that Mr. Geach's argument appeals to me, having myself, some time ago,[2] used a similar one and tried to show that the direct method of language analysis as practised by many contemporary British philosophers is not reliable since one of its leading exponents made on one single occasion so many blunders.

Though the arguments are similar, indeed, it seems to me that it would not be difficult to point out the essential differences between a mistake within a rigorous discipline and a mistake in interpretation of "correct" language. But, fortunately enough, no much effort on my side is necessary, as Mr. Geach's argument is almost completely unjustified. My discussion will follow Mr. Geach's criticisms point by point. Carnap's *Logical Syntax of Language*, *Introduction to Semantics*, and *Meaning and Necessity* will be referred to as LS, IS, and MN, respectively, Mr. Geach's note as RS.

1. Mr. Geach accuses Carnap of using dots and dashes as a device to avoid certain difficulties. Carnap himself explains this use quite clearly: "The context is indicated only by dots instead of by a second-level variable, in order to make the definition applicable also to systems not containing such variables." (MN, p. 147, n. 5.) Mr. Geach argues: "But these dots *are* a sort of variable; only it is left obscure whether they are, after all, a second-level variable of the object-language, or are rather a variable of the meta-language".

The facts are simple and obvious. The dots and dashes *function*, in this case, as second-level variables of the object-language (and *function*, in other cases, as sentence-variables or as many other things) but they *are not* second-level variables. Their function is explicitly given or implicitly understood in the meta-language. It may be that certain difficulties are connected with such usage. But Mr. Geach has not succeeded in pointing them out, nor has he succeeded in showing another

[1] "On Rigour in Semantics", MIND, October 1949, pp. 518–522.
[2] In "Analysis of 'Correct Language'", MIND, N.S., vol. lv., 1946, pp. 328–340 [reprinted here as Ch. 19].

equally simple, if not simpler, way of transcribing Russell's definition of the class-symbol into a language-system which does not contain second-level variables, and such systems are frequently studied. (By the way, there are two inaccuracies — or misprints — in Mr. Geach's rendering of Carnap's 33.2.)

2. Mr. Geach accuses Carnap of giving two inconsistent definitions of the sign of definition on pages 17 and 20 of IS, namely

(2:1) A definition has the form '... = Df – – –'; this means; " '...' is to be an abbreviation for '– – –' ",
and

(2:2) ' = Df' is to mean 'is (hereby defined to be) the same as' or 'if and only if'.

It is hard to understand why Mr. Geach calls these explanations belonging to a brief survey given of certain elementary parts of symbolic logic 'definitions'. At the end of (2:1), Carnap refers to his §24, where 'definition' is more extensively dealt with, though still not defined, in any rigorous sense of this word.

But what is "inconsistent" about these two explanations? I quote:

Now 2:2 expounds the sign '= Df' in terms of an expression, 'if and only if', which can stand only between sentences or sentential functions; 2:1 expounds it in terms of the expression 'is to be an abbreviation for', which can stand only between *names* of expressions, not between sentences or sentential functions.

So what? At the best, we have here one more instance of Mr. Geach's failure to observe the distinction between the *use* and *mention* of expressions.[3] The reader will verify that 'is to be an abbreviation' appears in Carnap's first statement (without quotes), but " 'if and only if' " in his second statement (with quotes), so that Mr. Geach's putting them on the same foot by using the same expression 'expounds it in terms of the expression' is more than misleading.

3. Mr. Geach's third accusation boils down to this: Carnap regards the expression 'Des$_G$ ('drei', three)' as a sentence of the meta-language he uses in his §12 of IS; "but this is certainly not an English sentence".

Well, we need only reproduce Carnap's words in the first passage of §12:

We use as meta-language in this section the English language supplemented by variables.... Instead of 'u designates v in S' we write 'Des$_G$(u,v)'....

---

[3] Cf. the note of R. M. Martin, "Mr. Geach on Mention and Use", MIND, October 1949, pp. 523–524.

'Des$_G$ ('drei', three)' *is* a sentence of (supplemented) English, since introduced as an abbreviation of a sentence in what is doubtless good English. 'Des$_G$('drei', three)' is hence an example of an English sentence having the form $\mathfrak{pr}_i\ (\mathfrak{A}_j, \mathfrak{A}_k)$.

This is the kind of argument by which Mr. Geach tries to show that "there is a recurrent error in Carnap's use of letters"!

4. Mr. Geach is indeed right in pointing out that the definition given by Carnap for the adequacy of a predicate $\mathfrak{pr}_i$ in M for the concept of truth with respect to an object language S holds good only in the case that M is English (supplemented by certain variables). But this point is so trivial that no reader (with a certain minimum of understanding and good will — and such a minimum is required even by the most formal and rigorous expositions!) should feel any unhappiness about it; he will surely be able to make the necessary alteration for the case where M is some other language or does not contain variables.

5. Once again Mr. Geach is right. Carnap made indeed two grave mistakes.

a. His use of quotes around syntactical variables or variable expressions *might* mislead. But I am sure nobody will be misled. Carnap himself has already pointed out (IS, 7) an exact method of dealing with cases where misunderstandings are possible.

b. There is really a misprint on p. 22 of LS. A pair of quotes are missing. They are missing in the English translation only; in the German original, they appear at their proper place. Now, there are very few misprints in Carnap's publications, and we are grateful to Mr. Geach for having detected one more. But we have already shown our gratitude by pointing out *two* misprints in his article. There are, by the way, a few more, and to one of them we shall call attention later.

6. Mr. Geach simply has not grasped the full import of Carnap's distinction between variables, constants of undetermined meaning, and constants of determined meaning. If 'B' is an abbreviating constant of an object-language with undetermined meaning, then it *makes sense* to write "for any 'B' " in the meta-language, and the sense is very obvious.

7. Mr. Geach criticizes Carnap for introducing the null thing a_o as the common descriptum for those descriptions which do not satisfy the uniqueness condition (a_o is the descriptum, by the way, and not 'a_o', as Mr. Geach has it on p. 521 of RS, line 4 from below, a rather curious "misprint").

He compares this convention with the following "really similar mathematical" one:

It is possible to count among natural numbers also the *standard number*, characterized as that finite integer which is the least common multiple of all natural numbers....

But is Mr. Geach indeed unable to see what must be a very obvious difference? It can easily be proved that no natural number is a common multiple of all natural numbers; but can Mr. Geach, or anybody else, prove that there is no thing which is part of every thing? Perhaps he can, starting from certain definitions of 'thing' and 'part of thing' which are suitable to him. But this does not prove that it is impossible to show the existence of the null thing from other definitions which are not less suitable, to other persons and for the purposes.

Mr. Geach's comment, "in plain English", on Carnap's making the null thing correspond to the null class of space-time points as describing it "as existing nowhen and nowhere" speaks for itself.

There are, of course, serious reasons for *not* introducing a null thing, but these are of a philosophical and not logico-semantic nature.

BOLZANO'S PROPOSITIONAL LOGIC[1]

1848 is a remarkable year not only in general history; in the history of human culture and thought it will be remembered also as the birth year of *G. Frege*, "the greatest logician of the 19th century",[2] and should be remembered as the year in which the death of the greatest logician between *Leibniz* and *Frege*, the Czech Bernard *Bolzano*, occurred. So far, little has been done to evaluate his important contributions to logical theory,[3] and I hope that the present article will help to undo this undeserved wrong.

The purpose of this article is very restricted: only a small part of Bolzano's investigations will be dealt with, i.e. his propositional logic, and even this in a limited degree. This theory is in my opinion not only a master-work of outstanding historical interest, I also believe that it contains many features neglected even by modern symbolic logic and nevertheless worthy of close study. I am convinced that such a study will considerably enrich our logical technique and terminology.

Since our principal aim is to emphasize the impact which Bolzano's ideas should have on contemporary logic, I shall allow myself to depart, sometimes considerably, from his original account and even to disregard parts of his theory unacceptable to us which do not play any decisive role in its construction, all this, of course, after due warning shall have been given.

---

[1] This article has been written as an outcome of conversations with Professor Hugo Bergman of the Hebrew University, Jerusalem, and a joint reading of the relevant passages of Bolzano's *Wissenschaftslehre*. It is to Professor Bergman that I owe the general ideas on which this paper is based.

[2] According to A. Tarski, *Introduction to Logic*, 1941, p. 19.

[3] The following is a list of the most important articles dealing mainly with Bolzano's contributions to logic which have appeared in the last two decades:

W. Dubislav, "Bolzano als Vorläufer der mathematischen Logik", Philosophisches Jahrbuch der Görres-Gesellschaft, vol. 44 (1931), pp. 448–456.

H. Scholz, "Die Wissenschaftslehre Bolzanos", Semesterberichte, 9. Semester, 1936/37, pp. 1–53.

H. Scholz, "Die Wissenschaftslehre Bolzanos", Abhandlungen der Fries'schen Schule, n. s. vol. 6 (1937), pp. 399–472.

H. R. Smart, "Bolzano's Logic", The Philosophical Review, vol. 53 (1944), pp. 513–533.

I have not been able to get hold of Scholz's second article, but since it is, according to the Journal of Symbolic Logic, only a somewhat broader version of his first article, the loss is probably not too great. My quotations from Scholz will therefore refer always to his first article.

I shall summarize the contents of §§ 147, 154–160 of Bolzano's *Wissenschaftslehre* (1837), with which alone this study is concerned, in 28 definitions and 95 theorems. Most of these theorems will not be proved, for the sake of brevity, but the reader will, in general, be able to supplement the proofs by himself. Many definitions and a few theorems will be illustrated by simple examples. Major departures from Bolzano's original account will be specially mentioned and justified.

In the second part of the study I shall outline the place of Bolzano's contribution within the framework of modern semantics, by its detailed comparison with the corresponding parts of *R. Carnap*'s two volumes of *Studies in Semantics*. This comparison will give us a certain perspective on the bearing of Bolzano's highly original innovations for modern research, and on the other hand enable us to see clearly the precise nature of some of his shortcomings.

I

§1. Informal Exposition of Basic Concepts

The basic concepts of Bolzano's logic are "proposition", "term", and "variation of terms". A *proposition*,[4] in Bolzano's usage, is that which is expressed by a sentence, its objective content; since most authors now use this term in the same sense,[5] we need not dwell upon it. A *term*[6] is any constituent of a proposition which is not itself a proposition.[7] Whereas every proposition is either true or false, by varying one

---

[4] I have found considerable difficulty in rendering Bolzano's sometimes antiquated German terms into current English. I decided to translate rather freely and to give the German original terms only in the notes, with some comment, if necessary.

Bolzano's term for 'proposition' is 'Satz an sich'. This complicated expression originates in the fact that in his times, logicians used to deal either with sentences, Sätze, spoken or written, or with judgments, Urteile, sentences thought of. Bolzano's fight against what we might call today the descriptive syntactical and pragmatic versions of logic is well known, since Husserl chose him as a major ally in his "anti-psychologism". Cf. Smart, op. cit.

[5] Cf. R. Carnap, *Introduction to Semantics*, 1942, pp. 235–236. I do not intend to deny that this sense is still very vague.

[6] "Vorstellung an sich". I chose the neutral 'term', wishing to avoid, in accordance with Bolzano's intentions, any psychological associations. My choice fully corresponds with Russell's usage in *The Principles of Mathematics* (1903), pp. 43–44: "Whatever... may occur in any true or false proposition... I call a *term*..." But whereas Russell's terms, under the influence of Frege and Meinong, are Platonic entities, Bolzano's attitude is ontologically more cautious.

[7] This definition is, of course, extremely vague, since, in addition to its reference to the obscure 'proposition', it refers to the even more obscure notion of a "con-

or more of its terms, i.e. by replacing[8] them by other suitable terms belonging to their respective *ranges of variation*,[9] we get several classes of propositions showing "most remarkable" properties — as Bolzano has it — which serve as the starting-point for the further development. Nobody will fail to see that the *variation of terms* is Bolzano's equivalent of the *propositional functions* of modern symbolic logic.

According to the truth-behaviour of the *variants*[10] of a given proposition with respect to a class of terms which may contain none, one or more (but not all[11]) of the terms of the proposition, this proposition

stituent" of a proposition. This notion has not been clarified even by Russell, in whose logic it occupies a central position.

[8] Scholz, op. cit., p. 35ff., finds fault with the expression '*Vertauschung* (Austausch) zweier Vorstellungen', since terms such as, for instance, numbers are not the kind of objects which can be replaced. (Incidentally, Russell uses the same criticized mode of expression very often, e.g., in "Logical Atomism", *Contemporary British Philosophy*, I, p. 371.) He therefore proposes to use instead, in effect, the expression 'replacing a designation of a term by a designation of another term in a sentence which expresses a proposition', thus forcing Bolzano's theory into a semantic framework. Whereas the general question of the domain to which Bolzano's investigations belong will be discussed later (§ 12), I want to remark here only that we might as well, or even better, look upon Bolzano's expression as a *façon de parler*, which can be easily avoided without entering the domain of semantics. Instead of, say, 'p′ results from p by replacing a by b in p', we might say, e.g., 'p′ is like p except in containing b where p contains a'. We shall therefore continue to use the convenient 'replace', always carrying in mind that nothing semantic, or even anthropological, is to be connected with this word.

[9] Bolzano shares with almost every other logician up to the most recent times the opinion that all terms may be exhaustively classified into mutually exclusive ranges of variations, types, domains of things, spheres, semantic categories, or genera — to mention a few of the terms used to render this concept —, such that all elements of these ranges are mutually and significantly replaceable in all contexts, and no one is replaceable in any context by an element of another range. This opinion is unfounded, and its breaking down has rather important consequences for logic and philosophy alike. I have dealt with this question in "On Syntactical Categories", *Journal of Symbolic Logic* 15 (1950), pp. 1–15. It is easy to see that Bolzano's whole further treatment is gravely affected by this basic failure.

[10] This convenient term has no counterpart in Bolzano's exposition. Its introduction considerably simplifies subsequent formulations.

[11] Bolzano's reason for not allowing variation of *all* terms is that thereby every proposition may be obtained from any other. This reason is obviously faulty, since from $2 = 2$, e.g., we cannot obtain $3 > 4$, as every occurrence of 2 has to be replaced by occurrences of the *same* term. This failure is partly responsible for certain peculiarities of Bolzano's conception of *analytic* propositions. Cf. my paper "Bolzano's Definition of Analytic Propositions", *Methodos* 2 (1950), pp. 32–55 and *Theoria* 16 (1950), pp. 90–117 [reprinted here as Ch. 1].

has a certain (degree of) *validity*,[12] defined as the ratio of the number of true variants to the total number of variants. If all the variants are true, its validity is 1, and the proposition is *universally valid*.[13] If all its variants are false, its validity is 0, and the proposition is *universally contravalid*.[14] Normally, some of the variants will be true and some false, and the validity of the proposition therefore some fraction between 0 and 1.[15]

Let us stress that validity, as defined by Bolzano, is a *relative* concept, that one and the same proposition may have different validities, according to the number and nature of the varied terms. It follows immediately from the given explanations that with respect to any *foreign*[16] class of terms, i.e. a class none of whose elements is contained in the given proposition, the validity of any proposition is either 1 or 0, depending on whether the proposition is true or false.

Three examples, drawn from elementary arithmetics, will illustrate the concepts explained so far.

The proposition

(1) $\qquad\qquad\qquad 2 + 3 = 2 + 4$

is false and therefore universally contravalid with respect to any foreign class of terms. So it is with respect to the class which contains 2 (the number, not the numeral!) as its sole element. The validity of (1) is still 0, if we enlarge the class by the term $+$,[17] provided that the range of variation of this term contains, besides itself, only the terms $-, \cdot, :$. But any further enlargement of the varied class by a term occurring in (1) will increase its validity; we may even determine its exact value if we restrict the variation[18] of the numbers occurring in it to, say, the natural numbers up to and including 100. Incidentally, we see that the defined concepts are relative in a double sense, first with respect to the

---

[12] "Grad der Gültigkeit".

[13] "Allgemeingültig", "vollgültig", "ihrer ganzen Art nach wahr", or "ihrer ganzen Form nach wahr".

[14] "Allgemein ungültig", "durchaus ungültig", "ihrer ganzen Art nach falsch", or "ihrer ganzen Form nach falsch".

[15] This is true, of course, only if the class of variants is finite. We need not enter here a discussion of Bolzano's treatment of the case where this class is infinite, since the numerical value of the validity of a proposition is of no importance for the core of that part of Bolzano's theory to which we confine our study.

[16] Our term.

[17] Bolzano had, in 1837, no troubles with type restrictions.

[18] The idea to deal with restricted variation occurs in Bolzano's writings, in a somewhat different context.

class of varied terms, second to their ranges of variation. Normally, however, when no special restriction is mentioned, the range of variation is meant to be the maximum one, so that no term not contained in it may significantly replace the varied term. I, however, shall continue to work in this section with the mentioned restrictions, so as to allow for exact evaluation of the validities.

The validity of (1) with respect to $\{2, +, 3\}$ — to use the customary symbol of the theory of sets for the class which contains 2, +, and 3 as its sole elements — is $1/100$ ($= {}^{400}/_{40000}$), as the reader may easily verify for himself. By a further enlargement of the varied class to $\{2, +, 3, 4\}$, the absolute number of the true variants of (1) is increased, but its validity remains unchanged. No further increase of the varied class is possible, since it is not allowed to contain *all* terms of the given proposition.

The proposition
$$9 - 5 = 8 + 3$$
has validity 0 with respect to $\{5\}$, validity $1/2000$ ($= {}^{5}/_{10000}$) with respect to $\{5,8\}$, since only 5 out of its 10000 variants with respect to this class are true, as the reader will easily verify for himself. Its validity with respect to $\{9\}$ is $1/100$, etc.

The proposition
$$7 + 3 = 3 + 7$$
is universally valid with respect to $\{7\}$, $\{3\}$, even $\{7,3\}$, but not with respect to $\{7,3, +\}$; in the last case, its validity in only $1/2$.

§2. Variant, Validity

The mathematician's instinct for generalization now leads Bolzano to extend the range of the arguments of the functor 'validity of' so as to contain not only propositions but also propositional classes. Before proceeding to this extension, let us introduce some abbreviations and other conventions. The symbolism used is meant only as a kind of shorthand, designed to abbreviate longer expressions of ordinary language, and should by no means be understood as an attempt to formalize Bolzano's theory.

    p, q, r, p′, q′, r′, . . .   will stand for undetermined constant propositions,

    A, B, C, A′, B′, C′, . . .   will stand for undetermined ordered classes of terms,

P, Q, R, P′, Q′, R′, ... will stand for undetermined propositional classes,

$\bar{P}, \bar{Q}, \ldots$ will stand for the classes whose elements are the negations of the elements of P and Q, respectively,

'prop(s)' will abbreviate 'proposition(s)',

'propcl(s)' will abbreviate 'propositional class(es)',

'$=_{\text{def}}$' will abbreviate 'is, by definition, the same as'.

Further abbreviations will be introduced as occasion arises.

We assume that the range of variation of every term is determined. If A and B contain the same number of terms, and corresponding terms belong to the same ranges of variation, the expression 'the replacement of A by B in P' will be used as short for 'the replacement of every occurrence of an element of A in every element of P by an occurrence of the corresponding element of B'.

Whenever a concept applies to a unit-class of props, we shall apply the same concept to the prop which is its sole element.

We may now proceed to establish the formal definitions:

D1*[19] (Definition 1). P′ is a *variant of P with respect to A* (to be abbreviated to: $\text{var}_A′P$) $=_{\text{def}}$ there is an A′ such that P′ results from P by the replacement of A by A′ in P.

> E1 (Example 1). Let A = ⟨3, +⟩, P = {9 − 5 = 8 + 3, 7 + 3 = 3 + 7}; then P′ = {9 − 5 = 8:2, 7:2 = 2:7} is a $\text{var}_A′P$; A′ = ⟨2, :⟩.
> As already remarked, not all elements of A need occur in P, not even a single one. In the last case, P itself is, of course, the only $\text{var}_A′P$.

D2. The (*degree of*) *validity of P with respect to A* ($\text{val}_A′P$) $=_{\text{def}}$ the ratio of the number of the true $\text{var}_A′P$ to the number of all $\text{var}_A′P$. (A propcl is called true, if all its elements are true, otherwise — false.)

> E2. Let A, P, and A′ be as in E1. Then $\text{val}_A′P = 0$, since to the only two true variants of the first element of P, resulting from replacement of A by A′ and A″ = ⟨4, −⟩, respectively,

---

[19] When I introduce a definition or theorem not given by Bolzano and not substantially equivalent to a definition or theorem given by him — and this happens sometimes for the sake of a simpler and clearer exposition or to facilitate comparison with recent systems —, the respective definition or theorem will be marked by an asterisk.

there belong false corresponding variants of the second element of P.

E3. Let A and A' be as in E1, P = {9 − 5 = 8 + 3, 2 + 3 = 3 + 2}. Then $val_A'P = 1/400$, since out of the 400 $var_A'P$ just one is true, namely that one in which A is replaced by A'.

T1* (Theorem 1). val'P is either 1 or 0 with respect to any foreign A. In the future, we shall omit the clause 'with respect to A' and the corresponding subscript, whenever misunderstandings will not be likely to arise.

D3. P is *universally valid* (uval) $=_{def}$ val'P = 1.

E4. Let P = {7 + 3 = 3 + 7, 5 − 3 = 3 − 1} and A = ⟨7,8⟩. All the 100 $var_A'P$ are true, P therefore $uval_A$.

T2.* Every true P is uval with respect to any foreign A.
D4. P is *universally contravalid* (uconval) $=_{def}$ val'P = 0.

E5. Let P be as in E3 and A = ⟨5,2⟩. Then P is $uconval_A$, since no $var_A'P$ is true.

T3.* Every false P is uconval with respect to any foreign A.
D5.* P is *consistent*[20] (cons) $=_{def}$ val'P ≠ 0.

E6. Let P and A be as in E3. Since $val_A'P ≠ 0$, P is $cons_A$.
E7. Let P be as in E4 and A = {3}. Since val'P ≠ 0 — $val_A'P$ = 1/100, P being the only true $var_A'P$ —, P is $cons_A$.

T4.* P is cons if and only if P is not uconval.

§3. Compatibility and Incompatibility

After having introduced the three basic properties of propcls, we now proceed to define and deal with some relations between them.

D6. P is *compatible*[21] (comp) with Q $=_{def}$ P ∪ Q (i.e. the class whose only elements are all the elements of P and all the elements of Q) is cons.

E8. Let P = {9 − 5 = 8 + 3}, Q = {27 − 9 = 8 + 3}, A = {9}. Then P is comp with Q, since the replacement of A by A' = {16} will yield a true var_A' (P ∪ Q).

---

[20] Bolzano has no single corresponding term. He uses 'nicht allgemein ungültig' or, for propcls, 'ein Inbegriff miteinander verträglicher Sätze'.
[21] "Verträglich", "einstimmig", or "einhellig".

T5. comp is symmetric (i.e., if P is comp with Q, Q is comp with P).
T6.* If P is comp with $Q \cup R \cup \ldots$, then Q is comp with $P \cup R \cup \ldots$, R is comp with $P \cup Q \cup \ldots$, etc.

We shall therefore also use the expression 'P and Q are comp (with one another)' and 'P, Q, R, ... are comp (with one another)'.

D7. P is *incompatible*[22] (incomp) with $Q =_{def}$ P is not comp with Q.

> E9. Let P and A be as in E8, and $Q = \{26 - 9 = 8 + 3\}$. Though P and Q are cons$_A$, $P \cup Q$ is not, hence P is incomp$_A$ with Q.

Since theorems corresponding to T5 and T6 hold with regard to incomp, we shall write also 'P and Q are incomp (with one another)' and 'P, Q, R, ... are incomp (with one another)'.

T7.   P and Q are incomp if and only if $P \cup Q$ is uconval.
T8.   If $A \neq B$, then P and Q may be[23] comp$_A$ and incomp$_B$.

> E10. Let P, Q, A be as in E8, $B = \langle 3,8 \rangle$.

T9.   If A is an initial segment[24] of B ($A \langle B$) and P and Q are comp$_A$, they are comp$_B$.

> *Proof*: Variation of additional terms cannot diminish the number of true variants (though it may diminish the validity), since replacing the additional varied terms by themselves yields the previous variants.

T10.   If $A \langle B$ and P and Q are incomp$_B$, they are incomp$_A$.

> The converses of T9 and T10, resulting from exchanging their second antecedent with their consequent, do not hold. This is shown by the following counterexample.
> E11. Let P and Q be as in E8, $A = \{3\}$, $B = \langle 3,9 \rangle$.

T11.*   If P is cons for any A, it is true.
T12.*   If P is false, there is an A for which P is uconval.
T13.   If P is false, it is uconval for any A which is foreign to the false elements of P.
T14.   If P is a subclass of Q ($P \subset Q$) and P is uconval, then Q is uconval.

---

[22] "Unverträglich", or "misshellig".

[23] A good deal of Bolzano's theorems is of the "may be" and "need not be" kind. They are valuable as a pedagogic protection against careless inferences.

[24] e.g. $\langle 2, - \rangle$ is an initial segment of $\langle 2, -, 3 \rangle$.

The converse of T14 does not hold. This is shown by
E12. Let P and A be as in E8, and $Q = P \cup \{26 - 9 = 8 + 3\}$.

T15. If $P \subset Q$ and Q is cons, P is cons.
T16.* If P is cons, it is comp with itself,[25] and conversely.
T17.* If P is uconval, it is incomp with itself, and conversely.
T18.* comp is not totally-reflexive (i.e., neither reflexive nor irreflexive).
T19. comp is non-transitive (i.e., neither transitive nor intransitive, in other words, when P is comp with Q and Q is comp with R, P may or may not be comp with R).

Since the transitive case is trivial, we shall give an example only for the intransitive case.

E13. Let $P = \{2 + 3 = 6\}$, $Q = \{9 - 6 = 4\}$, $R = \{4 \cdot 6 = 14\}$, $A = \langle 6,4 \rangle$. Then P is comp with Q — take $A' = \langle 5,4 \rangle$ —, Q is comp with R — take $A'' = \langle 2,7 \rangle$ —, but P is incomp with R.

We shall illustrate the second case of this important theorem in two more examples, the one taken from algebra, the other from geometry.

E14. Let $P = \{x + y = 8\}$, $Q = \{x - y = 4\}$, $R = \{x + y = 12\}$, $A = \langle x, y \rangle$. P is comp with Q, in other words, the system of the first two equations is solvable, Q is comp with R, but P is incomp with R, the system of the first and last equation is unsolvable.

E15. Let Q be the Hilbertian set of axioms for Euclidean Geometry with the exception of the Axiom of Parallels, let P be (the set whose only element is) this axiom, let R be the negation of this axiom, all of them reduced to primitive terms, A be the class of these primitive terms. Then, as is well known, $P \cup Q$ is $cons_A$ — and this not only in the customary sense of *logical consistency*, but even in Bolzano's sense of *having a model*, either of mathematical or empirical nature—, so is $Q \cup R$, and this independently of whether physical space is Euclidean or not, since hyperbolic geometry has Euclidean models and Euclidean geometry hyperbolic models, whereas $P \cup R$ is evidently $uconval_A$.

T20.* incomp is non-reflexive.
T21. incomp is non-transitive.

[25] There is nothing like self-compatibility or self-incompatibility in Bolzano's writings. These concepts have been introduced for the sake of comparison.

Since the intransitive case is trivial, we shall give an example only for the transitive case.

E16. Every two of the following three props are incomp with respect to {7}:
7 is a power of 2, 7 is a power of 3, 7 is a power of 5.

T22. If p is comp with q, $\bar{p}$ may be incomp with $\bar{q}$.
A trivial example is the case where p is true and A is foreign to p.

T23. If all the classes resulting from the replacement of any one of the elements of P by its negation are cons, then a class resulting from P by replacing two of its elements by their negations may still be incomp, and this even if P itself is cons.

E17. Let p = 3 is a prime number, q = 3 is odd, r = 3 is identical with 2 or 3 or 9, P = {p, q, r}, A = {3}. Then P itself is clearly $cons_A$, but so is {$\bar{p}$, q, r} — replace 3 by 9 —, so is {p, $\bar{q}$, r} — replace 3 by 2 —, and so is {p, q, $\bar{r}$} — replace 3 by 7, but there is no true var_A' {p, $\bar{q}$, $\bar{r}$}.

§4. Derivability

Whereas the changes introduced so far into Bolzano's exposition were only technical ones (improvements, I hope) that stood nowhere in direct opposition to Bolzano's own words, we feel ourselves obliged to change his definition of the central concept of his logic, the concept of *derivability*, in deliberate contrast to his explicit formulation. I believe there are strong reasons for this departure and shall present them shortly.

Bolzano's definition is:

D8A. P is *derivable*[26] from Q $=_{def}$ Q is cons and whenever a var'Q is true, the corresponding var'P is true.

Our definition will be:

D8.* P is *derivable* (der) from Q $=_{def}$ whenever a var'Q is true, the corresponding var'P is true.

The difference is, of course, this: Whereas according to Bolzano's original definition *no* propcl is der from a uconval Q, according to our definition *every* propcl is der from such a Q. This state of affairs reminds us strongly of the now classical controversies concerning the "paradoxes of material implication", and, indeed, material implication is a special case of our derivability, namely that case where P and Q

---

[26] "Ableitbar".

are unit-classes and A is foreign to both of them. Since the settlement of these controversies has shown the basic importance of "material implication", which of course must be carefully distinguished from "logical implication",[27] we cannot afford to do without its analogue in Bolzano's logic. Bolzano's derivability would, in the mentioned special case, coincide with compatibility.

Our second reason for the departure is the much greater simplicity of the formulation of further definitions and theorems which can be achieved by the omission of Bolzano's first clause in the definiens.

The third reason is that we are interested in derivation not only from *false* propcls — this case is provided for even by Bolzano's definition, if only the A with respect to which P is der from the false Q is such that Q is cons$_A$ — but also from *uconval* propcls, in the case of a reductio ad absurdum argument, for instance. Bolzano apparently missed this point. He explicitly mentions the "great remarkability" of the derivability relation, since it enables us to infer immediately the truth of P from the truth of Q, but does not care that *his* definition does not enable us to infer from the universal contravalidity of P the universal contravalidity of Q.[28]

E 18. Let P = {5 is divisible by 2}, Q = {7 is divisible by 4}, A = $\langle 5,7 \rangle$.

T24.* der is reflexive (it is non-reflexive under Bolzano's original definition.
T25. der is neither symmetric nor asymmetric, in other words, if P is der from Q, Q may or may not be der from P.
T26. der is transitive.
T27. If P is der from Q and Q is uval, P is uval.
T28.* If P is der from Q and P is uconval, Q is uconval.

---

[27] For a lucid and elementary treatment of this complex of problems, see Tarski, op. cit., p. 23ff.

[28] Dubislav, op. cit., p. 452 ff., deals at some length with the differences between Bolzano's concept of derivability and the corresponding modern one and adduces more reasons for the superiority of the latter. Scholz introduces the same change in Bolzano's definition without mentioning however that an amendment has been made. It is true that, in §164, Bolzano himself does not postulate the consistency of Q in the definiens of 'P is derivable from Q', but he does so explicitly in §155, where derivability is introduced for the first time. When Scholz states, p. 40, that the relation of derivability, *as defined by Bolzano*, is reflexive (cf. our T24), this statement is, therefore, simply false.

This theorem is *not* given by Bolzano, of course, but its importance may be illustrated by the following famous example:

E19. Let Q = {83 is the greatest prime number}, P = {83 is the greatest prime number, there is a prime number greater than 83}, A = {83}. Since P is der$_A$ from Q and P is plainly uconval$_A$, Q is uconval$_A$.

T29.* If p̄ is der from p, then p is uconval. (Bolzano has: p̄ is not der from p.)

Proof: Under the hypothesis and T24, {p, p̄} is der from p, hence (T28) p is uconval.

T30.* If p is der from p̄, p is uval.

Proof: p̄ is uconval (T29), hence p is uval.

T31. If P is der from Q and there is a uval subclass R of P, then P is der from Q − R (the class whose only elements are all the elements of Q except those which are also elements of R).

T32. Let Q be the class of all props which are der from P; if Q is true, P is true.

Proof: P ⊂ Q.

We now come to a series of theorems dealing with the relations between der and the previously defined concepts.

T33. If P is der from Q and Q is comp with R, then P is comp with R; the relative product of der with comp is included in comp. In the usual symbolism of the Theory of Relations: der/comp ⊂ comp.)

T34. If P is der from Q and P′ is der from Q′ and Q is comp with Q′, then P is comp with P′ (der/comp/der ⊂ comp).

T35. If P is der from Q and P′ is der from Q′ and P is incomp with P′, then Q is incomp with Q′ (der/incomp/der ⊂ incomp).

The converses of T34 and T35, resulting from exchanging their third antecedents with their consequents, do not hold. This is shown by

E20. Let P = P′ = {5 ≠ 3}, Q = {5 > 3}, Q′ = {5 < 3}, A = ⟨5,3⟩.

T36. If p is not uval and p is der from q, it is not der from q̄.

T37.* If p is der both from q and from q̄, it is uval; and conversely.

The following theorem is to be contrasted with T36.

T38. If p is der from Q, then, even if p is not uval, p may be der from any Q' resulting from Q by replacing one or more, even all, of the elements of Q by their negations.

> *Proof*: Whereas one of corresponding variants of p and p̄ must be true, corresponding variants of Q and Q' may well both be false.
> E21. Let p = 7 is not identical with 2, Q = {7 is prime, 7 is odd}, Q' = {7 is compound, 7 is even}, A = {7}.

T39. If p̄ is comp with Q, p is not der from Q; and conversely, if p̄ is incomp with Q, p is der from Q.

> *Saccheri* tried to prove that Euclid's axiom of parallels is der from the remainder of his set of axioms by showing that its negation is incomp with this remainder; *Gauss* proved that this axiom is not der from the remainder by showing that its negation is comp with it.

T40. If P is der both from Q − {p} and from Q − {p̄}, then P is der from Q; and conversely.

> Since the theorem that every angle exterior to a triangle is greater than any other of the two non-adjacent interior angles of this triangle can be derived both from a Euclidean axiom set and from a set in which the axiom of parallels has been replaced by its negation, this theorem can be derived from an axiom set of so-called absolute geometry which contains neither.

T41.* If P is uval, it is der from the null-class of premisses; and conversely.

> This theorem has *not* been given by Bolzano. It follows immediately from T40 and T37. He missed this theorem, which looks so strikingly modern, only very nearly when he said: "A uval prop is not dependent for its truth upon the condition of the truth of its premisses". But a null class was apparently a concept too daring even for Bolzano's untraditional mind.
> The following theorem stands in contrast to T40.

T42. If P is der both from Q − {p, q} and from Q − {p̄, q̄}, then it need not be der from Q.

> E22. Let Q = the null class (of props), P = {7 is not identical with 2}, p = 7 is prime, q = 7 is odd, A = {7}. P is der both

from $\{p, q\}$ and from $\{\bar{p}, \bar{q}\}$ (E21), but not from Q, since it is not uval (T41).

T43. If p is der from Q, then, for any premiss q, $\bar{q}$ is der from $Q' = Q - \{q\} \cup \{\bar{p}\}$.

Proof: If q were not der from Q', q would be comp with Q' (T39), hence $\bar{p}$ comp with $Q - \{q\} \cup \{q\}$ (T6), i.e. with Q, therefore p not der from Q (T39).

T44. If P is der_A from Q and $B < A$, then P is der_B from Q.

The converse of this theorem, resulting from exchanging its first antecedent with the consequent, does not hold.

T45. If P is der from Q and P' from Q', then $P \cup P'$ is der from $Q \cup Q'$.

§5. Superalternation and Subalternation

D9. P is *superaltern*[29] (super) to $Q =_{def}$ P is der from Q but Q is not der from P.

D10. P. is *subaltern*[30] (sub) to $Q =_{def}$ Q is super to P.

Bolzano justifies these definitions which stand in straightforward opposition to customary usage by pointing out that if P is super to Q, the val'P is *greater than* val'Q, though P has smaller content, says less, is weaker than Q.

Let us state the connections which hold between the validities of two propcls and the last three defined relations between them in special theorems.

T46. If P is der from Q, then val'P > val'Q.
T47. If P is super to Q, then val'P > val'Q.
T48. If P is sub to Q, then val'P < val'Q.

The converses of theses theorems do not hold.

For the sake of completeness we define the converse of der and state the corresponding theorem with regard to the validities.

D11.* P *implies* (impl) $Q =_{def}$ Q is der from P.
T49.* If P impl Q, then val'P < val'Q.

---

[29] "Übergeordnet", "höher", "von ausgebreiteterer Gültigkeit", "von grösserer Gültigkeit", "weniger sagend", "einseitig ableitbar". The third and fourth of these terms are not happy ones, since greater validity is only a necessary, but not a sufficient condition for the holding of super. Cf. T47.

[30] "Untergeordnet", "niederer", "von beschränkterer Gültigkeit", "von geringerer Gültigkeit", "mehr sagend".

Two further theorems with regard to super will end this short section.

T50.* super is irreflexive, asymmetric and transitive.

T51. If P is super to Q, there is an R which is comp with P but incomp with Q.

> *Proof*: By hypothesis and D9, Q is not der from P, hence there are true var'P for which the corresponding var'Q are false. Let S be the class of all those elements of Q, the variants of which are rendered false, and let R be S. Then P is comp with R, but R is evidently incomp with Q.

§6. Irredundant and Redundant Derivability

D12. P is *irredundantly derivable*[31] (irreder) from Q $=_{def}$ P is der from Q but is not der from any proper subclass of Q nor from a Q' which results from Q by weakening any of its elements (i.e., by replacing some element of Q by a super prop).

D13. P is *redundantly derivable*[32] (reder) from Q $=_{def}$ P is der from Q but not irreder from Q.

> E23. Let P = {7 is divisible by 10}, Q = {7 is divisible by 15, 7 is divisible by 2}, Q' = {7 is divisible by 5, 7 is divisible by 2}, A = {7}. Since the first element of Q' is weaker than the first element of Q — its validity is, under plausible assumptions, 3 times greater! – and P is irreder from Q', P is reder from Q.

T52. If P is irreder from (a non-null) Q, then
    (a) P is not uval, and
    (b) Q contains no uval elements.

> *Proof*: (a) T41 (b) T31.

T53. If p is irreder from Q and R is a proper subclass of Q, then p̄ is comp with R.

D14.* P is *irredundant*[33] (irredun) $=_{def}$ there is a Q which is irreder from P.

D15.* P is *redundant*[33] (redun) $=_{def}$ P is not irredun.

---

[31] "Steht in einem genauen, genau bemessenen oder adäquaten Verhältnis der Ableitbarkeit", a somewhat clumsy mode of expression, even in German. "Genau ableitbar" would have been as clear and much shorter.

[32] "Steht in einem überfüllten Verhältnis der Ableitbarkeit".

[33] We have introduced these two properties of propcls, since their definition is obvious and their use simplifies things considerably. In addition, they play important roles in modern axiomatics.

E24. Let P, Q, Q', and A be as in E23, and let P' = {7 is divisible by 30}, Q" = {7 is divisible by 15, 7 is divisible by 6}. Then not only is Q' irredun, P being irreder from it, but so is Q, because, in spite of P being reder from it, P' is irreder from it; but Q" is redun, since all R which are der from Q" are already der from Q.

T54. If P is irredun, then P is irreder from P, i.e., no element q of P is der from $P - \{q\} \cup \{q'\}$, where q' is super to q.
T55. If P is irredun and q is an element of P, then $\bar{q}$ is comp with $P - \{q\}$.

The following theorem stands in contrast to T55.

T56. If P is irredun and $\{q, r\}$ is a subclass of P, then $\{\bar{q}, \bar{r}\}$ need not be comp with $P - \{q, r\}$.

§7. Equivalence

D16. P is *equivalent*[34] (equiv) to Q = $_{def}$ P is der from Q and Q is der from P.
T57. If P is equiv to Q, then val'P = val'Q.
T58. If P is equiv to Q, P and Q need not be equinumerous.
T59. If P is equiv to P' and Q is equiv to Q', then $P \cup P'$ is equiv to $Q \cup Q'$.
T60. If P is equiv to P' and Q is der from P, then $P \cup Q$ is equiv to P'.
T61. If P is der from Q and P' is der from Q' and Q is equiv to Q', then P need not be equiv to P'.
T62. If P is equiv to P' and $P \subset Q$ and $P' \subset Q'$ and P' is equiv to Q', then $Q - P$ need not be equiv to $Q' - P'$.
T63. If p is equiv to p', then $\bar{p}$ is equiv to $\bar{p}'$.
T64. If P is equiv to P', then $\overline{P}$ need not be equiv to $\overline{P}'$.
T65.* equiv is reflexive, symmetric and transitive.
T66. The left and right hand relative products of equiv with any one of the relations comp, incomp, der, super, sub, impl, equiv are included within these relations, respectively.

---

[34] "Gleichgeltend".

§8. Independency and Dependency

D17.* P is *independent*[35] (indepen) of Q = $_{def}$ P is comp with Q but not der from Q.

D18. P and Q are *independent*[36] (indep) (of each other) = $_{def}$ P is indepen of Q and Q is indepen of P.

Let us add two more obvious definitions, not given by Bolzano.

D19.* P is *dependent* (depen) upon Q = $_{def}$ P is not indepen from Q.

D20.* P and Q are *dependent* (dep) (upon each other) = $_{def}$ P is depen upon Q and Q is depen upon P.

T67. If p and q are indep, then either p̄ and q̄ are indep or p̄ is incomp with q̄.

> E25. Let p = 6 has even prime factors, and q = 6 has odd prime factors, A = {6}. Then p and q are indep, p̄ and q̄ are incomp (provided that 1 is excluded from the range of variation of 6), hence dep.

T68. P and Q are dep if and only if P is incomp with Q or P is der from Q or P impl Q.

T69. The left and right hand relative products of equiv with indep and dep are included in these relations, respectively.

§9. Exclusion, Biexclusion, Contradictoriness, Contrariety

D21. P is *excluded*[37] (excld) by Q = $_{def}$ P̄ is der from Q.

D22. P *excludes* (excls) Q = $_{def}$ Q is excld by P.

D23. P and Q are *biexcluded*[38] (biexcld) (by one another) = $_{def}$ P is excld by Q and Q is excld by P.

Exclusion is, in general, a much stronger relation than incompatibility, and biexclusion is, of course, even stronger, though all three relations coincide with regard to unit-classes.

T70. If P excls Q, P is incomp with Q (excls ⊂ incomp).

---

[35] This concept of unilateral independency is not given by Bolzano, who defines immediately the bilateral independency. Only this relation is symmetric. This simple fact is often overlooked, even in modern textbooks.

[36] "Verkettet", "verschlungen", or "unabhängig". The first two designations have been transferred from Bolzano's theory of terms.

[37] "Ausgeschlossen".

[38] "Wechselseitig ausgeschlossen".

The converse of T70 does not hold; {p, q} is incomp with {p̄, q̄}, but is not excld by it.

D24. P and Q are *contradictory*[39] (condi) or *contra-classes*[40] (concls) $=_{def}$ P is equiv to Q̄ and Q is equiv to P̄.

D25. P and Q are *contrary*[41] (contr) $=_{def}$ P and Q are biexcld but not condi.

> E26. Let P = {7 is even, 7 is prime}, Q = {7 is divisible by 3, 7 is compound}, A = {7}. Then P excls Q, but is not excld by it — take 6 for 7 —.
>
> E27. Let P and A be as in E26, Q = {7 is odd, 7 is compound}. Then P and Q are biexcld but not condi — 6 for 7 makes P̄ true but Q false —, hence contr.

None of the four conditions with regard to der which are embodied in the definiens of 'condi' is redundant. One case in which three of them are fulfilled, but the fourth not, is illustrated in the following example.

> E28. Let P = {9 is even, 9 is prime}, Q = {9 is compound or odd [or both]}, A = {9}. Then P is der from Q̄, Q̄ is der from P, Q is der from P̄, but P̄ is not der from Q — take 8 for 9 —. P and Q are not even biexcld, since P̄ is not der from Q, hence not contr. P only excls Q, but P̄ and Q̄ are biexcld.
>
> Condi is rather trivially exemplified by {p, q} and {p̄, q̄}. It is not easy to construct less trivial examples, but Bolzano himself gives one. Let P = {a + b + c = 3m, 2b + c = 3m, 2c + b = 3m, a + b + d ≠ 3m, 2d + a ≠ 3m, 2a + d ≠ 3m}, Q = {a + d = 2m, 2b + d = 3m, 2d + b = 3m, b + c = 2m, 2c + a[42] = 3m, 2a + c ≠ 3m}, A = ⟨a, b, c, d, m⟩.

T71. p and p̄ are condi with respect to any class whatsoever.

T72. If P and Q are condi, then P̄ and Q̄ are condi.

I come now to a rather serious blunder made by Bolzano in the otherwise generally admirable development of his theory. Bolzano has a theorem[43] stating, in effect, that if P is equiv to P' and Q is equiv to Q' and P' and Q' are condi, then P and Q are condi; in other words,

---

[39] "Widersprechend", "contradictorisch".

[40] "Widerspruch" in a specially peculiar usage: If P and Q are condi, then "P ist ein Widerspruch von Q".

[41] "Widerstreitend", "conträr".

[42] Bolzano has 'c', but this is obviously a misprint.

[43] §159, subsection 9.

that the left and right hand relative products of equiv with condi are included in condi. This theorem is false and its proof is mistaken — as a matter of fact, Bolzano gives no direct proof but refers to the proof of the analogous theorem with respect to der.[44] But der and condi behave differently, and it is very important to dwell upon the reasons of their different behaviour. Whereas der is a *truth-relation* — by this term, formed in analogy with the customary *truth-function*, we mean that the truth of the prop "P ist der from Q" depends only on the truth-values of the arguments of der, in our case on the truth or falsity of P and Q—, condi, as well as all the other concepts defined in this section, is *not*, since P (or Q) which enters its definition essentially is not a truth-function of $\bar{P}$ (or $\bar{Q}$); the falsity of P is a necessary condition for the truth of $\bar{P}$ but not a sufficient one. The truth-value of $\bar{P}$ is not unaffected by the replacement of P by an equivalent propcl, a fact which, astonishingly enough, was well known to Bolzano himself (T64).

A simple example will make the state of affairs clearer.
E29. Let P = {7 is even, 7 is prime}, P' = {7 is identical with 2}, Q = {7 is odd, 7 is compound}, A = {7}. Then P and Q are plainly condi, P and P' evidently equiv, but P' is not condi with Q, since Q is not der from $\bar{P}'$.

At the end of the formal development of Bolzano's theory, we shall state in special theorems which of the introduced properties, relations and functions of propcls are *extensional* — we shall use this term as a convenient abbreviation for 'truth-property or truth-relation or truth-function' —, and which are *non-extensional*. So far, we already know that all the relations mentioned in T66 are extensional.

T73. If P and Q are condi and Q and R are condi, then P is equiv to R; the second power of condi is included in equiv (condi^2 ⊂ equiv).

T74. If P and q are condi, all elements of P are equiv.

T75. If P and Q are condi and P contains at least two non-equiv elements, then there are subclasses of P and Q which are comp.

The fact that $\bar{p}$ is a truth-function of p, but $\bar{P}$ is, in general, not a truth-function of P, finds its expression in the following three pairs of theorems.

T76. If p is equiv to q, then p and $\bar{q}$ are condi.

T77. If P is equiv to Q, then P and $\bar{Q}$ need not be condi.

T78. If p is der from q and $\bar{p}$ is der from $\bar{q}$, then p and $\bar{q}$ are condi.

---

[44] §156, subsection 4.

T79. If P is der from Q and $\bar{P}$ is der from $\bar{Q}$, then P and $\bar{Q}$ need not be condi.

T80. If P and q are condi, then corresponding var'P and var'q have different truth-values.

T81. If P and Q are condi, then corresponding var'P and var'Q need not have different truth-values.

T81 shows that the extension of the classical relation of contradictoriness between props to propcls causes a deviation from the classical theorem that exactly one number of this relation must be true. The following theorem, on the other hand, corresponds to the classical theorem, even in the extended case.

T82. If P and Q are contr, then corresponding variants of P and Q may both be false.

T83. If P is der from q, then every concl of {q} is der from every concl of P.

T84. If p is incomp with q, then every concl of {p} is comp with q and even der from q.

T85. If P is comp with Q, then P may be comp with any R which is biexcld by Q and P may even be der from both.

T86. If P and Q are condi and P is comp with R, then Q is not der from R.

T87. If P and Q are condi and Q is not der from R, then at least one element of P is comp with R.

§10. Exhaustiveness, Disjunctness, Exclusiveness, Alternateness

D25.* If P contains at least two elements, then
P is *exhaustive* (exh) = $_{def}$ at least one element of every var'P is true.

The elements of an exhaustive class are called *disjunct*[45] (disj) (with one another).

D26.* If P contains at least two elements, then
P is *exclusive* (excl) = $_{def}$ at most one element of evey var'P is true.

T88. If P is excl, then every element q of P excls P–{q}.

D27. P is *alternate*[46] (alt) = $_{def}$ P is exh and excl.

---

[45] "Einander ergänzend", or "einander aushelfend".

[46] If P is alternate, then its elements stand "im Verhältnis der eingliedrigen Ergänzung", or "im Verhältnis der Disjunktion". Bolzano defines in this paragraph many

T89.   P is alt if and only if exactly one element of every var'P is true.
D28.   P is *exhaustive in relation to* $Q^{47} =_{def}$ whenever a var'Q is true, at least one element of the corresponding var'P is true.

> E30. Let P = {7 is divisible by 2, 7 is divisible by 3, 7 is divisible by 5, 7 is divisible by 7}, Q = {7 is less than 10 and greater than 1}, A = {7}.[48]

§11. Extensionality and Non-Extensionality

T90.*   val' is an extensional function.
T91.*   uval, uconval, and cons are extensional properties.
T92.*   comp, incomp, der, super, sub, impl, equiv, indepen, indep, depen, dep, and disj are extensional relations.

(Though disj has been defined with the help of the non-extensional concept exh, it is extensional, and it is easy to see how an equivalent definition using only extensional concepts could have been formulated.)

T93.*   var' is a non-extensional function.
T94.*   irredun, redun, exh, excl, and alt are non-extensional properties.
T95.*   irreder, reder, excld, excls, biexcld, condi, concl, contr, and exh-in-relation-to are non-extensional relations.

II

§12. The Place of Bolzano's Theory in Modern Logic

I come now to the second part of this paper: the evaluation of Bolzano's contribution to the logic of propositions, propositional classes and propositional functions. I do not intend, as already remarked, to elaborate Bolzano's exact place in the history of logic, though this is certainly a task worth undertaking. I shall content myself by pointing out that a good deal of the preceding theory is highly original, and even where Bolzano did not invent the definitions or prove the theorems for the first time, he mostly generalized previous achievements to a degree unheard of in his time.

All concepts defined in the previous sections are *absolute radical*

---

more interesting properties and relations but their discussion would require too much space.

[47] The elements of P "helfen einander aus unter der Bedingung" Q.

[48] In the annotation to this paragraph, Bolzano remarks that two props are sub-contrary, according to the classical terminology, if they are comp and disj according to his own terminology.

concepts in Carnap's terminology,[49] where 'absolute' means roughly the same as 'not dependent upon language' and 'radical' means, even more roughly, 'not further specified with regard to being logical or factual'. They belong to the *non-semiotical* part of the metalanguage of the object-language dealt with, which was colloquial German for Bolzano and is ordinary English with us. They do *not* belong to the *semantical* part of the metalanguage, and in their definition no mention is made of any semantical concepts such as 'designate', 'express', etc. (Even the concepts "true" and "false" appear in their absolute, non-semantical sense.) *H. Scholz's* contrary statement, in which he hails Bolzano as a forerunner of modern semantics,[50] is therefore unjustified. There is no difficulty at all, however, in raising Bolzano's absolute theory to a semantical level; this can be done simply by replacing 'proposition' by 'sentence', 'term' by 'expression', property' and 'relation' by 'predicate (of degree 1, 2 or higher)'. But Bolzano did not do it. He worked, of course, with semantical concepts (like almost every other logician from Aristotle onwards) such as 'the linguistic expression of a proposition', but these concepts do not appear in that part of his logic which has been dealt with in the preceding sections. Let us also note, in passing, that there would be no difficulty in constructing a syntactical counterpart of Bolzano's absolute logic.

The easy reconstructibility of Bolzano's logic on a semantical level leads us to attach no major importance to its absolute character — for somebody interested in the ontological implications it may be otherwise —, but its second feature, its radicality, has surely decisive consequences. The concepts appearing in it are not logical at all, paradoxically as it sounds, but only what we might call *prelogical*. If there are two blue books on my table, then 'this book on my table is blue' is uval with respect to 'this' and 'This book on my table is green' is uconval with respect to 'this'. 'Jerusalem is the capital of Israel' is der not only from '2 + 3 = 6' with regard to any foreign class A, but also from '2 + 3 = 5', which is a paradox only so long as one does not distinguish between material and logical relations. Bolzano himself would not have consented to this "paradox of material derivability", as already remarked. This does not mean that radical concepts are worthless, but it does mean that a theory of radical concepts has to be supplemented by a theory of the corresponding logical concepts, Carnap's L-concepts.[51] Bolzano

---

[49] op. cit., §9 and §17.
[50] Cf. note 8.
[51] op. cit., §14.

tries, in fact, to do this, at least with regard to the central concept "derivability". He even makes, for the first time – according to his own assertion –, a distinction between logical derivability, for which no empirical knowledge is necessary, and factual derivability, for which logic alone is not sufficient. However, his account of L-derivability is not satisfactory, though we have no space to discuss his elaborate theory of inference.

We shall therefore confine ourselves to the following question: "What can we learn from Bolzano's theory of the absolute radical concepts?" Since he unites in one theory four parts which usually receive distinct treatment — if they are treated at all —, namely the logic of propositions, of propositional classes, of propositional functions and of classes of propositional functions, we shall first inquire into the implications of Bolzano's unusual combined treatment for each part separately and only afterwards return to the unified theory.

§13. The Logic of Propositions and Propositional Classes

Since all our definitions were framed with regard to propcls, we shall start with them and only later on deal with unit-classes of props, i.e., with single props. We get this specification from the general theory by choosing as the A, to which all definitions refer, a class foreign to the respective propcls. Bolzano himself refers sometimes to this case of *vacuous* variation by adding to some of his concepts the adjective '*material*', in contradistinction to '*formal*' which applies to cases of real variation. He does not distinguish, strangely enough, between material and formal derivability, but he does so, for instance, with respect to a closely related concept, that of *consequence*.[52] Since we cannot see any reason to the contrary, we shall extend this familiar looking usage of 'material' and 'formal' to all defined concepts.

We have already remarked that Bolzano defined two kinds of concepts, extensional ones, the application of which to their arguments depends only upon the truth-values of these arguments, and non-extensional ones, the application of which is, in general, dependent upon additional information such as the truth-values of the elements of their arguments.

Let us deal first with the extensional concepts. As standard works

---

[52] "Abfolge", the most important concept of the subsequent sections of *Wissenschaftslehre*.

of comparison Carnap's *Introduction to Semantics* and *Formalization of Logic* (cited as 'IS' and 'FL', respectively) will be used.

1. No other comment is needed for val'P (T90), except that in our case its values can be only 1 or 0 (T1).

2. Of the three basic properties (T91), (materially) uval and cons coincide and correspond simply to *true* (IS: D9–1), whereas uconval corresponds to *false* (IS: D9–2).

3. Of the twelve defined relations (T92), (materially) incomp corresponds to *exclusive* (IS: D9–6), comp to *non-exclusive* (or *conjunct*), der to *implicate* (IS: D9–3), impl to *implies* (IS: D9–3), equiv to *equivalent* (IS: D9–4), disj to *disjunct* (IS: D9–5); no concepts corresponding to super and sub appear directly in IS, but they may be easily implemented. Out of the four remaining material relations, indepen and indep are *empty* since two comp propcls are always der from each other; depen and dep, on the other hand, are *universal*, holding between any two propcls. In IS, therefore, the corresponding radical concepts are only casually mentioned, whereas one of the corresponding L-concepts, namely *L-dependent* (D14–3) occupies an important position.

We come now to the non-extensional concepts.

1. A syntactical concept, corresponding to $var_A'P$ (T93), but only with regard to single sentences and single expressions, appears in FL (D28–3) as 'instance of S_1 with respect to i_k'. But it would be easy to generalize Carnap's concept to full correspondence, and other logicians make indeed use of the generalized concept of multiple simultaneous replacement.

2. Only one of the five non-extensional material properties is dealt with by Carnap. But before dealing with this extremely interesting correspondence, let us finish with the other four cases. Irredun and redun are in our special case rather trivial, since there is only one true irredun propcl, namely the null-class (of props), every true propcl being der from it (T41); any other true propcl is redun. excl and alt, on the other hand, are important concepts, though even more so in the case of classes of propositional functions; we shall therefore deal with them later on.

There remains exh. It is a non-extensional property of propcls, since P and Q may both be false, hence equiv, and P exh, containing one true element, but Q need not be exh, all its elements being false. Though exh is, therefore, not a truth-property, it nevertheless depends only on the truth-value of something, to wit, not upon the truth-value of a propcl, but upon the truth-values of its elements. It should therefore be also *extensional*, in some other sense of this term. We have before us one more case of a certain lack of symmetry in the usual construction of propositional logic, to which attention was called by Carnap, both in IS and in FL.[53] The source of this asymmetry is our custom to look upon the class-concept *"conjunctively"*, i.e., to understand by the assertion of a propcl the assertion of all its elements. This common procedure entered our exposition of Bolzano's theory, when I accepted the common definition, by which a class is called true, if *all* its elements are true, and false, if at least one element is false (D2). Carnap has shown[54] that it is convenient for certain purposes to use another conception of a propcl, the *disjunctive* one according to which asserting a propcl means the same as asserting that at least one of its elements is true. For a class, conjunctively understood, he coined the term 'conjunctive', for a class, disjunctively understood, the term 'disjunctive', and distinguished both from the *"neutral"* conception. Many definitions and theorems would have got a simpler formulation with the help of these new and important terms. I decided not to employ them before, so as not to deviate too much from the customary terminology. But now I intend to show in just one example the potential fruitfulness of the "junctive"-terminology.

If we designate with Carnap by 'P^v' the disjunctive which corresponds to the neutral P, we can reformulate D25 in the following simple way: D25A. If P contains at least two elements, then

$\qquad$ P is exh $=_{def}$ P^v is true.

exh failed to be extensional, since Bolzano defined his equiv conjunctively. Let us agree to call two propcls P and Q *disjunctively equiv*, if P^v and Q^v have the same truth-values, to rechristen Bolzano's equiv, which holds between P and Q when $P^\bullet$ (the conjunctive corresponding to the neutral P) and $Q^\bullet$ have the same truth-values, as *conjunctively equiv*, and to call finally two propcls (strongly) *equiv*, when they are both conjunctively and disjunctively equiv.

It is now easy to see that exh is what we may call *disjunctively extensional*, i.e., whenever P is exh and P and Q are disjunctively equiv, Q is exh. The abolishment of the asymmetry mentioned has helped us to find a new sense of 'extensional', to our intuitive satisfaction. There is, of course, a third sense of 'extensional', namely '(strongly) extensional', the definition of which is clear. This success must not cause us to overlook the fact that we have not yet exhausted all the plausible senses of 'extensional'; excl, for instance, a property depending only on the truth-

---

[53] See, e.g., FL, p. 105.
[54] For the whole discussion, cf. FL, p. 104ff.

values of the elements of the given propcl, is still not extensional in either of the mentioned senses.

As a matter of fact, we already made use of a device with a somewhat similar effect as the introduction of the junctives. Our '$\overline{P}$ is false' means the same as 'P^v is true', and we could have defined 'disjunctively equiv' by 'P is *disjunctively equiv* to Q $=_{def}$ $\overline{P}$ is equiv to $\overline{Q}$'. Lack of space prevents us from entering deeper into this subject.

3. With regard to the nine (conjunctively) non-extensional relations (T95), we shall content ourselves to remark that with the exception of irreder and reder, which are trivial for the same reasons as the corresponding properties, all of them are disjunctively extensional. More will be said in the next section.

Since the three class-conceptions coincide with regard to unit-classes, there remains for this case only one sense of 'extensional'. The reader will easily verify that in this special case excld, excls, and biexcld all coincide with incomp, condi and concl correspond to *non-equivalent* in IS; no specially defined term in IS corresponds to contr, but *non-disjunct* would be suitable; exh-in-relation-to, finally, coincides with der. The three (conjunctively) non-extensional properties have all been defined with respect to propcls containing at least two elements and hence do not apply at all to single props.

To get an impression of the degree in which Bolzano exhausted his subject, let us take a broader survey of its possibilities. Corresponding to the sixteen extensional binary semantical propositional connections[55] — for the sake of brevity, we shall not deal with the singular connections —, there are sixteen binary propositional truth-relations. Only eight of the connections have more or less agreed upon special names and signs in modern symbolic logic. Bolzano discusses *all* corresponding truth-relations and in addition two more! We shall give the comparison in the form of a four-columned table, the first column containing Bolzano's term, the second containing one or two current terms, the third stating the condition for the holding of this relation in the form of the truth of the corresponding connection-prop, the fourth the symbolic counterpart of the third column in one of the current systems of notation.

[55] FL, p. 38.

(1) Bolzano's term	(2) Current term	(3) Truth of connection-proposition	(4) Symbolic Counter-part
p is compatible with q	p is conjunct with (non-exclusive of) q	the conjunction of p and q is true	$p \cdot q$
p is incompatible with q	p is exclusive of (non-conjunct with) q	the exclusion of p and q is true	$p \mid q$
p is derivable from q	p is an implicate of (implied by) q	the inverse implication of p and q is true	$q \supset p$
p is superaltern to q	—	(p alone is true)	$(p \cdot \bar{q})$
p is subaltern to q	—	(q alone is true)	$(\bar{p} \cdot q)$
p implies q	p implies q	the implication of p and q is true	$p \supset q$
p is equivalent to q	p is equivalent to q	the equivalence of p and q is true	$p \equiv q$
p is disjunct with q	p is disjunct with q	the disjunction of p and q is true	$p \vee q$
p is contradictory to q	p is non-equivalent to (exclusively disjunct of) q	the non-equivalence (exclusive disjunction) of p and q is true	$p + q$
p is contrary to q	p is non-disjunct with (bi-negated by) q	the bi-negation of p and q is true	$p \downarrow q$

§14. The Logic of Propositional Classes continued

There exists no logic of propcls. It apparently has not occurred to any logician to use connectives not only with (sentences expressing) props but also with propcls. It is true that to the first usage more or less corresponding counterparts may be found in everyday language, whereas no such counterparts exist for the second usage. One says 'If it rains, the street is wet', and one does not say 'If Newton's theory then Kepler's laws'. But we need not attach too much weight to this fact. Ordinary usage is none too consistent. Let p be the prop expressed by the first sentence of this section; then 'if p then such a logic should be erected' is quite good (though somewhat technical) English, but 'if the prop expressed by the first sentence of this section, then such a logic should be erected' is contrary to customary English syntax. We believe therefore the lack of correspondence with ordinary language should by no means impede us to construct a logic of propcls if only such a logic should turn out to be fruitful and important.

Part of this task is rather trivial. All the rules governing the use of the four singular and sixteen binary extensional connectives between single props can be extended to hold between propcls, conjunctively understood. 'P . Q' would mean therefore, e.g., 'P (is true) and Q (is true)'; P . Q is, of course, a prop and not a propcl, hence not homogeneous with its constituents, a fact which must be borne in mind when one comes to appraise the proposed logic of propcls. But with regard to propcls other possibilities arise. It might, for instance, be important in certain circumstances to have a concise expression for 'if all props of P (are true), then at least one prop of Q (is true)'. Such circumstances have indeed arisen, and such an expression plays an important part in one of the possible ways to construct a full formalization of propositional (and functional) logic which have been outlined by Carnap.[56] *Bolzano has a corresponding expression.* He would say 'Q is exh in relation to P'. Using the junctive-symbolism, we may write instead 'P$^\bullet \supset$ Q^V' or invent a new symbol. Carnap did the last thing, writes 'P ⊣ Q', and reads 'P involves Q'.

This example shows us the way to get a much richer, but therefore also much more complicated, theory of propcls. We must, apparently, take into account not only the truth and falsehood of the corresponding conjunctives but also of the corresponding disjunctives or, alternatively and equivalently, work not with two truth-values of propcls but with three. We might call P 'fully true' in the case that P$^\bullet$ is true, i.e., all props of P are true, 'fully false', in the case that P^V is false, i.e., all props of P are false, and 'partly true' (or 'partly false'), in the case that P$^\bullet$ is false but P^V is true, i.e., some props, but not all, of P are true. In such a logic, there would be 8 ($= 2^3$) singular connections and 512 ($= 2^{3^2}$) binary connections, otherwise expressed, 8 truth-properties and 512 truth-relations. This state of affairs recalls the so-called three-valued propositional calculus, but the analogy is only partial and superficial, the main difference being, of course, the above-mentioned heterogeneity of the connection props. It is perhaps not superfluous to stress that the three truth-values of the propcls are based on a strict two-valuedness of their elements.

[56] FL, §32.

This is not the place for a full discussion of the possibilities sketched. I shall confine myself to giving generalized truth-tables for six Bolzanian conjunctively non-extensional relations, together with the tables for five of the most important Bolzanian conjunctively extensional relations, and the tables for two more relations, namely disjunctively equiv and strongly equiv, which we have defined above. The three 'truth-values of the propcls, which are the members of these relations, "fully true", "partly true", and "fully false", will be designated by 'A' ("all"), 'S' ("some") and 'N' ("none"), respectively; the truth-values of the props stating these relations by 'T' ("true") and 'F' ("false"), as customary.

P	Q	conjunctively non-extensional relations						conjunctively extensional relations					disjunctively equiv	strongly equiv
		excld	excls	biexcld	condi	contr	exh-in-relation-to	comp	in-comp	impl	equiv	disj		
A	A	F	F	F	F	F	T	T	F	T	T	T	T	T
A	S	T	F	F	F	F	T	F	T	F	F	T	T	F
A	N	T	T	T	T	F	F	F	T	F	F	T	F	F
S	A	F	T	F	F	F	T	F	T	T	F	T	T	F
S	S	T	T	T	T	F	T	F	T	T	T	F	T	T
S	N	T	T	T	F	T	T	F	T	T	T	F	F	F
N	A	T	T	T	T	F	T	F	T	T	F	T	F	F
N	S	T	T	T	F	T	T	F	T	T	T	F	F	F
N	N	T	T	T	F	T	T	F	T	T	T	F	T	T

We shall now state, without proofs and further comments, some features of this extract of the generalized truth-tables for the 512 binary truth-relations between propcls.

1. In the *characteristics*[57] of all conjunctively extensional relations — the characteristic of impl is, e.g., TFFTTTTTT —, and only in them, there occur the same truth-values in the second and the third place, the same in the fourth and seventh place, the same in the fifth, sixth, eighth and ninth place.

2. We get from the nine-place characteristic of the conjunctively extensional relations their customary four-place characteristic, if we take only the values occurring in the first, third, seventh and ninth place. So we get from the mentioned nine-place characteristic for impl the customary four-place TFTT.

3. The customary truth-table forms therefore a proper and rather small part of the generalized truth-table.

[57] FL, p. 37.

4. The four-characteristics of incomp, excld, excls, and biexcld coincide, but the nine-characteristic of incomp is "weaker" — in an obvious sense of this word — than the nine-characteristics of excld and excls, which in their turn are weaker than the nine-characteristic of biexcld, which is finally weaker than the nine-characteristics of either condi or contr (Cf. T70).

§15. The Logic of Propositional Functions

Our exposition of the third part of Bolzano's theory, his treatment of the *formal* properties and relations of *varied props* — 'varied props' is an abbreviation for Bolzano's 'props in which one or more constituent terms are varied' —, in modern terms, of *propositional functions* or *attributes*, will be comparatively short. There exists, once again, a high degree of correspondence between Bozano's definitions of the basic concepts and those of Carnap. The following table will show this correspondence for properties:

Bolzano's properties of varied props	Carnap's properties of attributes[58]
(formally) universally valid	universal
universally contravalid	empty
consistent	non-empty

Bolzano often emphasizes the high degree of similarity which exists between his theories of the properties and relations of terms and those of varied props, and thereby justifies the common terminology which he proposes, even when it deviates considerably from the then common usage. It is a pity that he failed to see that this similarity is in fact — an identity (at least partially). Had he recognized this fact, his so astonishingly unifying treatment would have been even more comprehensive, and instead of the far-reaching correspondence which he established between varied props and terms he would have developed a single theory.

As for relations between varied props or attributes, only four of them are mentioned explicitly by Carnap,[59] namely 'implicate', 'implies', 'equivalent', and 'exclusive', corresponding to Bolzano's 'der', 'impl', 'equiv', and 'incomp', but it presents no difficulties to extend the whole table of §13 to the case of attributes.

[58] IS, p. 41.
[59] loc. cit.

Let us finally note that cons, which coincided with uval with regard to props and propcls, gains independence and importance in its application to varied props. Raised to the semantical level, it plays a central role in various logistic systems by Hilbert, Gödel, Tarski, Carnap and others as 'satisfiable',[60] 'fulfillable', 'having a model', 'non-empty', etc. Russell paraphrases it as 'possible', 'uconval' as 'impossible', 'uval' as 'necessary';[61] this is rather unfortunate with regard to radical concepts, but quite satisfactory for the corresponding L-concepts.

§16. THE LOGIC OF CLASSES OF PROPOSITIONAL FUNCTIONS

Coming now to the last special part of Bolzano's general theory, the logic of classes of varied props, we find ourselves once again on almost untrodden ground. Though a set of propfus — thus I shall henceforth abbreviate 'propositional functions' — is one method of formulation of an axiom-system,[62] one works normally with the conjunction of these functions instead of their class. I believe to have shown, in the treatment of propcls, that this procedure, far from being equivalent to that of conjunctions, as most logicians believe even now, essentially limitates the possibilities. We need not dwell any longer on this subject, since Carnap has already shown[63] that working with classes of props and propfus is indispensable for certain purposes.

It is with regard to classes of varied props that Bolzano's definitions and theorems gain their full weight; some concepts which have been trivial, empty or universal before, come now to fullblooded life, especially those concepts which resisted to become extensional even after our widening of this term to include disjunctive extensionality. For P to be irreder fom Q it is not enough that whenever a var'Q is true the corresponding var'P is true, neither will the truth-values of the variants of the elements of P and Q decide whether or not irreder holds between them. Nevertheless irreder is not an *intensional* relation, in the sense that its holding depends upon something more than truth-values; for as soon as the truth-values of *all* props are given (and with them ranges

---

[60] Carnap, in the preface to FL, p. XI, calls attention to the fact that the terms 'universally valid' and 'satisfiable', as used e.g. by Gödel in his 1930 theorem, are not of a syntactical nature, as Gödel himself probably believed at that time, but of a semantic one. With Bolzano, they are absolute.

[61] This is his "philosophical" interpretation; his normal terms are "always true", "always false", and "sometimes true and sometimes false".

[62] See Carnap, *The Logical Syntax of Language*, 1937, p. 272.

[63] FL, p. 114.

of variation of all terms), it is thereby completely decided whether irreder holds between P and Q or not.

From this point of view, Bolzano's work may be looked upon as a treatise in axiomatics — probably the first of its kind —, which not only deals extensively and precisely with some of its concepts, now regarded as most important, such as consistency, independency, irredundancy, and develops the now usual model-method, but also introduces concepts, or better kinds of concepts, which have been neglected in current syntax and semantics, and only partly and apparently independently developed in the most recent studies of Carnap.

§17. Bolzano's Unified Theory

Great as Bolzano's merits are for the development of several special branches of logic, his most important achievement is perhaps the endeavour to deal in one stroke with what are commonly regarded even today as distinct logical theories. And there can be no doubt that his treatment was successful. Of course, some of the defined concepts fail to be interesting in one or more of the special branches, but this is a price which generalization must always pay.

This trend has only very recently be followed up by several logicians. To look upon props as a limiting case of propfus has proved to be fruitful in various respects.[64] But even Carnap who otherwise went very far in his attempt to create a unified terminology for the various branches of logic and indeed uses the same terms for relations between attributes as for relations between props and propcls, employs different terms for corresponding properties, as shown in the table of §13. He avoids thereby, of course, a too great deviation from customary usage; but whereas this is an appropriate procedure for works of expositional and general character, we should, in technical treaties, follow Bolzano to complete uniformity. It sounds unnatural to say of a propcl that it is uval when what is meant by this pompous expression is just that this propcl is true, but one can get used to it; and it pays to get used to it.

Let us end our evaluation with three disconnected remarks:

1. So far as I can find out, Bolzano does nowhere state anything with regard to the number of props contained in the propcls with which he deals; since Bolzano showed in other works great skill in dealing with infinite classes, it is not impossible that he did not wish to exclude the case of the transfiniteness of the propcls. There is, anyhow, no difficulty

---

[64] Cf. IS, p. 48.

at all in extending the application of his theory to this case. The vital importance of this extension need not be stressed.[65]

2. Of the many valuable historical remarks with which Bolzano surrounds his systematic exposition, I should like to mention just one. In the annotations to the paragraph dealing with equiv, he mentions various definitions given by logicians who lived in the 18th and the first half of the 19th century. He mentions not less than 16 such definitions. Some of them define equiv, in effect, as a relation which holds between two sentences which express the same prop – in effect only, since the actual formulations are much more vague. One defines two props as equiv when they are interchangeable *salvo sensu*, to which definition Bolzano remarks that two props which, as *two*, though equiv must be different, may never be interchanged without changing the sense, since one may call *another prop* only what has *another sense*, and that there are contexts in which plainly equiv props may not be interchanged as, e.g., in "The class of terms contained in the prop A ...", where A is "This is an equilateral triangle" and B is "This is an equiangular triangle".[66] Other logicians distinguished between *grammatical* equivalence of sentences and *logical* equivalence of props. Against those who defined equiv by 'having the same meaning', Bolzano recalls that only sentences, as linguistic expressions of props, have meanings, namely the respective props, whereas the meaning of a prop is just — the prop itself. *Two* props which have the same meaning are therefore *one* prop. Another defines *materially* equiv with respect to expressions of identical meaning such as 'Bill is Jim's father' and 'Jim is Bill's son', to which Bolzano replies that these two expressions are not different expressions of one prop but of two different props, their subjects and predicates being different.[67] Bolzano finally remarks that never before has the relation of equivalence been extended to hold between propcls, though just this extension is of great importance in science, especially in mathematics.

3. I have already mentioned that though Bolzano's theory of radical concepts is quite satisfactory, he has not succeeded in implementing it by a theory of the corresponding L-concepts. This is a very serious

---

[65] Cf. FL, §29.

[66] Is it necessary to draw very recent parallels to these arguments?

[67] This time I cannot resist the temptation to call attention to completely parallel discussions held recently. Cf., therefore, G. E. Moore, "Russell's 'Theory of Description'", The Philosophy of Bertrand Russell, 1944, pp. 210–211, C. Lewy, "Equivalence and Identity", Mind vol. 55 (1946), pp. 223–233, and Y. Bar-Hillel, "Analysis of 'Correct' Language", Mind. vol. 55 (1946), pp. 338–339 [reprinted here as Ch. 19].

drawback, since neither material implication nor even formal implication can for themselves serve as sufficient bases for logical inference, contrary to the opinion of many distinguished modern logicians. It would therefore be anachronistic to reproach Bolzano for having failed in this respect. On the contrary, let us note that from the systematic point of view, though not from the historic one, he missed the development of at least the foundations of L-semantics only very nearly. He developed, neatly and exactly, his highly original theory of the degree of validity of a propfu, saw clearly that a propfu has at least the same validity as another propfu from which it is der, and stressed the inverse proportion between validity and content. But the whole concept of validity degenerates in the case of props and propcls, since it receives with these arguments the values 1 and 0 only. Bolzano did not see that for props another concept strikingly analogous to that of validity may be developed, namely that of *range* – in the sense of Wittgenstein-Carnap.[68] Range shares with validity the inverse proportion to content, and just as smaller (or equal) validity is a necessary condition for formal derivability between propfus, so is range-inclusion a necessary condition for L-implication between props and propcls. But range has the additional decisive property that range-inclusion is a *sufficient* condition too, so that the whole L-semantics may be developed on range as its basic concept.

§18. Summary

I hope to have established the following assertions, or at least to have given good reasons for their probable truth:

1. Bolzano created, more than 100 years ago, a generally satisfactory unified theory of the absolute radical properties and relations of props, propfus, and classes of them. Such a degree of unification has never since been achieved. It should therefore be an important task of contemporary logic to regain it, using of course all the tools of modern semantics and syntax.

2. Bolzano laid the foundations for a logic of propcls. This branch of logic has only quite recently received independent treatment again, though in certain respects not in the extension reached by Bolzano. Of the many relations between propcls which have no counterpart in propositional logic, especially those which we specified as conjunctively nonextensional but disjunctively extensional, only one has gained major

---

[68] IS, §18.

importance in one of Carnap's recent semantical systems — all the others remain unexplored.

3. Though many of the relations dealt with by Bolzano would be classified under the customary conjunctive conception of propcls as non-extensional, the introduction of new concepts of disjunctive equivalence and disjunctive extensionality would restore to many of these relations the status of extensionality to which they are entitled from the point of view that their holding depends upon the truth-values of the elements of the respective propcls only. Since nevertheless some relations remain non-extensional even after this broadening of the concept of extensionality, Bolzano's logic is to be classified as non-extensional. This is further stressed by the fact that two props may be logically equiv without being identical. There is nothing remarkable in all this, since a non-extensional (meta-) language is probably the appropriate medium to deal with absolute concepts.[69] If there is something extraordinary in Bolzano's treatment, then it is the degree to which so many properties and relations, including the most important ones, adapt themselves to an extensional framework.

4. A certain part of Bolzano's theory may be looked upon as the first rudimentary treatise on axiomatics. Many important properties of axiom-systems, such as consistency, independency, and irredundancy are defined, their interrelations investigated, and the method of models outlined.

5. Bolzano's terminology is sometimes richer and more elaborate than that now customary, and the introduction of some of his "innovations" into current logical notation should therefore be seriously contemplated. Other terms, for which equivalents exist in current usage, should be taken into account as possible alternatives.

6. Though Bolzano himself has not given a formalization of his theory, it seems that no great obstacles should stand in the way of such a task. Nor will any difficulties be found in constructing an almost complete semantical analogue to Bolzano's absolute theory.

7. Bolzano did not erect a satisfactory theory of L-concepts. But it seems that by implanting the single concept of range, to which a highly analogous concept, namely validity, already exists in Bolzano's logic, such a theory could be developed.

As an historical by-effect of our primarily systematic exposition, I believe I have also shown that

---

[69] IS, p. 92.

1. Bolzano must be considered one of the most important forerunners of modern formal logic, even if he did not contribute to the development of symbolic logic,[70] and that

2. some current metalogical discussions have certain counterparts in discussions held more than a century ago on a level sufficiently high to be of current value.

Let me finally stress again that I have by no means intended to give a complete account of Bolzano's contribution to propositional logic (in its broad Bolzanian sense), and that even in the eight paragraphs of his *Wissenschaftslehre*, to which this study has been confined, many more interesting features may be found, especially of an historical nature.

---

[70] The expression 'mathematical logic' is not free from ambiguities, but if its component 'mathematical' is not to be devoid of any literal value, then we cannot assent to Dubislav when he calls Bolzano "a forerunner of *mathematical* logic". There seems to be among German logicians a certain understandable tendency to praise Bolzano beyond his certainly great merits. Even if he did not anticipate either semantics or mathematical logic, he did investigate topics far beyond his own time and created foundations for many disciplines of current value.

INDEXICAL EXPRESSIONS

I

Even very superficial investigation into the linguistic habits of users of ordinary language will reveal that there are strong variations in the degree of dependence of the reference of linguistic expressions on the pragmatic context of their production. Whereas, for instance, the sentence

(1) Ice floats on water

will be understood by almost every grown-up normal English-speaking person to refer to the same state of affairs (this statement needs, strictly speaking, some qualifications which, however, in view of their generality, do not disturb the distinctions we are going to make), what the sentence

(2) It's raining

is intended to refer to will be fully grasped only by those people who know the place and the time of its production, and the identification of the intended reference of the sentence

(3) I am hungry

will require the knowledge of its producer and the time of its production.

I hope that the reader has noticed various ambiguities in the first paragraph and I hasten to straighten them out. I shall use in this paper the term 'sentence' in its traditional grammatical connotation, so that (2), for instance, will be regarded as a full-grown sentence rather than a mere abbreviation of a sentence, as modern logicians like to have it. And, secondly, I have, of course, to introduce immediately the now well-known type-token terminology with respect to the various usages of 'sentence'. Using this terminology, we may say that all the tokens of the sentence-type (1) will be understood by almost every grown-up English-speaking person to refer to the same state of affairs, whereas nothing of this kind can be said with respect to the tokens of (2) and (3).

Assuming this to be the case, we are entitled, according to a common and extremely important procedure, to abstract from the pragmatic context of the production of the various tokens of (1) altogether and say that all the tokens of (1) have the same reference. Most people and many philosophers would even speak of the common reference of the sentence-type (1). I shall adhere – as I did already in the first paragraph – to this usage without any ontological commitments, i.e., I am ready to regard it merely as a form of speech. In any case, I am for the moment completely uninterested in the ontological status of the references of sentences.

What is, however, important, for our purposes, is that not all the tokens of (2) have the same reference, though some of them may have, and that we are therefore not entitled to speak of *the* reference of (2) even as a form of speech. With respect to (3), we might even safely say that no two of its tokens have the same reference, since even if they are produced by the same person, say A, their production takes place at different times, say t_1 and t_2, so that one token will have the same reference as (any token of) 'A is hungry at t_1' (where 'is' is to be understood tenselessly) and the other token will have the same reference as 'A is hungry at t_2'.

It follows that the abstraction from the pragmatic context, which is precisely the step taken from descriptive pragmatics to descriptive semantics, is legitimate only when the pragmatic context is (more or less) irrelevant and defensible as a tentative step only when this context can be assumed to be irrelevant. It is, therefore, just a mistake to deal with references of the sentence-types (2), (3) and their like. Though denying a *reference* to type (2), we might still say it has a *meaning* in this sense that its various tokens may fulfil the same pragmatic function (or the same pragmatic functions), say to draw attention to certain meteorological conditions in the space-time neighbourhoods of their producers (or in certain other specifiable neighbourhoods). It seems, however, advisable to avoid the overburdened term 'meaning' in this connection, and I propose, therefore, to use instead the term *'function'* (as short for 'pragmatic function').

Similar things hold with respect to truth. Every token of (1) is true, and since all the tokens of (1) have the same reference, we may say in short that (1) is true. That the 'since'-clause in the former sentence is necessary is shown by

(4) I am producing now a sentence-token,

every token of which is true but which, nevertheless, cannot be regarded as true itself, since it does not refer to anything. (This "paradoxical" situation and a similar one arising with respect to the next example (5) will be discussed somewhat fuller in section VIII.)

Not all (possible) tokens of (2) or (3) have the same truth-values; with respect to these types, it is even more obvious that it makes no sense to speak about their truth or falsity.

To simplify the terminology, I shall call a sentence-token which is either true or false a *statement*-token and its reference a *proposition*. If and only if each sentence-token of the same type has one and the same proposition as its reference, I shall call this type a statement(-type).

According to this usage, only (1) will be a statement, but neither (2) nor (3) nor (4), though all tokens of these sentences are statements and all tokens of (4) even true statements.

This is a disquieting situation, though rather obvious and therefore often noticed. I have, nevertheless, the impression that its implications have not always been understood and its consequences not often been drawn and certainly not to a sufficient degree.

But before I proceed to draw what seems to me to be the necessary consequences of our insight, I should like to point out that the account given so far is still oversimplified to such a degree that obviously relevant factors have been left out. Is it, for instance, really the case that *all* tokens of type (3) are statements? Would we like to regard as a statement the utterance of such a token by an actor on the stage? Or the writing of another token of (3) in the sand of the desert by some strange play of the winds? I certainly would not, at least when the pragmatic context of the production of these tokens were known to me. For a sentence to be a statement, it has to fulfil certain syntactic and semantic conditions, but we see now that, in addition, its production has to fulfil certain pragmatic conditions, too, such as being produced by a conscious being having a certain "propositional attitude"; we shall not enter a discussion of the specific required conditions. We learn also from these situations that sometimes a sentence-token which is not meant by its producer to be a statement is understood so by a listener or reader, and we can, of course, very well imagine the opposite situation.

The extraordinary status of (4) is a bit shaken by these considerations, because now it turns out that not all imaginable tokens of this type are true, as we assumed before somewhat rashly. The situation is similar with respect to another "paradoxical" sentence-type

(5) I am dead.

It is, once again, not exactly the case that all tokens of this type are false, as has been assumed by some authors, though we might still say that all those tokens which are capable of being either true or false, the statements among them, cannot fail to be false.

One is, of course, entitled to introduce the additional pragmatic conditions into the definition of 'sentence' itself and to deny this predicate to patterns which "look like sentences" but the production of which does not fulfil the mentioned conditions. Such patterns might then be called perhaps "sentence-like patterns". But I still would not agree to Gilbert Ryle's formulation[1] that an actor's utterance cannot be classified

---

[1] In " 'If', 'So', and 'Because' ", *Philosophical Analysis*, 1950, pp. 323–340.

as either "use" or "mention". It is true that an actor does, in one important sense, neither use statements nor state propositions, but he still uses and perhaps even mentions propositions. In another sense, however, he even uses ("fictitious") statements and states ("fictitious") propositions.

These considerations make no difference with regard to sentence-type (3). It is not a statement, anyhow. But what with regard to (1)? We decided before to call it a statement, assuming that *all* its tokens have practically the same reference. But now we see that this is not the case – there might be some tokens of this type which have no reference at all, are not at all statements. Well, I still believe that it is advantageous to stick to our former decision. The cases where a token of (1) is not meant to be a statement are surely rather exceptional and anyhow completely harmless, since in these exceptional cases the tokens of (1) do not have a reference different from that possessed by the regularly produced tokens but no reference at all, and to abstract from them, therefore, is still in line with common scientific procedure. But let us not forget these exceptions, else we shall find ourselves sometimes confronting self-created pseudo-problems.

Another preliminary clarification has to be given to the term 'sentence-token'. I shall use it in such a way that a sentence-inscription, for instance, will be regarded as "the same token" during its whole lifetime. More technically speaking, sameness of linguistic tokens will be defined by *genidentity*. Accordingly, we may say that many people read the same sentence-token, and this even at different times.

This procedure is by no means necessary, and it has rather awkward consequences, in certain cases. But other procedures will have their disadvantages, too, and it seems to me that for our investigation the decision chosen is the least evil.

II

Let us turn now to our main theme. Having grasped clearly that it is meaningless to speak about the truth, or even reference, of the sentence-type (3), a conviction we summarized in denying this type, and similar ones, the title 'statement', we may now ask about the reference and truth of a certain *token* of this type. To what, then, does a certain token of 'I am hungry' refer? To the fact that I am hungry? Is this token true if and only if I am hungry? Certainly not! Outrageous as this interpretation sounds, let us notice, in passing, that the truth of sentences of this kind does not fulfil the famous Leśniewski-Tarski criterion of adequateness, at least not in its unsophisticated version which is meant to hold for statements of type (1). We may even turn the tables and safely declare that the inapplicability of this truth-criterion to a given sentence-type is a critierion that this type is not a statement.

What then, to ask the question again, does a certain token of (3) refer to? I hope that the reader is now ready to see that no categorical answer can be given to this question, so long as the pragmatic context of the production of this token is not known. Only when we know that it had been produced by B at time t_3, when he was fully conscious, not reciting a part of a play, etc., can we say that it refers to the same proposition as any token of 'B is hungry at t_3', a type of statements for which we assume that all questions of reference and truth are settled, so that this answer will satisfy us. Not knowing the pragmatic context, we can answer only hypothetically, with the help of a subjunctive conditional, "If this token had been produced by C at t_4, it would have meant that C is hungry at t_4", or using a general conditional, "For every person X and every time t, if X produces a token of the type 'I am hungry' at t (in an appropriate mood) this token refers to the proposition that X is hungry at t". And such a token of 'I am hungry' produced by X at t will be true if and only if X is hungry at t.

But I am not yet satisfied. I am afraid that certain modes of expression which I have used so far and which are in full accord with the common ways of argumentation are dangerously misleading and have, in fact, misled many philosophers. I refer to the expression 'a token of (3) has a definite reference in a certain pragmatic context', which may be paraphrased as 'a token of (3), as produced by C at t_4, refers to the proposition that C is hungry at t_4'. The adverbial clause 'in a certain pragmatic context', or the sentential clause 'as produced by C at t_4' are logical danger signals. They give the impression of being not too essential qualifications which cannot change the intrinsically dyadic relation of reference holding between a sentence-token and the proposition expressed by it. But this would be a mistake. Since the pragmatic context is essential and its omission leaves the token without reference, we have before us an essentially triadic relation between token, context, and proposition. We are entitled, of course, to analyse, for certain purposes, the context further into producer, recipient, the time of production, the place of production, etc., and get thereby polyadic relations with 4, 5, or more terms. And we are, of course, entitled, if we wish so for certain purposes, to reduce the triadic relation to a dyadic one, but – and this is the essential point – in this case the one member of the relation would not be any more the token itself, but the ordered pair consisting of the token and the context. Shifting the context to the other side of the relation, though formally completely correct, would be less in agreement with our usual linguistic habits and would anyhow change nothing at all.

There is nothing new in my point. It has been stressed often enough that it is not a sentence-token that refers to a proposition, but that it is a person who refers to something by this token (or a person-like machine, to keep up with the latest developments of communication-theory). And this is certainly true. But it is, on the other hand, also admissible and fruitful to speak about the reference of a sentence-token, if the context is irrelevant. And I am not sure whether this vital distinction, though nothing more than a restatement of the conditions which allow the transition from descriptive pragmatics to descriptive semantics, has always been fully understood.

The whole situation deserves more careful study with the help of an appropriate symbolism. Let me hint here at one possible start. Taking the triadic relation "(the sentence) a refers-pragmatically-to (the proposition) b in (the pragmatic context which includes also a reference to a language) c" as an undefined primitive concept – in symbols: $RP(a, b, c)$ – one could define "a refers-pragmatically-in-c-to b" – in symbols: $RP_c(a, b)$ – and "a-in-c refers-pragmatically-to b" – in symbols: $RP^+((a; c), b)$ – as being synonymous with it and then define 'refers-semantically' on the basis of one of these concepts, e.g. $RS(a, b) =_{df} (c)(d)(RP(a, b, c) = RP(a, b, d))$.

I propose not to assign reference and truth to sentence-tokens of type (2), (3), and their like, but only to a sentence-token-in-a-certain-context, i.e. to the ordered pair consisting of the sentence-token and its context. For the purpose of shorter expression, I shall call such a pair a *judgment*, thereby distilling a new sense out of this old-fashioned term. I hope the reader will carry in mind that, in this article, a judgment is neither the judged sentence-token nor the process of producing this token, but nothing more and nothing less than just the pair consisting of the token and the context.

By this proposal, I have reversed my former decision to call all tokens of (2) to (5), inclusive, statements. To leave no doubt open and to round off my terminology, I shall now make my final terminological proposals:

I shall use '*sentence*' (with respect to ordinary languages) as it is customarily used by grammarians.

Ordered pairs of sentences and contexts, of which truth or falsity may be predicated, will be called *judgments*.

The first component of a judgment will be called a *declarative sentence*.

A declarative sentence which paired with any context whatsoever forms judgments which refer always to the same proposition will be called a *statement*, otherwise an *indexical declarative sentence*, shortened to *indexical sentence* whenever misunderstandings will not be likely to arise.

The terms 'proposition', 'judgment', 'declarative sentence', 'statement', and 'indexical sentence' can be easily defined on the basis of the mentioned primitive triadic relation, its derivatives, and 'sentence'. One example will do for the purpose of illustration:

$$a \text{ is a statement} =_{df} (Eb)(RS(a, b)).$$

The distinction between 'indexical' and 'non-indexical' could, of course, be drawn also with respect to other types of sentences. "Close the door!" would be an indexical, "A to close the door d_1 at t_1!" a non-indexical command. But I shall limit my discussion to declarative sentences only.

All the definitions given refer, of course, to tokens only. The definitions of 'sentence-type' and 'statement-type' are obvious. And it clearly makes no sense to speak about 'judgment-types'.

According to these definitions, all the tokens of (1) and none of the tokens of (2) to (5), inclusive, will be statements, but the pairs of all of them with their pragmatic contexts will be judgments.

With respect to most artificial interpreted language-systems, our terms 'sentence', 'declarative sentence', and 'statement' coincide, whereas 'indexical sentence' is empty and 'judgment' unimportant. These systems have been constructed so that the pragmatic contexts of the production of their sentences is completely irrelevant. I believe that Carnap was the only major logician who mentioned this point explicitly, when he decided[2] to restrict his discussion of General Syntax to languages featuring this property only. He also drew the important distinction between two types of context-dependency (Carnap's own term is 'extra-syntactical dependence' which might be somewhat misleading outside the framework of Logical Syntax): an inessential one where the relevant context consists of preceding sentences only exemplified by "Yes" as an answer to "Does ice float on water?", where "Yes" is immediately replaceable by the statement (1); and an essential one, where the relevant context is extra-linguistic, which is much more interesting and therefore the main one discussed in this paper.

Owing to the restriction to non-indexical languages – voluntary and explicit with Carnap, unconscious with most other logicians – the tre-

---

[2] In *The Logical Syntax of Language*, London, 1937, § 46, p. 168.

mendous development of Logical Syntax and Semantics in the last two decades has had only limited bearings on indexical languages, and no satisfactory *logic of judgments* has been proposed so far, although judgments with indexical components play an extremely important role both in common and in philosophical discourse. I have no statistics available, but I guess that more than 90 per cent of the declarative sentence-tokens we produce during our life-time are indexical sentences and not statements; it is plain that most sentences with tensed verbs are indexical, not to mention all those sentences which contain expressions like 'I', 'you', 'here', 'there', 'now', 'yesterday' and 'this'.

What can be the explanation of this strange neglect of such very obvious traits of ordinary languages? I venture the following hypothesis: Since a judgment with an indexical sentence as first component can always, without loss of information, be transformed into a judgment with a statement as a first component, keeping the second component intact, we might easily be tempted to drop the common phrase 'a judgment with . . . as first component' from both sides of this transformability statement and arrive at the result that any indexical sentence can be transformed into a statement, a patent falsity, according to our former analysis. I guess that this illicit dropping is the main cause for the mentioned neglect, which is then in its turn the main cause for the grave mistakes made sometimes by good philosophers and logicians in the use and mention of indexical sentences.

Assuming that our psychological explanation holds for those cases in which treatment of the indexical traits of ordinary languages has been unconsciously neglected, we still have to face the deliberate neglect practised, for instance, by Carnap. I believe that the two main reasons behind his decision were: First, non-indexical languages are sufficient for the formulation of any given body of knowledge; second, the logic of non-indexical languages is complicated enough and should be developed before we proceed to deal with the incomparably more complicated logic of indexical languages. He was right in both reasons, in their time. But now, since the development of a satisfactory logic of non-indexical languages is well under way and since formulation of given bodies of knowledge is obviously not the only function of language, we can no longer shun the more formidable task of analysing the complicated functioning of indexical expressions.

But is not the formulation I gave to the first reason weaker than necessary? Could we not assert much more, namely that non-indexical languages are sufficient for *every* communicative purpose? If this were true, if one could always express every cognitive content in a non-indexical language, the urgency of an investigation of the logic of indexical languages would be somewhat reduced, though it would still be of extreme importance for the analysis of common and philosophical discourse as it is historically given.

Let us try to answer this question with the help of the following *Gedankenexperiment*. Assume that Tom Brown is a logician interested in our problem who has decided to find out whether he could get along, for just one day, the first of January 1951, using the non-indexical part of ordinary English only. He told, of course, his wife about this experiment. At the morning of the mentioned day Tom awakes and since it is a holiday, he decides to have breakfast in his bed. His watch is under repair and he, therefore, does not know the time. How shall he inform his wife about his wish? He is forbidden to say 'I am hungry', but even 'Tom Brown (is) hungry on January 1st, 1951' will not do, since nothing in this sentence (though, of course, many things outside the sentence) indicates that he is hungry then, rather than that he has been hungry before or will be hungry in the afternoon. And he has told his wife to react only to the sentences themselves and to nothing else. Shall he say, then,

Tom Brown is hungry at the momont when Tom Brown utters this sentence-token?

Certainly not. He is not allowed to use 'this'. Well, then perhaps

Tom Brown is hungry at the moment when Tom Brown utters 'Tom Brown is hungry'.

or, say,

Tom Brown is hungry at the moment when Tom Brown utters 'tweedledum',

or, even,

Tom Brown is hungry at the moment when a fly is sitting on his bed

will do? No, still not. There is nothing in the 'when'-clauses which ensures the uniqueness of the described situation, and Tom Brown, as a good logician, could not even use the definite article 'the' before 'moment'. Does there exist another uniqueness-ensuring 'when'-clause? Perhaps. I must admit that if I had been in his place, I would not have managed to make myself understood to my wife (or should I say 'to his wife'?) to the same degree as a simple 'I am hungry' would have done under ordinary circumstances. (This point should not be exaggerated. For successful communication it is not necessary that the event-class described in the 'when'-clause should be logically unique. A plausible empirical uniqueness will do in most cases. And it is a grave mistake to suppose that indexical expressions function always better in this respect. It is well known that many failures of communication are due to an excessive use of 'this'.)

But even if Tom Brown had a good watch and were able to say

Tom Brown is hungry on January 1st, 1951, at nine o'clock in the morning,

but his wife had none and no other means to check the time, he would have failed to communicate what he wanted to.

We see that effective communication by means of indexical sentences requires that the recipient should know the pragmatic context of the production of the indexical sentence-tokens. (Sometimes other contexts are relevant – but I shall waive their discussion.) To communicate the same information by using non-indexical sentences only, knowledge of the context by the recipient is not required, but in its stead additional knowledge of some other kind may be necessary. Not in every actual communicative situation could every indexical sentence be replaced, without loss of information, by a non-indexical sentence; but there is, on the other hand, no indexical sentence which could not be replaced by a non-indexical sentence, without loss of information, in some suitable communicative situation.

Since our knowledge is limited, the use of indexical expressions seems therefore to be not only most convenient in very many situations – nobody would doubt this fact – but also indispensable for effective communication. Indexical language will continue to be used by scientists, philosophers, and everybody else alike. Recipients of indexical communication will not always be able to know its original context and hence not be able to find the statement to which the received sentence, paired with its context, is logically equivalent. Interesting and important problems with regard to successful or unsuccessful communication are certain to arise. I believe, therefore, that the investigation of indexical languages and the erection of indexical language-systems are urgent tasks for contemporary logicians. May I add, for the sake of classificatory clarity, that the former task belongs to *descriptive pragmatics* and the latter to *pure pragmatics* (in one of the many senses of this expression)?

III

Our investigation was so far carried on mainly on the level of sentences. It can be repeated on the level of non-sentential expressions, of course only with respect to reference and not with respect to truth.

This has been the customary procedure, so far. It was C. S. Peirce who introduced the terms 'indexical sign' and 'index', Bertrand Russell used instead 'ego-centric particular', Nelson Goodman coined 'indicator', and Hans Reichenbach 'token-reflexive word'. I decided to use Peirce's term since it provides an adjective easily combined with 'sign', 'word', 'expression', 'sentence', 'language', 'communication' alike. I already made use of these combinations before, without any formal definition. Since these definitions are more or less obvious, on the semi-strict level of our exposition, I shall skip them. Let it be stressed, however, that an indexical sentence need not necessarily contain a non-sentential indexical expression as a part: 'Rain', for instance, can serve, in suitable contexts, as an indexical sentence.

IV

Let me deal, though only in a few lines, with some of the problems in communication arising out of the use of indexical language. One major problem lies in the fact that the pragmatic context, as it is known to the producer of the expression and which is, *nota bene*, not formulated but assumed to be tacitly understood in any act of communication, need not be understood in this way by a recipient and may be understood in various ways by various recipients. The depth of the pragmatic context which is necessary for the full understanding of various sentence-tokens is different, of course, from case to case and cannot even be brought into a linear order. To grasp the reference of a token of (2), for instance, one has to know more in one respect but may also know less in another respect than with regard to (3). To understand a token of (2), we have to know *where* this token has been produced, which is not necessary with regard to a token of (3); but we need not know *who* has produced it, which is necessary in the other case. (I use the expression '*the* reference of an indexical sentence' for the reference intended by the producer of this token, although I have doubts as to the usefulness of such an expression. I also use 'understand' in its strong sense of 'fully understand', i.e. 'understand in the way intended by the producer'; in another weaker sense, one can "understand" a token of (2) or (3) if one knows only that it has been produced by somebody in an appropriate mood. (2) will then be understood to mean that it is raining sometime somewhere and (3) as 'Somebody is hungry sometime', which are good 'statements' though, of course, of extremely poor content; in another weaker (or broader) sense still, *mis*understanding will also be a kind of understanding, and somebody who, for some reason or for no reason, took M to be the producer of a token of (3), whereas this token was produced by N, will still have "understood" this token'.)

Let me also just mention a brand of dependency which embraces even the non-indexical sentences. I mean the fact that any token has to be understood to belong to a certain language. When somebody hears somebody else utter a sound which sounds to him like the English 'nine', he might sometimes have good reasons to believe that this sound does not refer to the number nine, and this in the case that he will have good reasons to assume that this sound belongs to the German language, in which case it refers to the same as the English 'no'. In this sense, *no* linguistic expression is completely independent of the pragmatic context. But just because this kind of dependence is universal, it is trivial, and we shall forget it for our purposes. (May I, nevertheless, add in parentheses, that all expressions dealt with in our investigation belong to ordinary English, if not specifically mentioned otherwise.)

Though indexical communication is in so many cases much more convenient than non-indexical and often even indispensable, it carries with it additional possibilities of misunderstanding. Mistaking A for B as the producer of a token of (1) will not cause misunderstanding of this statement. But this will happen with respect to (3). There might arise cases in which both indexical and non-indexical transmission of information or commands will be possible. Weighing the respective advantages and disadvantages in such cases would be an important problem in applied semiotics. Usually, but not always, additional possibilities of misunderstandings will be a price not too high paid for shortness, straightforwardness, and other advantages of indexical communication. The main danger in indexical communication is, however, not in *this* obvious fact but in another one, namely that the dependence upon pragmatic context might sometimes be forgotten so that the recipient will tend to supplement unconsciously some context, but not the intended one, to the received expression-token and so get the impression of having received a statement-token with no special problems of reference.

I have left the central concept of this paper, namely *pragmatic context*, in rather thorough vagueness, and this for the very simple reason that I see no clear way to reduce this vagueness at the moment. From a technical point of view, it seems to me preferable to replace the contexts by *context-descriptions*. (Contexts are non-linguistic events, context-descriptions are linguistic entities.) This procedure would have the advantage that the pairs would be more homogeneous, consisting now of two linguistic components instead of one linguistic and one non-linguistic component. But, as against this, it should be borne in mind that a context-description might be more specific than the context which the producer might have had "in his mind". The vagueness in which I left the expression 'pragmatic context' is partly due to the fact that its reference is often intrinsically vague itself.

Let me also call attention to the fact that of two tokens, belonging to the same type, the one may be indexical and the other not and that sometimes the very same token may be understood indexically by A and non-indexically by B. A token of 'Socrates has an ugly wife' (with a tenseless 'has') will be understood by most educated people in the year 1951 non-indexically, but there may be a few people who have acquaintances called 'Socrates' – with or without ugly wives – and would therefore like to know the pragmatic context of the production of this token before they are able to make up their mind with respect to the reference and truth of this token. To say that what the grammarians call 'proper names' in ordinary languages are not always (or perhaps never?) "really" or "logically" proper names is just one way – and not the best one – of explaining this somewhat inconvenient fact.

V

The question of the interdefinability of the various indexical expressions has been discussed quite often in recent years. It is, however, still not customary among philosophers to distinguish such a question in descriptive pragmatics of ordinary languages where 'interdefinability' would be synonymous (more or less) with 'universal replaceability without loss of information' from verbally the same question with respect to a language-system supposed to stand "in close connexion" with ordinary language. In the second case, the question would belong to pure special pragmatics, if the language-system is pragmatic, or to pure special semantics, if the system is semantic. With all the vagueness left by this non-distinction in mind, let us now turn to an investigation of some of the answers given.

Russell[3] believes that all indexical expressions can be defined with the help of non-indexical expressions plus the single indexical word 'this', and he is followed in this respect by Reichenbach,[4] Arthur Pap,[5] and others, sometimes with slight variants. Russell says, for instance, at one

---

[3] In *Human Knowledge*, London, 1948, ch. iv, pp. 100 ff.
[4] In *Elements of Symbolic Logic*, New York, 1947, § 50, pp. 248 ff.
[5] "Are Individual Concepts Necessary?", *Philosophical Studies* I (1950), p. 22.

place that "I" means "the person experiencing this" and defines in another place "I" as "the person attending to this". It is, however, pretty obvious that Russell's statement, understood in the sense that 'I' can always and without loss of information be replaced by 'the person experiencing this', is false, and this because it is simply not at all the case that "given the speaker and the time, the meaning of 'this' is unambiguous", as everybody will verify immediately: Knowing *only* the speaker and the time of utterance of 'The person experiencing this is hungry', we would not yet be justified in understanding that the speaker was hungry at the time of the utterance of this token (though we would probably fail only seldom if we understood it in this way), whereas we could do so unhesitatingly on hearing 'I am hungry' and knowing once again the speaker and the time of utterance only. It is a very plain fact that whereas the *function* (not, of course, the *reference*) of 'I' is unambiguous, the function of 'this' is decidedly not so. 'This' is used to call attention to something in the centre of the field of vision of its producer, but, of course, also to something in his spatial neighbourhood, even if not in his centre of vision or not in his field of vision at all, or to some thing or some event or some situation, etc., mentioned by himself or by somebody else in utterances preceding his utterance, and in many more ways.

VI

Sometimes the question of reducibility of the indexical expressions to just one of them has been discussed together with the question of their complete eliminability, a problem we discussed before (in section II). And, indeed, a positive solution of the first would simplify the solution of the second since the eliminability of one indexical expression only had now to be brought under consideration.

When I arrived at the result that indexical communication is indispensable, I was in good company. Peirce,[6] Russell, Arthur W. Burks,[6] and Pap came to the same conclusion. But their arguments seem to me to be wrong and of sufficient interest to be discussed here. If I have understood them rightly, their main argument is that replacing 'here' or 'now' by co-ordinate-descriptions does not eliminate the indexical space and time descriptions since the origin of the co-ordinate-system,

---

[6] Peirce's theory of indexes is given a good exposition and critical discussion by Burks in "Icon, Index, and Symbol", *Philosophy and Phenomenological Research* ix (1949), pp. 679 ff. Burks' own later treatment of the problem shows decisive advances towards better understanding of the specific functioning of indexical expressions.

to which the replacing co-ordinates refer, the directions and the units of its axis can be taught and learned only with the help of indexical, linguistic or non-linguistic, signs. But this seems to me to be a very obvious *non sequitur*, based on a *confusion between using language and learning how to use language*. There can be little doubt that learning how to use co-ordinates, just as learning how to use words like 'red', involves the use of indexical signs. But, nevertheless, a co-ordinate, just as the word 'red', is non-indexical in the clear and definite sense we used this term in our discussion, namely, to say it again, in its reference being independent of the pragmatic context of its production. A token of 'This book is red' will not be understood in the way intended by its producer by anybody who does not know the context of its production, even if he has an encyclopedic knowledge and an arsenal of tools; a token of 'The book at location l_1 and time t_1 is red' will be understood in exactly the same way by anybody having a certain knowledge (which he might have got with the help of indexical signs) and perhaps other tools.

Reichenbach, if I have understood him rightly, claims to have developed a method for complete elimination of indexical expressions (p. 287). Since this method is very intricate and interwoven with his peculiar theory of token-quotes, a criticism of which is beyond the limits of this paper, I shall state only somewhat dogmatically that a thorough investigation of this method has shown me that an elimination according to it requires additional knowledge on the part of both producer and recipient, in conformity with our former results.

With respect to Reichenbach's contribution to our whole topic, I fully agree with Nelson Goodman when he states[7] that "Reichenbach goes considerably beyond Russell's remarks on ego-centric particulars" but that this "treatment is still incomplete and faulty in some respects. Nevertheless, the approach is essentially correct, and there is probably no equally adequate discussion of the matter in print." (The 'is' in the second clause of the last sentence is tensed and refers, in its context, to 1947. And my agreement with Goodman's evaluation holds, therefore, only with respect to this date.)

---

[7] In his review of Reichenbach's *Elements* in *Philosophical Review* 57(1948), p. 102. Goodman's own treatment of the problem in his *Structure of Appearance*, Harvard University Press, 1951, ch. xi, was published too late to be discussed at this place.

VII

P. F. Strawson, in a recent paper in MIND,[8] dealt with many of the topics discussed here, and I believe that our evaluations of the functions of indexical discourse coincide to a high degree. Strawson draws admittedly rough and ready distinctions between a sentence (understood to be always in this context short for 'a sentence having a uniquely referring expression as its subject'), a use of a sentence, and an utterance of a sentence (325). Whereas his sentence corresponds to my sentence-type and his utterance of a sentence to my sentence-token, his use of a sentence is apparently somewhat more specific than my judgment. According to Strawson, only by producing utterances of the *same* sentence, can one make the same use of this sentence. The question when two judgments are the same has been left dependent, by me, on the question of identity between propositions. And usually this identity is defined in more liberal terms than identity of the sentences referring to them. According to one of these more liberal definitions, two judgments can be identical without their first components belonging to the same sentence-type. I have no intention to enter here any more the discussion about the merits of the various possible decisions; whether the propositions referred to by the sentences 'The sun is larger than the moon' and 'The moon is smaller than the sun' should be considered as identical has already been discussed *ad nauseam*, and I have no radically new solutions to offer.

I agree completely with Strawson when he warns us of the danger of confusing talk about sentences with talk about uses of sentences, and he is right when he charges Russell with making sometimes just this confusion (329). But I do not agree with him that this kind of confusion is responsible for the alleged mistakes in Russell's theory of description. With respect to the sentence, "The king of France-in-1872 is wise", it is obvious that all its utterances – to adopt for the moment Strawson's terminology – have the same character, whether they are all true or all false or perhaps neither, that therefore all its uses are the same, and that we are, finally, entitled in this case – as with respect to any non-indexical sentence (I am not saying 'statement' because Strawson intends apparently to deny this sentence its statement-character) – to apply the same predicate to the sentence itself. Whatever the reasons Strawson may have for denying that by uttering this sentence one intends to

---

[8] "On Referring", MIND lix (1950), pp. 320–344.

imply – in the customary sense of this word – that there exists a king of France-in-1872, they are not justified by his analysis of indexical expressions. I personally, had I happened to utter this sentence and were I asked by somebody whether I intended to assert by this utterance that there existed a king of France-in-1872, would have rather impatiently answered: "Sure, what else?" And since I believe, in spite of Strawson's testimony, that this is the general attitude, I see no reason to avoid the formulation that the mentioned sentence entails – in the ordinary sense of entailing – the sentence, "There exists a king of France-in-1872", and is therefore false. Whether a corresponding rule of formation is convenient, with respect to an envisaged artificial language-system, is another question which has been discussed often and competently by other authors. Incidentally, Strawson's answer to the question, "Do Russellian or Aristotelian rules give the exact logic of ordinary language?", is not: "This is a pointless question; for ordinary language has no exact logic." Instead he closes his paper with the straightforward assertion (to which I wholeheartedly agree): "Neither Aristotelian nor Russellian rules give the exact logic of any expression of ordinary language; for ordinary language has no exact logic" (344). Let me stress that I do not wish to deny that, in other cases, the predicate 'pointless' might be more suitable than 'false', though final judgment on this matter will have to await a much more elaborate treatment of this predicate.

VIII

A clear understanding of the functioning of indexical expressions can be helpful both in avoiding pseudo-problems and in solving genuine philosophical problems (though the borderline between these two cases is somewhat vague). I shall give just one example for each of these two types of application.

Sentences like

(6) I believe he has gone out, but he has not

or like (5) ("I am dead") have given headaches to some philosophers and the discussion of the so-called "pragmatic paradoxes" connected with them is still going on. On the other hand, there is nothing mysterious in sentences like

(7) Dick believes Bill has gone but Bill has not

or

(8) G. B. Shaw is dead in 1949.

G. E. Moore[9] has tried hard to destroy the mystery surrounding the sentence (6), but lack of appropriate terminology made his task very difficult. Since I have already discussed once Moore's attempt at length,[10] I shall now show only how the new terminology will allow us to dissolve the puzzling situation simply and effectively.

Let us notice that though the sentences (7) and (8) look completely innocent, certain assertions of tokens of them would be puzzling, e.g., an assertion of a token of (7) by Dick himself or of a token of (8) by G. B. Shaw himself. In the second case, we could have explained Shaw's *prima facie* strange assertion as one of his jokes and would perhaps have investigated the situation a bit more to find out what exactly might have provoked such a joke. In the first case, however, knowing nothing specially about Dick, we would be seriously puzzled and if not able to find a rational explanation for Dick's behaviour might be entitled to call it *absurd*. And that is all that is to be said in this situation. Many people behave absurdly sometimes. But it is the psychiatrist's business to deal with their behaviour and not the logician's. But is it not different with respect to (5) and (6)? Only very few exceptional assertions of (8) are absurd, but *every* assertion of (5) (which cannot be explained away as an "apparent" assertion) is absurd. Is therefore not (5) paradoxical to a degree that (8) is not? Our answer is, of course: No, not at all. That *all* assertions of (5) are absurd is due to the peculiar character of 'I' in this case, a character which has to be studied and understood much more than it has been done so far; philosophers have spent too much time in studying instead the I.[11] But there are also non-indexical sentences *all* assertions of which are absurd, e.g.:

(9) Nobody has ever uttered a sentence-token.

Let us summarize the discussion of this section: There are false statements (like (9)), all assertions of which are absurd; there are false statements (like (8)), some assertions of which are absurd; there are indexical sentences (like (3)) which as such are neither true nor false but such that some judgments containing them as first components are (possibly) false; there are indexical sentences (like (5)) which as such

---

[9] In "Russell's 'Theory of Descriptions'", *The Philosophy of Bertrand Russell*, The Library of Living Philosophers, vol. v (1944), pp. 177-225 and in "A Reply to my Critics", *The Philosophy of G. E. Moore*, The Library of Living Philosophers, vol. iv (1942), pp. 542-543.

[10] In "Analysis of 'Correct' Language", MIND, 55, 1946, pp. 333-338 [reprinted here as Ch. 19].

[11] *Cf.* Gilbert Ryle, *The Concept of Mind*, London, 1949, ch. vi, pp. 186 ff.

are neither true nor false but such that all judgments containing them as first components are false and all assertions of them absurd. (In our terminology, an assertion is a kind of behaviour and a judgment a pair of a sentence and a context.) That such linguistic situations arise is interesting enough and deserves careful study, but there is nothing in them which should disturb the logician's mind and make him start worrying about "pragmatic paradoxes".[12] (I do not intend to deny that there might exist situations of a different kind which deserve the time-honoured title of "paradox".)

IX

As an example of a solution of a genuine philosophical problem I shall now give a *proof of the impossibility of any strictly phenomenalistic language*. I am not the first to try to show this, but I believe that my approach is the simplest. To prove that the expression 'phenomenalistic language' is a *contradictio in adiecto* or, more precisely, that the property expressed by it is logically empty, I have to start of course from the meanings of the two components of this expression. I believe that the partial meanings from which I shall derive a contradiction are standard. If I am mistaken in this belief, then my proof will hold for only such interpretations of 'phenomenalistic language' which exhibit these partial meanings.

Now, I think that for a system of expressions to be called a *language*, as this term is commonly understood, it is necessary, though not sufficient, that logical relations such as derivability, contradiction, etc., should hold between at least some of the sentences of this system. I believe, in addition, that for a language to be *phenomenalistic*, as this term is commonly understood, every sentence must contain essentially, i.e. uneliminably, at least one indexical expression and therefore be an indexical sentence. Since no indexical sentence is a statement and since logical relations, as commonly understood, hold only between statements (or between the propositions referred to by them) and not between other types of sentences (at least not between other types of declarative sentences; whether or not logical relations obtain between non-indexical

---

[12] As a paradigm of the queer arguments to which philosophers have been led by misunderstanding the functioning of indexical expressions can serve the discussion on "pragmatic paradoxes" which took place recently in MIND. *Cf.* D. J. O'Connor: "Pragmatic Paradoxes", MIND, 57(1948), pp. 358–359, L. Jonathan Cohen: "Mr. O'Connor's 'Pragmatic Paradoxes' ", MIND, 59, 1950, pp. 85–87, and P. Alexander: "Pragmatic Paradoxes", MIND, 59, 1950, pp. 536–538.

commands, for instance, is an issue to be settled by decision – I mean, there are important relations between commands which require study by logicians, but whether they should be called 'logical' or some other term is a verbal issue – and of no importance for my proof), no logical relations can hold between any sentences in a phenomenalistic language, which concludes my *reductio ad absurdum*.

HUSSERL'S CONCEPTION OF A PURELY LOGICAL GRAMMAR

The assumption that there exists a common grammatical core which is valid for all languages and which can be determined by *a priori* insight is an old and venerable speculation of both linguists and philosophers. This assumption is not fashionable any more, and the old arguments adduced for it could not withstand the onslaught of the empirical evidence provided by the study of "exotic" languages. Nevertheless, in a certain sense, to be more closely determined later on, it has been taken up by no less a man than Rudolf Carnap, one of the leading logicians and antispeculative philosophers of our time.

It should therefore be of more than purely historical interest to investigate into what one of the most influential philosophers of this century, Edmund Husserl, had to say on this topic. Carnap studied some time with Husserl and it is not impossible that at least part of the impact that led him later on to write his *Logical Syntax of Language*[1] originated at that time.

I intend to deal almost exclusively with the fourth chapter of the first part of the second volume of Husserl's *Logische Untersuchungen*, in the revised version of the second edition of 1913. Husserl himself insists in the preface to this edition that he did not change his point of view relative to the first edition of 1900. He improved the text in a few respects and added a few points that were to be elaborated in later publications. The major changes seem to be due to the impact of Anton Marty's criticisms of the text of the first edition in his *Untersuchungen zur Grundlegung der allgemeinen Grammatik und Sprachphilosophie*, Halle a.S., 1908.

I

I have no idea who was the first man to ponder about the fact that certain sequences of words in a given (natural) language make sense, whereas other sequences of these very same words do not make sense. This is not as silly as it sounds. As a matter of fact, it has been taken up again recently by very sophisticated people within the framework of a new science, the Theory of Communication, and has found there an interesting and rather surprising explanation which is, however, irrelevant

---

[1] R. Carnap, *Logical Syntax of Language* (New York and London 1937). This is an enlarged and revised translation of *Die Logische Syntax der Sprache* (Vienna, 1934).

for our purposes.[2] Husserl, at any rate, who ponders about this very fact (327), claims that, though a very considerable part of the restrictions on the significance of word sequences is due to accidental linguistic habits, there is another part which is rather due to the fact that within the realm of meanings there are *a priori* laws of connection and change of which the grammatical incompatibilities, that exist in every developed language, are only the more or less articulated manifestations.

Now, this is certainly not a very novel doctrine. As a matter of fact, it is hardly more than common sense, if the technical jargon of its formulation is discounted. Aristotle would have doubtless said that the word sequence 'Grammar is winged' does not make sense, since being-winged is not a possible characteristic of a science. He did not say so in so many words, because the distinction between significant and non-significant word sequences was not made at his time, at least not in these terms. He did say, however, that 'winged' is not predicable of 'grammar',[3] for the reason stated above. This grammatical incompatibility has its roots in the ontological circumstance that the differentiae of different *genera* that do not stand in the relation of subordination are *toto coelo* different.

I do not think that Aristotle ever considered the question how he came to know this ontological circumstance. Returning to Husserl and asking this question of him, we get the answer: through *apodictic evidence*. "The incompatibility of the connection is an essential [wesensgesetzlich] one, i.e., not merely subjective, and it is not due merely to a factual inability (by forces of our "mental organization") that we are unable to perform the unity [die Einheit vollziehen]. In those cases which we have here before our eyes, the impossibility is rather objective, ideal, based in the "nature", in the pure essence of the realm of meanings, and may be grasped as such through apodictic evidence" (318). That's it. Those of us who are not much impressed by an appeal to "apodictic evidence" will be put on their guard by this appeal and will perhaps become even more suspicious than they were before towards the attempt of explaining grammatical incompatibilities through incompatibilities in the realm of meanings, or in the realm of (non-linguistic) entities, respectively. These two realms should by no means be confounded: there may

---

[2] See, e.g., G. A. Miller, *Language and Communication* (New York, 1951), especially chapter 5.

[3] Aristotle deals with this topic in chapter 3 of *Categoriae*. For a critique of Aristotle's treatment, see my doctoral thesis *Theory of Syntactical Categories* (in Hebrew) (Jerusalem, 1947), pp. 4–5.

be an incompatibility in the realm of entities when there is none in the realm of meanings. The expressions 'wooden iron' and 'round quadrilateral' are significant, their meanings exist, though there exist no corresponding entities, nor could they possibly exist. The sentence 'all quadrilaterals have 5 vertices' is an honest-to-God significant sentence, though it does not denote a possible state-of-affairs (327). Husserl is certainly more sophisticated than Aristotle in the treatment of significance, but this is not sufficient to persuade us to accept his appeal to apodictic evidence as a good answer to a good question.

Let us now see in greater detail what Husserl did grasp with the help of his apodictic evidence. The word sequence 'this careless is green' makes no unitary sense. Though each word by itself is significant, the combination of their meanings in the order indicated by the sequence is not — this much tells us our apodictic evidence. The non-significance of 'this careless is green' is of a different type from that of, say, 'this blum is green' which lacks significance because one of its constituent words lacks significance. But — and now comes an insight of Husserl's which, though not spectacularly deep and revolutionary, may well have been expressed here for the first time, with a tolerable degree of clarity — having convinced himself of the non-significance of the sequence 'this careless is green,' one is immediately sure also that any other sequence *of the same form* is non-significant: non-significant are also 'this hot is green,' 'this green is hot,' etc. All these sequences have the same form since (a) the meanings of their constituent words, insofar as their meanings are *forms* [Formen], i.e., meanings of formative expressions like 'this', 'is,' 'if,' 'and,' etc., are the same, and (b) the meanings of their constituent words, insofar as these meanings are matters [Materien], *belong to the same categories*. Since 'hot' and 'careless' belong to the same meaning category, the replacement of one of these words by the other within a given expression will leave this expression significant if it was so before and leave it non-significant if it was so before. Replacing a word within a given significant expression by a word belonging to a different meaning category will always turn this expression into a non-significant one. The significant 'this tree is green' turns non-significant, if 'tree' is replaced by 'careless,' by 'slowly,' by 'goes,' or by 'and.' (This need not be the case the other way round, of course. Replacing 'green' in 'this careless is green' by a word belonging to a different category will not *always* turn this non-significant expression into a significant one, as the reader will readily verify for himself.)

Let us not discuss here the question how to distinguish between words signifying forms and words signifying materials. This is a notoriously difficult question and still under discussion. Hence one should perhaps not take Husserl to task for his optimism in assuming this distinction to be clearer than it is. Let us only note in passing that 'this' is regarded by Husserl as a formative word (319).[4] But we must certainly ask ourselves what Husserl's meaning categories are supposed to be. And here an unpleasant surprise is awaiting us: these categories turn out to be nothing else but the objective counterparts of the grammatical categories that were regarded as standard in Husserl's time (at least for Indo-European languages)! "Where a nominal matter stands, there may stand any arbitrary nominal matter, but not an adjectival or a relational or a whole propositional [ganze propositionale] matter" (319). It follows that in order to decide which words (or expressions) can significantly replace a given word in a given context we have just to determine its grammatical category — the whole detour through the realm of meanings is at the best completely superfluous and at the worst positively damaging by misleading the inquirer into a labyrinth from which he might not find his way out again.

There can be no doubt that Husserl's apodictic evidence is, in our context, nothing but a certain kind of grammatical intuition. If Husserl's intuition in this field were sound, we would still have gained with its help certain insights, in spite of their misleading formulation. Unfortunately, Husserl's intuition was not sound and has been found lacking in at least two respects. I shall state these respects somewhat dogmatically here, as I already discussed this question at some length elsewhere.[5] First, it is simply not the case, at least not *prima facie* so, that an adjectival matter appearing in a significant text can never be replaced by a nominal matter, yielding again a significant text. It is beyond doubt that 'this tree is a plant' is significant and still is obtainable from 'this tree is green' by just such a replacement. Now I think that this objection can be met by a sufficient number of additional *ad hoc* grammatical rules, but Husserl does not discuss such rules. Nor is it clear that the overall system resulting from these additions will be a sufficiently simple one. Second, it can at least be doubted whether most speakers of English would regard 'this algebraic number is green' as a significant sentence at all. It seems hardly to be even a matter that could be settled simply by

[4] It is almost unbelievable in how many different ways the functioning of the particle 'this,' and of the other demonstratives, has been misunderstood by philosophers. Bertrand Russell regarded 'this' at one time as the only logically proper name.

[5] In my thesis mentioned in note 3.

statistical investigations. The terms 'sentence', 'significant,' 'silly,' and 'ridiculous' are not sufficiently univocal to attach much significance to the results of a questionnaire in which the testees will have to tell whether according to their intuition the word-sequence 'this algebraic number is green' is a sentence and, if so, whether it is non-significant or significant but silly or ridiculous. Husserl's assertion that "through the free replacement of matters within their category there may result false, silly, or ridiculous meanings (whole sentences or possible sentence-parts), but still necessarily unitary meanings...," as a factual statement, is therefore of doubtful validity. However, if understood as a proposal for the syntactical categorization of the expressions of German (and Husserl's examples are always taken from that language), i.e., for the erection of a language-system, closely connected with ordinary German, it has to be judged by its intrinsic merits. And here it should be stressed that, in spite of all the shortcomings in the details, Husserl has got hold of a basic insight into the techniques of language investigation. He may well have been the first to see clearly the fundamental role played in linguistic analysis by what modern linguists call *commutation*.

In summing up the first part of our critique, we may say that Husserl was one of the initiators of the technique of commutation in logico-linguistic analysis but failed in two respects: first, he did not realize that the traditional parts of speech were not useful syntactical categories beyond a first crude approximation; second, by leaving unnecessarily the linguistic level, he misled himself and others into believing that something can be achieved by exploring the realm of meanings with the help of an apodictic evidence. No support for this belief is supplied by Husserl, and the few positive theses he formulates in this field are hopelessly wrong.

II

Just as Husserl's treatment of meaning categories is an important though not always adequate anticipation of the modern theories of syntactic (or semantic) categories, so there is to be found in his distinction between *nonsense* [Unsinn] and *countersense* [Widersinn] an interesting anticipation of the modern conceptions of *rules of formation* and *rules of transformation*. To be more exact, there seems to exist a far-reaching parallelism between Carnap's conception of these two major kinds of semantic[6] rules of a language-system — a conception now almost univer-

---

[6] In *Logical Syntax*, only syntactical language-systems (non-interpreted calculi) were treated, and these rules were therefore regarded as syntactic. Later, however, as is well-known, Carnap began to study also semantical (interpreted) language-

sally accepted — and Husserl's conception of the major kinds of laws of meaning: the *laws of avoiding nonsense* [Gesetze des zu vermeidenden Unsinns] and the *laws of avoiding formal countersense* [Gesetze des zu vermeidenden formalen Widersinns] (334–335).

Nowadays, the L-emptiness of the predicate 'is-a-round-quadrangle,' i.e., the fact that, for logical reasons, there can be no entity that is a round quadrangle, will be confused only by few philosophers with the non-significance of the word-sequence 'is-a-round-or,' i.e., with the fact that this word-sequence is not well-formed. In other words: hardly anyone will now treat on a par the L-falsity of the sentence 'G is a round quadrangle', i.e., the fact that, according to the rules of transformation of (a certain formalized counterpart of) English, this sentence cannot be true, with the non-sententiality of the word-sequence 'G is a round or', i.e., with the fact that, according to the rules of formation of (this formalized counterpart of) English, this word-sequence does not form a sentence. It was otherwise fifty-one years ago. At that time the distinction between these two types of meaninglessness [Sinnlosen] seems not to have been the philosophical commonplace it is today, and Husserl goes to great lengths in stressing its importance. It is not implausible that the present conception of this distinction is to a large measure due to Husserl's efforts, though perhaps mainly through indirect channels.

However, Husserl does not formulate his distinction in the clear-cut way it is done by Carnap, for instance, nor should we expect this thirty-five years before Carnap's relevant publication. Again he makes the fatal transition from the straightforward formulation in terms of the well-formedness of certain sequences of signs to the formulation in terms of compatibility, complication, and modification of meanings. If we are ready to forget Husserl's detour through the realm of meanings and "translate" his insights into the purely syntactical idiom, we shall not hesitate to accept his evaluation that the rules of avoiding nonsense are logically prior to the rules of avoiding countersense, that the statement of the rules of formation of a certain language-system has to precede the statement of its rules of transformation. This should not have been a very deep insight since it is only trivial that the definition of the consequence relation between sentences — the major point of the transformation rules — should be based upon the definition of sentence itself — the major point of the formation rules.

systems. For such systems, he now prefers the terms 'rules of truth' or 'rules of ranges' to 'rules of transformation.' See *Introduction to Semantics* (Harvard University Press, 1946).

I think that Husserl was right in his claim that the basic role played by the rules of formation in the construction (or description) of any language had not been clearly realized by other logicians and that the classical theory of terms and judgments that used to be presented in preparation for the treatment of inference was entirely inadequate (329, 331, 342). And I think that he was right when he stressed the legitimacy of the idea of a *universal grammar*, as conceived by the rationalists of the 17th and 18th centuries (336). But not before Carnap's investigations into General (Logical) Syntax has this idea been realized to any appreciable degree of adequacy, and certainly not by Husserl himself. Though Husserl stresses the distinction between the "prescientific private conceptions of the grammarians about the meaning forms" and "the empirically distorted ideas that historical grammar, say of Latin, presents him," on the one hand, and "the pure system of forms that is scientifically determinate and theoretically coherent", i.e., Husserl's own theory of meaning forms (339), on the other hand, no real indication whatsoever is given where and how to draw this distinction. Husserl regards it as an *a priori* property of all languages to have forms for the plural, for instance, thereby justifying the significance of the question, how "the" plural is expressed in German, Latin, or Chinese. But it seems that he would regard it as illicit to ask a similar question with respect to, say, the ablative. I do not deny that there seems to exist some distinction between these two features, that we somehow have the feeling that all languages should contain some simple means of expressing "the" plural but do not feel the same with respect to "the" ablative. Modern psychologically trained linguists are, I think, in a position to explain this difference of attitude on behalf of the linguistically innocent speakers of Indo-European languages. But this does not justify by any means Husserl's distinction.

There is only one way of arriving at the common ideal grammatical framework of all empirical languages, namely by departing from the very definition of language. Nothing belongs to that framework that does not follow from this definition. The justification for an *a priori* statement that all languages contain, say, words and sentences can only be that this must be so by definition. But whether all languages contain nouns, or negation-signs, or modal expressions, after a general definition of noun etc. has been given, if this definition forms no part of the definition of language, can only be established by empirical investigation. Pure Syntax, in Carnap's sense, is a formal science whose statements, if true, are analytically so. Though Carnap defines in a general way[7]

[7] *Logical Syntax*, p. 202.

when a symbol of any given language is, say, a negation-symbol, it is, of course, quite possible that a certain language should contain no negation-symbol. (As a matter of fact, certain language-systems, well-known to formal logicians, contain no such symbol.) But it is still a theorem of General Syntax that *if* a language contains, say, a (proper) negation-expression and a (proper) disjunction-expression, than it contains also a (proper) conjunction-*expression*, though it is of course quite possible for a language to contain a negation-symbol and a disjunction-symbol without containing a conjunction-*symbol*. Just as it is a theorem of General Syntax that for each language containing proper negation, disjunction, and conjunction, the principles of traditional logic such as those of excluded middle and of contradiction are valid.[8]

The *a priori* fundaments of language which linguistics has to become conscious of, according to Husserl's challenge (338), are nothing but analytic consequences of the definition (or conception) of language. Husserl was right when he defended the non-psychological character of his purely logical syntax — as well as of logic proper — against Marty's psychologistic arguments (341), and many variants of such a syntax such as combinatorial, arithmetized, and structural syntax, have proved their value. However, the last word about the exact relationship between logical syntax and the empirical sciences such as psychology and sociology, has not been said yet.

There seems to be one point in which Husserl was not radical enough. He concedes (341) that the "upper" part of logic which — in Carnap's terms — is based upon the rules of transformation is irrelevant for (descriptive) grammar. He is satisfied with having shown that the "lower" part of logic — the rules of formation — is theoretically relevant for grammar though of little practical value. I have tried to show elsewhere,[9] in elaboration of the basic insights of Carnap, that rules of transformation are no less relevant for linguistics than rules of formation, thereby counter-balancing Husserl's stress of the relevance of the formation rules for logic. Therefore, I shall say no more here one this topic.

In conclusion, we may say that Husserl's conception of a purely logical grammar has to be regarded, in a very essential and pregnant sense, as a forerunner of Carnap's conception of a general logical syntax. One has "only" to omit the detour through the realm of meanings and

---

[8] *Logical Syntax*, p. 203.
[9] "Logical Syntax and Semantics," *Language* (1954), pp. 30, 230–237 [reprinted in LI as Ch. 2].

the reliance upon an apodictic evidence and to add a mastery in modern symbolic logic and its philosophy in order to perform the transition from Husserl to Carnap. These three steps seem to me essential improvements, but I shall not try here to justify this opinion.

ON LALIC IMPLICATION AND THE *COGITO*

G. E. Moore, in a well-known and much-discussed paper,[1] dealt with a certain sense of 'implies' which I proposed shortly after to call 'pragmatically implies' and tried to explicate.[2]

In a recent paper[3] Castañeda takes up the issue again and introduces three new kinds of implication (and of inconsistency) called, respectively, lalic, phemic, and phrastic. He makes, however, a few mistakes which he might have avoided (I hope) had he taken account of the earlier discussions.[4]

Castañeda defines: "A sentence P *lalically* implies a sentence Q if and only if even the mere fact that P is used, i.e., uttered, in whatever mode and variety and context within its type of discourse, requires the truth of Q."[5] A few lines later he illustrates: "Any sentence P uttered by me lalically implies that I am a speaker, that there exists an object or person at the time of utterance . . ." The shift from 'sentence' in the definition to 'sentence uttered by me' in the illustration is probably unconscious but nevertheless illegal. If Castañeda uttered at some time t the sentence 'I am hungry' then even if the sentence-(token-)uttered-by-Castañeda-at-t lalically implies that Castañeda is a speaker — I shall return to this presently — this does not illustrate that the sentence(-type) 'I am hungry' lalically implies that Castañeda is a speaker. I had already the opportunity to point out that phrases of the kind 'uttered by me' (my example was 'as expressed by C at t_4') are logical danger signals.[6] It is a pity that one more author fell into the trap.

Castañeda makes the same mistake in his treatment of 'I never use language' (my example was 'I am dead') and 'I went to the theater last night, but I don't believe it' (my example was, following Moore, 'I believe

[1] "Russell's 'Theory of Descriptions'," *The Philosophy of Bertrand Russell*, The Library of Living Philosophers, Vol. V (Evanston and Chicago: Northwestern University, 1944), pp. 147–225, especially p. 204.

[2] "Analysis of 'Correct' Language," *Mind*, 55: 328–40 (1946), especially p. 334 [reprinted here as Ch. 19].

[3] "Some Non-Formal 'Logical' Relations," *Philosophical Studies*, 8: 89–92 (December 1957).

[4] In addition to my paper mentioned in note 2, I discussed the issue again in "Indexical Expressions," *Mind*, 63: 359–79 (1954), especially pp. 376 ff. [reprinted here as Ch. 5].

[5] "Some Non-Formal 'Logical' Relations," p. 91.

[6] "Indexical Expressions," pp. 363 ff.

he has gone out, but he has not'). In addition, however, Castañeda's discussion of these examples suffers from his disregarding the indexical character of these sentences, something which in such contexts will never be done with impunity. Though I would now want to formulate my own treatment of the issue in a terminology different from the one I used before, I think that Castañeda's innovations, because of his double failure to distinguish between sentence-types and sentence-tokens as well as between non-indexical and indexical sentences, must be rejected as confused and confusing.

One final remark (incited by Castañeda's last footnote): *Cartesius cogitat, ergo Cartesius est* is a valid argument whatever Descartes himself might have thought (under certain natural assumptions about the meaning of sentences of the form 'X *est*' where 'X' is replaced by a proper name). But this argument is so utterly trivial that it is hard to believe that it could have made the impression that was made by *Cogito ergo sum*. This sentence is indeed not a valid argument, or an argument at all, but only for the simple reason that the partial sentences of which it is composed, *Cogito* and *sum*, are indexical. Three features, each of only mild interest by itself, combined to impart to the *Cogito ergo sum* that almost magical fascination it has exerted since on the minds of so many good people: (1) Every argument of the form 'X *cogitat, ergo* X *est*' is valid. (2) Each time someone utters (a token of the type) *Cogito* in what Castañeda calls a *normal* context,[7] the statement he thereby makes is true. (3) The truth of these statements is establishable on nothing more than an understanding of the sentence by means of which it was made — *ex vi terminorum* — (and the knowledge that it was uttered in a normal context). It is easy to see how disregarding the distinction between declarative sentence and statement, on the one hand, and misunderstanding the functioning of indexical expressions (quite natural in 1637 though somewhat less excusable in 1957) would yield together the illusion that *Cogito* is a (logically) necessary statement, which combined with the illusion that *Cogito ergo sum* is a valid argument yields that *Sum* is a (logically) necessary statement.

---

[7] "Some Non-Formal 'Logical' Relations," p. 90.

ON MR. SØRENSEN'S ANALYSIS OF "TO BE" AND "TO BE TRUE"

§1. Mr. Sørensen's recent paper[1] carries the subtitle "A Linguist's Approach to the Problem", presumably with the intention of indicating that the paper was not only written by a linguist but also by someone *qua* linguist. I was greatly intrigued by this subtitle, but the greater was my disappointment when it turned out that Sørensen's paper was just a regular philosophical one, containing absolutely nothing which bore out the implied promise.

I have no objection to Sørensen's conclusion (which I put however in my own words) that the statement usually made by an utterance of a sentence of the form "A is" is identical with the statement usually made by an utterance of the sentence of the form "'A' denotes" (though I still hope a linguist will give us some time an exhaustive description of the situations in which such odd sentences are likely to be uttered). Neither do I object to the equivalence (in this sense) of "It is true that p" and "S denotes p and p" (where 'S' is a name of 'p') or to the equivalence of "S is true" and "There is a p such that S denotes p and p."

But I do object to almost everything else Sørensen says in his paper. Most of it is literally wrong and non-literally misleading.

§2. Sørensen claims to have shown in his article the following three points:

1. "To be" and "to be true" are *relation* signs, i.e., whenever we say that something A is or is true, we say that a relation R holds between A and something else B, R being the relation that is expressed by "is" or "is true".

2. The relations that are expressed by "to be" and "to be true" are the fundamental relations between (linguistic) *signs* and what signs are signs for. (The sign "Churchill" is a sign for (the person) Churchill.)

3. The relations expressed by "to be" and "to be true" are one and the same relation; "to be" and "to be true" are, in effect, one and the same sign.

None of these claims make literal sense. It seems that Sørensen believes that they follow from what I called above "Sørensen's conclusions". However, he arrives at this belief by a series of prejudices, misunderstandings and blunders.

---

[1] 'An analysis of "to be" and "to be true"', Analysis 19.6 (June 1959).

§3. At the beginning of his §5, Sørensen says: "I said above: The statement "A does not exist" implies the statement "A exists — as the subject of discourse". If there were no subject of discourse, there would be no discourse. Since we do speak about something when we say "Anderson does not exist", there must be a subject of discourse". The belief that whenever one makes a statement, one has to speak about something, in the sense of some thing — because otherwise "there would be no discourse" — is rather popular but not quite as harmless as it might look. I know of no justification for it. It seems, in addition, that Sørensen jumps from one meaning of "subject", i.e., *topic*, for which the prejudice is at least plausible, to another, namely *subject term* (of a subject-predicate-type sentence). However, even he who would like — for whatever reasons — to *stipulate* that every statement must have a subject, *qua* topic, would not be obliged at all to conclude, as Sørensen does, that the subject of the sentence "Anderson does not exist" must be a linguistic entity since it cannot be the non-linguistic entity Anderson; he could claim that the subject is the non-linguistic entity Anderson's existence. (What is predicated of this subject? Nothing. It is a subject *qua* topic and you don't have to predicate anything of a topic in order to make a statement.) Whatever reasons one may have for regarding locutions of the form "A exists" as quasi-ontological[2] or pseudo-object[3] — and I think that both Ryle and Carnap have given, directly or indirectly, good reasons for these conceptions, though Sørensen gives no indication of knowing them — none of these reasons gives the slightest support to Sørensen's formulations. Berkeley's and Quine's *To be . . .* slogans are literally somewhat misleading — as are presumably all slogans — and may be wrong in their intention; Sørensen's slogan *To be is to denote* (p. 127) is only outrageous.

§4. In his §6, Sørensen writes: "It follows that it (what is expressed by "exist") is a relational property, or simply: a relation." Not that Sørensen had really established that "exist" expresses a relational property. But this identification of a relational property with a relation is very strange. The consequences are, as one might expect, disastrous.

§5. Russell may well have failed to clear up millennia of muddle-headedness about "existence", as he claimed to do with his theory of descriptions. But surely not for the "simple reason" Sørensen gives in his §10. Russell does not retain *exist* as a predicate of non-linguistic

---

[2] See G. Ryle, "Systematically Misleading Expressions", *Logic and Language*, First Series, ed. A. G. N. Flew, pp. 15 ff.

[3] See R. Carnap, *The Logical Syntax of Language*, pp. 285 ff.

entities — notice another jump in Sørensen's argumentation from *predicate* qua grammatical term to *predicate* qua name of a property — and "there is no entity c", which leads off Russell's well-known rephrasal of "The golden mountain does not exist" as "there is no entity c such that "x is golden and mountainous" is true when x is c, but not otherwise", does not mean at all the same as "an entity c does not exist"; except in the rather trivial sense that neither of these phrases means anything, though for different reasons, the second phrase because 'c' is a variable, the first phrase because "there is no entity c" is not a categorematic expression at all but only a non-autonomous part of "there is no entity c such that" which is still not categorematic. (All this has of course been said many times before.)

§6. In his §12, Sørensen first claims that when one makes a statement that "Churchill smokes cigars" is true, one does not make a grammatical statement. This is doubtless true. He then goes on to say that this statement is not semantic either, "for it is not a statement concerning the meaning of "Churchill smokes cigars". On the contrary, it is a statement which presupposes that we know the meaning of "Churchill smokes cigars". We could not verify the statement unless we knew the meaning of "Churchill smokes cigars"."

This is a strange argument. Why should a statement which presupposes that we know the meaning of "Churchill smokes cigars" not be a statement concerning this meaning? (There are some reminiscences of the standard refutation of the verification theory of meaning in what Sørensen says. But it is difficult to reconstruct his train of thought.)

After having "shown", on the basis of this and similar arguments, that "is true" expresses a *relational property*, Sørensen repeats the transition to the claim that "is true" expresses a *relation*. Well. (All this has, of course, nothing to do with the well-known proposal to use, in some appropriate language system, the term 'is-true-in' as expressing a relation between a sentence and the language.)

§7. Confusions pile up in §13. This section starts off: "I have now shown that "to be" (= "to exist") is a synonym[1] of "to denote", and I have shown that "to be true" is a synonym[1] of "to denote". I have thus shown that "to be" and "to be true" are one and the same sign", with the footnote: "[1]With the qualification, that substitution of "denotes" for "exists" in "A exists" entails substitution of ""A"" for "A" (and similarly for "is true")." What Sørensen had "shown" before was that "to be" and "to denote" were *partial synonyms*, in the sense that "denotes" in certain contexts is replaceable, *salva veritate*, by "is" — of course,

Sørensen could not have possibly shown this at all, as is clear from his own quoted footnote which he refuses, for some reason, to take seriously — and that "to be true" and "to denote" are partial synonyms in the sense that "denotes" in certain contexts, but different from the previous ones, is replaceable, *salva veritate*, by "is true". Since partial synonymity is clearly not transitive, it does not follow from the premises that "to be" and "to be true" are partial synonyms, still less that they are synonyms, still less that they are one and the same sign, in any ordinary sense of the term 'sign'. However, Sørensen subscribes to the odd (*pace* C. I. Lewis) conception according to which a sign is a combination of a designator (a sign, in ordinary terminology) and a meaning. It is possible that Sørensen intends to imply, though he nowhere says that much, that two signs are the same if their second components are the same, i.e., if their first components are synonymous. This is not only a noteworthy deviation from the expected, since ordered couples are, in general, regarded as identical only if both their first and second components are identical, respectively, but would cause the whole conception to become a purposeless complication.

§8. In spite of Sørensen's paper I continue to cherish the belief that linguists could positively contribute to the explication of philosophically important locutions such as "to be" and "to be true".

CRITICAL COMMENTS ON THE INTRODUCTORY PAPERS ON LOGIC, LANGUAGE AND COMMUNICATION

These comments are restricted to the introductory papers by Perelman and Ayer. I could not persuade myself that I understood Forest's contribution to a degree sufficient for commenting.

Let me frankly state from the outset that I found both papers somewhat disappointing in what they did contain as well as in what they did not contain. Both contributions came very close to the formulation of highly important problems; unfortunately, they lost their way in irrelevancies. The real problems were never formulated and hence not even a hint for their possible solution was given.

1. I agree completely with Perelman's conclusion that "on ne peut pas traiter des problèmes de logique, de langage et de communication dans une perspective qui se limite aux enseignements fort précieux, mais partiels, que l'on peut tirer de l'étude exclusive de la logique formelle" (135),[1] though I wonder who among the attendants of this Congress would think otherwise. But the arguments by which he intends to support this rather trivial conclusion seem to me singularly irrelevant. It is not worthwhile to show this in full detail. My procedure, instead, will consist in first criticizing a few minor points, taken more or less at random, each of which is perhaps of little weight by itself but which do sum up, I think, to a substantial justification of my claim of irrelevancy, and then take up some issues of heavier weight.

On various occasions (125, 129, 130) Perelman stresses the particular role played by the principles of identity and non-contradiction. I did not understand why this fact — if a fact it is — furthers his argument. The justification Perelman gives for the special stress is unconvincing. I quote: "Pour que l'on puisse interpréter un formalisme non pas comme un calcul quelconque, mais comme une logique, il faut exclure a priori la possibilité de déduire le faux à partir du vrai; ceci impose le respect des principes d'identité et de non-contradiction" (125). My only comment: Why just these principles? Perelman doubtless knows that adding the

---

[1] The numbers in parentheses refer to the pages in the volume *Relazioni Introduttive* of the *Atti del XII Congresso Internazionale di Filosofia* (Venezia–Padoa, 1958).

negation of any axiom or theorem of the classical propositional calculus to *any* of its axiom systems will enable us to derive the false from the true. So in which respect do these two principles excel?

Again: "pour admettre l'application, dans le formalisme, du principe d'identité, chaque nom, et chaque expression, doit avoir un seul sens, parfaitement défini, ne variant ni selon le contexte, ni d'après les usages du langage formalisé" (130). Now, the advice to use symbols always in the same sense in a given argument is certainly very sensible, and Aristotle already discussed the fallacies into which one might fall by not paying heed to it. But what has this to do with the principle of identity? Sure, 'Johnny = Johnny' will not only not be logically true if the two occurrences of the word 'Johnny' do not refer to the same person but even empirically false. But the same holds for 'if Johnny is hungry, then Johnny is hungry'. Or does Perelman take the mentioned advice itself as the principle of identity? I remember having seen logic texts where this is done, but I can't believe that Perelman would want to follow their lead, certainly not without warning.

The last quotation in this connection: "Le système logistique que nous avons présenté contient une autre imperfection, c'est qu'il ne mentionne pas le rôle particulier du principe de non-contradiction" (129). Since I can nowhere find the logistic system which Perelman claims to have presented, I interpret, with some hesitation, his words as referring to the characterization he gives of logistic systems in general (126) and which he adapts from Church's recent standard textbook of mathematical logic.[2] Church indeed does not require a logistic system to be consistent by definition. But there are obviously very good reasons for doing so. Otherwise we would have been obliged to formulate the highly important problem whether, in Church's terms, a given logistic system is consistent as something like "is the given golistic system S a logistic system?", where a golistic system is like a logistic system except for not being necessarily consistent. I fail to see the gain in this formulation. As to the importance of consistency for logistic systems, who but formal logicians have put the greatest stress on this feature (perhaps a little bit too much so)?

The next quotation seems to me not only irrelevant and obviously wrong in part but also somewhat obscurantist: "Une théorie de la logique et une théorie de la connaissance sont incomplètes et insuffisantes si

---

[2] A. Church, *Introduction to Mathematical Logic*, Princeton University Press, 1956.

elles ne parviennent pas à rendre compte de cette supériorité de l'esprit sur la machine à calculer" (129). I agree that epistemology should deal with the problem of the relationship between the intellectual faculties of a human being and of electronic computers, and I am sorry that the only remarks I find on this fascinating topic in the *Acts* of the Congress are the completely insufficient remarks of Perelman himself (128–129) to which I shall return presently. But I don't see with what justification Perelman regards an epistemology that does not arrive at the conclusion he likes as incomplete and insufficient, though he might have reasons — I think wrong ones — to regard such an epistemology as wrong. But surely the discussion of this problem is not the task of logic (or of metalogic, if this is what "théorie de la logique" is meant to refer to), unless this term is so watered down that it does become synonymous with "epistemology".

Let us now turn to the only justification Perelman gives for his belief that the human mind is superior to an electronic computer: "...une machine à calculer... est incapable de corriger des fautes et des erreurs de calcul, *du moins quand elles n'ont pas été prévues par le constructeur*. Or l'esprit humain placé devant un calcul quelconque, régi par des règles, en est parfaitement capable" (128; italics added). On what errors is Perelman talking here? Those made by the machine itself? But Perelman surely knows that electronic computers can be constructed, and many are, to detect and correct their own errors. Or does he mean that the machine should be able to correct errors made by 10-year old Johnny in his copybook? Assume that an electronic computer has been told that Johnny has in his copybook '5+3=7' and has been *programmed* (not constructed; there is no need for any special-purpose machine, general-purpose machines as they are mass-fabricated nowadays, are easily able to handle the problem) to check whether there is an error in this formula. Does Perelman doubt whether the machine would do this? But could the machine also correct the error and replace '7' by '8', as Johnny himself would do spontaneously, according to Perelman's claim? I hope not. The machine I would program would not correct anything but only suggest that the *three* correct statements from which the erroneous statement would result by a "first-order" mistake (I hope the meaning of this term is self-explanatory) are, in addition to the one given spontaneously by Johnny, also '4+3=7' and '5+2=7'. But I do not claim that this proves that the electronic computer is intellectually superior to a human being, even a ten-year old one.

And now to the major issues. Perelman points out that the formal logicians are unable to determine whether the sentence "Tu ne tueras point" — I'd better stick to the French rendering of the fifth commandment, its English version would kill Perelman's point from the start — is a declarative sentence. But which formal logician — or any logician, for that matter — of any reputation (and I don't think that Perelman should bother with "logicians") during the last 50 years (and Perelman is surely not interested in this context in prehistory) has claimed that it is the business of formal logicians to determine whether a given French word-sequence is a declarative sentence or not? What kind of strawmen is Perelman fighting here and for what purpose? True enough, I always spend some time in my introductory freshman course in logic in telling my students that one often uses declarative sentences to utter commands (and imperative sentences to make statements) but it should go without saying — I shall say it, however, — that the determination whether a given word-sequence is a sentence and, if so, whether it is a declarative sentence, is the linguist's business (unless treated on a common-sense level, in which case it is everybody's business) and that the determination whether a given declarative sentence was uttered on a certain occasion in order to make a statement or to give a command or for any other old purpose is the psychologist's business (unless...). It is possible that many logic-teachers don't care to tell these things to their audience but which logician does tell his students (or does write in his textbooks) that these determinations are the logician's business?

My comment on the second major issue will be very short. I utterly fail to see what the problem of platonism versus nominalism, to the discussion of which Perelman dedicates much space, has to do with Perelman's conclusion. Quine's insight that there exist great differences between bindable and non-bindable variables (together with his proposal to call the latter schematic letters rather than variables) is certainly of major importance, but what is its connection with the limitations of formal logic?

The problem which Perelman missed formulating and discussing in his paper and which — I hope — was in the back of his mind (and which he takes up in other publications of his) is: Is extant formal logic, deductive and inductive (it is amazing that Perelman does not mention inductive logic even once), sufficient for the formalization of all arguments, of whatever degree of conclusiveness, that are used in ordinary language, or at least in the sciences, or at least in the natural sciences (where by formalization I mean now "those preparatory operations in applied logic, whereby sentences of ordinary language are fitted to logical forms by interpretation and paraphrase"),[3] or is some better-developed formal logic necessary for this purpose, or is formal logic altogether insufficient for this purpose? It is a pity that this problem, which I regard as one of the major philosophical problems of our time, has only been scratched in Perelman's concluding remarks.

2. With regard to Ayer's paper, let me again start my critique with a couple of minor animadversions before I come to the only major one which I have space to discuss. Ayer says: "To refute the logical atomist theory, in its extreme form, it need only be remarked that a sentence which consisted entirely of logically proper names could not be used to say anything false. Either it would express a truth or it would be meaningless" (143–144). I don't know why Ayer should bother to refute today the extreme form of logical atomism since I do not believe that there still exists today a philosopher who adheres to this view. At any rate, I fail to understand Ayer's refutation. He does not bother to tell us the rules of formation by which a concatenation of logically proper names would form a sentence — and these rules are certainly not self-evident for such a strange language — and a fortiori not the rules of interpretation that would determine the meaning of the sentences. Why does Ayer think that the sentences of this odd language could be used to say something true but not something false? I remember having read some old discussions which might throw some light on what Ayer might have intended to say, but I don't think it is fair of him to assume that the readers of his paper will have read and remembered these discussions. He provides no references whatsoever.

I don't know who the "philosophers" are who, according to Ayer, take the view "that singular nouns mean individual concepts; common nouns mean class concepts; adjectives mean universals; indicative sentences mean propositions" (145). The philosophers that come immediately into one's mind in this connection are Church and Carnap who were the first to use (or revive) the term 'individual concept' (and I hope again that Ayer would want to criticize views of first-rate philosophers rather than those of lesser rate). But if so, then Ayer's formulation is at best a very doubtful rephrasing of their professed views. Neither of them uses the word "means" in this context, Carnap's preferred way of putting the issue being 'has as its intension (or extension)' and Church's being 'has as its sense (or denotation)'. The distinction Ayer makes here

---

[3] This quotation is from the highly relevant paper of W. V. Quine, *Mr. Strawson on Logical Theory*, "Mind", LXII (1953), p. 438.

between common nouns and adjectives is utterly foreign to Carnap and, I think, to Church, too. Are class concepts universals? What are universals? Ayer fuses — or confuses? — here extensions and intensions, senses and denotations, as Carnap and Church would have put it. On purpose? Because he believes that their distinctions are wrong? Irrelevant? Who, then, to repeat, are the "philosophers"?

And now to the major point: let me continue the series of questions of the last paragraph. By whom are concepts and universals and propositions "held to be real" (145)? Is Ayer really unaware of the fact Carnap and Church never (I did not really check all of Church's writings in this connection, and I might be mistaken, though I would be surprised) say that propositions are real (or unreal) or that numbers are real (or unreal) and that Carnap has often had to say illuminating things about the uses of 'real' in this connection, the last time in a publication two years old?[4] Carnap is certainly not one of the philosophers who claim that universals are not physical. As if to stress the pointlessness of Ayer's attack (always under the assumption that Carnap is one of its targets), Carnap states very clearly and explicitly: "...the properties of things are not meant as something mental, but as something physical the things have".[5] But Ayer seems to believe that philosophers who don't say that properties exist in space and time (but rather say that they, the thing-properties among them, are had by things, i.e., by spatio-temporal entities) thereby commit themselves to saying that they are not physical. Why?

Should some philosopher, for some reason or for no reason, want to say that properties and classes and propositions and individual concepts (all or only some of them?) are real, I don't see why someone's credulity would be too heavily strained by it (145). What is wrong with there being an infinite number of objective falsehoods? I am fully aware of all that talk about Ockham's razor and the robust sense of reality but don't see the slightest reason why I, or anybody else, should be frightened by it into using a language which is less convenient for scientific purposes (though I, following Carnap, don't see the slightest reason why I should want to use 'real' in this context).

But Ayer has a second argument against the reality of universals;

---

[4] See the penetrating discussion on pp. 44 ff. of R. Carnap, *The Methodological Character of Theoretical Concepts*, in *The Foundations of Science and the Concepts of Psychology and Psychoanalysis*, Minnesota Studies in the Philosophy of Science, Volume I, 1956, pp. 38–76.

[5] See R. Carnap, *Meaning and Necessity*, University of Chicago Press, 1947, p. 20.

they serve no explanatory purpose. I have no idea what the use of at least second-order functional calculus — which alone commits (according to Quine) or "commits" (according to Carnap) one to the existence of universals — is supposed to explain, and if one were to decide to use such a calculus for a certain purpose, in preference to a first-order one, the reasons would have been not that it explains something or other but that it is more convenient and fruitful. Ayer himself points out that the question "what do words mean?" is not serious and requires no explanation (146). What Ayer may be driving at is perhaps that the very serious question "how do words acquire the meaning they have for A?" is often answered by: "by having a meaning", which is clearly much worse than a tautology.

Since my space is running out, I shall not comment on Ayer's own tentative solution of what seems to him to be the major problem in connection with meaning, namely the problem how to define "the sentence s means the proposition p to A" in non-intentional terms. Let me only say that this problem, and the clarification of the status of intentional verbs in ordinary language, has been more helpfully treated by Quine and in a recently published exchange of letters between Chisholm and W. Sellars.[6]

Let me use the remaining space first for formulating once again the two serious problems, to the formulation of which Perelman and Ayer should have been led but were not, and for voicing a protest. The problems are:

(1) *Is extant formal logic, deductive and inductive, sufficient for the formalization of all arguments in ordinary language?*

(2) *How do words acquire the meaning they have (for a given person A)?*

The protest refers to the fact that neither Ayer nor Perelman found it necessary to give if only a hint that there exists an enormous recent literature on logic, language and communication which, alas, has been written by linguists, psychologists and, more specifically, psycholinguists. I am aware that the combined efforts of these scientists have so far yielded only partial insights into the second of my problems (and related ones) and that some philosophers who are out for quick answers do prefer to arrive at them by armchair reflection rather than by patient observation, experimentation and theorizing, aided by methodological

---

[6] See W. V. Quine, *Quantifiers and Propositional Attitudes*, Journal of Philosophy, LIII (1956), pp. 177–187; *Appendix to Concepts, Theories and the Mind-Body Problem*, Minnesota Studies in the Philosophy of Science, Volume II, 1958, pp. 507–539.

analysis. I am also aware that ours is a Congress of Philosophy and not of Psycholinguistics, Communication Engineering or Information Theory. But just as I am convinced that methodologically trained philosophers could contribute to the solution of the mentioned and related problems, I am convinced that disregard of the relevant scientific literature must deprive our discussions of any serious impact. If we'll continue to keep ourselves aloof of what scientists have to say on the subjects in which we are interested (and let me add, in parentheses, that I do warn scientists, on other appropriate occasions, of the disastrous effects of their failure to cooperate with trained methodologists), we should not be astonished if people looking for enlightenment on logic, language and communication turn to all kinds of places and meetings but Congresses of Philosophy.

CAN INDEXICAL SENTENCES STAND IN LOGICAL RELATIONS?

1. When Professor Castañeda, in a condensed paper he published a few years ago,[1] tried to introduce various types of nonformal logical relations in order to disentangle the issue often run together under the name 'pragmatic implication,' I criticized[2] this attempt as confused and confusing because of his double failure to distinguish in his paper between sentence-types and sentence-tokens as well as between nonindexical and indexical sentences, two distinctions I myself had drawn and shown to be essential in the second of my two papers[3] in which I had previously discussed the issue of pragmatic implication.

In a recent reply to my criticism,[4] Castañeda expresses his belief that my "charges are unfair" but is kind enough to continue the discussion on an almost purely substantive basis (a move for which I am sincerely obliged). He goes on to argue that my prior discussions of the issue are "mostly irrelevant to a study of nonformal logical relations" and that my objections to his own study are unfounded since they were based on my "claim that indexical sentences cannot stand at all in logical relations" which he would show to be false.

2. I readily admit that my own prior treatment of pragmatical implication was leaky in some respects. As a matter of fact, I had myself realized at least some of these leaks before. I hinted at them in my 1960 paper when I said there (p. 24) that "I would now want to formulate my own treatment of the issue in a terminology different from the one I used before." Again as a matter of fact, I had already started revising my terminology in another paper published in 1957,[5] where I gave some indications of the changes in the formulation of the argument relevant to the present issue.

---

[1] H. N. Castañeda, "Some Nonformal 'Logical' Relations," *Philosophical Studies*, 8: 89–92 (December 1957).

[2] Y. Bar-Hillel, "On Lalic Implication and the Cogito," *Philosophical Studies*, 11: 23–25 (January–February 1960) [reprinted here as Ch. 7].

[3] Y. Bar-Hillel, "Analysis of 'Correct' Language," *Mind*, 55: 328–40 (1946); Y. Bar-Hillel, "Indexical Expressions," *Mind*, 63: 359–79 (1954) [reprinted here as Ch. 19 and 5, respectively].

[4] H. N. Castañeda, "Professor Bar-Hillel on Nonformal Implications and Phenomenalism," *Philosophical Studies*, 12: 85–90 (December 1961).

[5] Y. Bar-Hillel, "New Light on the Liar," *Analysis*, 18: 1–6 (October 1957) [reprinted here as Ch. 21].

Since nobody is particularly interested in who was wrong when and where, but both of us seem vitally interested in the question *whether indexical sentences can stand in logical relations*, let me immediately restate my point in the terminology of my 1957 paper. I said there (p. 3): "Truth and falsity ... apply directly only to *statements* and not to (declarative) sentences. And a statement can, but need not necessarily, be made by uttering a declarative sentence." Two pages later, I went on to say: "It is, of course, much simpler to manipulate sentences in logical arguments than the incomparably more elusive and less definite statements. It is indeed often perfectly safe to deal not with certain statements but with sentences that are usually uttered when one wants to make these statements. In scientific matters especially it does little harm and a lot of good to work with sentences and assign them truth-values, so long as it is kept in mind that this is a matter of convenience only and that one must be prepared to return to statements as soon as trouble arises. But this procedure is suicidal when working with context-dependent sentences. Applying logic to context-independent sentences of ordinary language has been on the whole fairly successful; applying logic to context-dependent sentences by treating them as entities that are either true or false must occasionally lead to spectacular failures, as we can now say by hindsight."

My claim is, then, that, with respect to ordinary language, *logical relations hold primarily between statements, derivatively between the non-indexical (context-independent) sentences that can be used to make them, but not at all, in any nontrivial sense, between indexical sentences* (whereas, with respect to formalized language-systems, *logical relations hold, without any distinction in priority, between both the sentences among themselves as well as between the propositions expressed by them among themselves*).

It is obvious that my claim is partly a statement, partly a proposal. I hope that it is not necessary, for our present purpose, to try to separate out these parts. It should also be obvious that the claim still requires plenty of elaboration and qualification.[6]

3. Now, does Castañeda claim otherwise? I venture to say, very definitely, that he *does not*, and this in spite of the fact that Castañeda

---

[6] One such qualification would deal with the fact that nontrivial logical (or "quasi-logical," if one insists) relations hold also between commands (and, therefore, derivatively, and between nonindexical imperatives, but not between indexical imperatives), between questions (and therefore, derivatively, between nonindexical interrogatives, but not between indexical interrogatives), etc.; cf. my 1954 paper, pp. 378-79.

very clearly *says* that he *does*. This is a strange situation, so let me elaborate.

The point is that what Castañeda means by claiming that indexical sentences can stand in logical relations is that (i) primarily, *indexical sentences qua used in a certain context* (or *indexical-sentences-cum-context*, or *ordered pairs of indexical sentences and contexts*) can stand in logical relations, but that (ii) in a derivative sense, indexical sentences (plain, without any of the three synonymous qualifiers mentioned right now) can stand in such relations inasmuch as the ordered pairs into which they enter as first components stand in logical relations.

But indexical-sentences-cum-context (or . . .) are exactly some of the things I now call statements (and called, unfortunately, judgments for reasons that looked good to me at the time but which are no longer attractive, apparently creating some confusion by *not* saying explicitly that judgments stand in logical relations).

On the other hand, Castañeda's derivative sense of standing in logical relations seems to me utterly trivial and misleading. It is as if one would want to say that, "in a derivative sense," 2 is equal to 3, since there exist two numbers, *e.g.*, 5 and 4, which when added to 2 and 3, respectively, yield numbers which are equal in a primary sense.

4. Though I do not think at all that my proposal not to speak about indexical sentences standing in logical relations "flies in the face of the facts of the common use of the English language" — the term 'indexical sentence' being a highly technical one, which has no common use at all, and hardly anybody talking about logical relations between sentences at any rate, but rather between statements and propositions, in the non-technical sense of these terms — this is surely irrelevant in view of our agreement that such locutions make no primary sense. Whether it is worth saving the "derivative" sense in philosophical-logical discussions, the reader will judge.

5. Let me repeat that there is a trap in the use of such phrases as "indexical sentence qua used in a certain context." It is difficult to realize that indexical sentences qua used in a certain context are not sentences (an ordered pair never being identical with its first number), just as painted cocks (i.e., representations of cocks on a painting, not cocks covered with paint) are not cocks, as Aristotle noticed quite some time ago. I am afraid that Castañeda is still not out of the trap. This seems to me to be the explanation for the fact that Castañeda still goes on omitting the required qualifier even in crucial contexts.

6. It is perhaps worthwhile remarking, say in an introductory logic

class, that all statements that can be made by uttering "I am hungry" in normal contexts are consistent with all statements that can be made by uttering "Peter will come tomorrow" in normal contexts, but I would discourage formulating this point by saying that all the tokens of the first sentence are consistent with all the tokens of the second sentence. It is similarly worth pointing out, on suitable occasions, that some statements made by uttering "Bar-Hillel is older than I" entail some statements made by uttering "I am not older than Bar-Hillel" (in particular, this is true for all those contexts in which these sentences are uttered by the same person), but it is equally worth pointing out that some statements made by uttering "Bar-Hillel is older than I" entail some statements made by uttering, say, "You are not older than Bar-Hillel" (the reader being invited to formulate the appropriate context). It is plainly misleading to say, instead, that some tokens of "Bar-Hillel is older than I" entail some tokens of "I am not older than Bar-Hillel."

7. It was indeed awkward of me, and totally unnecessary for my, or anybody else's purposes, to pair sentence-tokens with contexts.[7] I should have paired sentence-types, and this is what shall be done hence. The tokenness is sufficiently taken care of by the context. There is no problem in pairing one sentence(-type) with many contexts.

---

[7] In my 1954 and later papers.

REMARKS ON CARNAP'S *LOGICAL SYNTAX OF LANGUAGE*

After I had accepted the task of evaluating Carnap's *Logical Syntax of Language*[1] for the present volume, I cherished for some time the thought of both presenting the main ideas of the *Logical Syntax* and of criticizing them in the light of the progress made in logic and methodology during the last twenty years. But one more careful reading of the book made me realize the absurdity of my original intention. How could one possibly summarize, and critically evaluate, the contents of a book in a few dozen pages, when every single one of its sections contains such a wealth of ideas, painstakingly elaborated, carefully explained and illuminatingly illustrated? Not all of these ideas were original with the author, but even when he adopted somebody else's flashes of genius — his debts to Frege, Russell, Wittgenstein, Hilbert, Gödel and Tarski are acknowledgedly great — he made them change their character and often gain in importance by incorporating them into his own general framework. How would one go about condensing a book when he is convinced that often not a single word can be omitted, not a single illustration discarded, not a single historical aside passed over, without becoming involved in some serious loss, and when he has, moreover, every few pages the impression that the author could and should have said much more on a certain subject and that only lack of space prevented him from giving us the enlightenment for which we now have to struggle all by ourselves. There are many pages containing short remarks that carry convincing proof that Carnap must have deeply thought about the problem treated there but would have needed many more pages to expand his ideas. (As a matter of fact, I myself have already had twice the opportunity of publishing papers whose content is essentially nothing more than a series of footnotes to pp. 168–170 of *LSL*.[2])

---

[1] The following abbreviations will henceforth be employed: *LSL* for *The Logical Syntax of Language* (London and New York, 1937), being an expanded and corrected translation of the German original *Die logische Syntax der Sprache* (Vienna, 1934); TM for "Testability and Meaning," *Philosophy of Science*, III (1936), 419–471, and IV (1937), 1–40, reprinted by Graduate Philosophy Club, Yale University, New Haven, Connecticut (1950); ESO for "Empiricism, Semantics, and Ontology," *Revue Internationale de Philosophie*, IV (1950), 20–40, reprinted in *Readings in Philosophy of Science*, ed. P. P. Wiener (New York, 1953), 509–522 (and quoted according to this reprint).

[2] These papers are "On Syntactical Categories," *The Journal of Symbolic Logic*,

The only rational way, that was left open to me, of discussing Carnap's masterwork within the frame of this volume could therefore consist of choosing almost at random a couple of what I regard as the most important insights gained by Carnap and evaluating their impact as of today. I would like to show on the one hand that in spite of the intense study which *LSL* has undergone in the hands of many competent students much has been left that still awaits understanding, elaboration and application, and that, on the other hand, in order to encourage this application, certain revisions in some formulations might be indicated.

I

The *Logical Syntax of Language* should have exercised a decisive influence on modern linguistic research. It didn't. Part of the fault was Carnap's. Not because what he had to say was couched in a language no linguist without many years of logico-mathematical training could understand; this could not be helped. But because he left them with the impression that the content and methods of *LSL* were of little relevance for their issues, so that it was not worthwhile for them to undergo this kind of training. I believe this to be the only case in Carnap's teaching where his cautiousness betrayed him. He did not write *LSL* in order to provide a framework in which to discuss ordinary languages. He wrote it in order to create a tool, at least the outlines of a tool, with which one could efficiently handle constructed language-systems of science. But he did not forcefully enough drive home the point that the tool he created was almost equally efficient for the treatment of the vernacular. He discussed this application many times throughout the book, but the conclusions at which he arrived were somewhat ambivalent. In the introduction he says:

In consequence of the unsystematic and logically imperfect structure of the natural word-languages (such as German or Latin), the statement of their formal rules of formation and transformation would be so complicated that it would hardly be feasible in practice (2).

A few pages later he makes the following claim which, though not exactly contradicting the former passage, still shifts the emphasis considerably:

XV (1950), 1–16 [reprinted in LI as Ch. 1], which belabours pp. 169–170 of *LSL* and "Indexical Expressions," *Mind*, LXIII (1954), 359–379 [reprinted here as Ch. 5], in which Carnap's tantalizingly condensed remarks on p. 168 of *LSL* are expanded.

> The method of syntax ... will also help in the *logical analysis of the word-languages*. Although here ... we shall be dealing with symbolic languages, the syntactical concepts and rules — not in detail but in their general character — may also be applied to the analysis of the incredibly complicated word-languages (6).

The reconciliation of these two slightly antithetic views is then effected as follows:

> The direct analysis of these [word-languages], which has been prevalent hitherto, must inevitably fail, just as a physicist would be frustrated were he from the outset to attempt to relate his laws to natural things — trees, stones, and so on. In the first place, the physicist relates his laws to the simplest of constructed forms; to a thin straight lever, to a simple pendulum, to punctiform masses, etc. Then, with the help of the laws relating to these constructed forms, he is later in a position to analyze into suitable elements the complicated behaviour of real bodies, and thus to control them. One more comparison: the complicated configurations of mountain chains, river frontiers, and the like are most easily represented and investigated by the help of geographical coordinates — or, in other words, by constructed lines not given in nature. In the same way, the syntactical property of a particular word-language, such as English, or of particular classes of word-languages, or of a particular sub-language of a word-language, is best represented and investigated by comparison with a constructed language which serves as a system of reference (8).

That this reconciliation is still not unambiguously clear can be seen from the fact that one of the leading American structural linguists, Zellig Harris, derived from it a conflict of attitudes between logicians and linguists. After quoting from the last-mentioned passage of Carnap's he continues:

> Linguists meet this problem differently than do Carnap and his school. Whereas the logicians have avoided the analysis of existing languages, linguists study them.[3]

One sees clearly how a nice little and completely superfluous and unwarranted controversy of logicians versus linguists is in the making. It is true that logicians, i.e. Carnap, avoided large-scale analysis of existing languages, but they did this very deliberately, not because they wanted to meet this problem differently than do linguists, but quite simply out of a certain division of labour. Carnap finishes the last-quoted passage with the following characteristic sentence: "Such a task, however, lies beyond the scope of this book" (8). But from a division of labour neither a difference in belief nor even a difference in attitude should be derived. I admit that Carnap's formulations lack here their usual clean-cut

---

[3] *Methods in Structural Linguistics* (Chicago, 1951), 16, n. 17.

pregnance and I complained myself about this fact before. I imagine that many a linguist who, attracted by the title of the book, was looking through its preface and introduction in order to determine whether it might not contain some new tools for linguistic analysis closed it in desperation when, after the stirring remarks of p. 1 of the introduction (which we shall quote presently), he read, on p. 2, the discouraging sentence we quoted first. After that he might well have decided that reading and trying to understand the whole book with its strange symbolism was not worth the trouble. He did not care whether logic and mathematics were to be constructed simultaneously or the one on the basis of the other. He was not at all impressed by the differences of two language-systems, consisting in the fact that the one allowed for limited operators only whereas the other admitted also unlimited operators. It must be understood, though still deeply deplored, that the *Logical Syntax of Language*, after this discouraging opening, did not touch the heart of the linguists.

This is the more deplorable since at approximately the same time at which Carnap conceived his book and tried to incorporate in it his deep conviction that it is worthwhile, nay necessary, to deal with languages qua *calculi*, i.e. uninterpreted formal systems, and to disregard, for the investigation of their syntax, the meaning of their expressions, their connections with actions and perceptions, and their sociological status in communication, many linguists arrived at the very same conviction utterly independently and out of a quite different historical development. Logical syntax originated with the efforts of the Hilbert School to prove the consistency of mathematics by treating it as a calculus and the partly simultaneous, partly subsequent generalizations of this approach by the Polish logicians, especially by Leśniewski and his pupils, to language-systems in general. Not a single professional linguist is mentioned by Carnap in his extensive bibliography to *LSL* (with the exception of Bréal and Bühler, who are mentioned once, on p. 9, in connection with a minor terminological discussion). American structural linguistics, on the other hand, started off as a revolt against mentalistic linguistics but arrived at the conviction that it is worthwhile to study the regularities in the distributional relations among the elements of speech, in abstraction from the various other observable regularities. In Leonard Bloomfield's book *Language*, that appeared in 1933, no mention is made of any work by Carnap or the Polish logicians.[4]

---

[4] Later on, however, there was a considerable rapprochement between Carnap and

In spite of this entirely different background, there might still have been a complete convergence of linguists and logicians towards a new approach to linguistics (a partial rapprochement took indeed place in the late Thirties), were it not that Carnap's attitude did little to encourage linguists to study his work, leaving them without the benefit of a major insight of his, the lack of which caused them, and is still causing them, many quite superfluous troubles.

The irony of this failure of convergence is the greater since that insight of Carnap's which would have, in my opinion, helped the structural linguists immensely, is to be found on the very first page of the introduction:

The prevalent opinion is that syntax and logic, in spite of some points of contact between them, are fundamentally theories of a very different type. The syntax of a language is supposed to lay down rules according to which the linguistic structures (e.g. sentences) are to be built up from the elements (such as words or parts of words). The chief task of logic, on the other hand, is supposed to be that of formulating rules according to which judgments may be inferred from other judgments; in other words, according to which conclusions may be drawn from premises.... In the following pages, the view that logic, too, is concerned with the *formal* treatment of sentences will be presented and developed. We shall see that the logical characteristics of sentences (for instance, whether a sentence is analytic, synthetic, or contradictory; whether it is an existential sentence or not; and so on) and the logical relations between them (for instance, whether two sentences contradict one another or are compatible with one another; whether one is logically deducible from the other or not; and so on) are solely dependent upon the syntactical structure of the sentences. In this way, logic will become a part of syntax, provided that the latter is conceived in a sufficiently wide sense and formulated with exactitude. The difference between syntactical rules in the narrower sense and the logical rules of deduction is only the difference between *formation rules* and *transformation rules*, both of which are completely formulable in syntactical terms (1–2).

The thesis that rules of transformation are as much syntactical as rules of formation has been completely missed by all structural linguists and, to my knowledge, not even been mentioned if only to be refuted. That it is up to Engligh syntax to tell us that any sequence of two English statements 'a' and 'b' with 'and' or 'or' in between is a statement, was, of course, perfectly recognized by all linguists. But that it is up to the same English syntax to tell us that 'a' is derivable from 'a and b' but not

Bloomfield. In 1939, Bloomfield published *Linguistic Aspects of Science* for the International Encyclopedia of Unified Science, of which Carnap was an Associate Editor.

from 'a or b,' escaped their attention. Since it is only by this and similar rules of transformation that the difference in functioning between 'and' and 'or' can be formally described, structural linguists were either obliged to relegate the treatment of this difference in function to some non-formal part of linguistics or else to embark on the *prima facie* utterly hopeless task of explaining this difference in terms of rules of formation. A similar situation prevails with respect to the relationship between say, 'loves' and 'is loved by.' In terms of rules of transformation, this relationship is easily determined: 'A loves B' and 'B is loved by A' are mutually interderivable. It should be rather obvious that it is beyond the rules of formation to provide for an equivalent determination. Leaving for some other occasion the detailed criticism of one such heroic attempt by a distinguished structural linguist[5] to get along with rules of formation alone, let us be satisfied to state here that it is at least highly plausible that the neglect of the rules of transformation has led structural linguists either to restrict unduly the field of application of their methods or to embark on futile attempts to achieve the impossible with inadequate tools.

That the vital importance of the rules of transformation in formal linguistic description was overlooked is, of course, due to the fact that for structural linguists, not appreciably less than for linguists of other brands, "the prevalent opinion is that syntax and logic, in spite of some points of contact between them, are fundamentally theories of a very different type" (1). This opinion is prevalent among linguists in 1954 no less than in 1934, and Carnap's work, for reasons stated above, did not succeed in changing it. There existed, of course, quite valid motives for linguists to want to uphold this cleavage. The brand of logic which was taught at the universities in the Twenties or early Thirties was surely not something a self-respecting structural linguist would have wanted to have to do much with. Psychologism and introspectionistic insistence on "meaning" was exactly what they tried to avoid in their own work. It was Carnap's brand of logic, his *LSL*, which was congenial to their approach — but they missed it.

I have no intention to claim that every logician should undergo an extensive linguistic training or vice versa. Even when the fundamental unity of syntax and logic is recognized, there still remain large parts in linguistics, such as phonology, for which logical training would be of little practical value, and large parts in logic, for which linguistic field

---

[5] Zellig S. Harris, "Discourse Analysis," *Language*, XXVIII (1952), 1–30, see esp. p. 19.

training woud be of no help whatsoever. I do however believe that a straightforward claim by Carnap that his work should serve as a methodological and terminological basis for structural linguists and a similarly straightforward recognition by structural linguists that Carnap's investigations, in spite of their so completely different background and motivation, are of immediate importance for their work, especially the recognition of the vital part played by the rules of transformation in language description, should have a healthy impact. Another artificial barrier, this time between logic and linguistics, would be brought down, and a few more linguistically trained logicians, a few more logically trained linguists, a few more logicians and linguists cooperating, should be able to arrive in the near future at many interesting new results.

Logical syntacticians and structural linguists have in common the aim of providing for a structural description of natural languages (in addition to other aims which are specific for each group). The achievement of this aim requires both the development of efficient and reliable techniques of elicitation in order to get the data, and the development of a conceptual and terminological framework in which can be analysed those constructed language-systems from which in ever increasing approximation those data can be derived. Since rather different qualifications seem to be required for practical work in these two branches, the existing division of labour between linguists and logicians may well be justified. It would surely be detrimental to the common aim to transform this division of labour into an antagonism.

In developing his General Syntax, Carnap's major aim in *LSL* was definitely and admittedly not the construction of language-systems that could serve as systems of reference with which to compare particular natural languages. "Such a task lies beyond the scope of this book" (8). Therefore, though he claims in the first section of chapter B of part IV, where he opens the discussion of "the syntax of any language" — this is the title of this chapter — that

in this section we shall attempt to construct a *syntax for languages in general*, that is to say, a system of definitions of syntactical terms which are so comprehensive as to be applicable to any language whatsoever (167),

he immediately qualifies this somewhat sweeping claim in three ways.

Firstly,

We have, it is true, had chiefly in mind as examples languages similar in their principal features to the usual symbolic languages, and, in many cases, the choice of the definitions has been influenced by this fact. Nevertheless, the terms defined are also applicable to languages of quite different kinds (167).

Secondly,

The outline of a general syntax which follows is to be regarded as no more than a first attempt. The definitions framed will certainly need improvement and completion in many respects (167).

Thirdly,

In what follows, we shall deal only with languages which contain *no expressions dependent upon extra-linguistic factors*. The logical character of all the sentences of these languages is then invariant in relation to spatio-temporal displacements; two sentences of the same wording will have the same character independently of where, when, and by whom they are spoken. In the case of sentences having extra-syntactical dependence, this invariance can be attained by means of the addition of person-, place-, and time-designations (168).

It must be perfectly clear that especially the last qualification restricts highly the immediate applicability of Carnap's General Syntax to natural languages. The overwhelming majority of the sentences in these languages are *indexical*, i.e. dependent upon extra-linguistic factors, and their transformation into a context-invariant form poses formidable problems, which are only touched upon in the last-quoted sentence. These problems, moreover, cannot be solved any more within the framework of *LSL*, their solution lying clearly within what became known as *pragmatics* a short time after the appearance of *LSL*.[6]

Though Carnap himself did little to apply his General Syntax to natural languages, there were a few logicians who did some work along this line. Among them are some British analyticists, though doubtless from a somewhat different angle and from certain particular motives. Many analyses in Gilbert Ryle's *Concept of Mind*,[7] to mention just one recent influential book emanating from this school, should have very straightforward linguistic value — in addition to its philosophical significance — and his notion of category mistakes (which could still stand some refinements) is based on the observation that two expressions may have some linguistic environments in common without thereby necessitating that their total distributions should be identical.[8] This is a piece of distributional analysis, and distributional analysis is at the heart of present structural linguistics.

Hans Reichenbach was very definitely of the opinion that the incredible

---

[6] Some of the problems posed by the indexical character of most ordinary discourse were discussed in the second paper mentioned in footnote 2.

[7] *The Concept of Mind* (London, 1949).

[8] This point touched upon in *LSL*, 169–170, is extensively analysed in the first paper mentioned in footnote 2.

complication of natural languages was no sufficient obstacle to the search for regularities in these languages. His *Elements of Symbolic Logic*[9] already contained a chapter, wholly devoted to the application of the techniques and terminology of modern logic to the analysis of natural languages, and in his posthumous work, *Nomological Statements and Admissible Operations*,[10] he makes a strong plea for the possibility and necessity of such applications.[11] Though he does not mention Carnap by name in this context, it is fairly obvious that his remarks were, at least partly, directed against Carnap's attitude. I think that Reichenbach was basically right and I would be glad to learn that Carnap would not fundamentally disagree with him.

W. V. O. Quine's excursions into the analysis of natural languages have become more and more frequent recently, and his last volume of essays, *From a Logical Point of View*,[12] contains many incisive remarks, revealing both a mastery of the fundamental teachings of structural linguistics and a clear insight into the role logic is dedicated to play in the future linguistics.

Now, however, it is time to notice that with the last-mentioned logicians it is, in general, no more Logical Syntax whose techniques, terms and methods are invoked for the analysis of ordinary languages, but rather Logical Semantics, if I am allowed to coin this term, the adjective 'logical' serving to distinguish this science from the various other occupations that are also known under the name 'Semantics.' There can, of course, be no doubt that Carnap would approve of this development. This would mean not a repudiation of the teachings of *LSL* but rather an implementation. It was Carnap himself who reintroduced semantic considerations into the logic of science, even before the ink of the English edition of *LSL* was dry. The reasons for this development will probably be discussed in other contributions to this volume. Let me notice here only the fact that no parallel development has taken place in structural linguistics to such a degree of overtness, though there are many indications that the high tide of anti-semantic feeling is slowly but surely subsiding. The return of semantics into modern, scientific linguistics will not be a capitulation before the good, old ways of thinking, but a recognition of the fact that this branch of the theory of signs has come of age and has

---

[9] *Elements of Symbolic Logic* (New York, 1947).
[10] *Nomological Statements and Admissible Operations* (Amsterdam, 1954).
[11] *Ibid.*, 14.
[12] *From a Logical Point of View* (Cambridge, 1953); see esp. essay III on "The Problem of Meaning in Linguistics."

finally turned from an introspectionistic art into a publicly controllable science, whose basic concepts are about as rigidly definable as those of any other science, including syntax. But since I dealt with this aspect at some length elsewhere,[13] no more will be said here.

II

During the first half of the twentieth century, more and more thinkers became increasingly aware of the fact that certain types of linguistic behaviour tended to be misevaluated by many people who were professionally engaged in putting this behaviour under rules through the customary scientific procedures of abstraction and generalization. As a result, paradoxes and antinomies were generated, whose resolution required much mental energy that might otherwise have been put to more fruitful and creative work, and pseudo-problems formulated that would continue to be discussed without end unless their baselessness could be convincingly pointed out, thereby causing their dissolution rather than their solution.

For lack of space, we shall not deal with the interpretation of Russell's and Wittgenstein's teachings under this aspect but turn immediately to the discussion of what Carnap had to say on this topic in *LSL* and some later works and compare it with Gilbert Ryle's approach as expressed in "Systematically Misleading Expressions".[14]

The term Carnap used for characterizing some of this misevaluated linguistic behaviour was '*the material mode of speech*'. This term has become widely known and applied, and the method of resolving certain philosophical problems by showing that they were based on formulations in this mode of speech but disappeared when the underlying issue was reformulated in *the formal mode of speech* has since been repeatedly discussed and criticized. It was less noticed that Carnap himself regarded the material mode of speech only as a special kind of *transposed mode of speech* (*LSL* 308). Though Carnap deals, both prior to this passage and afterwards, mainly with the material mode of speech and its dangers, and in the systematic treatment of this topic in Part IV of *LSL* with this mode and the autonymous mode of speech exclusively as the only

---

[13] "Logical Syntax and Semantics," *Language*, XXX (1954), 230–237 [reprinted in LI as Ch. 2].

[14] I shall quote from the version printed as chapter II in *Logic and Language*, First series, ed. by A. G. N. Flew (Oxford, 1951), 11–36. The paper originally appeared in the *Proceedings of the Aristotelian Society* for 1931–2. It will hereafter be quoted as SME.

possible interpretations of *quasi-syntactical sentences*, there can be no doubt that he was aware of the possibility of running into obscurities, inconsistencies, pseudo-questions and the other undesirable by-products of the material mode of speech also through the use of other kinds of transposed mode of speech.

I am quite ready to accept the thesis that many philosophical troubles are due to a failure of recognizing the transposed character of a certain formulation, but I am in some cases hesitant to accept Carnap's specific suggestions that the responsibility for these troubles rests in the fact that the transposed mode of speech takes the specific form of the material mode of speech rather than some other form. However, even if I am right, this does not reduce the value of Carnap's method but, in my opinion, rather enhances it, since it suffices to show, in order to exhibit the "pseudo"-character of a given formulation, that this formulation is *transposed*, though not necessarily *material*.

But before we proceed to the exposition of Carnap's views on this topic and our criticism of them, it is necessary to be somewhat more precise than we were so far. First, the term 'transposed mode of speech' has to be explained. Carnap's own explanation — which, he insists, is not meant to be an exact definition — is:

> By a transposed mode of speech we mean one in which, in order to assert something about an object a, something corresponding is asserted about an object b which stands in a certain relation to the object a (*LSL* 308).

It is obvious why Carnap is so cautious about this characterization. Too many expressions that occur in it are either vague or indefinite (or both) to a rather high degree. This holds not only for the deliberately vague 'corresponding' and the deliberately indefinite 'certain' but also, perhaps less deliberately so, for 'to assert something about an object'. (I am not even sure whether the term 'assert' is to be taken very seriously. It is surely worthwhile to extend the analysis of transposed modes of speech also to speech-acts other than assertions, e.g. to questions, commands, etc. Carnap's choice of 'assert' is due, of course, to his customary self-restriction to the treatment of the assertive aspects of language.) But, even taking all this into account, I find it difficult to interpret these terms in such a way that every metaphor will turn out to be an expression in the transposed mode of speech, as Carnap claims in the sentence immediately following the quoted characterization. I think that the sentence 'I am dead' (for 'I am very tired') would commonly be regarded as a metaphor. I cannot see what is the object b about which something is asserted in this sentence, when I am using it, in order to assert something about the object *a*, which is, in this case, obviously myself. Or is perhaps identity included in the range of indefiniteness of 'certain'? This, I must say, seems to me extremely unlikely.

Let us then start afresh. What Carnap wants to put his fingers on is clearly the fact that not all expressions are always used by all people in a way which is standard, by some criterion, for a certain class to which these expressions belong. To illustrate: Most English sentences of the form '... is ——' (with a proper name instead of '...' and an adjective instead of '——') are used most of the time by most people so as to convey to the receiver (listener or reader) that the object denoted by the proper name substituting '...' has the property (or quality, or character) denoted by the adjective substituting '——'. If we are ready to regard this usage as *standard*, then divergent usages are *non-standard*. When using 'John is clever' in order to convey that John is dull — for instance, when speaking "ironically" — this usage is non-standard. When using 'John is dead' in order to convey that John is beyond his apex in creative work — i.e., when speaking "metaphorically" — this usage is non-standard. (This is true, of course, only if we consider being-dead as *the* (only) character denoted by 'dead'. To be a metaphor is relative to a set of semantic rules. This needs further expansion, which will, however, not be undertaken here.)

On the other hand, when someone is using 'John is popular' in order to convey that John is popular or, more cumbrously, that John has the property of being popular, his usage is standard. But is it? Is being-popular a property (or quality, or character) at all? This question, of course, is itself a likely candidate for turning out to be a pseudo-question or, at least, a "verbal issue." I do not know of any sufficiently standard usage of 'property' for which this question could be decided one way or the other. The point is, however, that being-popular and being-clever are sufficiently different to necessitate some difference in terminology, perhaps best by adding some qualifying adjective to 'property'. This difference can be roughly put in the following way: If someone is clever at t_0, he will be so at t_1, with $t_1 > t_0$, unless some "changes" occurred in him, whereas someone may be popular at t_0 and cease to be so at t_1, with no changes having occurred in him. (That the term 'changes' begs the question, at least partly, is obvious. It is believed, however, that enough meat is left in the preceding statement to justify the introduction of a discriminating terminology — leaving a fuller justification for deeper investigation.) One might perhaps decide to use the qualifier 'categorical' for properties of the "clever"-type and 'relational' for properties of the "popular"-type. — The situation can be described also, and perhaps better, in the following way: 'John is popular' and 'Many people like John, and many more like him than either dislike or are indifferent to him' (cf. SME 33) can be anticipated to be sufficiently pragmatically equivalent; this anticipation could be checked, in principle, through a study of the linguistic behaviour of English-speaking people. If this anticipation is right, the overtly relational form of the expanded statement can be taken to be a hint for the hidden relational character of the adjective 'popular'. No such reformulation is in view for 'John is clever' (at least not on an unsophisticated level — on a more sophisticated level, 'John is clever' may be taken to be pragmatically equivalent to 'John is more clever than most other people (in his community)'), hence being-clever to be a relational property, too; indeed one could envisage John ceasing to be clever at t_1 through a sudden rise in the intelligence of the other people in his community between t_0 and t_1, without there having occurred any "interior" changes in John himself).

Should now careful observation of linguistic behaviour lead to the establishment of the fact that most people are strongly disposed to expect that a sentence starting with 'John is' and ending with an adjective will end with an adjective denoting a categorical property — the psychological analysis of this disposition will again be dodged here — then the ordinary usages of 'John is popular' will be non-standard. This formulation sounds somewhat paradoxical. It seems as if at least a misuse of terminology is involved, when an "ordinary" usage is treated as "non-standard." But the pseudo-problem created here is, of course, nothing more than another illustration of the issue under discussion. A sentence of the form 'A certain ordinary usage is non-standard' looks as if by it the property of non-standardness is assigned to usages that have already the property of ordinariness, creating thereby the feeling of self-contradiction. But the term 'non-standard' is a relational term involving a certain class of sentences to which the treated sentence belongs. And no contradiction is involved in saying that an ordinary usage of a given sentence is extraordinary (or non-standard) for the members of a given sentence-class to which this sentence belongs.

Non-standard usages serve as a constant and obvious source for failures in communication (though they may, and indeed often do, serve as a source for especially successful communication, if this peculiar effect is judiciously anticipated), but it seems that only non-standard usages of the second kind are philosophically dangerous. The fact that a given sentence may, within a specific context, be used differently from its standard usage is too well known to create any theoretical troubles. But the fact that even the *ordinary* usages of some sentences should be non-standard does not seem to be as generally recognized by the language theoreticians and, consequently, constitutes a fertile breeding ground for pseudo-problems.

I now propose to christen those sentences whose ordinary usage is non-standard (with respect to a certain sentence-class, to be determined on a pragmatic basis) *sentences in the transposed mode of speech*. This is still not an exact definition but is, I hope, more exact and helpful than Carnap's characterization. I also hope that Carnap will agree that my characterization is an adequate expansion of his intention. Should this hope turn out to be unwarranted, some other definiendum for the above-given definiens will have to be found. Tentatively, I shall proceed as if my proposed usage is adequate to Carnap's intentions.

But whether this characterization is adequate for Carnap's intentions or not, it seems to me that it coincides almost completely with the intentions of Gilbert Ryle when he introduced his term 'systematically misleading expressions'. This does not mean that I agree with the way Ryle himself characterizes these expressions. On the contrary, I think that his own characterization is not very helpful and is itself misleading to a degree, though not systematically so.

Let us first notice that Ryle talks about 'systematically misleading *expressions*', where 'expression' is used "to cover single words, phrases, and sentences" (SME 14). However, when Ryle gets to characterize these expressions, he talks in terms of being "couched in a syntactical form improper to the facts recorded" (SME 14), a formulation which is proper only for statements, i.e. sentences in the indicative, and even only for true statements. It seems therefore that what Ryle was up to was primarily a characterization of systematically misleading sentences (or perhaps statements) and only on this basis also of other kinds of expressions that are systematically misleading, though he nowhere gives us this secondary characterization. At any rate, I shall deal only with systematically misleading *sentences*, and the claim I made before that my characterization of sentences in the transposed mode of speech is more or less identical, in spirit if not in words, with the one given by Ryle, is meant to hold with this restriction.

Let me quote in full the passages in which Ryle introduces his conception of systematically misleading expressions:

The gist of what I want to establish is this. There are many expressions which occur in non-philosophical discourse which, though they are perfectly clearly understood by those who use them and those who hear or see them, are nevertheless couched in grammatical or syntactical forms which are in a demonstrable way *improper* to the states of affairs which they record (or the alleged states of affairs which they profess to record). Such expressions can be reformulated and for philosophy but not for non-philosophical discourse must be reformulated into expressions of which the syntactical form is proper to the facts recorded (or the facts alleged to be recorded)... When an expression is of such a syntactical form that it is improper to the fact recorded, it is systematically misleading in that it naturally suggests to some people — though not to 'ordinary' people — that the state of affairs recorded is quite a different sort of state of affairs from what it in fact is.

...expressions... which occur and occur perfectly satisfactorily in ordinary discourse, but which are, I argue, *systematically misleading*, that is to say, that they are couched in a syntactical form improper to the facts recorded and proper to facts of quite another logical form than the facts recorded. (... And when I call a statement 'systematically misleading' I shall not mean that it is false, and certainly not that it is senseless. By 'systematically' I mean that all expressions of that grammatical form would be misleading in the same way and for the same reason.) (SME 13–15.)

Ryle's talk of the "logical form" of facts and of syntactical forms being proper and improper to the facts might cause the impression that being systematically misleading is for him a semantic property of certain classes of sentences, and therefore quite different from our conception of sentences in the transposed mode of speech. But Ryle himself voices some misgivings about "what makes an expression formally proper to a fact" (SME 34). In spite of his scruples, Ryle was not ready at that time — though he might be so today — to repudiate the whole notion of the logical form of facts and was satisfied with stating his view

that the propriety of grammatical to logical forms is more nearly conventional than natural though I do not suppose it to be the effect of whim or of deliberate plan (SME 34).

That the semantic characterization of systematic misleadingness is not to be taken too seriously seems also to follow from the passage, already quoted, in which the term 'systematically misleading' is justified

in that it naturally suggests to some people — though not to 'ordinary' people — that the state of affairs recorded is quite a different sort of state of affairs from that which it in fact is (SME 14).

If we take *this* passage seriously — and I would prefer to do just that — then it seems that the whole talk about "logical form of fact" and "propriety" to these forms should better be completely forgotten and systematic misleadingness directly and non-misleadingly characterized in terms of what expressions exhibiting this feature "naturally suggest" to people, as I tried to do with respect to sentences in the transposed mode of speech. Should Ryle be ready to accept this interpretation, then my claim that there is an essential coincidence between these two terms would be vindicated.

There are still a few more minor points where I would disagree with Ryle. I think that sentences in the transposed mode of speech do sometimes mislead also "ordinary" people, hence do not always "occur perfectly satisfactorily in ordinary discourse" — the child looking for the equator, having probably been misled by sentences of this type — though the problems created by such misunderstandings will usually be of a rather harmless character. (This much, however, seems to be admitted by Ryle himself when he qualifies his contention that the non-philosophical author of systematically misleading expressions is not ignorant or doubtful of the nature of the state of affairs which his expression recorded, by a parenthesized "save in a special class of cases" (SME 17).) Ryle is still essentially right when he claims that only people professionally engaged with theorizing and generalizing about language are apt to be seriously misled by these sentences to a degree that whole theories might be created by them in order to solve pseudo-problems generated by their own short-sighted generalizations.

Carnap and Ryle both clearly see the important role played by sentences in the transposed mode of speech, or systematically misleading expressions, in the creation of philosophical pseudo-problems. But though Ryle displayed great ingenuity and acute insight into the workings of ordinary language in his classification of systematically misleading expressions into quasi-ontological statements, quasi-platonic statements, quasi-descriptive sentences, quasi-referential 'the'-sentences, etc., and in providing convincing illustrations of these various transposed modes of speech, he did not succeed in crystallizing what seems to be the philosophically most interesting class of sentences in this mode of speech, i.e. the sentences in *the material mode of speech*, though he came on occasion (SME 19) very close to this discovery.

If I had to point out what I regard as the greatest single achievement of Logical Empiricism (and of Analytical Philosophy in general), I would not hesitate to declare that this greatest achievement consists in establishing and corroborating the thesis that many, if not most, philosophical controversies are not, as they are commonly regarded by participants and onlookers alike, theoretical disagreements on questions of fact (of a scientific, or ethical, or aesthetical, or... nature) but rather disagreements (whose exact nature will be discussed later on) on the kind of linguistic framework to be preferably used in a certain context and for a certain purpose. That it took so long to develop this thesis and that so many thinkers are still so reluctant to accept it, is easily explained by the fact that philosophers, like scientists, ordinarily use the indicative mood in their sentences and that the standard use of this mood — and the one adopted almost unexceptionally by scientists in their scientific writings — is that of making statements about the entities denoted by their subjects, or so at least one was accustomed to assume unquestioningly until very recently.

If one philosopher of mathematics writes that

(1) Numbers are classes of classes of things

and another that

(2) Numbers belong to a special primitive kind of objects

(cf. *LSL* 300), then these sentences look very much like contrary statements of which at most one can be true. But looking upon the controversy of these philosophers in this way is perhaps unkind to them. No scientifically acceptable method is in view by which this controversy could be decided, if the dispute is taken to be about the ontological status of numbers. It might perhaps be kinder to interpret their intentions, when using these sentences, not as making assertions but rather as making proposals to look upon numbers as classes of classes of things or as objects of a special primitive kind, respectively. Putting the situation this way would, however, be of little help, since the reader's reaction would probably be: "What do you mean by *proposing to regard* numbers as classes of classes? Either this is what they are, then your proposal is superfluous, or they are something else, then your proposal is preposterous." In any case, one would be led back to an investigation of what numbers "really" are, an attempt of whose futility we convinced ourselves before.

It is at this stage that Carnap's great insight comes to our help. Uses of the sentences (1) and (2) are still interpreted as proposals and not as assertions, but not as proposals to regard certain entities as belonging to the one or the other category of entities, but rather as proposals to construct (or use) a language in which certain expressions belong to the one or the other category of expressions. More specifically, (1) is interpreted as being used for proposing to construct (or for suggesting to use) a language-system in which numerical expressions are class-expressions of the second level, (2) for proposing to construct a language-system in which numerical expressions are expressions of the zero-level and of a special sort. Under this interpretation, sentences (1) and (2) are treated as being formulated in a special kind of transposed mode of speech, namely in the *material mode of speech*. Though they look like ordinary sentences dealing with certain objects treated in the object-language, Carnap insists that it is more profitable to regard them as *pseudo-object sentences*. Their "true" character is revealed by putting them into the *formal mode of speech*.

(1a)   Numerical expressions are class-expressions of the second level

and

(2a)   Numerical expressions are expressions of the zero-level

are nice syntactical sentences in the metalanguage of . . . Well, of what object-language exactly? Here we come to the major point of the reformulation: it forces us to relativize these formulations with respect to some object-language, already in existence or to be constructed. Without such a relativization, formulations (1a) and (2a) are just incomplete, whether their uses are interpreted as assertions or suggestions. What looked before as a grim disagreement about facts, the grimmer since no way of coming to terms on these "facts" was in view, becomes now a disagreement about which language-system is to be preferably used. This disagreement need not be less intense for that shift, but the outlook for coming to terms is not so hopeless any more.

So far, we described Carnap's insight as involving a double reinterpretation of certain sentences: their apparent use for *making assertions* is reinterpreted as being one for *making suggestions*, and their apparent subject-matter is shifted from that of the objects belonging to the universe of discourse of the object-language, their properties and relations, to that of the designations of these objects, properties, and relations, and *their* properties and relations. So far, we stressed rather the first shift, involving the reinterpretation of many philosophical disagreements as being of a practical rather than of a theoretical nature. This point should, however, not be overstressed. Though a sentence like (1), whose use, if standard, would have been that of making assertions about certain objects, might be used for making suggestions about the construction of a certain language-system in which numerical expressions will belong with a certain syntactical category, this is by no means the only obvious interpretation, under which the character of this sentence will be changed from a philosophical pseudo-thesis to something more interesting. At least two other interpretations are in view. Under both, the sentence is assumed to be used for making assertions; the asserted statements, however, are rather different. The first interpretation, already mentioned in *LSL*, would transform (1) and (1a) into

(1b) There is a language-system in which numerical expressions are class-expressions of the second level,

the second interpretation would result in

(1c) It is fruitful and expedient to construct a language-system in which numerical expressions are class-expressions of the second level

or perhaps rather in

(1d) It is more fruitful and expedient (for certain purposes) to work with a language-system in which numerical expressions are class-expressions of the second level than with differently constructed language-systems.

There is of course an enormous difference between these interpretations. (1b) is an innocuous and almost trivial statement that nobody would want to dispute. Its rival statement

(2b) There is a language-system in which numerical expressions are expressions of the zero level and of a special sort

would turn out to be equally innocuous and trivial, completely blunting the point of the original dispute. Under the second interpretation, however, and especially for its second variant, we would get as the counterpart of (1d) the statement

(2d) It is more fruitful and expedient (for certain purposes) to work with a language-system in which numerical expressions are expressions of the zero level and of a special sort than with differently constructed language-systems,

a statement that may or may not contradict (1d), depending upon the exact meaning of the parenthesized clause 'for certain purposes'. Should the proponents of (1d) and (2d) agree that the purposes are the same, a genuine theoretical disagreement would exist between them, though *toto coelo* different from the theoretical disagreement that seemed to exist between them before this analysis. Instead of a dispute about the intrinsic character of certain spurious entities, with no indication in view on the kind of scientifically acceptable evidence that might be relevant for deciding between the rival theses, we now have a dispute about the relative merits of two language-systems, an interesting affair, difficult but certainly not hopeless. Though there exist no generally accepted criteria for the comparison of two language-systems — and here lies an important task for present-day methodology — one can easily imagine conditions under which a dispute of this kind could be definitely settled.

For our illustrative sentences (1) and (2), three interpretations have been discussed here altogether. As a matter of fact, Carnap himself mentioned in *LSL* (299) *eight* different interpretations of sentences in the material mode of speech. As these are only variants of the first two interpretations discussed here, there is no need to go into further details, for our purposes. It should, however, be noticed that our third interpretation, in either of its variants (c) and (d), is not mentioned in *LSL* though it appears in essence in the much later publication ESO. In a sense, this interpretation is only a variant of that in terms of proposals and one may insist — rightfully, I think — that discussing the utility of a proposal is essentially the same as discussing the truth of the assertion that this proposal is useful. This would confirm my contention, at which I hinted above, that out of the various advantages, which Carnap claims for the translation of controversial philosophical theses from the material into the formal mode of speech, that of forcing the participants to clarify whether they intended to make an assertion or a suggestion is probably of minor importance. The decisive advantage is in the transition from "ontological" disputes to methodological controversies.

When I mentioned just now the formal mode of speech, I was still talking the language of *LSL*. It should be noticed, however, that the translation of (1) into (1c) or (1d) is not, strictly speaking, a translation into the formal mode of speech, since (1c) and (1d) do not deal with purely syntactical properties of linguistic entities but rather with their pragmatic properties. Under this interpretation, (1) is not a *quasi-syntactical* but rather a *quasi-pragmatic sentence*.[15] This way of putting the situation transcends, of course, the lines of thinking adopted by Carnap in *LSL*. There, it is well known, Carnap made great efforts to show that it is not necessary, for philosophical discussions, to go beyond syntax. This attitude makes it understandable why our third interpretation

---

[15] Cf. Charles W. Morris, *Foundations of the Theory of Signs, International Encyclopedia of Unified Science*, I, no. 2 (Chicago, 1938), esp. 40–41.

does not occur as such in *LSL*. As soon, however, as one is ready to accept semantics and pragmatics as fields standing on a par with logical syntax — and Carnap was ready to do this at the time the English edition of *LSL* was published — we have much greater freedom in the interpretation of pseudo-object sentences, and there can be no doubt that our third interpretation, for instance, is rhetorically superior to the others; it does neither transform a seemingly theoretical controversy into a pair of theoretical assertions which do not contradict each other at all — an interpretation that might well look as an affront to the intelligence of the disputants — nor into a disagreement on a practical issue — an interpretation which involves a loss of prestige, in another sense — but rather into a different theoretical controversy, which is both real and interesting.

I am again pretty much convinced that Carnap would now agree to all this. I also think that he would now be ready to reformulate some of the statements he made in *LSL* on traditional philosophical controversies in a way which would be both less offensive and more correct. I believe, for instance, that he would no longer want to regard

the controversy between positivism and realism ... [as] an idle dispute about pseudo-theses which owes its origin entirely to the use of the material mode of speech (*LSL* 301).

Though certain theses maintained by positivists, such as

(3) A *thing* is a complex of sense-data,

and the corresponding theses maintained by realists, such as

(4) A *thing* is a complex of atoms,

are systematically misleading, being formulated as pseudo-object sentences, and may hence be characterized, in a sense, as pseudo-theses, they can be transformed, by translation into what we might call the *pragmatic mode of speech*, to the following antithetical statements

(3d) It is preferable to use as a language of science a phenomenological language (in which sentences containing thing-designations are reducible to a class of sentences containing only sense-data descriptions)

and

(4d) It is preferable to use as a language of science a physicalistic language (in which sentences about things are reducible to a class of sentences containing space-time coordinates and certain descriptive functors), creating thereby a dispute which is by no means idle and in which, as a matter of fact, Carnap himself actively participated (TM).

It is worthwhile to see how the method of pseudo-object sentences fared in Carnap's later publications, especially in ESO. The distinction there made between *internal* and *external questions* is somewhat related to that between the material and the formal (or pragmatic) mode of speech. Internal existence questions, such as questions as to the existence of numbers in general, of prime numbers, of prime numbers greater than one trillion, of prime number twins greater than one trillion, or of elephants, are in any case philosophically uninteresting, since the answers to such questions are to be obtained either by ordinary scientific methods, as used in the empirical sciences, or by logical proof — trivial in the case of numbers, less trivial in the case of prime numbers, and far from trivial in the case of prime number twins. Of philosophical interest is only the external question of the acceptability of the linguistic framework for, say, natural numbers. The traditional opinion seems to have been that this framework is acceptable if and only if natural numbers "exist," above and beyond any linguistic framework. Since this traditional approach leads nowhere, the only way out of this impasse is, according to Carnap, to interpret the seemingly theoretical external question of the existence of numbers as a practical question of the acceptance of certain linguistic forms to be solved by decision, which "is not in need of a theoretical justification (except with respect to expedience and fruitfulness)" (ESO 519).

Later on (ESO 521), Carnap proposes to replace alleged ontological questions of the existence of abstract entities in general by the question whether the use of certain abstract linguistic forms is expedient and fruitful for certain purposes. He does not state, however, that he proposes the latter question as a possible interpretation or reformulation of the original ontological question. The difference is, of course, very slight and probably no more than a matter of politeness and skill in controversy. I still believe that Carnap's position would be practically greatly strengthened if he were to express his readiness to interpret some or all ontological theses as theoretical theses about the expediency of the corresponding linguistic frameworks. It would, of course, be unduly optimistic to assume that many adherents of the original ontological theses would accept Carnap's reinterpretation as congenial.

III

So far, the two topics I selected from *LSL* for evaluation in this paper have been completely unrelated. I propose to discuss now an issue which is perhaps basic for Carnap's philosophy in general and which combines these topics, i.e., the applicability to natural languages of a terminological framework originally designed for language-systems and the method of transposed modes of speech.

The question that will be raised here is very simple and straightforward: Granted that for a given pair of language-systems, L_1 and L_2, such that L_2 is the syntax-language of L_1, each sentence of the object-language L_1 is either a real object-sentence or a pseudo-object-sentence (though these properties need not be definite so that there might not exist a method by which the specific character of any given sentence could be decided), what is the exact balance of gains and losses that results from a direct application of this dichotomy to natural languages?

It is well known that analogous questions arise with respect to other dichotomies such as object-language versus metalanguage, descriptive versus logical, synthetic versus analytic,[16] etc., and it is obvious that all these questions are methodologically strongly interconnected. To these one may add the pair introduced by Carnap in ESO, viz. internal versus external. All these dichotomies may be regarded, loosely speaking, as ramifications of the age-old dichotomy, *reality versus language*.

That adherence to this dichotomic conceptual framework is valuable at least as a first approximation is clear from the simple fact that common sense adheres to it and fares pretty well with it. The point is, therefore, whether this attitude will fare well enough in matters where a first approximation is not sufficient, e.g. in philosophical discussions. Should one even there insist on applying these dichotomies and explaining obvious non-conformities as residual effects due to mixtures, impurities, or noise (in the communication-theoretical sense), or should one, for this purpose, replace the whole methodological framework by a new and probably very complex one?

Assume, to give a rather simple-minded illustration, that John hears Bill utter the sentence, "All ravens are black," and that circumstances are such that there are good reasons to believe that this utterance was meant to be an assertion. Is it now fruitful for John to require from Bill

---

[16] Since this will be discussed elsewhere in this volume, no references will be given here.

to make clear whether his statement was meant to be analytic or synthetic by explicitly stating whether in his, i.e. in Bill's, usage the meaning of 'raven', which in the everday language in general is rather vague, is such that it entails 'black' or not and, if he did not think of it before in this light, to make up his mind on this point?[17] And should Bill regard John's request as a really helpful one and try to comply with it? Will communication be improved by such procedures? (It is clear that the request "State your meaning-postulates!" — which is, of course, nothing but a highly refined version of the old "Define your terms!" — will be made and taken seriously only if the issue is serious enough; extending this request to everyday situations would annihilate communication.)

Assume, now, that Bill replies to John's suggestion as follows: "Well, I understand your point completely. I know from my studies in the semantics of language-systems how important the distinction is between statements whose truth is analytic and those whose truth is synthetic. However, with regard to the statement, "All ravens are black," I made just now I cannot see why I should commit myself. You see, I made this statement because you asked me a minute ago whether the bird we both saw sitting on the nearby tree was not a raven. You will probably recall that the bird had some red plumage on its neck. My statement was meant to indicate that the bird we saw could not have been a raven. I assume that the aim of this statement has been achieved. What point is there now in committing myself as to the *character* of this statement? And what would you gain even if I committed myself? You are hardly interested in the character of the sentence, "All ravens are black," according to *my* usage, but rather in its character according to the *general* usage and if this usage is vague as to whether 'black' is entailed by 'raven', then this is all there is to be said about it and the analytic-synthetic dichotomy is simply inapplicable. The ordinary meaning of 'raven' is vague and being-black lies within its region of vagueness, though being-a-bird does not lie within that region, or at most only at its fringes so that the sentence, "All ravens are birds," is analytic according to the general usage, at any rate much more analytic than the sentence, "All ravens are black," if you allow me to express myself this way. A better way of expressing this situation would avoid the semantic term 'analytic' altogether and make use of some corresponding pragmatic

---

[17] For the following discussion, see R. Carnap, "Meaning Postulates," *Philosophical Studies* III (1952), 65–73, esp. 68.

term, say Quine's 'central'. We could then say that the sentence, "All ravens are birds," occupies a much more central position in the system of sentences which are generally believed to be true than the sentence, "All ravens are black," though this sentence is itself pretty central, too. The partial indefiniteness of meaning of the predicate 'raven', notice well, does not interfere at all, for almost all practical purposes, with successful communication in which this predicate is used. My conclusion is, then, that though the customary analytic-synthetic dualism is helpful enough as a first approximation even for the treatment of natural languages, this instrument is not fine enough for a higher degree of approximation. To leave it at the stage I mentioned, i.e. to say that common usage is too vague to allow for an application of this dichotomy, is surely not very fruitful, and to state one's meaning postulates is beside the point. What we need is a more elaborate methodological framework in which positive things can be said even of only partially meaning-determined expressions. I admit that no such framework exists so that for the time being we shall have to go along with the usual one as far as it goes, but I am afraid that it does not go far enough for a really interesting discussion of philosophically important questions. By the way, whatever I said so far for the analytic-synthetic dichotomy holds also, and for exactly the same reasons, for the logical-descriptive, external-internal, object-language-metalanguage dichotomies and for the determination of the synonymy of two expressions in natural language. When I say "Five is a prime number," I am not only talking about the number five, and when I say "Five is a number," I am not only talking, though in a transposed way, about the number-word 'five'. To put it this way may be good enough as a first approximation but it is far from an exact description of the whole situation. In whatever I say, both reality and language are involved, though sometimes the one and sometimes the other component may be practically neglected. To be more exact: the communicational process is a unity whose separation into a reality and a language component is an artifice which is immensely helpful in almost all practical situations but which nevertheless may break down under certain critical circumstances. Any attempt to enforce this separation beyond certain limits must lead to unsatisfactory formulations. I admit, however, that I have no conceptual framework ready in which to treat these critical situations."

I am afraid that Carnap would regard Bill's long speech — with which I am in considerable sympathy, as the reader has probably guessed — as just another embodiment of philosophical obscurantism. Indeed, this attitude is, at least for the time being, wholly negative. The fruitful applicability of the customary dichotomic methodological terminology to sophisticated theoretical issues is denied beyond a first approximation but nothing is proposed instead. There is even a flair of paradoxality in this denial itself since it is formulated in natural language, in which the reality-language dualism is so firmly rooted. By refusing to commit yourself, Carnap might argue, you simply put yourself outside of rational argumentation altogether. Ordinary logic, as you admit, is not applicable to expressions whose meaning is only partly determined, but there is no other logic in existence. On which basis shall we then go along discussing these issues?

It is very difficult to answer these objections. I shall not try to do it here, if only for lack of space. Let me then remark only this. Carnap put his method of the material mode of speech to a most powerful use in pointing out the pseudo-character of many traditional philosophical disputes. I do not think that it would do much good to the adherents of the philosophical theses under discussion to seek refuge from this criticism by claiming that this method is too crude to handle their theses.If they are right, then their theses lie already in that region where the separation of reality from language is no longer operational. But in this case the significance of these theses becomes totally blurred, since no tools are known of rationally manipulating statements in this region. Ontology might be saved from becoming either a collection of platitudinous pseudo-object statements or a set of theses about the expediency of certain linguistic frameworks (or a set of proposals to use certain linguistic frameworks) but only to become a self-defeating attempt to say something significant about pure reality at a level of sophistication where this simply cannot be done any more.

This last section might contain too much loose talk for Carnap to want to react to it. But he still owes us a general statement about the methods of explicating philosophically important concepts for natural languages. I hope that my last remarks, with all their crudeness and indecisiveness, will induce him to give us this statement.

(Added in January, 1962). In view of the fact that close to eight years have passed since the present paper was submitted to the editor, the following supplementary remarks, which, for obvious reasons, have been kept at a minimum, should be of help:

1. In the meantime, I saw an early version of Carnap's Reply and tend to agree almost completely with its content. However, in order not to detract from its value, no changes were made in the paper.

2. The promise I made in the text to which Footnote 5 belongs was fulfilled in

the paper mentioned in Footnote 13. I would like to acknowledge that a good part of Noam Chomsky's defence of Harris' position, undertaken in "Logical Syntax and Semantics: Their Linguistic Relevance," *Language* XXXI (1955), 36–45, was well taken and that many more linguistic facts than I had originally thought of can be adequately described with the help of rules of formation. Among these facts belong, e.g., also those relating to the active-passive relationship. However, those formation rules which can handle these facts are of a type which has only recently been analysed and understood, a development in which my critique might have played some slight role. It is interesting that this novel type of formation rules has been called by Harris and Chomsky (and is now being called by everybody else) "rules of transformation", and the reader should beware of confusion. Cf. Zellig Harris, "Co-occurrence and Transformations in Linguistic Structure," *Language* XXXIII (1957), 283–340, and Noam Chomsky, *Syntactic Structures* ('s-Gravenhage, 1957). The last book is a living corroboration of my claim that the incredible complications of natural languages are no sufficient obstacle to the search for formal regularities in these languages (cf. above, p. 117).

3. For refreshingly new light on the issues discussed on pp. 123–124, above, see Paul Ziff, *Semantic Analysis* (Ithaca, N.Y., 1960).

4. For the issue discussed above under II, cf. also my recent paper, "A Prerequisite for Rational Philosophical Discussion," *Synthese* XII (1960), 328–332 [reprinted here as Ch. 22].

ET TU, DIODORUS CRONUS?

In a recent article (Analysis, March 1965, pp. 137–141), Diodorus Cronus, in what seems to be a latter-day reincarnation residing in New York City, saw fit to take up again the second-oldest profession of *épater le bourgeois* and tried to show, among other amazing results, that the statement (made by someone at time t_3)

(1)   Stilpo was able at t_1 to render S false

(where S is the statement

S   Stilpo walks through the Diomean Gate at t_2,

and where t_1 is earlier than t_2 and t_2 earlier than t_3) must be false, if Stilpo was indeed walking at t_2 through that fateful gate.

Unfortunately, Diodorus Cronus arrived at this truly astonishing conclusion only after a whole series of fallacies, some of which will be exposed here. I hope Diodorus Cronus (DC, for short, henceforth) will not commit suicide again. It could become a habit.

S has the form

(2)   M does A at t,

'wherein M designates a specific person, A a specific action and t a specific time' (p. 137). DC calls statements of this form R-statements. R-statements are context-independent, so that, at least *prima facie*, the Tarski truth criterion applies to them: the statement 'M does A at t' is true if and only if M does A at t. S, in particular, is true if and only if Stilpo walks through the Diomean Gate at t_2. In what seems to be an innocuous paraphrase, one may then also say that Stilpo, by walking through the Diomean Gate at t_2, *renders* S true, and this is then also clearly the only way in which Stilpo can render S true (pp. 137–138).

Having said, in effect, that much, DC continues: 'For someone to be able to render an R-statement true, consists simply of his being able to do something which is *logically* both necessary and sufficient for the truth of the statement to the effect that he does the thing in question at the time in question'. Very benevolently interpreted, this is an extraordinarily cumbersome paraphrase of the truism, 'For someone to be able, at t_1, to render, at t_2, an R-statement (with time-reference t_2) true, consists of his being able, at t_1, to do something, at t_2, that renders this R-statement true'. However, by consistently omitting, by inadvertency or negligence, the time-adverbs, DC manages to fall very quickly into the trap he created for himself by his elliptical formulation. (There is an important general lesson to be drawn from DC's failure, and this is the main reason for my writing this little exercise: elliptical transformations, as discussed in recent theory of generative grammars,[1] are many-one; those who do not pay attention to this simple fact — and there is a general tendency in this direction — will indeed often wind up with logico-linguistic fallacies.) He clearly replaces in his mind the truism by 'For someone to be able, at t_1, to render an R-statement (with time-reference t_2) true consists in his being able, at t_1, to do something, at $t_1(!)$, that renders this R-statement true', and the road to hell is wide open. This replacement may well have happened in three easy stages: 'For Stilpo to be able, at t_1, to render S true consists in his being able, at t_1, to do something, at t_2, that renders S true' (truism)→ 'For Stilpo to be able, at t_1, to render S true consists in his being able, at t_1, to do something that renders S true' (ellipsis of a truism which — if one knows how to read it! — is still equivalent to that truism)→ 'For Stilpo to be able, at t_1, to render S true consists in his being able to do something, at t_1, that renders S true' (so long as the second occurrence of 'at t_1' is enclosed by commas, this can still be interpreted, with extreme benevolence, as equivalent to the original truism)→ 'For Stilpo to be able, at t_1, to render S true consists in his being able to do something at t_1 that renders S true'. (Omitting the commas now makes the benevolent interpretation psychologically well-nigh impossible; cf. p. 140, lines 21–22.) Though DC himself had insisted that for Stilpo to render S true, the only thing for him to do is to walk, at t_2, through the Diomean Gate, DC now has to face the self-created problem of determining an act Stilpo can perform at t_1 to the same effect. He therefore first arrives at the curious formulation quoted above and then takes two pages to demolish it. By falling now into the same trap from the opposite direction (if I may be allowed to use this wild simile), DC arrives at the conclusion that (1) cannot possibly be true.

But on his way to this conclusion, he manages to commit a further fallacy (which has again considerable general logico-linguistic interest). By a seemingly utterly innocent linguistic transformation, DC manages to turn the triviality, 'Stilpo is unable, at any time prior to t_2, to do *something that renders* S false' (since the only way in which Stilpo can do this is by not performing, at t_2, the act A) into the fatalistic monstros-

---

[1] See, *e.g.*, N. Chomsky, *Syntactic Structures*, The Hague, 1957.

ity, 'Stilpo is unable, at any time prior to t_2, to do *something to render S false*'. Not even committing suicide will do, as DC is very careful to expound. The simple truth is, of course, that there are innumerable acts that Stilpo can perform, prior to t_2, to render S false — committing suicide at t_1 only being a particularly radical one while also certainly being particularly effective — just as there are innumerable acts that Stilpo can perform, at t_1, to render S true, though, by the definition stipulated by DC himself (and perhaps also by common usage), none of these acts renders S false (or true, respectively).

Let us summarize: If someone advocates an atemporal use of 'is true' (and I for one should applaud, particularly in logico-philosophical contexts), he should refrain from using, in the same context, the phrase 'to render a statement true', since this phrase almost automatically implies that what has been rendered true was not so before. If, nevertheless, anyone wants to use this phrase, *e.g.* by saying that M, by performing act A at time t, renders the statement 'M performs act A at time t' true, he has no right to find fault with the expression 'M renders a R-statement true', since, for certain kinds of statement, this means no more nor less than that M performs the act described in this statement. Nor should he find any fault with the expression 'M is able at t_1 to render, at t_2, true the statement "M performs A at t_2"' (where t_1 is prior to t_2). He may even, at his own risk, omit 'at t_2' from this expression, but it is then up to him to beware of interpreting the resulting ellipsis as 'M is able at t_1 to render, at t_1, true the statement "M performs A at t_2"'. Nor is there anything faulty with 'M is able, at t_1, to do something, at t_1, in order to render true the statement "M performs A at t_2"'. He must of course distinguish carefully between this faultless formulation and the nonsensical formulation of the preceding sentence, and this in spite of the fact that in order to render the statement 'M performs A at t' true, M has to do something at t, namely to perform A. If someone, and be he a reincarnated Diodorus Cronus, manages to confuse all these things, then we should not be surprised if he arrives at very strange results indeed. Fatalism remains in need of stronger arguments.

IMPERATIVE INFERENCE

The recently revived discussion of so-called imperative inference by Messrs. Williams, Rescher and Robison, Gombay and Åquist[1] impressed me as being held, like so many other recent logical discussions, in a kind of Never-Never-Land whose exact location it is impossible to determine. Given their failure to distinguish, at least with sufficient clarity and consistency, between imperative sentences, acts of uttering (tokens of) such sentences, acts of issuing commands and the commands issued in such acts, general confusion is an almost inevitable consequence. This quadruple non-distinction mirrors, of course, the quadruple non-distinction between declarative sentences, acts of uttering (tokens of) such sentences, acts of making statements, and the statements made in such acts. These distinctions can be safely neglected for systematized languages, for obvious reasons, but are indispensable with regard to natural languages, the languages with which the above-mentioned authors are concerned, or so at least it seems, since examples with imperative English sentences are freely drawn upon.

To illustrate: Gombay tells us (p. 62) that 'Surely, if Williams is told "Take one of these pieces of cake, but don't take the larger", he knows perfectly well what to do', while, so we may infer from the context, had he been told 'Take one of these pieces of cake; don't take the larger', Williams would have been at a loss what to do. The difference, according to Gombay, is that in the first case only one command was issued, whereas in the second case two commands were issued which were 'sequentially inconsistent'. That replacing 'but' by a semicolon (or rather by whatever corresponds in speech to a semicolon — and Gombay shows not the slightest awareness that there is a problem here) should make such a difference, is *a priori* not very likely. Actually, of course, the whole story is entirely different. I do not know Mr. Williams, and I do not happen to know the people who might say to him, on some appropriate occasion, 'Take one of these pieces of cake, but don't take the larger'. But I am unable seriously to envisage situations in which Mr. Williams could be tempted to interpret an utterance of this deviant sentence as

---

[1] B. A. O. Williams, 'Imperative Inference' (Analysis Supplement, Vol. 23 (1963), pp. 30–36); N. Rescher and J. Robison, 'Can One Infer Commands from Commands?' (Analysis, 24.5 (1964), pp. 176–179); A. Gombay, 'Imperative Inference and Disjunction' (Analysis, 25.3 (1965), pp. 58–62); L. Åquist, 'Choice-offering and Alternative-presenting Disjunctive Commands' (Analysis, 25.5 (1965), pp. 182–184).

intended to convey a command. On many occasions, he would have interpreted it as an *encouragement* to help himself, expressed in some kind of jocular form. It is possible that Williams would have known, on each such occasion separately, what to do, but I can envisage situations where Williams, instead of taking the smaller piece — which is clearly what Gombay expects him to do — would have grabbed the larger piece, in full compliance with the actual intention of his host, other occasions where he would have taken neither, still in compliance with his host's intention, but would instead have helped himself to a nearby caviar sandwich, and still others where he might have reacted just with an icy look, having reasons to regard his host's joke as a bad one. In neither situation, and whatever his reaction might have turned out to be, would Williams have either complied with his host's command or disobeyed it, for the simple reason, mentioned above, that no command was issued. Even if he had interpreted his host's utterance, appropriately or inappropriately, as encouraging him to take the smaller piece, it would be utterly inappropriate to describe this mental act as an inference from two commands issued by his host and not much less inappropriate to describe him as having *inferred* the encouragement to take the smaller piece from two encouragements given by his host, though the fact that the encouragement was made by uttering a sentence that had some formal resemblance to sentences in which one presents premises for inferences to be made is, of course, an essential feature of the joke.

Or take the illustration given by Rescher and Robison (p. 179, n. 1):

> An example [for a situation where a 'disjunctive' command is issued which does not offer a choice but rather presents alternatives] might be as follows: Teacher: 'John, stop that foolishness or leave the room!' John gets up and starts to leave. Teacher: 'Don't you dare leave this room!' Here, Teacher's second order is neither incompatible with the first nor an abrogation of it, but gives a clarification by excluding one of the initial alternatives.

But Rescher and Robison's description of what happened is surely ridiculously wrong. Though Teacher doubtless had uttered a disjunctive imperative (English) sentence, she equally doubtless did not issue, on that occasion, a disjunctive command (whether choice-offering or alternative-presenting, leaving aside the question of the importance of this distinction) but rather a single categorical command followed by a threat, a combination of linguistic acts that a more pedantic Teacher could have performed by uttering something like 'John, stop that foolishness or *else* you will have to leave the room', or even 'John, stop that foolishness! If you won't do so, I shall order you to leave the room'. The fact that she chose (as many other Teachers would have done in her place) to perform her acts by uttering a disjunction of imperative sentences is, of course, highly interesting and deserves a close analysis by sensitive experts (who should preferably have some, though perhaps not too much, logical training) and it was this fact that enabled John to react in the startling way described. John must have been very stupid to misinterpret his Teacher's utterance, though it is more likely that he was rather of more than average intelligence but singularly mischievous, and only played the part of having received a choice-offering command. When Teacher shouted at him: 'Don't you dare leave this room', she did *not* clarify her original command by excluding one of the original alternatives but only countermanded by a new order the overstupid (or overclever) reaction of John to her first order. (It would be a good exercise for the reader whose linguistic sensitivity has been blunted by the way he has become accustomed to look at logic, to figure out Teacher's reaction if John, rather than rising immediately after having heard Teacher's utterance, had continued his foolishness for another minute and then risen to leave the room.)

How out of focus all this choice-offering and alternative-presenting business is in the given illustration becomes immediately clear when one realizes how oddly Teacher would have behaved had she said 'John, leave the room or stop that foolishness!' I wouldn't have wanted to be in her shoes then. Her class would probably have been justified in thinking that John's horsing around must have so enraged Teacher as to drive her out of her mind, at least temporarily. That disjunctive imperative sentences (in English) are not always commutative (in a sense that should be sufficient clear not to necessitate further elaboration) should, of course, be no more surprising than that conjunctive declarative English sentences are not always commutative. Recall only that stock example, 'Paul and Mary got married and a son was born to them' *versus* 'A son was born to Paul and Mary and they got married', though the non-commutativity is due to different reasons, if reasons are called for.

There exists no logic that covers all English imperative sentences, just as there exists no logic that covers all English declarative sentences. But just as there exists a logic of statements made by uttering English declarative sentences (or by uttering French sentences, or in innumerable other ways), underdeveloped as it may be, so there exists a logic of commands (and of instructions, and of encouragements, *etc.*) issued by uttering English imperative sentences (or appropriate other English sentences, or certain French sentences under appropriate circumstances, or in innumerable other ways), though this logic has hardly been developed at all, partly due to misconceptions of the type illustrated above. In order to develop such a logic formally — and there seems to exist no other way of doing it that deserves serious attention — the commands (and statements) have to be presented first in some normalized form, preferably in some formalized language, but at least in some 'natural' language that has been sterilized and exempted from all disturbing pragmatic features (the reader will forgive me this condensed and metaphorical account — expanding it would require a volume and would be worth one). This, of course, now poses the double problem of, firstly, specifying the exact nature of this normalization and, secondly, and still more formidably, establishing the 'rules of normalization', governing the transformation from ordinary speech into the normalized language. The second task can surely not be performed by logicians as such. One should, therefore, not be surprised to find clever logicians writing slightly foolish papers when they succumb to the temptation of not paying sufficient attention to certain distinctions in their treatment of natural languages just because these distinctions are immaterial for language systems.

REVIEW OF *THE STRUCTURE OF LANGUAGE**

The term PHILOSOPHY OF LANGUAGE has again become respectable. This is not the place to discuss the reasons why so many serious students of the field shied away from its use for some four decades. During that time, the term LOGIC carried so much more prestige and overtones of responsibility that relevant publications appeared under titles such as *The Logical Syntax of Language* or *Logic and Language*, although written mostly by members of philosophy departments. When the editors of the book under review published their article, 'What's wrong with the philosophy of language?' (1962) — an adapted version of the first half of which serves as the introduction to the present book — their criticisms were directed against authors who had hardly used the term PHILOSOPHY OF LANGUAGE at all. Often, the term LINGUISTIC PHILOSOPHY was employed as a generic name for philosophical views that were strongly determined by linguistic considerations. When these considerations referred to natural languages and ordinary speech, the term ORDINARY LANGUAGE PHILOSOPHERS was often used and is so used by the present authors, though LINGUISTIC NATURALISTS, a phrase advocated by Rudolf Carnap in this connection (Schilpp 1963:933), would probably be better. When the considerations were based upon constructed language systems, the term LOGICAL POSITIVISTS was used in the early thirties, later to be replaced by LOGICAL EMPIRICISTS. It is unfortunate that the editors saw fit to continue the use of POSITIVISTS in their introduction, since POSITIVIST nowadays carries a mostly negative connotation (which, I suppose, was exactly the reason they used it). The best term seems to be LINGUISTIC CONSTRUCTIONISTS, as suggested by P. F. Strawson and used by Carnap (Schilpp, ch. 16).

The 'primary incentive in compiling this anthology has been to bring to the attention of philosophers basic papers in the theory of language which suggest a new approach to philosophizing about language' (vii). It is hoped 'that the present collection of papers will help persuade philosophers that only an approach which integrates with empirical linguistics can succeed where current philosophy of language fails' (vii). Current philosophy of language fails because the linguistic naturalists, though sensitive to quite subtle nuances in ordinary speech, are incapable

---

* *The Structure of Language: Readings in the Philosophy of Language.* Edited by Jerry A. Fodor and Jerrold J. Katz. Pp. xii, 612. Englewood Cliffs, N.J.: Prentice Hall, Inc., 1964.

of providing an acceptable theory of language, due to their animosity to systematicalness and theorizing in such matters. The linguistic constructionists, on the other hand, although fully aware of the need for a systematic theory, have a tendency to get so enamored of their constructed language systems that they become insensitive to the need for methodological controls, and to the need for empirical evidence for their claims that these systems are (more or less) close approximations to natural languages; they therefore apply their results directly and uncritically to natural languages and ordinary speech.

The present anthology 'is primarily dedicated to presenting the recent work in linguistics which is most relevant to the development of a methodologically sound philosophy of language' (viii). A secondary incentive is to supply 'a source book in which the research worker in language studies will find those papers that have contributed the new insights into the nature of language and the new conceptual frameworks to the theory of language which have emerged from recent investigations in linguistics and philosophy' (viii). The anthology is meant to serve by itself as a text for courses in the philosophy of language as well as, in conjunction with others, a text for courses in grammar, semantics, linguistic theory, and psycholinguistics.

The material selected is not intended to be representative of ALL current views, not even of the most popular ones. Indeed, the extent of editorial license is rather extraordinary for a book that claims, in its title, to provide readings in the philosophy of language, without any qualifications. Of the twenty-three chapters of the book, nineteen were written by Noam Chomsky, his teachers (Willard V. Quine, Zellig S. Harris), collaborators (Morris Halle, Kenneth N. Stevens), or students (Paul M. Postal, Edward S. Klima, and the editors themselves). The four remaining chapters were written by Carnap, Alonzo Church, Paul Ziff, and Eric H. Lenneberg. All authors are living Americans. Six of the chapters are published here for the first time, others have been revised for the occasion.

To the question whether the anthology achieves its professed aims, I shall return at the end of this review. Let me, however, state immediately that my review may not turn out to be as objective as I (and the reader) would wish, since I find myself, on the one hand, in considerable general agreement with the 'new approach to philosophizing about language' that the editors set out to promote; but I strongly feel that in their own contributions they have seriously mishandled this approach. It is therefore likely that I shall be more lenient with certain shortcomings than differently inclined reviewers would have been, and less lenient with others.

The book consists of six parts. The first part is the introduction which, as already mentioned, is a revised version of part of an older paper by the editors. The second part, entitled 'Linguistic theory', contains five chapters, as does the third part, 'Grammar'. The fourth part is entitled 'Extensions of grammar' and contains four chapters. The fifth is 'Semantics', and four of its six chapters are written by philosophers and logicians, the remaining two by the editors. The sixth and last part is 'Psychological implications' and consists of three chapters.

In their introduction, the editors make two claims in support of their main thesis regarding the need for a new approach to the philosophy of language. The first claim is to the effect that Naturalists and Constructionists 'have failed to offer satisfactory solutions to traditional problems concerning language or to provide an understanding of the nature of language' (1). I think that they succeed in substantiating this claim, although I would not agree with all their arguments in full detail. However, I am less inclined to accept their second claim to the effect 'that any approach combining features of each to form a better philosophy of language than they have severally offered is precluded by the incompatibility of their basic claims' (1). Carnap and myself, for instance, have on many occasions tried to show that there exists no essential incompatibility between our basic claims and those of such Naturalists as Gilbert Ryle and Strawson (cf. Schilpp, ch. 17 and pp. 933 ff.), although we have not always felt satisfied with certain specific formulations. Carnap would claim that the basic concerns are complementary to rather than inconsistent with each other. The editors' arguments supporting the inconsistency do not seem to be conclusive. Rather, what they do succeed in substantiating is that both parties have underestimated the possibilities of erecting a systematic and comprehensive theory of natural languages, both because of lack of sufficient knowledge of modern linguistics and because of the rather sorry state of theoretical linguistics up to the midfifties. From this common (and not unjustified) evaluation, the two parties drew DIFFERENT, but not INCONSISTENT, conclusions: the Constructionists concentrated on dealing with constructed language systems for which they and their logician friends had developed extraordinarily powerful theories, while the Naturalists in their despair turned to meticulous but unsystematic (occasionally, it should be admitted, even antisystematic) investigations into the usage of specific words or short expressions in the vernacular, in particular of those that played an important role in philosophical discourse.

I see, then, no difficulty in forming a synthesis of the two approaches; the synthesis seems to me to be rather a necessary condition for a full understanding of language. But such a synthesis is not SUFFICIENT. It must be supplemented by, and based upon, a comprehensive and systematic linguistic theory. It is this insight which is the essence of the novelty in the approach of Chomsky and his associates. (If the reader concludes from this formulation that my differences with Fodor and Katz are 'purely verbal', I will not object, as long as he agrees with the gist of my remarks, as I hope they themselves will do.)[1]

It is not quite true that 'Positivists contend that the structure of a natural language is illuminatingly like that of a logistic system' (1). SOME Constructionists might have thought so — perhaps Bertrand Russell and Hans Reichenbach — but Carnap claimed only that the syntax of natural languages is 'best represented and investigated by comparison with a constructed language which serves as a system of reference', as the editors themselves quote (6, n. 6); this is a different story, and may perhaps be paraphrased as contending that natural languages are illuminatingly DIFFERENT FROM constructed languages rather than ILLUMINATINGLY LIKE them. Carnap was rather pessimistic, even over-pessimistic, in my opinion, as to the application of his findings to natural languages (Schilpp 520–7, 931, 941). Like most other Constructionists, he was not really interested in natural languages as such but only in the language(s) of science, his major philosophical interest lying in providing foundations for science (or for the sciences). The language of science may indeed be said to 'function primarily in the statement of truths' (2), and it is therefore only natural that Constructionists should have been concerned primarily with the assertive function of language. When the Naturalists so forcefully called the attention of their fellow philosophers to the other functions of language, their claims were not inconsistent with those of the Constructionists but, as said before, complementary to them (although, as happens so often under similar circumstances, difference of interest frequently turned into opposition of interests).

When the editors claim, as opposed to the Constructionists, that 'if an artificial system is chosen arbitrarily, it cannot be supposed to offer solutions to philosophically important problems' (4), this claim is trivially true. But the Constructionists' artificial systems were not chosen arbi-

---

[1] As a matter of fact, Katz (1966) expresses himself in a similar vein; cf. in particular chapter 2.

trarily. They were intended to be adequate for science, not reconstructions of all features of natural languages. Though the successful Constructionists' constructions can therefore not be said to offer solutions for ALL philosophical problems, they may, if successful, provide solutions for problems in the field of philosophy of science, and therefore cannot be totally disregarded.

The editors are right, it seems, in criticizing the mode of speech, customary among Constructionists, that considers constructed language as 'idealizations' of natural languages, but for the wrong reasons. They point out that while it is possible to state in what ways a certain 'real' gas deviates in its behaviour from that of 'ideal' gases, no such comparison is possible with regard to natural and ideal languages, unless one has a prior theory of natural languages. To this argument one could retort that no comparison between ideal and real gases is possible without a theory of real gases, or rather that the theory of gases is itself meant to be a theory of real gases, although the application of this theory to actual gases will require rather complex rules of interpretation. I would rather say that all discussion about 'ideal' so-and-sos, whether in physics or in linguistics, is equally misleading and a remnant from a period when the nature of theoretical entities and rules of interpretation was not as well understood as it is today.

Most disturbing to me is the opposition which the editors seem to erect between developing formal semantics and constructing a systematic theory of the semantic structure of a natural language. Let me quote at length, since I regard the whole paragraph as very misleading, particularly for linguists who might know very little about the extensive philosophical background of these remarks.

> Systems of formal semantics interconnect concepts in the theories of meaning and reference to their mutual illumination only if the primitive concepts are empirically interpreted. For example, given an operational characterization of synonymity, a system may explain analyticity in terms of the substitution of synonymous expressions in truths of logic and entailment in terms of analyticity of the conditional. But beyond such interconnections these systems can afford no more clarification of their primitives than is provided by the results of behavioral tests for their application. Thus, the question whether two expressions are synonymous in a natural language might be answered by a behavioral test, but clearly a system of formal semantics contributes nothing to answering this question. If the concepts of a system of formal semantics are not otherwise empirically interpreted, then the tests themselves must provide the full account (7).

Would the editors also have said that 'the question whether two lots have the same area might be answered by a few measurements and computations, but clearly a system of formal geometry contributes nothing to answering this question'? Would one not rather say that although a system of formal geometry BY ITSELF cannot answer this question (surely nothing more than a monstrous triviality), this system clearly contributes to answering the question by either providing the theoretical justification for the measurements and computation, or by intimating which measurements and computations should be performed for the purpose at hand? A formal system of semantics, as any other formal system, is not meant to 'clarify its primitives'. In Carnap's well-known terminology (1950a, ch. I), CLARIFICATION OF THE EXPLICANDUM (conceivably resulting in the finding that there is more than one explicandum) has to precede the erection of the formal theory (system) that is meant to provide the explication of this explicandum (and perhaps others). Nor do behavioural tests provide any clarification. What they (or rather the rules of correspondence, of which the behavioural tests form only a special subclass) do provide, together with the formal system, is a (perhaps partial and indirect) INTERPRETATION of the primitives. When an adequate formal system of semantics is available, then the answer to the question whether two expressions are synonymous need not be provided exclusively by performing a certain behavioural test on the use of these expressions but could be forthcoming in many other ways — perhaps even without including any new behavioural test at all but only by relying on the results of older tests performed on other expressions, just as, in the determination of the area of a certain lot, the need for new measurements will not always arise, in view of the existence of a well-confirmed geometry. However, since my argument seems to be known to the editors (cf. their following paragraph), perhaps I have not fully understood the whole issue.

I certainly concur with the editors that Quine's direct behavioural test for grammaticality, i.e., that a certain sequence of phonemes, say S, is grammatical if and only if S could be uttered by a speaker of the language without eliciting a bizarreness reaction, is inadequate. (I would moreover say that NO such direct test has any chance of being adequate.) But one counter-argument of the editors is clearly fallacious. They think they have refuted Quine by stating that 'almost any fully grammatical sentence could occur in a situation where it WOULD produce a bizarreness reaction' (8). (I do not quite understand the 'almost'. It should be obvious that for any fully grammatical sentence there will be innumerable situations where an utterance of this sentence will produce a bizarreness reaction.) But Quine only requires, as quoted by the editors themselves, that there be situations in which this sentence could be uttered without bizarreness reactions.

To repeat: What the editors have succeeded in showing in their introduction is not that the approaches of the Naturalists and Constructionists were wrong, but only that they were one-sided, and that for a really fruitful Philosophy of Language they should be synthesized and based upon a systematic and comprehensive theory of language.

In their introduction to Part II, the editors make it clear that they understand the term LINGUISTIC THEORY as 'a metatheory dealing with the properties of linguistic descriptions of natural languages' (19). I am not happy with two aspects of this statement. First, I doubt whether the self-restriction to NATURAL LANGUAGES, presumably to the exclusion of CONSTRUCTED LANGUAGES such as those invented by logicians for their purposes, or those produced by computer scientists and known as PROGRAMMING LANGUAGES (and perhaps even such ARTIFICIAL LANGUAGES as Esperanto?), is really justified. Though there are doubtless many decisive differences between natural and constructed languages, they also have a lot in common, and one wonders which field should deal with the metatheory of them all, if 'linguistic theory' is restricted in the way the authors propose. Secondly, I have misgivings as to the term 'Linguistic Theory' as such. If they shy away from using METALINGUISTICS, perhaps because this term has already been pre-empted by some linguists for some entirely different concept, it is not clear why the incomparably more descriptive term METHODOLOGY OF LINGUISTICS should not be used. The term THEORY is by now definitely overworked. On the previous page (18), the editors use 'theory of language' in a sense which is quite different from that of 'linguistic theory' (with which it will doubtless become confused, if their terminology is accepted). The intended sense is rather something like CONCEPTION OF LANGUAGE or, on a more sophisticated level, PHILOSOPHY OF LANGUAGE. On other occasions, a grammar of some given language is regarded as 'a theory' of this language, and the confusion should be complete. I am aware, of course, that the editors did not invent the term 'linguistic theory' — it is extremely frequent in Chomsky's writings — but I would still propose a moratorium on the use of the word 'theory' in all three contexts mentioned.

The first chapter of Part II, taken from a well-known book by Quine (1961), is entitled 'The problem of meaning in linguistics' and was originally a lecture presented before the Linguistics Forum at Ann Arbor in August 1951. As far as I know, it has made no noticeable impact on linguistic methodology. This is deplorable, indeed, and the editors should be congratulated for including this chapter in their selection. Quine's lecture was an extraordinarily clever attempt, made in a vivid and appealing style that never sacrificed lucidity and precision for persuasiveness, to impress linguists with the fact that they need not busy themselves with MEANING-IN-GENERAL but only with LIKENESS-OF-MEANING, or SYNONYMY, and possession-of-meaning, or SIGNIFICANCE, the division of labour being such that the grammarian should deal with significance and the lexicographer with synonymy. Though Quine agrees that the grammarian is able, in principle, to reproduce — the more fashionable term today would, of course, be 'generate' — the class K of all significant sequences of some given natural language, in a purely formal, i.e. semantics-free, way, he claims that evaluating the success of his attempt, i.e. determining the degree to which the class of generated sequences matches the class K, presupposes a prior independent determination of the semantic notion of significant sequence. Chomsky's arguments (1957) are well known.

But Quine's restriction of the task of the semanticist to establishing synonymy, revealing as his discussion may be about the length of strings in the synonymy in which he is interested, is indefensible. As a matter of fact, Quine never uses the term SEMANTICIST at all. He constantly confronts the grammarian with the LEXICOGRAPHER, apparently assuming without much further ado that their combined efforts will take care of all linguistic matters. Surely this requires at least a good deal of stretching the 'lexicographer's' task, but Quine is evidently quite ready to do so. The lexicographer not only focuses 'on a class of short forms capable of enumeration', providing genuine synonyms for them or, more often, 'a mixture of quasi-synonyms and stage-directions', but he also explains 'as systematically as he can how to construct genuine synonyms for all sufficiently long forms compounded of those short ones' (28–9). But this is something no present-day lexicographer does, though lexicographers might do so in the future, if and when dictionaries get a new look as advocated, for instance, by the editors in another paper in these *Readings*. Even then, the lexicographer will not yet handle all of the semanticist's tasks. It is not easy to see how even an extended monolingual dictionary will exhibit the meaning of such LOGICAL terms as *or* or *all* in English, in partial justification of the validity of the inference from, say, *All Athenians are Greeks* and *Socrates is an Athenian* to *Socrates is a Greek* — and merely providing quasi-synonyms such as *every* or *each* for *all* can't help, of course. Nor can one easily see how dictionaries will handle so-called 'theoretical terms', for which no synonym in observational terms might be available. It is conceivable, e.g., that *raven* (in its professional zoological usage) is such a theoretical term, for which neither synonyms nor quasi-synonyms in purely observational terms are available but which is used in such a way that from *A is a raven* one is entitled to deduce *A is a bird*, *A is black*, etc. In other words, *bird*, *black* etc. might be hyponyms to *raven*. (But I do not wish to intimate that by adding hyponymy lists to synonymy lists, the task of the semanticist would be exhausted.) For terms whose meaning is theory-dependent, nothing short of providing the whole (interpreted) theory is, in principle, sufficient for determining their meaning; and this, or even any approximation to it, is obviously well beyond the lexicographer's responsibilities (and abilities). Of course, it is at the moment far from clear how the semanticist will go about discharging this responsibility. Part of the task, e.g. the treatment of the 'logical' features, may perhaps be delegated to a so far non-existent UNIVERSAL SEMANTICS; but as to the theoretical terms which are primitive (undefined) in some theory, the situation is very unclear. Arguments can be presented for the view that this treatment is simply not the responsibility of the English semanticist. But this defensible view will certainly induce a rather radical re-evaluation of the status of semantics in natural languages. (Or shall one perhaps decide to take 'natural languages' as not containing scientific theories?)

Quine himself has some doubts as to the legitimacy of speaking of synonymy between expressions of different languages (30), because he tends to accept the Cassirer-Whorf thesis of the interdependency of language and world-view. One may therefore assume that when the much less controversial theory-dependency of the theoretical expressions is drawn to his attention (Quine's talk, we recall, was delivered in 1951, long before the status of theoretical terms came under the close scrutiny of such philosophers as Braithwaite, Carnap, and Hempel), he will himself recognize that providing synonymy lists could not possibly exhaust the semanticist's occupation.

Harris's 'Distributional structure' (1954) is presumably well known to readers of LANGUAGE, and does not require extensive comments. The student of the philosophy of language, for whom this volume is after all mainly intended, will be greatly disturbed by the constant unclarity (discernible also in most other publications of Harris) as to what he means by 'language'. Quine, in his contribution, distinguishes four classes of sentences that can be of interest to linguists, from a corpus (a class of observed utterances) to the class of all sentences that could in principle have been uttered by the members of a speech-community (disregarding restrictions imposed by memory structure, shortness of life, etc.; cf. Bar-Hillel 1964:206). When Harris says, e.g., that 'the distribution of an element will be understood as the sum of all its environments' (33), it is not clear whether actual environments in a given corpus or possible environments in some larger class are meant. When he continues in the next section, saying that 'an environment of an element A is an existing array of its co-occurrents', the meaning of the qualifier 'existing' is obscure (to me, at least). Surely, dealing with a given corpus as such is extremely uninteresting, for a linguist. Finding distributional rules that will fit such a corpus is trivial. Non-triviality can only be obtained by extension to an infinite class of sentences. But on this Harris is completely silent.

Similarly, his treatment of the 'reality of a distributional structure' worked out by some linguist is highly unsophisticated, from the standpoint of a modern methodologist. Harris shows no awareness of the distinction between external and internal existence (or reality) questions drawn years ago by Carnap (1950b). It just won't do to say that the question whether such a structure really exists in the speaker is a question of fact (36). However attracted one may be to use such a phrase as 'really exists', it should by now be clear that this use, without any further precautions or preliminary explanation, can only confuse issues. Note that my objection refers only to the terminology used by Harris and not to the very real psycho-linguistic problems he discusses in these terms.

Harris's discussion of 'Meaning as a function of distribution' is unsatisfactory, partly for reasons already mentioned, partly for quite different ones. What does he mean when he says 'If we consider *oculist* and *eye doctor* we find that, as our corpus of actual utterances grows, these two occur in almost the same environments, except for...' (43)? What strange corpus is this? Who can exhibit it? Who 'found' anything of the kind in this corpus? It is my guess that for at least 95% of all the utterances of English speakers in the 20th century containing the word 'oculist', there just exists no utterance in this corpus containing *eye doctor* instead of *oculist*, and that this percentage will grow in time rather than diminish. True enough, there exist of course interesting, even decisive, connections between synonymy and distribution — in the total language, not in some given corpus — and these connections can in part be established by asking informants to perform substitutions, but the exact nature of these connections is still very much in need of further clarification. Harris's rule (or definition) — 'If A and B have almost identical environments except chiefly for sentences which contain both, we say they are synonyms: *oculist* and *eye doctor*' (44) — is unacceptable as such. Let me repeat the objection I made to a prior version of this rule in a paper published shortly before Harris's (Bar-Hillel 1954): If by 'environments' are meant actual environments in actual corpora, then the environments of *oculist* and *eye doctor* would show only a very slight overlap, so that these two expressions would turn out not to be synonyms. If the totality of all grammatical English sentences is meant, then *oculist* and *eye doctor* would be approximately as interchangeable as *oculist* and *lawyer*. The words *four* and *seven* would be almost totally interchangeable (as would be any two number expressions) — remember that interchangeability is meant by Harris SALVA BENEFORMATIONE or GRAMMATICALITATE, not SALVA VERITATE — but nobody would like to regard this as an indication of their synonymy.

Harris is ready to go to amazing lengths in this extremely interesting, original, and imaginative — but utterly vain — attempt to discuss discourse analysis in terms of substitutability relations within a given discourse. Consider, e.g., the following: 'For example, if one sentence contains noun A + active (transitive) verb B + noun C, and a neighbouring sentence contains C + verb + A, there is a certain likelihood that the verb will be the passive of B' (46). Of course, there is such 'a certain likelihood'. But there is an incomparably larger likelihood that the verb, in any rational discourse I can imagine offhand, will be something else. After *John hit Paul* I would expect *Paul hit John back*, *Paul cursed John*, *Paul looked accusingly at John*, *Paul was flabbergasted by John's violent reaction*, etc., but least of all *Paul was hit by John*. It is time to put the horse back before the cart. True enough, every competent English speaker knows that after *the pianist* there will occur — in the English language, not in the speech of some English speaker, or even of all English speakers — 'much the same verbs as after *the pianist who*' (48). But he knows this because he has internalized the rules of English grammar, not because of any actual or imaginary eliciting tests. Reduction of syntax or semantics to distribution in any serious sense is dead. It was a good try, though.

The next chapter, Chomsky's 'Current issues in linguistic theory', has been published in book form (1964), and deserves separate review.

Chapter 4, Chomsky's 'On the notion "Rule of grammar"' (1961b), was originally delivered as a talk before a symposium in applied mathematics, and most of its contents have in the meantime been incorporated in other publications by the author. Let me therefore mention only a few salient points. In this chapter, the role of self-embedding is somewhat overplayed. Later, Chomsky came to realize (1965:12–4) that it is rather the more general notion of nesting which is of major theoretical importance, unbounded nesting being incompatible with finiteness of memory and therefore not representable by finite-state grammars. Unbounded nesting implies, of course, also unbounded self-embedding. That self-embedding, even bounded, should create additional difficulties in comprehension (and production) over and above those created by nesting as such is an interesting phenomenon, and is still in need of some satisfactory explanation.

An important observation has been made by Yngve to the effect 'that a grammar may contain devices that partially overcome the limitation on memory by allowing reformulation of sentences' (1960:126, n. 14). He has shown, in effect, that certain passive sentences have a lower degree of nesting than their active counterparts. Chomsky gives Yngve his full due. He does not believe, though, that Yngve's own measure of syntactic complexity, called by him 'depth', is of particular importance. The assumption that 'depth' is a good measure of syntactic complexity rests on the hypothesis that utterances are produced by the speaker from top down, as it were; i.e., that the speaker invariably first selects the most general grammatical construction, then the sub-constructions, and finally the words (or morphemes). But there exists little evidence for the truth of this hypothesis.

Two comments are worth making. First, Chomsky's characterization of Yngve's measure as resulting from an equal contribution of left-branching and self-embedding is wrong. Depth is rather a certain combination of what might be called 'width' (of branching) and left-branching. A construction whose tree diagram is, say:

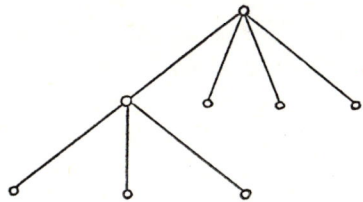

would have depth 6, according to Yngve, though its degree of left-branching is only 1 and its degree of self-embedding (or even nesting) is at most 1.

Secondly, the term 'reformulation' occurring in the passage quoted above should not be taken literally. It would, of course, be self-defeating to assume that we first formulate in our brain a sentence in the active, and thereafter, realizing the sad fact that its degree of nesting is beyond the tolerable, 'reformulate' it in the passive. The better picture is that, when confronting the decision whether to select the active or the passive form of the sentence, we select the passive, perhaps after having first determined that selecting the active would create difficulties with which our brain would be unable to cope. This picture also corresponds much better with the MIT school's most recent conception of the exact operation of transformations. Replace therefore 'reformulation' by 'different formulation'.

Chomsky warns (127, n. 16): 'It seems to me very likely that attempts to construct a model for the speaker or hearer are quite premature at this point, since we can hardly claim to have an adequate characterization of the form of the grammars that provide the devices that are employed, in some way, in the production and understanding of speech'. This warning has been largely unheeded, as might have been expected; some of Chomsky's students, indeed, were unable to resist the temptation. I personally am not sure that this temptation should be resisted. On the contrary, I tend to believe that the construction of grammars has to be accompanied by constructing models of producing and comprehending utterances — in the current terminology, that a theory of linguistic competence has to be developed simultaneously, more or less, with a theory of performance — since whether a language has been 'adequately' characterized can be seriously tested only by also taking performance into account. I would therefore interpret Chomsky's words as forewarning us that any attempt made at this stage of the game to present a theory of the speaker and hearer has little chance of survival, even for a short period. And to this one cannot but agree.

Postal's Chapter 5, 'Limitations of phrase structure grammars', does not contain much material that is not also covered in his monograph on constituent structure (1964). Let me mention only that Postal regards it as 'almost certainly true that such [context-sensitive phrase-structure] rules cannot enumerate the sentences of natural languages' (150), while Chomsky's more recent conjecture (1964: 61) goes in the opposite direction.

In their introduction to Part III, the editors stress, rightfully and persuasively, that the relationship between grammar and linguistic behaviour is exactly like that between, say, mechanics and certain phenomena in physical reality; i.e., that grammar is as much a partial theory of linguistic behaviour as mechanics is a partial theory of physical reality.

It is interesting that this remark had to be made at all. But there still seem to be linguists who understand the adjective DESCRIPTIVE in 'descriptive linguistics' very narrowly and atheoretically.

Chapter 6, 'Co-occurrence and transformation in linguistic structure' by Harris (1957) will not be reviewed here. Let me only stress, in view of recurrent misunderstandings, that Harris's notion of transformation has little substantial connection with Chomsky's notion and is, in my opinion, not very useful, since it is based on a wrong methodology (see above). That Chomsky himself should describe the relation of his own concept to that of Harris differently — and he does so, e.g., in the next chapter — may be explained as due more to a feeling of piety toward his teacher than to objective correctness. It would be more accurate to say that Chomsky developed his conception in opposition to Harris's. In spite of the inadequacy of Harris's basic notion, however, his paper contains innumerable pertinent observations on English grammar which no student of English would want to miss.

Chapter 7, Chomsky's 'A transformational approach to syntax' (1962) contains — if I am not mistaken — the first published sketch of a transformational grammar of English that can make any serious claim to relative exhaustiveness. Since its appearance, countless improvements and changes have of course been made to this sketch by Chomsky himself and others.

Chapter 8, Klima's 'Negation in English' (not previously published), is the longest paper in the volume. It is the most carefully thought out linguistic article in the collection, but by no stretch of imagination can I see why it has been included in this volume of *Readings in the Philosophy of Language*. But perhaps just because this chapter was written in such an utterly non-philosophical vein and has absolutely no philosophical axe to grind, any philosopher who from now on wants to write on negation (in general, or in English) will disregard this paper only at his own peril. This is the place where he will have to go to check his facts (if he is interested in such a pedestrian endeavour at all).

The next two chapters, 9 and 10, Halle's 'On the basis of phonology' and 'Phonology in generative grammar', are equally utterly unphilosophical. But with regard to them, I cannot even see why a philosopher of language, in this capacity, will ever want to study them. The second paper, however, is of extreme importance for linguists: in it, for the first time, a generative grammarian makes the claim that his theory has diachronic relevance and is therefore also historically testable.

Part IV deals with extensions of grammar. By this the editors mean, more specifically, the study of syntactic units longer than single sentences ('discourses') on the one hand, and the study of not completely well-formed strings on the other hand. Both topics have been traditionally shunned by linguists (for good reasons, it now seems, with hindsight). It remains to be seen whether the growing interest in these subjects is not premature.

The editors correctly stress the philosophical significance of both 'extensions'. In particular, they are right in stressing the importance of the concept of LOCAL SYNONYMY, i.e., synonymy within a discourse. But they are wrong in believing, with Quine, that synonymy alone 'would yield a well-defined notion of analytic sentence' (353).[2] What this means is that the self-restriction to local synonymy is unjustified. Adequate discourse grammars should enable us to clarify all kinds of 'local' grammatical properties and relations, of which local synonymy is only a single, though perhaps a particularly important, representative.

The philosophical interest in not fully grammatical and in otherwise deviant strings is very old, and the amount of nonsense written by philosophers on this topic is proportionally large. It is somewhat strange to see Paul Marhenke credited for having been the first philosopher to notice, in 1952, the consequences of grammatical ill-formedness for cognitive significance. In my paper, 'On syntactic categories' (1950), I discussed the history of this connection at some length (and at still greater length in my unpublished Hebrew dissertation, *The Theory of Syntactic Categories.* Jerusalem, 1947).

Thirteen years ago, when I first came across Harris's 'Discourse analysis' (1952), I scribbled some twenty pages of notes to it. That was the heyday of distributional, exclusively corpus-bound analysis, of which Harris was perhaps the most skillful and imaginative prophet. In 1966, I feel there is no point in flogging dead horses, so let my notes rest in peace.

The next three chapters, 12, 13, and 14, deal with semi-grammaticality, degree of grammaticalness, semi-sentences, etc., i.e. with linguistic entities that are not fully well-formed, according to some criteria, but are not fully ill-formed either. This is one of the most confused issues of recent linguistics, and these three chapters do not contribute much to its clarification; in fact, the last two contribute a great deal to its further obfuscation.

---

[2] It would take me too long here to justify this eminently important claim. For a forceful justification, see Kemeny 1963:64.

One root of the prevailing confusions lies in the almost universal disregard of the distinction between two kinds of linguistic entities. To use formulations that, in recent methodology of science, have become slogans,[3] one has to distinguish carefully between theoretical, abstract linguistic entities and the 'corresponding' observable, concrete entities; or still better, between theoretical and observational terms. I have already proposed to use SENTENCE, MORPHEME, etc. in technical discussions, exclusively as theoretical terms, while reserving the terms UTTERANCE, MORPH, PHONE, etc. for denoting observable entities (Bar-Hillel 1957). I would now propose to use such terms as GRAMMATICAL, SEMI-GRAMMATICAL, UNGRAMMATICAL, DEGREE OF GRAMMATICALNESS etc. in technical discussions, in connection with such theoretical entities as STRINGS (of appropriate units), SENTENCES etc., exclusively; such qualifiers as DEVIANT, ODD etc. would then be used only with UTTERANCE etc. (Incidentally, the distinction between string and utterance is by no means identical with that between type and token.) The relation between a string and an utterance 'of it' is, of course, by no means one-one or even one-many. Neither is it deterministic. The string which underlies a given utterance is never completely and uniquely determinable from the utterance as such, not even if we know the language to which the string is supposed to belong.

Utterances of (intuitively) perfectly well-formed strings may be odd, and this for many different reasons. (I am now talking about the utterance-act, not the utterance-product. This is another distinction not always drawn in places where it should be, in spite of the fact that it is otherwise well known.) Using what I hope to be a self-explanatory ad hoc notation: when A utters [It's raining], this may be taken by B as being an utterance of the indicative sentence /It is raining./ Nevertheless his act may be regarded as odd to some degree or other, and in certain circumstances even as extremely odd. This would, for instance, be the case if A and B were talking to each other under a blue sky, if they were running to find shelter from a torrential rain, if A were known to have been mute all his life, if A had never before uttered anything in English, etc. On the other hand, utterances of such perfectly ungrammatical strings as /rain Spain main plain/ will be treated, in appropriate contexts, as perfectly normal. To use other slogan terms, I would propose to restrict the term GRAMMATICALITY (and its cognates) to syntax and semantics,

---

[3] For details, consult any recent textbook on scientific methodology, the best such being Nagel 1961.

and DEVIANCY and ODDNESS (and their cognates) to pragmatics. In the established division of labour, grammaticality should be treated by linguists, deviancy by psycho-linguists. (Of course, there is no law against simultaneously being a linguist and a psycho-linguist.)

There exists no general decision procedure for oddness of utterances, nor for the problem of which string corresponds to a given utterance. Suppose that one is faced with an odd utterance (and it does not matter whether the product of this utterance is a sequence of phones, of graphic symbols, or is presented in any other mode), and that one is interested in 'understanding' this utterance (which is not imperative, since there is nothing inherently wrong in leaving odd utterances alone, though there often are certain social or other pressures toward 'understanding'). One has, then, in general and in principle, a choice between treating the product of this odd act as the realization of a grammatical or of a non-grammatical string (or of a string of an intermediate degree of grammaticality).

Assume that, on a certain occasion to be left unspecified here, I hear someone utter [Die Mädchen gehte auf dem Strasse.][4] I can take this to be an utterance of the ungrammatical string /Die Mädchen gehte auf dem Strasse./ If I have to, or wish to, I will then worry about what the 'utterer' really wanted to say. If I know the utterer to be a non-native speaker of German, and one who just recently started learning German, then a good guess would be to assume that what he wanted to say was /Das Mädchen ging auf der Strasse./ Under different circumstances, the best guess would be /Das Mädchen geht auf der Strasse./ Under still other circumstances it would be /Die Mädchen gingen auf der Strasse./ I would have no difficulty in telling a story where the correct interpretation would even be /Die Jungen standen auf dem Bürgersteig/ — or, with a still greater amount of imaginative effort, anything you like.

But some of these sentences can be taken to be not INTERPRETATIONS of the string the utterer realized by his utterance, but rather the sentences themselves that were realized by the utterer, perhaps only under appropriate conditions such as knowing about certain speech defects of the utterer, mechanical defects of his typewriter, or certain things about his mentality. There is just no single 'natural' counterpart to the mentioned utterance as such. Whether it makes good sense to look for the least unnatural counterpart, i.e. that fully grammatical sentence from which

---

[4] This illustration is taken from Schaechter 1935. In spite of its many shortcomings, this book, from a former associate member of the Vienna circle, contains much material which modern linguists could make good use of; cf. my remarks to this example in Bar-Hillel 1950, note 8.

the string realized by the utterer deviates 'least', is very doubtful, if what I have said so far is true. At any rate, any explication of this notion will require a combination of linguistic and psycho-linguistic features to be taken into account, and context and environment will remain decisive parameters. It is equally doubtful whether statistics will be of sufficient usefulness to warrant going through the trouble and expense of collecting them.

It is therefore not surprising that all three chapters dealing with this topic are rather unsatisfactory, though for quite different reasons. Chomsky's 'Degrees of grammaticalness'[5] does not draw any distinction between 'sentence' and 'utterance' (in these terms or others) and seems to use them more or less as synonyms. This presumably also indicates that he does not accept the view which I attempted to express by drawing this and other distinctions, or that he does not regard it as particularly important. However, most of what he says can best be understood as referring to the theoretical entities which I have suggested. He believes, doubtless rightly, that an ideally adequate grammar would work not with a binary family of qualitative predicates such as GRAMMATICAL and UNGRAMMATICAL — nor even with a ternary family, GRAMMATICAL, SEMI-GRAMMATICAL and UNGRAMMATICAL — but rather with the quantitative function DEGREE OF GRAMMATICALNESS. This is, of course, perfectly in line with the view of such methodologists as Carnap who have many times drawn our attention to the fact that scientific concept formation develops, by and large, from the qualitative through the comparative to the quantitative stage; the last-named, when achievable, forms the climax of such a development. It is interesting, however (and deplorable, I think), that in our case the comparative stage was skipped. Nobody, to my knowledge, explicitly proposed a definition (not to mention a whole theory) of MORE GRAMMATICAL (better-formed) THAN. Chomsky himself immediately jumped to the quantitative concept. When Katz, in his contribution to this part, 'Semi-sentences', rightly rejects Chomsky's particular (tentative) explication, he falls back to a qualitative conception, though he then tries to promote a ternary theory. Let me strongly suggest that somebody sit down and work out a theory of the comparative notion MORE GRAMMATICAL THAN. This concept should, of course, be a relation of the type known as PARTIAL ORDER; such a theory would not always determine, for any two given strings, which one is more grammatical than the other. And I for one would be quite content with this limitation,

---

[5] Originally published under a different title (1961a).

at least for a start. If, at some future time, a quantitative theory is developed that will somehow decide also, for a tolerable price, the intuitively incomparable cases, fine and good. Today, I repeat, this seems definitely premature.

Let me, at any rate, endorse Chomsky's conception voiced in the following passage:

> Thus, a generative grammar supplemented with a hierarchy of categories can assign a degree of grammaticalness to each sequence of formatives. If we could show how a hierarchy of categories can be derived from a generative grammar, then the latter alone would assign degree of grammaticalness. There are, in fact, several ways in which this might be possible (388).

I would definitely agree that, given a fully adequate generative grammar, it should be possible to define the term MORE GRAMMATICAL THAN in an intuitively adequate way, i.e. one that would establish this relation as holding between the right pairs of strings. But, tentatively, I have my doubts as to the possibility of coming up with a useful quantitative concept.

(Let me insist, in parentheses, that our intuitive judgments on such matters are very likely to be heavily marred by our confusing strings with utterances. Not only linguists do this, but the famous man in the street does it also, and this type of confusion is then not a professional disease but a rather common one. Thus these judgments can be taken into account only with many reservations.)

Chapter 13, Ziff's 'On understanding "Understanding utterances"' (not previously published), definitely deserves the booby prize as the worst article in the volume. Though the problem he attacks is, of course, of utmost importance, viz. an explication of the notion of understanding in general, and of understanding utterances in particular, his treatment is woefully inadequate and almost irresponsibly cavalier. The epigrammatic style of this article creates a certain atmosphere perhaps; but it is not conducive, I would claim, to presenting tight arguments nor to the understanding of the sloppy arguments presented. To illustrate:

(a) Ziff writes: 'Someone says, "hippopotami are graceful," and we understand what is said. In some cases we understand what is said without attending to the discourse the utterance has occurred in or without attending to the context of utterance. How do we do it?' (391) Since Ziff is talking about 'discourse' and 'context', he seems to use here 'utterance' (also) in the sense in which I propose to have this term always used in a technical discussion (which is, to repeat, not the sense in which it is used by Chomsky in the preceding chapter), though Ziff also talks about structure of utterances. But then, in at least one decisive sense of understanding, we can in NO case understand what is being said without attending to the discourse the utterance has occurred in as well as to its extra-linguistic context. 'What was said' could have been, with appropriate context and as part of an appropriate discourse, /Hippopotami are graceless./, /Flamingoes are graceful./, /After all, there is a certain amount of hidden grace even in the superficially utterly graceless movements of hippopotami./, perhaps even /Hippopotami are graceful./ What was actually said, then, can be determined ONLY by attending to discourse and context. Two different questions arise here, but they are completely fused and confused by Ziff: (i) How do we determine, for any given utterance, which is the 'corresponding' string? (ii) How do we know the meaning of the corresponding string (or strings, if our determination should not result in a practically unequivocal decision)? Whereas the answer to the first question must of necessity be extremely complex, to the second question a simple and adequate, though not very revealing, answer can be given: namely, that we know this by knowing the language (to a sufficient degree), i.e. by having internalized its syntactic and semantic rules. The answer to question (i) presupposes, of course, an answer to question (ii).

(b) 'Apprehending the syntactic structure of a nondeviant utterance is a matter of grasping the simplest relation between the utterance and the set of nondeviant utterances' (393). Just like that! What on earth can be meant by 'the simplest relation between an utterance and the set of nondeviant utterances'? Since a nondeviant utterance is a member of the set of all nondeviant utterances, why is not membership itself the 'simplest' relation? Strangely enough, Ziff's own conclusion from this state of affairs is that the 'simplicity of the relation... is essentially a matter of the internal simplicity of the set of nondeviant utterances.' Why? What does 'essentially' mean here? And this travesty of argumentation is not meant to be a joke.

(c) For deviant utterances, Ziff states categorically that they have 'that structure that constitutes the terminus of the simplest route from the regular grammar to the utterance in question' (393). Though it is not inconceivable that simplicity considerations of some vague nature may play a certain role in one's determination of what someone else wants to say by means of a certain odd utterance, Ziff's treatment is utterly inadequate (as Katz has no difficulty in pointing out in his contribution to the topic — and his misgivings are far from exhausting all the weak points in Ziff's remarks).

Ziff exhibits considerable naïveté in his talk about 'attributing' the deviance of an utterance to certain parts of it (395). He says, e.g., that '... the deviance of "He expressed a green thought" cannot be attributed to *thought*. It can only be attributed to *green*' (395). What he means is, clearly, that if one had to transform this sentence of doubtful meaning into one with a clear meaning by changing ONE WORD ONLY, the only candidate for such a change would be *green*. But this is a far cry from the way that Ziff actually puts it. Ziff draws from his own misleading formulation the conclusion that the given sentence is, in a certain sense, unambiguous, but that the utterance [That is a green thought] is ambiguous because it can be turned into a meaningful utterance by replacing either [green] or [thought] by a more suitable word.

Let me pass over in silence Ziff's own, admittedly tentative, proposals. I will only quote the last candid remarks he makes, after having discussed at some length 'simplicity of routes' leading from a regular grammar to deviant utterances:

No doubt the simplicity of a route must depend on the strength of the rule, the character of the classes involved, and so forth. But I can say nothing helpful about these matters here. Finally, I so far have said nothing about the significance of syntactically nondeviant utterances. If we relate a deviant utterance to the regular grammar by invoking certain rules, how do the rules serve to determine the significance of the utterance? To answer this question we must first consider how the structure of a nondeviant utterance serves to determine the significance of the utterance. That is a long and difficult story (399).

Such papers as Ziff's only make the story longer and more difficult.

Chapter 14, Katz's 'Semi-sentences' (not previously published), is written in the pretentious and cavalier style which one has unfortunately learned to associate with its author. A real understanding of it is almost excluded by its nondistinction between 'sentence' and 'utterance' and by its utterly careless use of 'understanding', 'intelligibility', and related terms — while Chomsky, for instance (1965:2, et passim), shows considerable sensitivity in this respect. The main point of Katz's paper is that the correlation between grammaticality and intelligibility is anything but perfect. Therefore, as I have already argued, an understanding of how deviant utterances are understood (or misunderstood, or partially understood) will, of course, take into account the ill-formedness of the string that will 'normally' correspond to this utterance (if this string is ill-formed at all, and Katz deals only with such utterances); but this will be only one factor among many others and, in many circumstances, not even the most decisive one.

The neologism 'semi-sentence' is to be deplored. It was born in confusion and will procreate further confusion. Katz says: 'A theory of semi-sentences, a theory that characterizes the set of ungrammatical strings that the speaker's knowledge of linguistic structure enables him to understand and explains why the members of this set are comprehensible is, therefore, to be regarded as an integral part of the description of a language, not as a bonus it is nice but not necessary to have' (400). In spite of the uncertainty in the interpretation of the terms KNOWLEDGE, UNDERSTAND, and COMPREHENSIBLE, as I understand Katz's intentions, what he calls A THEORY OF SEMI-SENTENCES belongs to psycho-linguistics and not to linguistics, while his theory is supposed to be a partial theory of linguistics. There is no urgent need for and no particular point in such a theory.

According to Katz, 'A semi-sentence is ... partly grammatical' (401), by which he means, it turns out, that parts of such a sentence are fully grammatical while the other parts are completely nongrammatical. He does not notice that the phrase 'part of a not-well-formed string' has not been formally defined at all and that our intuitions here are certainly vague and probably misleading. In what sense, for instance, does the semi-sentence *Scientists truth the universe* contain grammatical parts? Is this the case because it contains the two-word phrase *the universe*? Would then *Scientists truth universe* be utterly nongrammatical? Is it because it starts with a noun (which could therefore be a potential subject)? But what is then the justification of the 'part' terminology? Whatever 'enables a speaker [a listener?] to understand [an utterance of?] this semi-sentence' (401), it is probably not done 'in terms of its grammatical parts' (whatever this phrase may now mean), and this ability (which I would hesitate to call 'knowledge', as Katz does) is certainly not 'identically the knowledge of grammar that helps him understand "Scientists study the universe" ...'. However, in the absence of any distinction between sentence and utterance, it is almost impossible even to criticize coherently. Katz, like Ziff, is ready to say that 'the speaker knows that the semi-sentence "Scientists truth the universe" is ungrammatical because the word *truth* cannot appear in the context "Scientists... the universe"' (402). I have said enough about the doubtfulness and misleadingness of this *because*.

By not paying sufficient attention to the notorious complexity of the notion of understanding, Katz arrives at the conclusion that a standard generative grammar can account for how a speaker is able to understand sentences but cannot account for how a speaker is able to understand semi-sentences. However, when the meaning of *sentence* and *understand* is kept constant, this is just false. A generative grammar (interpreted as containing semantics, in accordance with the most recent usage of the MIT school) does not as such account for 'how a speaker is able to understand sentences', in the sense of comprehending utterances — this is accounted for rather by a psycho-linguistic theory of performance — and therefore could not possibly account for how deviant utterances are comprehended. But, when all this talk about intelligibility and comprehension and knowledge is interpreted 'quasi-psychologistically' — in Carnap's terminology (1950a) — in the framework of competence, to use Chomsky's term, then an adequate generative grammar will suffice for semi-sentences, too, as Chomsky has realized (see above).

Katz himself advocates a ternary system of classifying strings into sentences, semi-sentences, and nonsense strings. He even formally establishes a requirement, R1, to this effect. In addition, he requires, in R2, that an adequate theory of semi-sentences should 'explicate the speakers' knowledge of the patterns of deviation from grammaticality that preserve intelligibility' (403). Enough has been said above to establish that R2 is unreasonable. R1 is, on the other hand, arbitrary and internally inadequate. As a matter of fact, according to Katz, I cannot determine the status of an isolated word. It is certainly not a semi-sentence, probably not a nonsense string, and very likely also not fully grammatical — since presumably only whole sentences are fully grammatical. The same holds, of course, with regard to such strings as *my grandfather*, etc.

The arbitrariness of R1 resides in the preference it gives, without any further discussion, to the ternary classification, and this in spite of the fact that Katz constantly talks (informally?) about 'extent of deviation from full grammaticality', which indicates that he has some quantitative concept in mind. It is ironical, almost funny, that he rejects 'a theory that ONLY [my emphasis!] ranks strings in terms of their degree of departure from full grammaticality' because it does not fulfill his requirements, since it 'at best gives only approximate estimates of the membership of the set of semi-sentences of a language' (403). Katz does not realize that a rank-ordering is much stronger than a partitioning, and that partitions can always be obtained (and in many different ways) from rank-orderings but not vice versa.

Let me pass over Katz's criticisms of Chomsky's and Ziff's proposals. They are basically sound but rather obvious. His own tentative proposal in terms of what he calls COMPREHENSION SET and TRANSFER RULES is equally unacceptable. The fact that it fulfills requirements R1 and R2 certainly does not count in its favour.

Before Katz starts expounding his solution, there are some surprising moves. First, it turns out that the string *The of is likes the man*, is after all, not a semi-sentence, in spite of the fact that it contains well-formed parts, such as *likes the man*. After finishing his exposition, it turns out that, nevertheless, certain nonsense strings can be understood, e.g., Ziff's *The a man a that a I a saw a is a here a*. In a footnote to his discussion, Katz shows sufficient awareness of the possibility that ungrammatical strings are on occasion intelligible. But he does not realize that this destroys his own theory almost completely. I see no point in even summarizing it here.

Part V, containing six chapters, deals with semantics. The first four chapters are reprints from publications by leading logicians; the last two are contributions by the editors themselves. In their introduction, the editors state correctly that semantics of natural languages is today a programme rather than a field of substance, and they again explain the non-inclusion of contributions by 'ordinary language' philosophers as the result of technical difficulties and the lack of interest in the systematic and theoretical aspects of natural languages shown by those authors.

Chapter 15 is a selection from a booklet by Carnap (1939). After the woolly thinking exhibited in Ziff's and Katz's contributions, Carnap's old paper comes as a real respite. It makes its points in an incredibly clear, simple, careful, and pedagogically masterful way. (In this particular selection, Carnap, amazingly enough, manages NOT to use even the most elementary logical symbolism.) The famous tripartition of SEMIOTIC, the general theory of language, into SYNTAX, SEMANTICS, and PRAGMATICS is most clearly presented and illustrated with the help of a fictitious 'jungle' language.

I shall not try to summarize. Let me only express the hope that linguists will make a serious attempt to master the terminology and conceptual framework proposed here and think deeply on how to apply them to the study of natural languages. Carnap is, of course, primarily interested in scientific theories and their formulations. Having realized that for this purpose the language of scientific theories has to be studied, he embarked on his more general investigations into language and constructed language systems. But his basic interest in the language of science constantly shows through and, admittedly, greatly reduces the immediate applicability of his insights to natural languages. This explains why he restricts himself to assertion-making uses of languages to the exclusion of the myriads of other uses, and why he identifies making assertions with using declarative sentences. Such an identification, carried out for actual natural languages, would of course be intolerably naïve and lead to ridiculous conclusions. Nevertheless, such identifications were made in the past and resulted in creating among linguists a good amount of distrust against 'logical linguistics'. Although this distrust is indeed historically justified, it would be folly — and was folly — to throw the baby out with the bath water and to disregard altogether logical linguistics, i.e. logical syntax, logical semantics, and (the beginnings of) logical pragmatics.

Chapter 16, Church's 'The need for abstract entities in semantic analysis' (1951), is logical semantics at its best. Together with the preceding chapter, it should serve as an excellent introduction into what logicians have contributed to semantics. (For a further elaboration of the conceptual framework worked out by logicians for the treatment of semantics, Carnap's recent 'My conception of semantics' [Schilpp 900–5] should be carefully read.) Church's framework is an elaboration, simplification, and proliferation of the views of the nineteenth-century German logician Gottlob Frege, presented in an extremely lucid and precise style. It is impossible to summarize this chapter.

Church himself does not take his own ontologizing mode of speech ('introduction of abstract entities' and the like) very seriously. He believes 'that there are more important criteria by which a theory should be judged' (442). I would go still farther and insist that the so-called 'ontology' of a theory is entirely irrelevant as a criterion of evaluation. The ontological version of Occam's Razor, 'Entities should not be proliferated beyond necessity', is preposterous, silly, and misleading. Scientists and philosophers do not create, or annihilate, (abstract) entities through talking or writing. What they really do, and therefore should try to do to the best of their ability and professional training, is to create, confirm, and refute theories and conceptual frameworks.

Finally, Church's remarks on the relationship between formalized and natural languages — for him there is no difference in principle between the two — should be carefully studied. They are quite naïve, no doubt, but a linguist could do worse than try to make it perfectly clear to himself exactly where Church goes wrong.

Quine is the author of the next two chapters, Chapter 17, 'Speaking of objects', and Chapter 18, 'Meaning and translation'.[6] Since, to repeat, Quine is the leading philosopher of language of our time, a careful

---

[6] Originally written around 1957, these chapters were later incorporated in a book (Quine 1960).

study of these chapters is mandatory for all students of the field. Let me only state, however, that in two points I tend to disagree with Quine. I can put them in slogan form, since they have already been mentioned in various other connections. Quine's approach is, for my taste, too operationalistic and behaviouristic, on the one hand, and too ontological, on the other hand. Slogans, of course, are not arguments.

Chapter 19, 'The structure of a semantic theory', was authored by the editors themselves (1963), and has been widely discussed in the three years that have passed since its original appearance. The conception proposed in it, tentative as it was to begin with, has already undergone far-reaching changes by the authors themselves. I shall therefore confine myself to some general remarks.

I am afraid that my comments will have to mention the pretentious style of the article, which makes its reading an emotionally somewhat strained affair, in particular since the substantive contributions of the authors stand in no proportion to their claims. One cannot but admire the courage with which the authors deal with a field that has already many times before, in the history of philosophy and linguistics, been shown to be a real mine-field. It is very likely that their shortcomings will further the field much more than their actual positive achievements, and one should therefore be grateful for their effort. If the interest of linguists in semantics has sky-rocketed in the last three years, if courses on semantics (in the modern sense of the term) are now being offered in many linguistics departments that did not have them before, then this development is due to a large extent to the impact of this article. To put it in a nutshell, linguists have come to realize that semantics CAN be treated in a systematic way, with a degree of rigour and testability that need perhaps be no smaller than that already achieved in such more mature fields as phonology and syntax.

In its details, however, the semantic theory outlined by Katz and Fodor is a deplorable regression in comparison with the achievements of recent logical semanticists as exhibited, for instance, in the work of Carnap (Schilpp 1963). These semanticists, of course, did not even try to present an outline of a semantic theory of some natural language, simply because they had neither the training nor the desire to do so. But the general conceptual framework employed by such an author as Carnap, for instance, is vastly superior to and in many respects much more sophisticated than that of Katz and Fodor. To construct semantic rules in the form of DICTIONARY-PLUS-PROJECTION-RULES exclusively is a rather specialized conception of the form of such rules (called elsewhere MEANING RULES or MEANING POSTULATES) and would therefore, if defensible, indicate great progress over the usual less committal conception of the logical semanticists. But it is obvious to anyone trained in logical semantics that the Katz-Fodor programme is woefully inadequate. Innumerably many meaning rules cannot be put into Katz and Fodor's Procrustean bed, unless the bed is stretched out of recognition. (This stretching has, as a matter of fact, already begun in Katz's recent book [1966], where the so-called dictionary entry envisaged for *not* comes to look very much like one of the semantical rules that logicians would use.) The distinction between dictionary and projection rules is of no particular theoretical importance. Whether certain meaning rules can be given certain special forms, e.g. be presented in the form of tables, is of some practical importance, when learning, memorizing, or mechanical manipulation is envisaged, but I cannot see the theoretical impact of this question.

That Katz and Fodor should have restricted themselves, without warning and justification, to dictionary entries in the form of features (or components) that can be submitted to Boolean operations, is almost incredible, even if viewed as a first attempt. They must have heard of relational logic and therefore should know that relations are not reducible, in general, to properties, to mention only one aspect, which in itself is sufficient to make their approach utterly inadequate. (In Katz's recent book, this inadequacy is recognized and partly mended.)

The role of paraphrase is vastly overplayed. After all, the relation 'A is a paraphrase of B' ('A is logically, or cognitively, equivalent to B') is just one of the many logical relations that have been studied by logical semanticists. A 'lexicon', i.e. a monolingual dictionary, is indeed supposed to provide some kind of 'synonyms' or 'paraphrases' for words, and this presumably in the sense of the Katz-Fodor self-restriction. But this feature of lexicons is exactly one of the reasons why they are so inadequate as formulations of semantic rules. For so-called theoretical terms, but not only for them, paraphrases are usually non-existent, so that their 'meaning' has to be given in some other ways.

I have some 150 marginal notes in my copy of the Katz-Fodor paper, but I do not think it useful to go into them here. Let us thank the authors for their efforts, and then start afresh, with full utilization of the insights of the logical semanticists.

In chapter 20, 'Analyticity and contradiction in natural language' (not previously published), Katz claims to have found a 'solution to the problem of distinguishing analytic and synthetic truths' raised by Quine, and this on the basis of the framework introduced in the preceding chapter. This claim is preposterous. Katz's 'solution' is by orders of magnitude inferior to that of Carnap, for instance, for reasons hinted at above. It is based on the assumption, for which no justification is even attempted (had it been attempted, its futility would have become immediately obvious), that the meaning rules of English can be given in the forms stated above. It is annoying to read that Katz sees nothing wrong in the fact that the notion of analyticity he arrives at is essentially only a (very poor) explication of Kant's notion, which is notorious for its narrowness: 'Thus, the conception of analyticity and contradiction in natural languages developed in this paper draws the analytic-synthetic distinction at essentially the point where Kant sought to draw it' (543). Rather than realizing that this clearly indicates an essential vast failure of his explication, Katz is quite happy to throw empiricists back into 'the frying pan of unanalysed, synthetic necessary truths'. Let me assure Katz and the philosophically perhaps not particularly knowledgeable reader that empiricists are quite able to avoid the dismal fate prescribed to them by Katz without having to stay in 'the fire of dogmatism'. As a matter of fact, Carnap has recently been able to indicate a solution to the analyticity problem even for languages containing theoretical terms (Schilpp, 963–6). Whatever grain of validity remains in it is equally applicable to the Katz-Fodor approach, if not more so.

I realize that my present remarks are quite dogmatic, but a full discussion must be postponed for some other occasion.

In Part VI, psychological implications of linguistic theories are discussed. In their introductory remarks, the editors state, among other things, that '... no theory of learning which is unable to explain how grammars with transformational components are learned can be an adequate account of human learning' (545). This statement is true, of course, only if every adequate grammar of natural language MUST be transformational, a thesis which is still far from having been universally established. As a matter of fact, due to the still quite noticeable instability in the exact meaning of TRANSFORMATIONAL COMPONENTS, the precise force of the thesis is not yet really sufficiently determined. But let me insist that the following claim is of at least equal force: 'No theory of language is adequate unless there exists a theory of learning in accordance with which this theory of language can be internalized by adult etc. speakers.'

Chapter 21, Chomsky's review (1959) of Skinner, marks in a sense the beginnings of a new era in linguistic methodology. It expresses in unmistakable terms a conscious breakaway from operationalistic methodology, 'the hope that [linguistic] studies might ultimately be embedded in a framework provided by behaviourist psychology' (547), a hope that seems to have inspired much of American linguistics and philosophy of language during the last three decades. That this breakaway was made public on the occasion of reviewing 'the first largescale attempt to incorporate the major aspects of linguistic behaviour within a behaviourist framework' might strike many as ironical. The particular interest of this review is that its devastating critique is not a simple application of the insights arrived at in recent general methodology of science which have shown the insufficiency in principle of behaviourist, operationalist, atheoretical approaches, but rather the result of a detailed and, to a degree, even sympathetic investigation into Skinner's claims.

Skinner has repeatedly and confidently claimed that the overwhelmingly important factors in the determination of human verbal behaviour were the stimulation immediately preceding the behaviour studied and the history of reinforcement prior to it, that the contribution of the speaker is trivial and elementary, so that precise prediction of such verbal behaviour involves only specification of the few external factors that had been isolated experimentally in reinforcement studies with lower organisms. Chomsky has little trouble in demonstrating the untenability of Skinner's claims and the lack of any serious substantiation for them. That Skinner himself should have thought otherwise, namely, that he had created a rigorous scientific theory with a very broad scope, is explained by the fact that he relied heavily on analogous extensions of meaning. Chomsky counter-claims 'that with a literal meaning (where the terms of the descriptive system have something like the technical meanings given in Skinner's definitions) the book covers almost no aspect of linguistic behaviour, and that with a metaphoric reading, it is no more scientific than the traditional approaches to this subject matter, and rarely as clear and careful' (552). This counter-claim has been established with the utmost care and persuasion, at least in the view of one reader. No summary of the detailed argument will be attempted here.

Chapter 22, Lenneberg's 'The capacity for language acquisition',[7] has an aim similar to that of the preceding one. The author is out to demonstrate the likelihood that linguistic behaviour is not totally a learned and cultural phenomenon but is partly based upon highly specialized, biological propensities as deeply grounded in the natural constitution of

---

[7] Originally published under a different title (1960).

humans as, say, their predisposition to use their hands. Lenneberg's paper is by far the most elaborate and carefully demonstrated exposition of the view that linguistic behaviour is to a considerable degree a function of innate ('programmed') propensities. Lenneberg is fully aware that his argument in favour of this view is only able to show the high plausibility of the innateness conception. But this he has done with great persuasiveness. He has little trouble in showing that speech acquisition is much more like the acquisition of bipedal locomotion than of writing.

Chapter 23, Halle and Stevens' 'Speech recognition: A model and a program for research' (not previously published), seems out of place in this collection.

In summary, let me repeat the major points of my review:

(1) The editors claim to have shown that the philosophies of language held by the linguistic naturalists and by the linguistic constructionists are untenable and should be replaced by a NEW philosophy of language based upon the conception of natural languages held by the MIT school. What they have actually shown is, rather, that the naturalist and constructionist philosophies have to be synthesized and supplemented by the best available theories of natural languages.

(2) In view of the extreme bias in the selection of articles for the *Readings*, the book is anything but representative of the field. For any responsible course in the Philosophy of Language, it must be supplemented by other material. On the other hand, a good number of articles in the *Readings* have no conceivable direct philosophical impact whatsoever, and will be understood and appreciated only by students with a considerable linguistic background.

(3) The articles by Carnap and Church do give a good introduction into the field of logical semantics, but not more than that. The reader will not be able to realize from them the enormous wealth of insight and sensitivity shown by these and other authors in more detailed studies. While there have recently been published a number of readings in Ordinary Language Philosophy (Caton 1963, Chappell 1964), the only reader in logical semantics dates from much earlier (Linsky 1952).

(4) The most unfortunate aspect is that the reader may get an utterly distorted picture of what the new philosophy of language can contribute to the discussion of philosophical problems. The contributions of Ziff and Katz in the *Readings*, which were intended to discuss the eminently important philosophical problems of an explication of the notions of 'understanding' and of 'truth (and falsity) in virtue of meaning', respectively, are dismal failures. It would be unfortunate if the reader were to

regard the new philosophy of language as such as responsible for the failures, but many readers will doubtless draw just this conclusion. (It is close to catastrophic that Katz's new book (1966) will further reinforce this impression.)

(5) On the other hand, the selected *Readings* should give sufficient support for the claim that the operationalist, behaviouristic, anti-mentalistic, and anti-theoretical conceptions of language that dominated American linguistics for some three decades are definitely inadequate, so that any philosophy of language based upon them is very likely to be false.

Let me finish with two minor technical remarks which are in order for a book that was meant to serve as a textbook, is already in use as such, and will doubtless continue to be used for some time to come. These should be taken into account in a second edition: (a) There are a large number of misprints in the *Readings* although only very few of them create any problem in understanding. (b) The material selected is repetitious to a higher degree than could be justified by the editorial policy of reprinting whole articles rather than selections.[8]

[8] Carnap's recent book, *Philosophical foundations of physics* (1966), was published after this review was finished and could not be taken into account. The reader is, however, strongly advised to study it carefully, since it is by far the most readable presentation of this eminent philosopher's views of philosophy of science, and is often of direct relevance to the problems discussed here.

REFERENCES

BAR-HILLEL, YEHOSHUA. 1950. On syntactic categories. Journal of Symbolic Logic 15.1–15. (Reprinted, Bar-Hillel 1964, ch. 1.)
——. 1954. Logical syntax and semantics. Lg. 30.230–7. (Reprinted, Bar-Hillel 1964, ch. 2.)
——. 1957. Three remarks on linguistic fundamentals. Word 13.223–35 [reprinted here as Ch. 28].
——. 1964. Language and information. Reading, Mass., Addison-Wesley.
CARNAP, RUDOLF. 1939. Foundations of logic and mathematics. Chicago, University of Chicago Press.
——. 1950a. Logical foundations of probability. Chicago, University of Chicago Press.
——. 1950b. Empiricism, semantics, and ontology. Revue Internationale de Philosophie 4.20–40. (Reprinted in his Meaning and necessity, 2nd ed., Chicago, University of Chicago Press, 1956.)
——. 1966. Philosophical foundations of physics. New York, Basic Books.
CATON, CHARLES E. (ed.) 1963. Philosophy and ordinary language. Urbana, University of Illinois Press.

CHAPPELL, V. C. (ed.) 1964. Ordinary language. Englewood Cliffs, N. J., Prentice-Hall.
CHOMSKY, NOAM. 1957. Syntactic structures. The Hague, Mouton.
——. 1959. Review of Verbal behavior, by B. F. Skinner. Lg. 35.26–58.
——. 1961a. Some methodological remarks on generative grammar. Word 17.219–39.
——. 1961b. On the notion 'rule of grammar'. Symposia in Applied Mathematics, Proceedings 12.6–24.
——. 1962. A transformational approach to syntax. Proceedings of the 3rd Texas Conference on Problems of Linguistic Analysis in English, ed. by A. A. Hill, pp. 124–58. Austin, University of Texas Press.
——. 1964. Current issues in linguistic theory. The Hague, Mouton.
——. 1965. Aspects of the theory of syntax. Cambridge, Mass., MIT Press.
CHURCH, ALONZO. 1951. The need for abstract entities in semantic analysis. Proceedings of the American Academy of Arts and Sciences 80.100–12.
HARRIS, ZELLIG S. 1952. Discourse analysis. Lg. 28.1–39.
——. 1954. Distributional structure. Word 10.146–62.
——. 1957. Co-occurrence and transformation in linguistic structure. Lg. 32.283–340.
KATZ, JERROLD J. 1966. The philosophy of language. New York, Harper and Row.
KATZ, JERROLD J., and JERRY A. FODOR. 1962. What's wrong with the philosophy of language? Inquiry 5.197–237.
——. 1963. The structure of a semantic theory. Lg. 39.170–210.
KEMENY, JOHN G. 1963. Analyticity versus fuzziness. Synthese 15.57–80.
LENNEBERG, ERIC. 1960. Language, evolution, and purposive behavior. Culture in history, ed. by Stanley Diamond, pp. 869–93. New York, Columbia University Press.
LINSKY, LEONARD (ed.) 1952. Semantics and the philosophy of language. Urbana, University of Illinois Press.
NAGEL, ERNEST. 1961. Structure of science. New York, Harcourt Brace & World.
POSTAL, PAUL. 1964. Constituent structure. Indiana University Research Center in Anthropology, Folklore and Linguistics, Publication 30 (IJAL 30:1, pt. III). Bloomington, Ind.
QUINE, WILLARD V. 1960. Word and object. Cambridge, Mass., MIT Press.
——. 1961. From a logical point of view. 2nd ed. Cambridge, Mass., Harvard University Press.
SCHAECHTER, JOSEF. 1935. Prolegomena zu einer kritischen Grammatik. Vienna, J. Springer.
SCHILPP, P. A. (ed.) 1963. The philosophy of Rudolf Carnap. La Salle, Ill., Open Court.
YNGVE, VICTOR H. 1960. A model and a hypothesis for language structure. Proceedings of the American Philosophical Society 104.444–66.

UNIVERSAL SEMANTICS AND PHILOSOPHY OF LANGUAGE
Quandaries and Prospects

1. *Universal Semantics and Logic: A Critique of Some Recent Theories of Semantics*

The two Linguistic Institute Forum Lectures I presented in 1965 at the University of Michigan began with a historical sketch of the mutual relationship between logic and linguistics, starting with Aristotle. Since these lectures have not been published, and since the overlap between audiences is negligible, it might help to repeat briefly some of the points I made there before proceeding to my present topics.

At Ann Arbor I tried to stress the fact that, owing to certain extremely interesting but also highly unfortunate historical developments, argumentation in natural languages became a no-man's-land between logic and linguistics. Most logicians and linguists were equally eager to put the responsibility for the treatment of this important field — as a matter of fact, I can envisage few fields that are more important — squarely on the shoulders of their colleagues in the other discipline, with disastrous results. Occasional attempts by philosophers to invade this no-man's-land and to claim it for philosophical (or universal) grammar failed miserably because of utterly inadequate preparations, and served only to create distrust bordering on hatred among linguists, for many of whom "logic" and its cognates in time became almost dirty words.

The resulting splendid mutual isolation was perhaps not too bad for the field of logic. Unhampered by any need to care in particular for natural languages, logic, in the form of mathematical logic, reached incredible heights; recently, and rather unexpectedly, it even achieved a certain amount of applicability, if not in the critical evaluation of natural language arguments, at least in sometimes extremely sophisticated investigations into programming languages. On the other hand, while in the early nineteenth century this isolation put new life and ambition into autonomous, comparative, historical, and descriptive linguistics, in the end it succeeded in choking off linguistics almost completely, leaving its central part, semantics, in an atheoretical, sometimes even anti-theoretical, bloodless, and anaemic state, with anecdotes the only means of presenting a lifelike front.

Even the recent attempts by Katz, Fodor, Weinreich, Lamb, Hockett, and others[1] — and I shall refer here only to work done by American linguists, not out of parochialism, but because I do not think that linguists elsewhere (with the exception of Lyons[2]) have been able to do noticeably better, although they have certainly performed invaluably in creating new interest in semantics among linguists — were at best only a first step toward the theorization of the field; at worst they were so crudely executed as to harm rather than further the cause. What they all missed (with the partial exception of Weinreich[3]) was that meaning relations between linguistic entities are essentially deducibility relations and, therefore, logical relations. They missed this fact partly because a large number of the rules stating meaning relations can indeed be easily and practically formulated in the form of entries in traditional monolingual dictionaries (or lexica). Each such entry, so at least is the received view, tells that certain linguistic entities, usually words or short phrases, have the same meaning (perhaps only in certain contexts), are synonymous with each other (perhaps only partly so). Many linguists are aware of the innumerable problems that arise in this connection, but few are aware of the strong relationship that holds between synonymy and (mutual) deducibility, which is the basis of the successful performance of lexica. Unfortunately, the obvious efficiency of lexica has blinded almost all the linguists who gave any thought to that issue into believing that all of semantics is exhausted by lexicology, though a number of them paid some attention to the fact that other rules were needed at least for the purpose of determining how the meaning of longer linguistic entities is to be composed out of the meanings of their component smaller entities supposedly taken care of by the lexicon; but that the semantics of, say, English can be exhaustively presented in the form of a lexicon plus some meaning composition rules (called by Katz and Fodor, though

[1] I do not aim for bibliographical exhaustiveness. The contributions I have in mind are J. A. Fodor and J. J. Katz., eds., *The Structure of Language: Readings in the Philosophy of Language* (Englewood Cliffs, N.J., 1964); J. J. Katz and P. Postal, *An Integrated Theory of Linguistic Descriptions* (Cambridge, Mass., 1964); J. J. Katz, *The Philosophy of Language* (New York and London, 1966); U. Weinreich, "Explorations in Semantic Theory," in T. A. Sebeok, ed., *Current Trends in Linguistics*, Vol. III, *Theoretical Foundations* (The Hague, 1966), pp. 395–477; S. M. Lamb, "The Sememic Approach to Structural Semantics," *American Anthropologist*, 66, no. 3 (June 1964), pt. 2, pp. 57–78; and C. F. Hockett, "Language, Mathematics and Linguistics: Explorations in Semantic Theory," *ibid.*, pp. 155–304.

[2] J. Lyons, *Structural Semantics: An Analysis of Part of the Vocabulary of Plato* (Oxford, 1963).

[3] *Op. cit.*

not very helpfully, "projection rules"[4]), has seldom been doubted, though there has been a lot of discussion about the most appropriate form the lexicon should take, as well as a good deal of criticism of extant dictionaries.[5]

I shall presently repeat and further develop my arguments for the utter inadequacy of this conception. For the moment, let me only recall that in Ann Arbor I went on to say that linguists would greatly profit from the insights of such philosophers and logicians as Reichenbach,[6] Carnap,[7] Quine,[8] Curry,[9] and Putnam[10] (to mention again only Americans), who have lately paid much attention to logical semantics, although a crude application of these insights to linguistic semantics would again mean courting disaster. I voiced my apprehension that the long overdue *rapprochement* between logic and linguistics is in danger of being delayed and even stifled at the outset by overstatements and exaggerated and unsubstantiated claims. If we can beware of these lurking dangers, one may hope that linguists can be persuaded to accept that logic is linguistics' best friend, and that by judicious collaboration with enlightened logicians and judicious applications of their insights, linguistics will be able to reach an adequate degree of theorization. I did not propose a merger of logic and linguistics. There is nothing wrong with a division of labour, so long as it does not lead to a division of hearts and mutual distrust.

(When I discuss these problems before an audience of logicians, I try to present the other side of the picture and insist that logic can be brought back to its original task only by constant contact with linguistics: that logic, as it stands today, is quite inadequate to deal satisfactorily with that task, and that its development and expansion in the proper direction depends upon its receiving clues from linguistic needs.)

With this recapitulation behind us — and I hope that my original

---

[4] See, e.g., Katz, *op. cit.*, p. 153.

[5] See, e.g., Weinreich, *op. cit.*

[6] H. Reichenbach, *Elements of Symbolic Logic* (New York, 1952).

[7] In a very large number of contributions; for the latest, see Carnap's "Intellectual Autobiography," in P. A. Schilpp, ed., *The Philosophy of Rudolf Carnap* (La Salle, Ill., 1964), vol. 11 of *The Library of Living Philosophers*, pp. 53–66; and "Replies and Systematic Expositions," *ibid.*, pp. 809–943.

[8] Again in a large number of contributions; see, in particular, W. V. Quine, *Word and Object* (Cambridge, Mass., 1960).

[9] H. B. Curry, "Some Logical Aspects of Grammatical Structure," in R. Jakobson, ed., *Structure of Language and Its Mathematical Aspects* (1961), *Proceedings of Symposia in Applied Mathematics* 12: 56–68 (1961).

[10] H. Putnam, "Some Issues in the Theory of Grammar," *ibid.*, pp. 25–42.

talks contained more substance, fewer generalities, and less propaganda for a better world where logicians and linguists might live happily together ever after than this summary may have indicated — let us now turn to our first task, namely a critique of what has come to be known as the Katz-Fodor (KF) theory of semantics. I claim that this theory, even in its improved presentation in Katz's recent book,[11] is utterly inadequate as a whole, in spite of a large number of valid insights.

The major shortcoming of the KF theory has already been mentioned and briefly discussed: the identification of semantics with lexicology (supplemented by "projection rules"). True enough, Katz and Fodor were fully aware of the shortcomings of traditional dictionaries, but they definitely gave the impression that the dictionaries, with their format revamped, could still be made to carry the full burden of semantics — an idea that is disastrously misguided. Let me illustrate in some detail.

On page 152 of his recent book, Katz states: "The hypothesis on which we will base our model of the semantic component is that the process by which a speaker interprets each of the infinitely many sentences is a compositional process in which the meaning of any syntactically compound constituent of a sentence is obtained as a function of the meanings of the parts of the constituent." From this hypothesis he deduces (p. 153) "that the semantic component will have two subcomponents: *a dictionary* that provides a representation of the meaning of each of the words in the language, and a system of *projection rules* that provide the combinatorial machinery for projecting the semantic representation for all supraword constituents in a sentence from the representations that are given in the dictionary for the meanings of the words in the sentence." The hypothesis sounds extremely attractive, almost tautological (and the reader is invited to test this feeling of mine on himself and see offhand whether he can find a flaw in it); but it is, in its generality, just plain false. Since it is the basic hypothesis of Katz's theory of semantics, the theory itself simply collapses.

Katz's hypothesis (which has, of course, been formulated many times before) is far too atomistic even to stand a chance of being true. Each dictionary entry, in his view, "pairs a word with a representation of its meaning in some normal form" (p. 154), and "the information in dictionary entries must be full analyses of word meanings." The semantic part of the normal form consists of a set of "semantic markers" (and a "selection restriction"). The "semantic markers represent the conceptual

---

[11] *Op. cit.*

elements into which a reading decomposes a sense" (p. 155). Simply that! The reader will in vain look for any discussion of these "conceptual elements" or their "interrelations." I do not think I remember any recent treatise on philosophy of language in which the most basic notions are treated in such a cavalier and unsophisticated, not to say irresponsible, fashion. And what are these conceptual elements? Here the reader will be in for the surprise of his life! Not only are "physical object", "living", "human", and "male" conceptual elements, which would be reasonable enough for a philosophy of language of antiquity or the Middle Ages, but so are "serving under the standard of another", "without a mate at breeding time", and "having the academic degree for the completion of the first four years of college" (with Katz being parochial enough not even to mention that this holds only for the United States and perhaps a few other countries, but not, for example, for Israel, where we do not have colleges and where the bachelor's degree is awarded upon completion of three years of study at a university, with certain exceptions, nor for many other countries which have no bachelor's degree at all).

But this is not all. Has Katz really never heard of theoretical terms whose meaning is theory-dependent and, even within the framework of a whole theory, only partly and incompletely determined? He uses the term "theoretical construct" (p. 155), but without showing any awareness of the implication of this usage. Though he discusses at length Carnap's contributions to the philosophy of language prior to 1950 — not without a large number of distortions — he quotes, of the 1963 volume *The Philosophy of Rudolf Carnap*[12] (which, true enough, actually appeared early in 1964), only from Carnap's "Intellectual Autobiography", taking nothing from his "Replies and Systematic Expositions", which contain highly relevant and important views on semantics and the philosophy of language, views that make many of Katz's contributions look rather childish by comparison.

Nowhere does Katz show any awareness of the importance of semantic fields, a conception that makes it abundantly clear that, for innumerable terms, no individual, but only a collective, meaning specification is possible. His neglect is the more amazing since Chomsky has shown full awareness of this importance, though he apparently has had no time to discuss the topic at greater length. In *Aspects*[13] (which Katz mentions in his bibliography), Chomsky says (p. 164): "We have just seen that this account [similar to that of Katz but without the ridiculous commit-

---

[12] See n. 7, above.
[13] N. Chomsky, *Aspects of the Theory of Syntax* (Cambridge, Mass., 1965).

ment to such conceptual elements as "without a mate at breeding time"] is over-simplified in the case of semantic features, further structure being necessary in the lexicon to account for field properties", though not even he ever mentions the special problems posed by theoretical terms.

When Katz comes to the dictionary entry for *Neg* (the negation symbol), he conveniently forgets all about "normal forms" and presents it (on p. 201) without a word of excuse or explanation, as a sequence of three rules in eighteen lines — and I shall not here go into the adequacy of these rules or into the question of whether, even if adequate, they needed to be presented with such extraordinary complexity. Incidentally, the sense in which these three rules are "entries" for *Neg* is hyper-Pickwickian, as the reader is invited to check for himself.

After these few illustrations of the way Katz handles his tasks, let me come back to my major criticism. I claim that nobody has fully mastered the semantics of English who does not know that from *John is older than Paul and Paul is older then Dick* (with the occurrences of *Paul* referring to the same person) one can deduce *John is older than Dick*. A complete semantics of English must contain a rule to this effect, either as a primitive, explicit one, or at least as a derivative, implicit one. Such a rule might, for example, have the form: From *X is older than Y* and *Y is older than Z*, deduce *X is older than Z*. We also need rules to the effect: From *X is older than Y*, deduce *Y is not older than X* and *X is not as old as Y* and *Y is younger than X*, and so on. None of these meaning rules can be derived from traditional dictionaries. Any stretching of the notion of dictionary (or lexicon, for that matter) in order to incorporate them would be at best merely pointless and, at worst, a misleading adherence to outmoded terminology, even more than in the mentioned *Neg* example.

Notice that logicians have a way of compressing this multiplicity of rules into very compact formulations. One such formulation would be: *Is older than* denotes an irreflexive, asymmetrical, and transitive relation. A more compact formulation is: *Is older than* denotes a strict partial order. Still more compact and comprehensive is: *Is older than* and *is as old as* together form a quasi-order. (From this formulation it follows, among other things, that these two phrases fulfil the law of strong trichotomy: For any *X* and any *Y*, either *X* is as old as *Y*, or *X* is older than *Y*, or *Y* is older than *X*.)

Notice also that these meaning rules can be separated into two parts: one that is specific for a given language such as English, and one that is universal, holding for all languages, or rather is language-independent.

That *is as old as* and *is older than* form a quasi-order is, of course, peculiar to the English language, is a rule of specific English semantics; but the fact that, if they do, then *is as old as* is symmetrical, *is older than* is transitive, and so on, has no longer anything to do with English specifically. This implication belongs with "universal semantics" or "logic," depending upon the department you belong to. The first rule would best be published in a volume called *The Semantics of English*, the others in a volume entitled *Semantica Universalis sive Logica*. That *ist so alt wie* and *ist älter als* form a quasi-order in German belongs with German semantics, but the properties of this quasi-order are, of course, the same as those of any other quasi-order and are discussed only once, in the very same book, *Semantica Universalis sive Logica*.

Lest I be misunderstood, let me stress immediately that I do not believe that there exists a rigid borderline between special and universal semantics. The general tendency would be, for reasons of simplicity, elegance, economy, and "explanatory adequacy", to draw the line so as to include in universal semantics as much as possible. Following this maxim, one might, for instance, ask oneself whether one could not slice off from the mentioned rule of English semantics ("*is as old as* and *is older than* form a quasi-order") another universal ingredient. Let us first assume that not only does *is older than* denote a strict partial ordering, but that every English comparative does likewise. (This assumption is neither trivially true nor obviously false; but a more detailed discussion would require too much space.) Similarly, let us assume that every English *as Adj as* phrase denotes an equivalence (with a similar proviso). Then it should be clear how the semantics of English could be given a simpler form. But if the above assumption is correct (and I think that it could be enforced and therefore perhaps should be), then it is not unlikely that a similar situation should be made to prevail in all languages. (I would tend to believe that, but don't really know whether all languages have constructions that deserve to be called comparatives, or adequative constructions corresponding to *as Adj as*; but what still could be enforced is that no construction in any language should be called a comparative unless it denotes a strict partial order, or an adequative unless it denotes an equivalence.) Such universal similarity would allow the transfer to universal semantics of another part of the semantics of each specific language. We would then have as a rule of universal semantics (in a self-explanatory *ad hoc* symbolism): Compar (Adj) and Adeq (Adj) form a quasi-order. The phonological rules of English would state: Compar (Adj) is realized, depending upon some appropriate subclassification of adjectives, as *more Adj than*, or *Adj-er than*, or in both forms. Similar rules would indicate *Adj-er als* for German, *plus Adj que* for French, and so on.

English semantics must tell us that from *X is a parent of Y* one can deduce *Y is a child of X*, but for this purpose it would be sufficient to have a rule to the effect that *is a child of* denotes the relation converse to the relation denoted by *is a parent of*, with universal semantics (= logic) taking care of the rest. After being told that *is a pupil of* is the converse of *is a teacher of*, I would not only be able to deduce from *John is a teacher of Susan* that *Susan is a pupil of John* with the help of universal semantics, but would also be able to deduce from *Mary is a parent of a teacher of Susan* the statement *Susan is a pupil of a child of Mary*, with the help of my friendly logician who will call my attention to the rule (of universal semantics)

$$\widetilde{R/S} = \widetilde{S}/\widetilde{R},$$

after my equally friendly English linguist will have pointed out that, in accordance with a rule of English special semantics, *is an X of a Y of* denotes (perhaps with some qualification as to the membership of the categories *X* and *Y*) the relative product of the relations denoted by *is an X of* and *is a Y of*, respectively.

Let me point out that one must be careful not to push too many linguistic relationships into universal semantics. Husserl,[14] who was greatly impressed by the philosophical grammars of the seventeenth and eighteenth centuries, and was one of the last philosophers to take this conception seriously, regarded "How is the passive expressed in . . . ?" as a good question to ask for any given language. I doubt that many modern linguists will be ready to accept this notion. They would rather regard Husserl's view as one more attempt by a philosopher to impose his a priori schemes on linguistics, and resent his doing so just as much as their forefathers resented earlier such attempts. Indeed I see little justification for wanting to enforce the universal existence of passive constructions; but I think that what Husserl should have insisted upon was that the question "How does one express in . . . the converse relation of a given relation?" is a good one to ask. With this I would fully agree and am sure that attempts to answer this question will lead to progress. For some languages the answer will indeed somehow use the term "pas-

---

[14] E. Husserl, *Logische Untersuchungen*, Vol. II (Halle, 1900). Cf. my paper, "Husserl's Conception of a Purely Logical Grammar," *Philosophy and Phenomenological Research* 17: 362–363 (1957) [reprinted here as Ch. 6].

sive", but even for languages containing a passive this will by no means be the only way of expressing converse relations.

At this point it might be useful to propose not to treat the terms "general semantics" and "universal semantics" as synonyms, but rather to make use of the opportunity and, by fiat, give those terms, qua technical terms, different meanings. Whereas, I propose, *general* should be used to denote "accidental allness", *universal* should be reserved for "necessary allness". Whereas generality should therefore allow of degrees and enable us to say that certain linguistic phenomena are more or less general, or that such and such a feature occurs generally in all the Indo-European languages (but perhaps not in Semitic languages), universality would be absolute. A given linguistic feature would be termed universal, rather than just general, not simply because the state of affairs was such and not otherwise, but rather because we would not want to call something a language unless it contained that feature, in other words, if the occurrence of that feature was necessitated by the very meaning of the term "language". I realize that if my proposal is adopted, most of the "linguistic universals", including most of the "semantic universals", will have to be termed otherwise, though there are some obvious problems with "linguistic generals".

The semantics of a given language would be presented ideally not in one volume but in a number of them. One volume would contain universal semantics, another the special (idiosyncratic) semantics of the given language, while an indeterminate number of other volumes would contain the (more or less) general semantics of various classes of languages of which the given language is a member, with the optimum organization to be determined by a variety of pragmatic factors which I shall not go into here. The first volume, incidentally, would be written, according to the accepted division of labour, by logicians and, at least in principle, once and for all. Its contents, I submit, would not be subject to linguistic change.

With Katz's outline of a theory of semantics being such a complete failure, where do we stand? Are we back to chaos? Can anything sensible be said at the moment about restrictions on the forms that meaning rules should take? I am afraid that I, for one, have very little positive to say at present that might be of help in this situation. Though we can and should, in general, take many clues from Carnap (as well as, of course, from Reichenbach, Quine, Curry, Putnam, and others), he has very little specific to say about the form of what he calls "meaning postulates". This lack of specifics is not surprising in view of his avowed personal disinterest in the semantics of natural languages, though he fully realizes the importance of this field and merely takes, in the required division of labour, the other side.[15]

We need, then, a fresh start. As a first step, let us forget as quickly as possible Katz's theory; second, let us take it easy with semantic universals; third, let us realize that so far the only sound ingredient in universal semantics is logic, and, in consequence, let us press hard upon the logicians to spend some of their time (and even, for some of them, all of their time) in developing logic so that it will be able to answer the needs of linguists and of everybody else for a theory of deducibility in natural languages that should be as complete as possible and would then turn out to be a full theory of valid argumentation in natural languages. After that, we might perhaps be in a position to attack with better prospects of success the problem of the possibility of putting meaning rules into some normal form.

2. *The Future of Philosophy of Language*

Though I shall indeed discuss the future of philosophy of language, I shall not try to forecast this future but rather expand upon what I think should be its development. Though I do belong to a nation of prophets, we also have an old proverb to the effect that, since the destruction of the Second Temple (A.D. 70), the gift of prophecy has been restricted to infants and fools. I, however, plan to do slightly more than pronounce my predilections: I intend to do my share to make them come true.

Let me start with a terminological remark. In addition to the terms "philosophy of language" and "linguistic philosophy", recently also the term "philosophy of linguistics" has been propagated by the ubiquitous Katz-Fodor team (though with an interesting change of mind between 1962 and 1966 on the part of at least one member of the team[16]). I guess that one reason for this innovation was the existence of the triplet "philosophy of nature" — "philosophy of science" — "scientific philosophy"; but I have some doubts whether this particular triple distinction is worth imitating. "Philosophy of nature" is no longer an endeavour that is taken seriously, if I am not mistaken, as a result of the excesses of German *Naturphilosophie* in the early nineteenth century, and survives only in the periphery of philosophical thinking. It would be a pity if

---

[15] *The Philosophy of Rudolf Carnap*, p. 94.
[16] Katz, *op. cit.*, p. 4 n. 2.

the nice term "philosophy of language" would be reserved for wild speculations about the "nature" of language, its "origin", and so on. This seemed indeed to be the destination of the term during the 1930's and 1940's when it was scarcely used in English-speaking academic circles and was replaced by "logic of language" and the like. But now that this danger seems to be over, I at least would propose not to let the term "philosophy of language" go out of use but to apply it in approximately the same responsible way as the term "philosophy of science" is employed nowadays (perhaps adding to it the term "philosophy of communication", if this has not yet been done). On the other hand, for methodological investigations in linguistics and communication theory, the terms "methodology of linguistics" and "methodology of communication theory" (or "of communication science") seem to me apposite, so that I would propose discarding the term "philosophy of linguistics" (just as I am not in favour of such terms as "philosophy of physics", "philosophy of psychology", and the like). Not that the borderlines between these three disciplines, philosophy of language, methodology of linguistics, and linguistic philosophy are, or should be, rigidly determined: their interrelation is so strong that an extensive overlap is to be expected and encouraged, rather than frowned upon. It is, after all, one of the main contentions of KF that recent linguistic philosophy (as I propose to use the term), whether in the form of "(linguistic) constructionism" (as I shall hereafter call it, following P. F. Strawson and Carnap,[17] replacing KF's very unfortunate "positivism"), practised, say, by Carnap, or in the form of "(linguistic) naturalism" ("ordinary language philosophy"), practised by the late L. Wittgenstein, by the late J. L. Austin, and, at present, by G. Ryle, Strawson, J. O. Urmson, and a host of other Oxonians, suffers from neglect of the advent of theoretical linguistics and of its methodology, so that the philosophy of language on which they base their linguistic philosophy is too narrow, one-sided, and dated to serve its purpose well. Whether or not Katz and Fodor like my paraphrase of one of their main tenets, I like it and am ready to subscribe to it fully.

But exactly because I so heartily welcome this thesis and regard its acceptance as a necessary condition for a healthy development of philosophy of language, I am appalled by the extremely poor execution of this programme in the recent book by Katz. I fear there is a good chance

---

[17] Carnap, "Replies and Systematic Expositions," in *The Philosophy of Rudolf Carnap*, p. 933; P. F. Strawson's essay, *ibid.*, pp. 503–518.

that, because of the prestige acquired by its gifted and forceful author, both on his own and as the philosophical spokesman of the "MIT-niks" as a group, this book will be regarded by many readers as an authoritative exposition of "the new philosophy of language". They will turn away disenchanted, not from the book alone, but from the discipline as such, thereby possibly setting the clock back many years. Let me, therefore, make it perfectly clear that in my view all the many faults and shortcomings are the author's alone and carry no reflection on the discipline or even on his main thesis.

I shall first deal with an almost random selection of these shortcomings, and then turn to a list of problems which have been either entirely disregarded by Katz, or treated in an unsatisfactory manner, but which seem to me to deserve the closest study by future philosophers of language. No claim is made for the exhaustiveness of this list. After all, mine is a single lecture and not a book. As one more preliminary, let me mention that some of the points treated briefly in this presentation are discussed at greater length in my review of *The Structure of Language*.[18]

My first comment will be rather dogmatic, since I am addressing myself to linguists rather than philosophers, so that I cannot assume any particular familiarity with, for instance, the writings of Carnap. Let me then say that Katz's description of Carnap's views is anything but authoritative. The unquestioned adoption of Quine's well-known (to philosophers) criticism of Carnap's (older) treatment of analyticity (one of the two dogmas Quine so forcefully exposed and attacked in perhaps his most famous article, "Two Dogmas of Empiricism"[19]) is the author's privilege; but I must point out that, since the appearance of this article, many refutations of Quine's argument have appeared, not to mention Carnap's own reply — which for me was wholly convincing — in his "Replies and Systematic Expositions".[20] I already mentioned that Katz, perhaps for such respectable reasons as deadlines and other niceties that bedevil authors, gives no account of the highly significant articles dealing with philosophy of language in the Carnap volume, nor of the equally, if not more, significant "Replies" by Carnap himself. In particular, I can highly

---

[18] Review of Fodor and Katz, *op. cit.*, in *Language* 43: 526–550 [1967] [reprinted here as Ch. 14].

[19] W. V. Quine, "Two Dogmas of Empiricism, "*Philosophical Review*, vol. 60; reprinted as chapter ii in *From a Logical Point of View* (Cambridge, Mass., 1953); see also Quine's article, "Carnap and Logical Truth," in *The Philosophy of Rudolf Carnap*, pp. 385–406.

[20] *Ibid.*, pp. 917–919.

recommend a careful reading of Carnap's reply to Strawson (from which I took the terms "constructionist" and "naturalist").

I already commented on the strange and extremely old-fashioned atomistic conception of Katz of the role of elementary concepts in semantics. Since he does not make the slightest allusion to the vast philosophical literature on this topic, the linguist reader will probably end up with the impression that this conception is hallowed by philosophical consensus, while the philosopher reader might think that the existence of such concepts has been demonstrated by linguistic research. In fact, of course, this whole conception is utterly wanton and indefensible, as I showed in my first lecture.

Bordering on the ludicrous are some of the things that, according to Katz, can be done "simply". How, for instance, does one "obtain the *semantic categories of language*, i.e., the semantic categories for all natural languages . . ." (p. 234)? Nothing could be simpler. It is done in two easy stages. First, "to find the semantic categories of a particular natural language, we *simply* [my italics] check over the list of redundancy rules [i.e., rules stating that a semantic marker subsumes another semantic marker] in the linguistic description of L and pick out each semantic marker for which there is a rule saying that that marker subsumes other markers under it but for which none of the rules say that the marker is subsumed under other semantic markers" (p. 234). In the second stage, "the semantic categories of language are those concepts represented by the semantic markers belonging to the intersection of the sets of semantic categories for particular languages [Katz must surely mean "for *all* particular languages"], as obtained in the manner just described" (p. 235).

Should someone be worried by the fact that the semantic markers and the redundancy rules of a particular language have been defined only with regard to a given grammar, with no indication of how to get rid of this relativization (not to mention the fact that the whole idea that the semantics of any given natural language can be presented exclusively in terms of semantic markers, redundancy rules, and projection rules is ludicrous, as I tried to show at some length in the first lecture), Katz has a quick remedy: "Such justification for putative semantic categories is *simply* [my italics] a matter of empirically establishing that no simpler statement of the lexical readings for the dictionary of the language is provided by redundancy rules other than those which, by the given definition of semantic categories of L, yield the semantic categories in question" (p. 234).

Should now someone be uneducated or timorous enough to wonder whether it is so simple after all to establish that a certain set of rules is the simplest of *all* possible such sets, perhaps because this set seems to be so undetermined and is presumably infinite, which might create some obvious problems, his confidence is quickly restored by the remark that, after all: "This, it is to be noticed, is the same sort of empirical justification used in other branches of science when it is claimed that some theoretical account is best because it is based on the simplest set of laws describing the phenomena." Let me first state that this account of general scientific procedure is, to put it mildly, vastly oversimplified — I personally regard it as just plain false.[21] I do not deny that some scientists do on occasion use such formulations, but I do deny that there is any good reason to take such formulations seriously. Let me add, as an *argumentum ad verecundiam*, for whatever it is worth, that Chomsky has recently made it clear repeatedly that his appeal to simplicity as a criterion for evaluating competing grammars has nothing to do with the general notion of simplicity in the general methodology of science.[22] But I am already spending altogether too much time on this combination of browbeating and empty circular reasoning.

I shall pass over in silence Katz's treatment of analyticity (pp. 188–224), which he seems to regard as a kind of showcase for the superiority of his approach. If someone wants to see how this topic can be treated responsibly, let him read, for example, pages 963–966 of Carnap's "Replies" (though in order to understand these passages fully, he will have to read some preceding material) or Hintikka's recent series of four masterful articles,[23] one of which, incidentally, is called "Kant vindicated"; a comparison of this serious vindication of Kant's conception with Katz's attempts is a none too pleasant experience.

I come now to a brief list of real and underdiscussed problems that the future philosopher of language should investigate in depth.

A. *Utterance-Sentence-Statement*. I have many times[24] called attention to the necessity of carefully drawing certain distinctions that are

---

[21] See, e.g., my paper, "On Alleged Rules of Detachment in Inductive Logic," in I. Lakatos, ed., *Problems of Inductive Logic* (Amsterdam, 1968), pp. 120–128; see also the discussion on pp. 129–165.

[22] See, e.g., *op. cit.*, §7.

[23] J. Hintikka, "An Analysis of Analyticity," "Are Logical Truths Tautologies?" "Kant Vindicated," "Kant and the Tradition of Analysis," in P. Weingartner, ed., *Deskription, Analyzität und Existenz* (Salzburg and München, 1966), pp. 193–272.

[24] My latest attempt is "Do Natural Languages Contain Paradoxes?" *Studium Generale* 19: 391–397 (1966) [reprinted here as Ch. 24].

often slurred over even in places where they are required. I shall give it another try, since I would like to solicit help in this endeavour. I am quite sure that neither I nor anyone else has yet said the last word on this issue. None of these distinctions has been invented by me. On the contrary, each single one of them has been drawn on many occasions, and many authors are aware of them in some detached way; but when the chips are down, I have found time and time again that arguments suffer badly and sometimes decisively because of confusions between concepts whose distinctness is, in principle, well known.

Who does not know the distinction between an act — in particular, for our purposes, a linguistic act — and its product? Who does not know that the English word "utterance" (and innumerable other words, in English and, I am told, in very many other, and perhaps all, languages) denotes both a certain speech act and the (perhaps only a) product of the act? I believe that this distinction is part and parcel of high school textbooks. A statement can be quick, and it can be carefully formulated; but it is, of course, the statement-act, the particular act of stating, that is quick, and it is the statement-product that is carefully formulated, and any confusion (of categories) can be disastrous, and has been so on untold occasions.

Who does not know that one has to distinguish between a sentence, qua abstract linguistic entity, and the utterance of it, qua concrete physical product of some linguistic act, or even between a sentence and the set of all its actual and possible utterances? (One does not have to make this distinction by using these terms, of course; anything will do, so long as it is realized that one has to deal here with two entities that are different under any name.) But are you really sure that you know how to avoid the trap of regarding (as has been done quite often in the past) this distinction as being of the well-known type-token kind, or of the class-member kind? And are you really sure that you will know how to make this distinction when making it is crucial? I could give you hundreds of quotations, including recent ones from leading linguists, where it is obvious that the distinction was not made in places where it mattered.

Most, though not all, of the people I know understand rather quickly the existence of a difference between a declarative sentence, an abstract linguistic entity, and the statement, if any, that is made by an utterance of this sentence on some occasion. Statements are abstract, nonlinguistic entities that can be made by uttering declarative sentences but also in many other ways. The same statement can be made by uttering different tokens of the same sentence(-type), and also by uttering tokens of different sentences, in one language or in more, even by nodding one's head, and so on. It is statements that are the prime carriers of truth-values (i.e., that are true or false); and in natural languages, truth and falsity should be assigned to sentences or utterances only derivatively and with a number of precautions and provisos. I know quite well that this particular issue is still in flux and that what I said just now will not be generally accepted by all my philosophical colleagues, but it is precisely for this reason that I regard this topic as one of the major items that the future philosophy of language will have to discuss. Of course, many more refinements will need to be introduced and investigated. One will have to distinguish among, for example, the statement intended, the statement understood by some listener to have been made, the statement that is usually made by uttering a certain sentence under standard conditions (and, sometimes, these three statements may turn out to be different and thereby perhaps to be a major source of misunderstandings), and so on. More generally, for a given utterance, the questions of how one determines which sentence was intended to be uttered, which was understood to have been uttered, what kind of linguistic act was performed on that occasion (whether asserting, requesting, demanding, declaring, promising, swearing, or whatever), what was the product of this particular act, how was it intended, how was it understood, and so on, have only begun to be systematically investigated. It is amazing to see absolutely no awareness of this wealth of important issues in Katz's recent book; but I am afraid that even in Chomsky's *Aspects*, for instance, there are a number of points that rest upon nondistinction of distinguishables, and I return to one such point later.

B. *The Transposed Mode of Speech.* Even though linguists are aware of the problematics subsumed under such catch words as grammatical subject (logical subject) and psychological subject (but I agree with Chomsky that extant analyses of this issue are not particularly satisfactory and could not really have been so before some such distinction as that between surface and deep structure, under this or any other name, was made and clearly understood), they have unfortunately paid little if any attention to a phenomenon to which Carnap has, alas too briefly, drawn our attention under the somewhat forbidding name "transposed mode of speech".[25] Briefly and roughly, an utterance is in the transposed mode

[25] R. Carnap, *The Logical Syntax of Language* (London, 1937), p. 308; cf. my "Carnap's Logical Syntax of Language," in *The Philosophy of Rudolf Carnap*, pp. 519–543 [reprinted here as Ch. 11].

of speech if it seems to be about *A* but is really about some *B* different from *A*. Of course, certain subspecies of this mode of speech are well known and have been widely discussed by linguists, literary critics, and recently even by some philosphers of science under such headings as "metaphors" and the like. Yet what Carnap had in mind was something much more general than that which, however, still has enough interesting properties to deserve close study in all its generality.

To present just one, perhaps not too convincing, illustration, which has certainly nothing to do with metaphorical speech: One might want to say that, by uttering *LBJ is famous*, one is not really saying anything about LBJ at all, but rather something about people and their acts, in particular, perhaps, about their speech acts. Such a view may be defended by pointing out that a person may cease to be famous (or, for that matter, may become famous) without any change having occurred in him but rather, and exclusively, through some changes in his environment. All this raises innumerable problems, of course, some of which are well known to philosophers under such designations as "the problem of aboutness" or "the problem of external and internal relations". I would insist, though, that these problems are not really philosophical ones, and certainly not exclusively so, but should be the linguists' direct concern, and that no good understanding of language and speech is possible without an adequate understanding of their nature.

Let me also mention, in an aside, that some subspecies of the transposed mode of speech gained great fame among philosophers in the 1930's and 1940's and were discussed by them with great fervour and, in my opinion, deserve to be discussed some more. In particular, it was the material mode of speech which became, in the hands of Carnap and his followers, an extremely powerful technique for the dissolution of classical philosophical problems. To illustrate: *A rose is a thing* seems to say something about roses, namely, that they are things, but Carnap insists that what is really achieved by uttering (a token of) this sentence (in particular, when a philosopher is the utterer) is to claim of the word rose that it is a noun (a thing-word, *Dingwort* in German). And, believe it or not, this reinterpretation does make a decisive difference in matters philosophical, in particular in so-called ontology. Of course, there is nothing about all this in Katz's book.

C. *Indexical Expressions*. The problems created by the "indexicality" (or "context [-of-utterance] dependency") of most of our utterances — an indexical sentence is one that contains such words as *I, you, here, there, now, then, this*, and the like, or one that contains tensed verbs, but it is not limited in meaning to these two criteria — are numerous, all-pervading, and partly well known and understood. Indexical expressions are both ubiquitous means for effective communications (it is a nice philosophical standby to discuss whether communication is at all possible without them) and the source of many misunderstandings (i.e., of failures of communication). It is my personal view — which I shall, of course, not try to defend here — that this phenomenon is also a major cause of many philosophical pseudo-problems and pseudo-theses; and, in the confusion it creates when not fully understood, is partly responsible for the otherwise almost incomprehensible veneration in which the Cartesian *Cogito* is held.

Needless to say, nothing is said about indexical expressions in Katz's book. Standard dictionary entries for these expressions are altogether inadequate, and a KF-type lexicon is utterly unable to cope with them. To my knowledge, their treatment within such a framework has not even been seriously attempted, and all KF illustrations try to keep away from them, even though the reasons for this asceticism are never discussed. Semantic markers are clearly completely out of place in the characterization of their function, which is an almost exclusively pragmatic one. The occasionally quite confused, but sometimes also rather insightful, discussion by philosophers such as Peirce, Husserl, Russell, Reichenbach, Goodman, and many others is disregarded no less and no more than the treatment by such linguists as Stöhr and Karl Bühler — and I am just mentioning names at random, without any attempt to be even remotely exhaustive.[26] The terms used by linguists for this phenomenon are something like "deictic", but the phenomenon is simply under-discussed under any name.

D. *Degrees of Grammaticality*. The jungle of phenomena around degrees of grammaticality, semigrammaticality, semantic anomaly, oddness, bizarreness, category mistakes, type violations, and a host of other related concepts is now in a state of almost utter confusion, after a decade of intense and well-meant discussion which has exhibited linguists, logicians, and philosophers at their dogmatic and insensitive worst. Without the many distinctions I indicated above (under A) and a large number of additional ones, it is, in my opinion, almost hopeless to make inroads into that jungle. Because whatever positive statements I have

---

[26] More is said in my paper, "Indexical Expressions," *Mind* 63: 359–379 (1954) [reprinted here as Ch. 5]; see also my "Can Indexical Sentences Stand in Logical Relations?" *Philosophical Studies* 14: 87–90 (1963) [reprinted here as Ch. 10].

to make on this topic have already been made on another occasion,[27] let me turn to my fifth and last point.

E. *Incompletely Determined Meanings.* Carnap and other recent philosophers of science have brilliantly called our attention to the fact that scientists are constantly working, and successfully, with expressions whose meaning has only been incompletely determined. (The twin phenomenon of indirect meaning determination, decisive though it is for theoretical terms and the understanding of their methodological status, is so complex that it shall only be mentioned here.) This fact came as a surprise to many people whose conception of science included the notion that science abhors meaning indeterminacies, that in scientific writings each term, at least in principle, has a completely determined meaning. Wittgenstein, Waismann, and other philosophers of the British brand of analytic philosophy had said much about that many years before Carnap, with respect to expressions in ordinary, everyday speech, with Waismann coining the term "open texture" for this phenomenon. (Here, as often before, any identifications of intentions should be taken with a large grain of salt. Nobody will have any difficulties in finding any number of differences, even important differences, between Carnap's conception of partly interpreted theoretical terms and Waismann's conception of ordinary terms with open texture. I would still insist that, on a certain relevant level, they were discussing phenomena belonging to the same class.)

Unfortunately, the phenomenon of partial meaning is not reducible to full meaning in certain contexts and lack of meaning in all remaining contexts. It is only a whole theory that gets a kind of wholesale interpretation, usually through an enormously complex and, in practice, a never explicitly presented network of rules of interpretation whose exact functioning has never been satisfactorily analysed and understood. In general, there exists no retail basis for this global meaningfulness, so that the partial meaning of the particular theoretical terms cannot be characterized in terms of observational expressions in any more specific form. For a lucid and reasonably nontechnical presentation of the issue, let me refer to Carnap's recent, eminently readable volume, *Philosophical Foundations of Physics.*[28]

---

[27] In my review mentioned in note 18.
[28] R. Carnap, *Philosophical Foundations of Physics* (New York, 1966).

Postscript

Since my two lectures are being published two years after their delivery in June 1966, a certain amount of updating is mandatory. During the last sixteen months, a number of publications have appeared which change somewhat the picture described in the text. In particular, the new journal *Foundations of Language* contains a considerable number of highly relevant contributions. The most important of these is J. J. Katz's "Recent Issues in Semantic Theory" (3:124–194 [1967]) which is considerably more sophisticated than his previous contributions. It is Katz's reply to Weinreich's critique mentioned in note 1. (Cf. also Weinreich's short rebuttal in the August 1967 issue of that journal.) I still think my critique remains valid in essence, even with regard to Katz's more recent, improved formulations, but the sharp words I used in the text no longer apply to them. There has been considerable and welcome improvement, and it may be hoped that, by taking into account the achievements of the logical semanticists, this sophistication will soon be adequate to support a more serious scholarly undertaking.

ARGUMENTATION IN NATURAL LANGUAGE

At the International Congress for Logic, Methodology and Philosophy of Science held in Amsterdam in 1968 (at which a number of you have participated), we had an interesting Colloquium on the role of formal languages. I had the honour of being the coordinator of that Colloquium and, in this capacity, prepared the theses to be discussed, and also took an active part in the discussion. (Incidentally, I understand that a somewhat abbreviated version of this discussion is going to appear in one of the forthcoming issues of *Foundations of Language*.[1])

The discussion was, as I said — and this was not only my opinion — interesting but not conclusive; not that I had anticipated it to wind up with a general resolution. This being so, and since I continue to regard this issue as one of utmost importance — I have trouble envisaging issues of conceivably greater or more universal importance — let me use the time at my disposal to try to impress you with the fact that the neglect of this issue is much more of a scandal of modern philosophy than the many other issues that have been honoured with this title.

To put it then in a nutshell: one should think that the evaluation of arguments presented in a natural language should have been one of the major worries, if not the major worry, of logic since its beginnings. However, as I have argued at greater detail on other occasions,[2] the actual development of formal logic took a different course. It seems that, consciously or subconsciously, the almost general attitude of all formal logicians was to regard such an evaluation process as a two-stage affair. In the first stage, the original language formulation had to be rephrased, without loss, in a normalized idiom, while, in the second stage, these normalized formulations would be put through the grindstone of the formal logic evaluator. Aristotle, for instance, had his famous normal forms for sentences, on certain sequences of which he set loose his syllogistic apparatus. It seems that he was convinced that most, if not all, utterances of indicative Greek sentences could be losslessly rephrased

---

[1] [It has been published, in the meantime, in *Foundations of Language* 5 (1969), 256–284.]

[2] E.g. in my Linguistic Institute Forum Lectures presented in 1965 at the University of Michigan, a short summary of which is contained in "Universal Semantics and Philosophy of Language: Quandaries and Prospects", *Substance and Structure of Language* (J. Puhvel, ed.), University of California Press, Berkeley–Los Angeles, 1969, pp. 1–21 [reprinted here as Ch. 15].

in these normal forms. Unfortunately, most thinkers after Aristotle, philosophers, logicians and linguists alike, did not pay much more attention to the problems raised thereby than Aristotle himself, and contented themselves to further refine the second stage.

By now, it should have become amply clear that without substantial progress in the first stage even the incredible progress made by mathematical logic in our time will not help us much in solving our total problem. Again, as I said on other occasions, it is of no particular interest to decide who is more responsible for this unfortunate development, the logicians or the linguists. The point is that only by realizing the seriousness of the problem and by joining forces, can one hope to make any substantial progress. A lot of prejudices, created by concentration of effort on the second stage, will have to be given up and a wholly new conceptual framework will have to be created for the treatment of the logical aspects of what I propose to call, following Professor Richard Montague of UCLA, *pragmatic languages*, of which all natural languages form a subset.

One major prejudice, which the experience of Amsterdam, among others, has shown to be very difficult indeed to overcome, is the tendency to assign truth-values to indicative sentences in natural languages and to look at those cases where such a procedure seems to be somehow wrong, e.g., in the case of sentences containing indexical expressions, as being exceptional and in need of special treatment. The "justification" for this tendency is, of course, that formal logic is, by definition, able to deal only with entities that have a "form", i.e., with linguistic entities. This is perfectly valid for the output of the first-stage operations, the "normalized" sentences (as well as, of course, for sentences of constructed, interpreted calculi), but is perfectly misleading for the original sentences. Which true or false statement, if any, has been made on a given occasion (or referred to, since not on each occasion when a statement is referred to it is necessarily being "made" by the speaker, as Frege, among many others, was fully aware of, though with a different terminology), which statement, if any, has been understood by a given addressee to have been made on that occasion, which statement is "normally" made by similar utterances on such occasions (and these three kinds of statements need not at all be identical), these are all questions the answers to which may, on occasion, be very difficult to obtain and will hardly ever be determinable by just looking at the uttered sentence (if the statement was made by uttering a sentence and not, say, by a nod). Indexicality or context-dependency is only one of the many features of pragmatic languages that have to be taken into account. Another one, often neglected, is the background knowledge which the speaker presupposes to be available to the addressee, and this aspect, for instance, cannot be handled by the techniques being presently developed by Montague, Dana Scott and their associates in California, or by Mr. Asa Kasher in the Thesis he is writing for me in Israel.

What formal logic has to say about the validity of arguments will be no better than the adequacy of the normalization. Nothing short of the most sophisticated available approaches to the abstract theory of natural languages and the theory of communication with natural languages, sometimes dubbed theory of linguistic competence and theory of linguistic performance, respectively, combined with the most sophisticated approaches to philosophical semantics and pragmatics, will do for this purpose, and it is perhaps small wonder that until recently, not even serious attempts were made in this direction.

The difficulties for carrying out this programme are enormous indeed, and sometimes I find it very hard not to give up all hopes of ever solving them. In order to evaluate an argument presented in some natural language — and let us deal, for the sake of simplicity, with deductive arguments only, though this is indeed quite a simplification, the vast majority of such arguments being doubtless of the non-deductive variety— it is first necessary to determine which statements, if any, have been referred to on that occasion. I have still to see a really satisfactory discussion of the problems involved in this first step, not to mention a reasonably adequate solution of them. What has come to my attention so far in this respect is almost incredibly naive.

Next, it is necessary to formulate these statements in a "normal" (philosophical, universal) language in some canonical form. After 2,300 years of formal logic, we are still infinitely remote from having a clear idea of what such a language should look like — the classical concept of a *characterica universalis* having turned out to be so woefully inadequate — and, still more so (hoping that the set-theoreticians in the audience will forgive my mode of expression), from actually exhibiting such a language. It is now almost generally agreed upon that standard first-order languages won't do but I know of no agreement as to which kind of languages would do, and this would only be the easy part of the task.

The difficulties are of both a technical and, incomparably more importantly so, of a conceptual nature. What should be the logic of this language, to mention just one obviously decisive point? What will be its descriptive primitives? What will be its rules for introducing new terms? What will be its rules of interpreting, and to what degree will the circularity introduced by the necessity of using at some stage or other natural languages in their formulation spoil the whole endeavour?

Let me mention, for my final remark, that I have recently become more and more convinced that the rules in accordance with which utterances of sentences of natural languages will be normalized, will have to have a probabilistic character and thereby deviate still more from the dictionary and lexicon formats, so dear to the heart of modern semanticists of the MIT and related schools. On another occasion,[3] I have given a list of some problems which the modern philosophers of language and the logicians of natural language should busy themselves with. I would now like to add to that list the clarification of the problems connected with the probabilistic status of the semantic and pragmatic rules of natural languages.[4]

---

[3] Ibid.

[4] This suggestion has been taken up and insightfully developed in a thesis that Mr. Avishai Margalit is writing for me.

ARGUMENTATION IN PRAGMATIC LANGUAGES

Communication between humans proceeds along various channels, the most important of which is doubtless, at least for the time being, the uttering of sequences of sentences in natural languages ('utterance' includes here not only oral but also written and printed utterances). Most of the time communication achieves its purpose successfully. In general, we understand each other's statements, requests, orders, explanations, declarations and the thousands of other kinds of products of speech acts, often even with great exactitude and efficiency.

Should these facts create any surprise? I do not really think so. But certain doubts arise when reading some of the publications by leading authorities on this topic. Philosophers of language, or rather 'linguistic philosophers', whether subscribing to linguistic naturalism (better known under the names of 'ordinary language philosophy' or 'British analytic philosophy') or to linguistic constructionism[1] (better known as 'logical empiricism' or 'logical positivism'), have countless times complained about the chaotic character of the natural languages, which makes it so hard to frame rules about what is happening in them. The linguistic constructions drew from this 'fact' the conclusion that in order to treat truly serious issues of the kind arising in science or philosophy one has to switch to constructed language systems that will for ever remain under the control of their inventors and of those who will master their rules, fixed once and for all. The linguistic naturalists, on the other hand, tended to declare, in their despair, that there is no point in studying more than one linguistic unit at a time, or, at most, a restricted group of such related units, like words or short phrases; they themselves chose for such scrutiny units that for philosophical reasons aroused their interest (such as 'good', 'believes', 'real').

But here a question arises that seems to be a natural reaction to such defeatism: does there not stand at our disposal the science of logic — more specifically, of formal logic — whose professed aim is to put at our disposal *general* tools for dealing effectively with such a major

---

[1] For these two schools in the philosophy of language, see, e.g., my article 'Universal Semantics and Philosophy of Language: Quandaries and Prospects', published as Chap. I in: J. Puhvel (ed.), *Substance and Structure of Language*, Berkeley-Los Angeles 1969, pp. 1–21, and especially p. 12 [reprinted here as Ch. 15].

constituent of human communication as our ability to test the validity of arguments? The counterreaction to this reaction will surely be: true, but formal logic can be applied only after arguments have been reformulated in some *normalized* fashion. Responsible logicians have explicitly said this many times. While Aristotle himself, for instance, assumed that many, if not most, arguments can be forced into syllogistic form — unfortunately, for him and for us, without giving much thought to the clarification of the processes by which this is to be achieved in practice — and while most contemporary mathematical logicians and some philosophers of science tend to think that all mathematical, and perhaps even some scientific, discussions can without loss be put into a form that can be tested by the methods of present mathematical logic, yet with regard to the applicability of the methods of formal logic to argumentations in natural languages that deal with philosophical, ethical, political, legal and thousands of other topics, there exists in these circles a strange ambivalence between despair and shallow (I was almost tempted to say 'frivolous') underestimation of the difficulties of such applications.

In a lecture on 'The Betrayal by the Logicians',[2] I gave before this Academy six years ago, I dwelt at some length on this interesting development, but did not enter into a discussion of its causes, at any rate not in required depth. Last year, in Vienna[3] and Milan,[4] I touched once more on this subject, but again I could only scratch the surface. I shall try today to go below the surface, but, unfortunately, once again only limited time is available to me.

I believe I have succeeded, in the meantime, in isolating the decisive factor whose insufficient understanding is responsible, more than anything else, for the measure of irrationality in our approach to argumentation in natural languages and that disturbing wavering between despair and frivolity, namely, the essentially pragmatic character of these languages. This may be expressed, in other words, as the essential dependence of communication in such languages on *linguistic co-text*

---

[2] This lecture was published in *Iyyun*, XIV (1964), pp. 120–125 (in Hebrew).

[3] In a paper read before the Fourteenth International Congress of Philosophy, Vienna, 1968, on 'Argumentation in Natural Language', *Akten des XIV. Internationalen Kongresses für Philosophie*, III, Vienna 1969, pp. 3–6 [reprinted here as Ch. 16].

[4] In a lecture at a Symposium on Language in Society and the Technical World, Milan, 1968, organized by the Olivetti Company in commemoration of the hundredth anniversary of its founder; the Proceedings of this Symposium will be published soon.

(viz. the utterances, if any, that preceded the communicative act under scrutiny) and *extra-linguistic context* (the general background in which this communicative act was performed, the motives that brought it about, the cognitive and emotional background of the participants in it, etc.) — in short, to use for a moment the terminology of Communication Theory, on the fact that, in general, human communication proceeds in more than one channel at a time, that each channel has its own specific properties, and that their interaction creates possibilities whose number is greater than the sum of the possibilities of each channel taken separately, a fact which, of course, also raises questions as to the precise implications of this unusual situation.

Though for generations humanistic linguists and literary critics have dealt with this subject, scientific linguists and tough-minded philosophers of language were not particularly impressed by the impressionistic pronouncements of their tender-minded colleagues. Charles S. Peirce in the nineteenth century, Charles Morris, Rudolf Carnap and a few others in our century, stressed over and over again the priority of pragmatics (i.e. of that theory that studies the above-mentioned dependencies) in the investigation of natural languages. Indeed, it is difficult to imagine stronger and clearer statements than those made by Carnap[5] on this point.

Nevertheless, it seems that all these authors failed to do full justice to the fact that natural languages are essentially pragmatic languages, since they have not paid sufficient attention to the problematic character, in our special case, of a certain methodological step, which is, in general, in full accord with the best scientific traditions. They have all proceeded, with the greatest possible speed, to move away from the complex, complicated and multi-dimensional pragmatic aspects of human communication in order to move into the greener pastures of semantics, i.e. the theory that deals with the relations between language and the world, between signs and their *designata*, in deliberate disregard of the users of languages and their conditions of communication.

Let me repeat: abstraction is always a legitimate procedure, often very effective, sometimes even absolutely necessary in science. Modern science is inconceivable without it. To attempt abstraction is therefore always in order. But it is never *a priori* guaranteed that by abstracting one will be in a better position to solve a given set of problems, since for this purpose, sooner or later, the abstractive step will have to be followed

---

[5] E.g. in *Introduction to Semantics*, Cambridge (Mass.) 1946, p. 13.

by a concretive one — abstraction by *concretion*; otherwise, obviously, one will never come back to the original problems. Very often, but by no means always, will it turn out that solving problems by means of this double step of abstraction and concretion, which on first sight might appear to be a superfluous complication, is most effective, and sometimes, as said before, even absolutely necessary. But with regard to the field of problems involved in the theory of linguistic behaviour of humans, and especially of their argumentative behaviour, it is doubtful — to put it mildly — whether this two-step procedure has a great chance of success, and, in particular, whether the semantic theories of natural languages that have been proposed in the last decades, with various degrees of detailed formalization, will lead to a satisfactory division of labour.

It is not particularly difficult to invent some formal semantic theory and claim that this theory is *the* semantics (or model theory, to use a fashionable term) of some natural language, or at least *a* satisfactory and adequate semantics. But what exactly, or even not so exactly, has been claimed thereby? Has thereby the description of linguistic communication, in general, and of argumentative behaviour, in particular, been simplified? Have we not been asked to pay too high a price for the fact that a more or less convenient semantic theory has been put at our disposal? Shall we not run into great trouble as soon as we attempt to apply this convenient and smooth theory to a given communicative situation? Surely the frustrations that we shall doubtless experience as soon as we try to put actual communication processes into the straitjacket of a semantics that was conceived and born in the *a priori* will lead us quickly back to that vicious oscillating between despair and lighthearted optimism, already mentioned above, so that it will turn out that our only achievement will consist in just having climbed one more turn on that infinite magic screw!

Formal logic, formal semantics, formal model theory — all these can be applied to entities that have a form and, therefore, in these cases, though perhaps not necessarily in all, to abstract linguistic entities such as sentences. So long as we have not yet reached a state of such complete despair as absolutely to disregard formal logic when discussing natural languages — and I do not think that such an attitude is already justified today, since we have not yet really tried hard enough — we have to face the decisive choice: to apply formal logic either to the sentences of natural languages 'as is', or to sentences in one of the constructed language systems that 'correspond' (in a sense that has yet to be clarified) to the sentences that occurred in the original argument. Both methods are feasible, and neither need lead us into contradictions if only we employ them with adequate care, though both quickly lead us into trouble if we take even a single wrong step. I myself tend to believe that the second approach is more promising, more general, in a certain very important sense, more clarifying, and less in danger of being misapplied. But the last word has not yet been said on this all-important issue, and I do not intend, nor am I able, to say this word here and now. Nevertheless, we should at least attempt to catch a glimpse of how far we shall be able to advance along these two roads in the present state of affairs.

It is clear that the division of labour will be quite different according to whether we decide to use the 'direct' or the 'indirect' method. When a logician who decided to use the 'direct' method states that the English sentence

(1) 'Snow is white or red.'

(I would ask the reader to bear with my lack of imagination in choosing my illustrations; I hope that the tedium he may experience will be counterbalanced by the simplicity and clarity I need at the moment) is derivable from the sentence

(2) 'Snow is white.' —

what has he committed himself to with regard to linguistic behaviour? On this point alone, I could easily spend the rest of the time allotted to me. May I be allowed, then, to cut this discussion short (but I promise to expand it at some other occasion, or, at least, to take care that someone else expands it in due time) and to propose, skipping all Socratic preliminaries, the following rule of correspondence (bridging rule, rule of interpretation); which should be quite a good approximation to what is really needed:

> If sentence A is derivable from sentence B, then, whenever someone will be taken to have made, by assertively uttering B, the statement usually made by assertively uttering B in normal circumstances and thereby to have committed himself to the truth of B, he will also be taken, in general, to have committed himself to the truth of A, as an English sentence (i.e. to the truth of the statement usually made by the assertive utterance of A in normal circumstances).

Even this relatively cautious formulation harbours numerous problems, which I shall not even try to enumerate. At the moment, it is more important to indicate that there is need for many, many more of such rules of correspondence, amongst them also rules working in the opposite direction, i.e. from linguistic behaviour to logical derivability.

Let us now take another leap and turn directly to the most potent model theories known to me that employ the 'direct' method, viz. the theories that have been proposed during the last five years by Richard Montague and some of his colleagues and students.[6] According to their conception, logical relations hold not only between what W. V. Quine is accustomed to call 'eternal sentences',[7] i.e. sentences the meaning of whose utterances does not depend, in general, upon the context and co-text in which they were uttered — (1) and (2) migh well serve as illustrations for this point, too — but also between certain sentences that are context-dependent (indexical), such as — to continue with the type of illustrative sentences given above — between

(3) 'I am hungry.'

and

(4) 'I am hungry and thirsty.'

I shall not go into the details of the method by which Montague and associates succeeded in developing a logic, according to which Sentence (3) turns out to be derivable from Sentence (4). As a matter of fact, that (3) should be thus derivable from (4) is, of course, in accord with common-sense, so that a good amount of sophistication is needed to convince oneself that things are not as simple as that; that, e.g., it is certainly not the case that each utterance of (4) — or, rather, each statement made by an utterance of (4) — is derivable from each utterance of (3) — you have only to think of a case in which (4) was uttered by John and (3) by Paul — not to mention the necessity of carefully distinguishing between derivability of sentences and derivability of statements (perhaps even of utterances). One needs, therefore, a still greater amount of sophistication to convince oneself that such derivability can nevertheless be imposed, though only at the price of numerous relativizations and through the development of a logic that is much more complex than the one Aristotle, Kant, Frege or Russell, dreamt of. But all this is still not sufficient, and it is easy to realize that there still remain

---

[6] See, e.g., R. Montague, 'Pragmatics and Intensional Logic', *Dialectica*; idem, 'English as a Formal Language', *Proceedings of the Symposium on Language in Society and the Technical World, Milan, 1968*, to appear soon.

[7] See, e.g., his *Word and Object*, New York 1960, pp. 193 f.

many arguments that would be intuitively regarded as valid, but whose formal validity cannot be secured on the basis of the methods used by Montague and associates.

As to all those frequent cases in which it turns out that a certain argument is formally valid only after the sentences in which it had been originally formulated have undergone reformulation, or only after implicit premises have been supplemented (or, still more often, after both these operations have been performed) — there does not exist till this very day a theory of any weight that would throw light on them; and there are, of course, all those still more frequent cases in which it emerges, after we have carefully checked the structure and context of the argument, that we are not faced with a deductive argument at all, but that the arguer had in mind a weaker connection between the premises and the conclusion, a connection that may be characterized by the traditional term 'inductive', though giving it a name does not contribute much to its clarification.

For the time being, then, it seems that the theories of Montague and associates have only very limited practical applicability. The fields of application that come into consideration would be, first of all, the field of arguments as they occur in scientific books and articles — but a superficial check already shows that even there a direct application would definitely be the exception, and that, in general, even there one will need to apply extensively the advice 'Normalize before use!'

If I am right in my conclusion that even the most developed methods known today for a direct logical treatment of natural language sentences are of limited use only, though one can, at least, say this of them that they do not yield immediate contradictions when applied with care — something one cannot say of the many other theories I had the privilege of looking into on prior occasions — then there remains only the 'indirect' method. According to this approach, we always have to clarify to ourselves, as the first step in testing the validity of an argument presented in a natural language, what were the statements, if any, that were referred to on that occasion and intended to serve as premises in the argument. Since the English word 'statement' is so very ambiguous (though not more so than the corresponding words in other languages known to me), let me stress that I am using it here to denote a non-linguistic, abstract, theoretical entity, whose nature, like that of any other entity of its kind, can be clarified in principle only by presenting the whole theory to which it belongs; but I have no intention to present here such a complete theory. I shall, therefore, have to rely on only the partial understanding and good-will of the reader, and I admit that there is a good chance that I may fall down on both counts.

But one cannot apply formal logic to statements. Since they are non-linguistic entities, it is difficult, perhaps even impossible, to talk about the 'form' of statements. And if there is no form, there can be no formal logic. It is, therefore, necessary to take a further step, viz. to formulate these statements in some *normalized, sterilized, regimented, systematized* language to the sentences of which it is then possible to apply the rules of formal logic. This double step of transition from utterances of sentences in some natural language to statements, and from statements to sentences in some constructed language, will doubtless remind us of the double step mentioned at the beginning of my lecture — abstraction and concretion; and, indeed, there is a close connection between them, but I have no time to discuss it in detail. It is clear that one should not understand these two steps, the ascent to non-linguistic entities and the descent from them to new linguistic entities, as if they were being performed successively. It is close to impossible to deal seriously with statements referred to on a given occasion so long as one does not formulate them in some language.

I need hardly stress into what hornet's nest the indirect road leads us. My only consolation is that this nest has not been created by this approach, but rather exists independently, and that the indirect method only brings this existence into the open, while all other approaches, including some of those that have been proposed of late, only serve to conceal it. In the first place, three formidable questions immediately arise: (a) What is the exact nature of that language system in whose sentences all statements one can make in any natural language can be formulated, and to which formal logic can be applied? (b) What is the exact nature of that formal logic that will be applied to the sentences of that language system? (c) What is the theory that guides us in performing this fateful transition from utterances of sentences of natural languages to statements? Each of these three questions should be discussed in a whole series of lectures, and for each there exists an extensive literature. But I am not sure whether on any prior occasion all three of them have been discussed together, and I tend to believe that this is the crux of the matter. I can but touch lightly on each of these questions, but I shall do this from the vantage point of regarding them as part of a complex with strong internal bonds.

a. *What, then, is the nature of that magic language system in which all our problems will obtain their glorious solution?* The story of the attempts that were made to answer this question is long, tiresome and sad. The search after that unique language that preceded the construction of the Tower of Babel and became all confused on that occasion because of the sins of our forefathers, the search after the Adamic language, as it was sometimes called in the Middle Ages, underwent many metamorphoses and led from disaster to disaster. This striving for the universal, philosophical and logical language was responsible, among other things, also for the fact that from the beginning of the nineteenth century to this very day the adjectives 'universal', 'philosophical' and 'logical' are apt to vex many linguists, in particular when they are used to modify such nouns as 'language'. The linguists claim, and rightly so, that only after they had liberated themselves from the longing for the lost paradise and from the vain promises of the rationalist philosophers who insisted that they knew the road back, was their discipline able to develop and flourish and reach its present position.

But, in spite of all this, we are witnessing nowadays a revival of the term 'universal' amongst the linguists entirely of their own free will, no pressure being exerted by any external authority, philosopher or logician. The number of conferences dedicated to discussions of Linguistic Universals is constantly increasing; in particular in the school of Noam Chomsky, the greatest theoretical linguist of our time, the term 'universal' has reached new heights, with persistent stress being put on the continuity with the rationalist doctrines of the seventeenth and eighteenth centuries.[8]

True enough, one does no longer speak, even in these circles, of a 'universal language', and many who were happy to see the linguists return to the 'classical sources' do not pay sufficient attention to this fact. I do not know whether there is a single linguist, or a single scientist in any other field, who believes in all seriousness that there could be a language that would be 'ideal' for all the purposes of linguistic communication, whose syntax would preclude syntactic ambiguity, whose semantics would provide a unique interpretation for every well-formed sentence, that would allow for convenient communication under all conditions, and — what interests us most at this moment — that would permit a mechanical test procedure for the validity of the arguments advanced in it. But it seems to me that it has not yet been sufficiently clarified that these tasks cannot be attained with a single tool, and that our natural languages embody a compromise solution to all this, perhaps

---

[8] Cf., e.g., N. Chomsky, *Cartesian Linguistics*, New York 1966, and the literature quoted there.

even a close-to-optimum solution, but that just because of this feature of theirs they cannot be the ideal tool for accomplishing any of these tasks. As to our present needs, one should not really demand — and the absurdity of such a demand becomes obvious after a little thought — that arguments in natural languages should allow for a mechanical test of their validity. Since arguments are meant not only to *convince* supermen with unlimited capacities for thinking, concentrating and remembering, but also to *persuade* all-too-human beings who suffer from rigid restrictions on what they can store in their short-term memory, are full of irrational emotions and prejudices, and possess so many other 'pleasant' traits of this kind — it is but natural that man should use in his argumentations, as in his other communicative acts, additional channels to the one of pure reason. Without the use of these additional channels there can hardly be any doubt but that communication between humans, in a form similar to the one known to us, would be impossible. Let us not regret this, but, at most, only experience some kind of detached sorrow that the Lord did not create us as angels. Instead of feeling frustrated, we should try to understand better what price we have to pay for the fact that there stands at our disposal a communicative tool as wonderful as 'natural language'.

Conclusion: For the purposes of testing arguments in natural languages for validity, there just seems to be no way of going around their reformulation in some non-pragmatic language to which the rules of formal logic can be applied. Let us not hesitate to propose such languages while knowing perfectly well, first, that such languages are not fit to serve as tools for all-round communication, and, second, that one should not expect unanimity regarding the nature of these languages. If my partner will oppose a certain reformulation of mine in some regimented language — whether because he has some grudge against this language, or because he thinks that there is some fault or other in my particular reformulation — this does not necessarily mean the end of our conversation. I can still ask him to propose a regimented language of his own, I might still demand of him to give his own reformulation, one that he will regard as adequate, and to continue the discussion. Should he oppose regimented reformulation as a matter of principle — and there are those who are ready to give you a thousand reasons for such an opposition — then I am afraid that I, for one, would be non-plussed and could but see in a reaction like this a symptom of such a high degree of irrationality that it would make it fruitless for me to want to continue the discussion.

It might be that we could come to a certain preliminary agreement as to the character of certain regimented languages, one that endows them with the capability and privilege to serve as target-languages for the *depragmatization* of certain kinds of arguments; if so, well and good. But what the chances are that this will happen, I do not know. For certain circles, certain aims and a limited period, perhaps it is not quite a pipe dream.

b. *What is the nature of the logic that will rule in the regimented languages*? Let me stress again that putting the question in this form may create the impression that the same language could have different logics, as if logic were a dress that a language wears so that there could be 'evening logics' and 'cocktail logics', for instance. I do not want to deny the existence of such conceptions of language, or to deny that many linguists indeed believe that logic is a purely external matter, so that a language might wear any logic it wishes (or rather, its speakers wish), and that only for the sake of decency does it wear one at all.

On another occasion[9] I tried to make it clear that such a conception is very misleading and that it is responsible to a considerable degree for the confusion that is noticeable today among those linguists who dedicate some of their thinking to semantic matters. Here I shall only make the dogmatic claim that rules stating relations of deducibility and derivability, of implication and presupposition, are part and parcel of the semantics of any given language, of the set of meaning rules of that language, and therefore of that language as a whole.

Two languages that have the same vocabulary, the same syntactic rules and the same phonology, but differ in their meaning rules — and among them, say, in the meaning rules of their 'logical' words, i.e. in their logic — are *two* languages, be the degree of their similarity, according to appropriate criteria, as it may.

Therefore, the very formulation of the second question might mislead. There is no room for an independent selection of languages, on the one hand, and of logic on the other. What we should compare are languages-*cum*-logics, and then choose, for some purpose, one of them. Only for the purpose of division of labour is it possible, and sometimes even convenient, to perform an artificial separation between language and logic, and even then let us by no means forget that it is only a matter of division of labour.

I have already mentioned that Montague and associates find them-

---

[9] In the paper mentioned in n. 1, pp. 6 f.

selves obliged to call upon non-orthodox logics in order to widen, in accordance with the direct method, the applicability of logic to some further classes of sentences of natural languages. It is not inconceivable that for the indirect method this will not be necessary. But neither is it excluded that there will be need — or, at least, that it will be of help — to employ still more complex and exotic logics. As a matter of fact, the distinction between logic and meaning rules in general is getting blurred more and more, and there seems to be no longer any good reason not to regard logic, or logics, as systems of meaning rules for certain privileged sets of words, such as connectives and quantifiers (and/or as systems of meaning hyper-rules of a certain kind and a universal character).

If so, why should we not consider in this light also the system of meaning rules for the field of modal words ('possible', 'necessary', etc.), for the field of deontic words ('obliged', 'forbidden', 'allowed', etc.), for the field of epistemic words ('know', 'believe', etc.) and similar fields. It is difficult to distinguish between 'epistemic logic', for instance, and 'the system of meaning rules for the semantic field of epistemic expression'.

c. But the betrayal of the logicians to which I referred above found its expression not so much in the neglect of constructing ideal languages — the opposite complaint would be more appropriate — or in the neglect of the development of heterodox logics (during the last years, many such systems of logics have arisen, and it may be that here, too, one should begin worrying about the beginnings of an inflation, so that there might perhaps be a point in declaring a temporary moratorium) as in an astounding lack of linguistic sensitivity, a lack that still continues, in spite of a few rays of hope here and there, as to the rules of regimentation themselves. One feels as if philosophers and logicians have come to a silent agreement to the effect that the question of the transition from a natural language to a regimented one is either too trivial to deserve their attention or too difficult to be soluble in a rational way, but that in either case it should not be discussed; they seem also to have agreed that under no conditions should they approach a linguist in this matter, apparently because it cannot be assumed that he will be able to understand the very idea of employing a regimented language for logical purposes. At the same time the linguist, as I have intimated many times before on various occasions,[10] kept away from this question as from the pest, since it was redolent of 'logic'. In the meantime I came to realize that there was a further reason for this abstention, which is of no less

---

[10] E.g. in the articles mentioned in footnotes 1 and 2.

importance, namely, an insufficient understanding of the decisive role played by the pragmatic element in communication by natural languages.

That such an element existed was, of course, common knowledge, but again there was some kind of silent agreement that the prudent should keep away from it and leave its treatment to the neighbours on the left, who busy themselves with literature and style — the rhetoricians, the psycholinguists, sociolinguists, ethnolinguists and their kin — just as they had long ago left the treatment of logical issues to the neighbours on the right, those strange logicians.

In a famous article published by Katz and Fodor in 1963,[11] in which many see the beginnings of the New Semantics — I have already had an opportunity to express my doubts as to this evaluation[12] — the authors dedicate a page or two to a justification of their refraining from discussing pragmatic matters and of their opinion that one can deal effectively with the semantics of natural languages without having to take pragmatics into consideration — in our terms; they attempt to justify their conception that it is useful, indeed, to abstract from pragmatics.

I think that they have failed almost completely in this endeavour; elsewhere[13] I have dealt with this point at length. The issue seems to me to be of such importance that I shall now give it further formulation with the help of another pair of terms that have gained world-wide publicity of late, viz. 'competence' and 'performance', introduced as technical terms in our context by Chomsky.[14] In respect to these terms, the question is whether one can subject the theory of competence to effective and useful treatment if it is divorced from the theory of linguistic performance. We all know that a similar treatment proved to be immensely worthwhile when abstract geometry was treated in separation from physical geometry. I do not think that it could have been foreseen that what did work so well for geometry will not work for linguistics. But now that this has turned out to be the case — though there are still many who would not agree with my evaluation of the position — it is better to acquiesce in this situation as quickly as possible and start

---

[11] J. J. Katz & J. A. Fodor, 'The Structure of a Semantic Theory' *Language*, XXXIX (1963), pp. 170–210; reprinted in: J. A. Fodor & J. J. Katz (eds.), *The Structure of Language — Readings in the Philosophy of Language*, Englewood Cliffs (N. J.) 1964.

[12] In a review of the book mentioned in the previous note, which I published in *Language*, XLIII (1967), pp. 526–550 [reprinted here as Ch. 14].

[13] *Loc. cit.*

[14] See, e.g., N. Chomsky, *Aspects of the Theory of Syntax*, Cambridge (Mass.) 1965.

cooperating with each other more often, the logicians with the linguists, both with the psycholinguists (and let us not forget to consult from time to time the philosopher of language, who for a rather lengthy period has kept burning the fire of universal language and universal semantics — which upon investigation may well be seen to be identical with logic — and of a number of other universals, a fire in which his hands and those of his neighbours got burnt not once and which of late kindled the flame that inspired many linguists all over the world).

Let me conclude with two remarks.

1. The official title of our discussion is 'Argumentation in Pragmatic Languages'. But so far I have dealt with natural languages only. Are there pragmatic languages that are not natural? I will not deal here with artificial languages of the type of Esperanto and the problems they raise in our context. Likewise I shall not discuss language systems of the type of the language of *Principia Mathematica*. Such languages have, by definition, no pragmatics, and it is this feature, of course, that qualifies them for serving as target-languages in the process of depragmatization. But during recent years a new kind of languages has come to the fore: computer languages and programming languages of a bewildering variety, i.e. languages in which people converse with computers and computers with themselves and between themselves.

It used to be a kind of meta-axiom, which one did not in general even bother to mention explicitly, that such languages have to be devoid of any pragmatic elements and even of any semantic elements, in the sense that these adjectives apply to natural languages. And the reason for this restraint seems to be quite obvious: computers are just not equipped with those additional channels, at least for the time being, that we humans use for communication between ourselves, since computers are so far nothing but pure symbol manipulators.

But in time it emerged that the use of programming languages in vogue today, and be they 'high' as they may, restricts their communicative ability to a very high degree, so that for the moment the kind of problems whose solution we can require of computers is of very narrow scope, in spite of their amazing performance in solving those problems that lie within the range of their 'understanding'. One should, therefore, not be surprised by the fact that at this very minute hundreds of research groups all over the world should concern themselves with the problem of extending the scope of programming languages so as to bring it closer to that of natural languages. But it appears that in many cases these research workers want to attain two inconsistent ends simultaneously: on the one hand, to keep the programming languages free from any intrusion of pragmatic elements, and, on the other hand, to enable them to attain the full power of natural languages. I am afraid that very soon it will become clear to these research workers that they just cannot strive for both results simultaneously, at any rate not to their full extent. They will have to be satisfied with either working for one goal only or to diminish both aims. But the whole idea of a planned and gradual introduction of pragmatic elements into programming languages sounds so unorthodox that in general I speak about it only among friends. I cannot say that they are overjoyed with the idea. I understand their feelings, and only time will tell who is right.

2. My last observation is not a remark but a (true?) story. At the end of one of his lectures on ethics, the famous Roman Stoic philosopher, Epictetus, praised logic and recommended its study to the audience for its usefulness. During the question period, one of the listeners rose and asked: 'Well, Sir, could you *demonstrate* the usefulness of the study of logic?' Whereupon Epictetus just smiled and said: 'This is the point. How could you, without such study, test whether my demonstration would be valid or not?' I do not know what happened next. But if the questioner and the other listeners were convinced that it would be worthwhile paying Epictetus the tuition fees for the logic course that he had announced he would give the following term, then I am sure that they suffered a great disappointment. What Epictetus had shown them was only that there was need for a theory that would enable one to test the validity of arguments in natural languages. What he intimated on that occasion was that he himself was in a position to teach such a theory to whoever was ready to pay the fee. We know today that Stoic logic was by many orders of magnitude too weak to fulfil the announced aims of such a theory. As to myself, I even think I know the reasons, or, at least, some of the decisive reasons for this fact. Epictetus could not really have known them, and still less so his audience. Those listeners who attended his lectures in logic were in all likelihood disappointed, but I doubt whether they really understood where exactly lay the cause of their disappointment. It is possible that at the end of the course they started cursing Epictetus, all philosophers, and philosophy and logic as well, but I have no doubt that they could not possibly have managed to give a clear formulation of what it was that aroused their feeling of having been cheated. In this respect we are today in a much better position, but then we are also sufficiently polite not to express our dis-

satisfaction with the failures of the philosophers, the logicians and the linguists in such a coarse form. After all, we have at our disposal other, more refined forms, such as publishing one more paper or presenting one more lecture before the distinguished members of the Academy.

REVIEW OF THEODORE DRANGE'S
TYPE CROSSINGS *

The volume under review is an elaboration of a Ph.D. dissertation in philosophy submitted in 1963. Among the thirty-four authors quoted, all but two (Chomsky and Hill) are philosophers, though some are (at least part-time) philosophers of language or linguistic philosophers. Let me mention, as a curiosity — or is it, really? — that not only is the object-language of the booklet English, inasmuch as the author deals with type crossings in English, but that all the publications quoted by him are in English, as the original language or in translation; this may be the first time such a thing has happened in my reviewing career. Such predilection for English — if this is the right phrase — is not quite innocuous. It is likely that a number of authors, whose contributions to the subject are no less important than those of many of the authors quoted, were missed because they happened to write in German, for instance, and their works are not yet available in English; this is probably the case for Edmund Husserl and Stanislaw Leśniewski, who wrote in German (and, in the latter case, also in Polish).

Drange is worried, as were many other philosophers before him, by the 'meaninglessness' of such sentences as *The theory of relativity is blue, Quadruplicity drinks procrastination, Moral perfection is a prime number*. He himself presents (extralinguistic) cotexts and (linguistic) contexts, in which utterances of these sentences would be quite appropriate and uniquely understood by anyone who is sufficiently acquainted with the (cotext and) context; but he still points out, rightly, that in these particular contexts the uttered sentences are not interpreted literally, since literal interpretations of them just do not exist. This problem (which he calls a 'philosophical problem', for reasons which I do not understand, unless he means that he saw it discussed mostly in the philosophical literature) is then (p. 12): 'just WHY are these sentences unintelligible when taken literally?'

Literal interpretation is, of course, to be distinguished from 'normal' interpretation. The sentence *Necessity is the mother of invention* will be 'normally' understood non-literally, i.e. metaphorically. In its normal interpretation, people will not only understand it but even discuss the truth or falsity of the statement made by a particular utterance of it.

---

* Janua linguarum, series minor, 44. The Hague: Mouton, 1966, p. 218.

But in its literal interpretation, something which is applicable only to animate things, namely, being a mother, is said of necessity, a highly abstract notion. It, the sentence, is therefore called by Drange a 'type crossing', as are the sample sentences mentioned above for which the same analysis can be performed. Or, to be more precise, a sentence-in-a-literal-interpretation is a type crossing, under the mentioned conditions, while the very same sentence in a metaphorical interpretation will be meaningful, perhaps even true.

There would be little point in going over the tortuous arguments which Drange quotes from other authors favouring various solutions to the problem of type crossings (or category mistakes, or . . .) and the almost equally tortuous counterarguments he himself presents. And there is still less point in a detailed description of Drange's own 'new approach', based on the concept of unthinkability. The reason for my global rejection of such studies is that too many absolutely vital distinctions are not made, or at least not invoked in vital places. The distinction between a declarative sentence, an utterance of a declarative sentence, and the statement (if any) made by uttering a declarative sentence, should be so obvious that it is hard to understand why so many brilliant — not to mention less brilliant — philosophers frequently fail to make it. The distinction between a linguistic act and the product of such an act should be so clear that etc. — but in the present work the fact, e.g., that 'utterance' and 'statement' are systematically ambiguous in this respect is not taken into account. The fact that it is, for instance, extremely difficult, almost impossible, to work with a theory of natural languages in which truth is assigned to certain sentences (rather than to statements) — as I have argued on other occasions (1966, 1967, 1969) — is not even seen as a problem. Even more decisive is the fact that the importance of the distinction between deep and surface structure (which, in essence and under different names, was reasonably well known also to many philosopher-logicians such as Frege, Russell and Wittgenstein) is not realized. To apply logic to surface structures without greatest precautions cannot but lead to absurdities.

Let me then present a number of minor comments, not in order to persuade linguists how stupid philosophers can be — this would mean carrying owls to Athens — but to show how wrong and misleading seemingly trite and obvious statements and arguments can be.

(1) 'We can perfectly well understand what a person is saying when he utters the negation of a certain sentence without having to understand what he or someone else might be trying to say by uttering the sentence

itself. Nowhere is this more evident than in the area of type crossings. To say, "Socrates is a color" makes no sense at all; to say, "Socrates is not a color (but a person)" makes perfectly good sense. There could be point in saying something without there having to be point in denying it as well. Thus, a sentence could be meaningless even though its negation is not meaningless' (23). The connections between sentences, their negations, and the understanding of what one might be trying to say by uttering these sentences or their negations, is incomparably more complex than this. In almost all situations where it makes sense to say such a thing as 'Socrates is not a color', it makes sense to say 'Socrates is a color.' A typical situation for uttering 'Socrates is not a color' and being correctly understood would be, for instance, the following: Alexander reads in a story the sentence 'Aristotle wore a Socrates suit'; he turns to his wife Berenike and says, 'What do you know, Socrates is a color! Which color is it?' Berenike, pained but patiently, replies, 'Socrates is not a color but a person. The suit Aristotle wore on that occasion was cut along the fashion introduced by Socrates, my dear husband. It's really time you should know this after so many years of marriage to me.' But it is true that there are innumerable situations in which it makes no sense to utter a certain sentence, but good sense to utter its negation, innumerable situations in which the opposite is the case, and innumerable situations in which neither makes sense. Had I continued my manuscript at this point with either 'Two plus three equals five' or with 'Two plus three does not equal five', I can imagine the look on the editor's face.

(2) On p. 28, Drange uses in all seriousness the expression 'conventional definitions' for natural language expressions. One might have thought that in the sixties such usage would have become obsolete. The appropriate term, I take it, would now be something like 'meaning rule', which has all the desirable but few of the undesirable connotations of 'conventional definition'. Rather than saying, as Drange does, that 'All parents have children' is a definitional truth, it would be much less misleading to say that the statement usually made by uttering this sentence is true in virtue of the meaning rules of 'parent' and 'child' (plus, of course, a lot of other rules). Then it would never have occurred to Drange to worry (30) about how people 'CONVENTIONALLY DEFINE "theory" and "colored" '. But of course, Drange does not really mean what he seems to say. Otherwise he would not have said (33) that 'it still must be acknowledged that "abstract" and "concrete" are conventionally defined in opposition to each other'.

(3) On some occasions, Drange's linguistic naïveté borders on the ludicrous. On one such occasion (37, note), he states in all seriousness that 'it would be of great interest to learn whether there are natural languages in which type crossings cannot be formulated at all'.

(4) And what about such a claim (in 1963!) as that 'in language, things are designated by noun-morphemes' (38)?

(5) Drange sees 'no reason why a correct grammar of English should have to rely on a transformational analysis' (47). This is, of course, a pity. He surely must have seen a couple of reasons in Chomsky 1957 or in Fodor & Katz 1964, since he quotes these books.

(6) When Drange talks (51) about placing the expression 'it is not the case that' before a question or a command, he clearly means placing such an expression before an interrogative or imperative sentence. But then it might have helped some readers to say so.

(7) Drange is quite sure that 'there is an ordinary concept of grammar' (53) and that this concept 'does not warrant any grammatical distinctions among nouns except possibly in the case of count-nouns and mass-nouns'. As against Chomsky's suggestion (1964: 387) that (at least some) 'type crossings' are 'semi-grammatical', Drange has the decisive counter-argument that 'since type crossings have been shown to be grammatical..., they cannot be, as Chomsky suggests, semi-grammatical'. What could be more convincing?

(8) Drange (p. 59) credits Gilbert Ryle with the first mention of type rules in his article on categories (1937–38). The fact is, of course, that Carnap had already discussed the problem of Sphärenvermengung at length in 1928. The example used in my paper (1950:1) and mentioned by Drange (52, note), 'Aluminum weighs five pounds', was taken from Carnap and, of course, duly credited to him. But Carnap's book was written in German. The issue as such, as already mentioned, goes back much further.

(9) When Drange (77) criticizes Ryle for promoting a theory that could (almost) 'never be used to show of any sentence that it is NOT a type crossing', and which therefore 'provides no basis for classification', what he means is that this theory provides no decision procedure for such classification. But though it is nice to have such a procedure, the time has arrived when the lack of it in linguistic matters should no longer be regarded as a 'serious handicap'. Drange is not the only one who has not yet learned the lesson.

(10) 'A complex type crossing is a sentence whose translation into the language of symbolic logic ...' (136). There is of course no such

thing as 'the language of symbolic logic', and it is high time that people stop using this definite description. (Logicians, to my knowledge, never use it.) What Drange probably meant was 'an appropriate interpreted applied first-order predicate calculus' or something equivalent.

(11) 'Although the test for whether or not a number is divisible by 3 is to try to divide it by 3 ...' (153): this procedure is of course only A test, not THE test. I myself am accustomed to compute, for this purpose, the digit sum (in decimal notation) of that number, to repeat this procedure, if necessary, and see whether I wind up with 3, 6, or 9. The whole thing is a triviality, but the tendency among philosophers and linguists to use the definite article beyond responsibility is so common that any opportunity should be exploited to combat it.

(12) Drange has a good number of delusions as to his pet concept of unthinkability. He claims that 'with regard to the application of the term "unthinkable" to propositions, [philosophers'] opinion, at least as far as I know, has been quite uniform' (156). I am sorry to say that, in this respect, Drange knows very little. Defending this view against the obvious counter-example of the flatness of the earth by just claiming that 'no one ever held that to be self-evident in any relevant sense' hardly reduces the short-sightedness.

(13) Drange introduces (163) a certain technical sense of 'understanding' and calls it 'linguistic understanding', presumably intending to give an explication of one of the senses of this term, since it surely has been used before. His explication is: 'A person linguistically understands a sentence if and only if he knows the relevant meaning of each word in the sentence and also all the logical relations of the sentence with other sentences. In other words, all that is required for linguistic understanding of a sentence is knowledge of its vocabulary and syntax.' This 'compositional conception' of the meaning of a sentence as a combinatory function of the meanings of each single word of the sentence (plus the totality of all its linguistic relations to all other sentences) is either true but trivial, or non-trivial and false, and no less prejudiced by being very common. I have dealt with this elsewhere (1969: 4–5).

(14) Drange asks (170), 'What is the ordinary criterion for something, say x, liking drink A better than drink B?' His answer is, 'Roughly,... whenever x is to make a free choice between A and B..., x invariably chooses A rather than B.' This is, of course, wrong. The 'ordinary' criterion has something like 'most of the time' or 'normally', rather than 'invariably'.

(15) Drange adheres in all seriousness to the view that there exist logically simple properties (175), where 'logically' excludes 'relative to

some language'. Unthinkability is such a property, as redness is. This is the last refuge of dogmatism.

(16) One premise in a proof Drange uses (188) is: 'The package's being large is a case of being large.' This is one more case of the philosophers' myopia as to argumentation in natural languages, by carelessly transferring to these languages principles of Boolean algebra. 'The package's being large' means, of course, something like 'the package's being larger than the average package,' while 'being large' means 'being larger than the average thing'.

(17) The notion of 'intentional verbs', used by many philosophers, is regarded by Drange to be 'artificial and invented' (193). It is probably true that this notion was introduced by philosophers rather than by linguists; but it was linguists who have been able to show that intentional verbs have some definite interesting syntactic and semantic peculiarities which justify treating them as a separate class. Drange seems to know nothing of all this.

(18) 'That written declarative sentences cannot end in a question mark is a matter of convention' (206). Since I am not quite sure what Drange means here by 'written declarative sentence', I am not sure whether the statement he makes here is tautological or false. What about the sentence 'John is home?'? — 'But that theories cannot be blue is not a matter of convention.' No, indeed, it is rather a matter of non-convention. There exists no 'convention' (meaning rule) that would assign a meaning to such a sentence. But if it were decided to call a theory blue, if it is, say, well-confirmed, and red if disconfirmed, the world would not go to the dogs. Of course, there would be nothing wrong in saying that the concept of blueness would have undergone a change thereby, or that a different concept of blueness had been created, or many other things.

(19) Carnap's first name is consistently misspelled. It is 'Rudolf', not 'Rudolph'.

Let me finish with a quotation from Drange (209): 'I acknowledge that the positive parts of this book (in which I put forward my own theory of type crossings) are not as strong as the negative parts (in which I attack other theories).' I would only add that a much stronger attack on other theories could have been mounted on the basis of the recently achieved incomparably greater linguistic sophistication in these matters, and that Drange's own theory is, from this vantage point, on exactly the same level as the theories he criticizes.

REFERENCES

BAR-HILLEL, Y. 1950. On syntactical categories. Journal of Symbolic Logic 15.1–16 [reprinted in LI as Ch. 1].
——. 1966. Do natural languages contain paradoxes? Studium Generale 19.391–97 [reprinted here as Ch. 24].
——. 1967. Review of Fodor and Katz 1964. Lg. 43.526–50 [reprinted here as Ch. 14].
——. 1969. Universal semantics and philosophy of language: quandaries and prospects. Substance and structure of language, ed. by J. Puhvel, 1–21. Berkeley and Los Angeles: University of California Press [reprinted here as Ch. 15].
CARNAP, RUDOLF. 1928. Der logische Aufbau der Welt. Berlin-Schlachtensee: Weltkreis. (Second ed., Hamburg, Meiner, 1961.)
CHOMSKY, N. 1957. Syntactic structures. The Hague: Mouton.
——. 1964. Degrees of grammaticalness. In Fodor and Katz, pp. 384–9.
FODOR, J. A., and J. J. KATZ, (eds.) 1964. The structure of language: readings in the philosophy of language. Englewood Cliffs, N.J.: Prentice-Hall.

LINGUISTIC PHILOSOPHY

ANALYSIS OF "CORRECT" LANGUAGE

The purport of the following criticism of a recent article by Professor G. E. Moore[1] is to indicate the essential fruitlessness of the so-called "analytic method", as it is practised by a great many of contemporary British philosophers, especially of the Cambridge School.

I was able to find in this article, invented and (presumably) written by one of the most scrupulous and minute thinkers of our time, several mistakes, ranging from slight errors to quite serious and important blunders, but even the slightest of them of greater weight than that made by Bertrand Russell, to the discussion of which Moore dedicated almost two pages[2] of his contribution. This fact leads me to assume that there is something fundamentally wrong in Moore's approach. I shall return to this topic at the end of this article.

1. I doubt whether Moore's statement (p. 184) "The assertion, "The sentence 'The sun is larger than the moon' means neither more nor less than that the moon is smaller than the sun" is certainly true and yet anybody who asserted it would certainly not be *giving a definition* of the English sentence named", is certainly true and even if it is true at all. I can imagine an English class for foreigners where the teacher might use just this English sentence to introduce to his class the word 'larger' which had not been taught before. In this case, I believe it would be "good" usage to call this introduction 'giving a definition', because this sense of 'definition' as 'introduction of a new term or a new combination of terms' seems to me to be as "correct" as the sense of 'definition' as 'explanation (or explication or clarification or analysis) of a (perhaps only partially) known expression'. (I would even propose to restrict, by convention the usage of 'definition' to the former sense only and use, say, 'explication' for the second sense, at least in philosophical articles — a lot of confusion might thus be saved.)

2. It seems to me that Moore had not seen far enough when he stated (p. 197) "it is, so far as I can see, a sufficient condition for saying that, in making an assertion of the form "*s* means neither more nor less than

---

[1] Russell's "Theory of Descriptions", *The Philosophy of Bertrand Russell*, The Library of Living Philosophers, vol. v (1944), pp. 177–225.

[2] *Op. cit.* pp. 188–189. The point was that Russell used the word 'wrote' in his set of three propositions whose conjunction was to be equivalent to the "author of *Waverly* was Scotch", whereas the correct word should have been 'invented', as one might be an "author" of a literary composition without "writing" it.

p", one has *given a definition* (correct or incorrect) of s, that the sentence used to express p should (1) mention separately a greater total number of conceptions and objects than s does, and (2) should also not contain as a part of itself either s or any other sentence which has the same meaning as s".

According to this statement, in making every one of the following assertions, one would *be giving a definition* of the sentences which form the first part of these assertions:

(1) The sentence 'The sun is larger than the moon' means neither more nor less than that the sun is neither smaller than the moon nor as large as the moon.

(2) The sentence 'The sun is not smaller than the moon' means neither more nor less than that the sun is either larger than the moon or as large as the moon.

(3) The sentence 'A is a sibling of B' means neither more nor less than that A is either a brother or a sister of B.

(4) The sentence 'A is a brother of B' means neither more nor less than that A is a sibling of B but not a sister of B.

(5) The sentence 'A is a brother of B' means neither more nor less than that A is a male sibling of B.

I should say that, according to traditional logic, the three pairs of assertions, (1) and (2), (3) and (4), (3) and (5), yield circular definitions, and Moore would not recognise them as definitions at all.[3]

I found it hard, from the beginning, to believe that the greater total number of conceptions mentioned in the sentence used to express p should be a sufficient condition for regarding this sentence as a definition of s, disregarding the (relative) complexity of these conceptions. And the contradictions to which Moore's statement apparently leads but strengthened my doubts.

3. Moore's technique for using quotation-marks is somewhat strange and leads to confusions. The distinction between use and mention of signs should by now be commonplace, and the dangers of disregarding it have been sufficiently clarified and exemplified by Frege, Carnap, Tarski, Quine and others.

Here are some more examples of the confusions resulting from such disregard: After having decided (p. 195) to call the sentence "At least one person is a King of France, at most one person is a King of France,

---

[3] *Cf.* p. 197. I could, of course, have chosen much simpler examples such as defining 'large' by 'not small' and 'small' by 'not large', but I preferred to stick to Moore's examples.

and there is not anybody who is a King of France and is not wise" — "U", Moore says (p. 198): "Instead of writing U preceded by "that" and *not* putting inverted commas round it, I might have written, instead of "that", the words "the proposition", and followed these words by U *in inverted commas*". Whereas the expression 'writing U without inverted commas' is, though unfortunate, perhaps no more objectionable than 'writing 'burst' without 'r' ', the expression 'writing U in inverted commas' is really confusing, as Moore's intention apparently was simply 'writing U' (because, according to him, U has already inverted commas!). Connected with this mistake are two other confusing usages. U, "in inverted commas", can be *either a proposition or a sentence* (which are different concepts, as used by Moore, a sentence *expressing* a proposition), according to the last cited sentence, and to distinguish between these possibilities we must, apparently, always prefix the word 'proposition' or the word 'sentence', which is, to say the least, very cumbersome. And, according to Moore, U can be used sometimes "*merely* as a name of itself", whereas it is not so used when, "in inverted commas", it is preceded by the words, 'the proposition'. Now, a sign might be used *autonymously*,[4] though it is perhaps preferable to avoid, whenever possible, such usages. But, as a matter of fact, Moore did *never* intend to use U "*merely* as a sign of itself", because even when U, "in inverted commas", is preceded by the words 'the sentence' or 'the words', it is used as a name of the *proposition* U, which is, unfortunately, also written "in inverted commas". And I do not believe that it is "correct" English usage to say, in such a case, that U is used "*merely* as a sign of itself".[5]

4. Another objectionable formulation of Moore's is contained in his statements (p. 199) "We are never giving a definition, if we merely say of one expression that it means what is meant by another. For, if this is all we are saying, a hearer or reader can understand us perfectly without needing to understand *either* of the expressions in question" and (p. 200) "Since it is not necessary, in order to understand such a

---

[4] *Cf.* R. Carnap, *The Logical Syntax of Language*, 1937, p. 156f.

[5] For obvious reasons, I had to adapt my own usage of quotation marks in this article, partly, to Moore's standards. Therefore, most of the sentences of this paragraph and of the following one, would be either false or (syntactically) nonsensical, according to the standards of the above-mentioned logicians. But I hope that the careful and interested reader will be able to make the necessary transformations for himself. For the same reasons, my use of 'sentence' and 'proposition' will not be consistent, and in them lies the cause of my annoyingly frequent use of double inverted commas and italics.

statement,[6] that either sentence be understood, if follows that such a statement is *never* a definition". Now, it seems to me perfectly clear, that even if we *merely* say of one expression that it means what is meant by another, and do not, therefore, by this statement, give a definition to those who do not understand *either* of the expressions in question, we might nevertheless give by it a definition to those who understand *at least one* of the expressions in question. And though by such a statement[7] we may not give a definition to *every* hearer or reader, because it is not necessary, in order to understand the statement (in one sense of 'understand'), that either expression be understood (in another sense of this word), we might give by it a definition to those who should happen to understand at least one expression. In addition, I can hardly suppose that somebody who is given by Moore the definition "The expression 'is a triangle' *means* 'is a plane rectilinear figure, having three sides' " and understands this sentence *as a definition* (which entails that he understands the meaning of the expression 'is a plane . . .'), would not understand the statement "The expression 'is a triangle' *means what is meant* by the expression 'is a plane . . .' " *as a definition*. ('Being a definition' would accordingly be a *pragmatical* property of a statement, relative to the knowledge of the hearer or reader. But I think it is preferable to reserve this expression for the corresponding *syntactical* property together with 'being a possible definition', in analogy to a proposal made by Tarski[8] in a somewhat different context, and to use for the pragmatical property the expression 'being understood as a definition'.)

5. Moore, in trying to prove that the proposition W, namely "The sentence 'At least one person is a King of France' means that at least one person is a King of France" is *not* a tautology, as one might be tempted to think, gives two reasons. His first reason is (p. 202): "W is the same proposition as "*Les mots* 'At least one person is a King of France' *veulent dire qu'une personne au moins est roi de France*". But I think it is quite obvious that this proposition is not a tautology; and since it is the same proposition as W, it would follow that W is not either". Now, I think that Moore is right in denying the tautological character of the proposition W either in its purely English or in its mixed Anglo-French version, but I do not believe he is right in assuming

---

[6] Namely, the logical equivalence of two sentences written in a book in an unknown language.

[7] *Cf.* the preceding note.

[8] *Einige methodologische Untersuchungen über die Definierbarkeit der Begriffe*, Erkenntnis 5 (1935), p. 81. Tarski's term is 'eventuelle Definition'.

that, in the mixed version, the non-tautological character is more obvious than in the purely English one or, to put it otherwise, I think that Moore's psychological attitude is not justified by the "correct" usage of language. The trouble is that Moore consistently fails to indicate the language in reference to which he makes his statements, a procedure whose extreme importance has been sufficiently brought out by Carnap.[9] This failure is of no great importance in the greater part of Moore's article, as the reference-language is quite clearly understood to be the "correct" English everyday-language, but this conjecture is out of place, of course, in the case of the mixed version of W. I guess, therefore, that the reference-language in our case would be what we might call 'the "sum" of the "correct" English and French everyday-languages'. I think it is quite obvious that in reference to *this* language, the tautological or non-tautological character of the *mixed* version of W is *just as obvious* as the corresponding character of the *English* version in reference to the "correct" English everyday-language.

Moore's second reason is (p. 202):

I think it is also obvious on reflection, that the sentence Z ("At least one person is a King of France") *might*, quite easily, *not* have meant that at least one person is a King of France. To say that it does mean this, is to say something about the correct English use of the words which occur in Z and of the syntax of Z. But it might easily not have been the case that those words and that syntax ever were used in that way: that they are so used is merely an empirical fact, which might not have been the case.

Now, this argumentation seems to me so fantastically absurd and confused that I begin to doubt whether what appeared to me quite clearly understood up to this moment, namely, that Moore's normal reference-language is the "correct" or "established" English everyday-language, is after all the case. To put it in the form of a dilemma. Either (a) the reference-language is "correct" English. Now this contains the *semantic* rule: "If s is any sentence which expresses a proposition p, then s means p". In that case W is *semantically valid* though not *tautologous*; for the latter term designates, according to Carnap's and Quine's proposal and perhaps even according to "established" usage, only a certain sub-class of *syntactically* valid propositions. (This is *my* reason for denying the tautological character of W, but not Moore's!) It is true, indeed, that the proposition "W is semantically valid" can be validated only empirically. For the *sentence-event* W[10] (which is printed

---

[9] *Cf. e.g. Syntax*, p. 299.
[10] *Cf.* R. Carnap *Introduction to Semantics*, 1942, p. 6.

on pp. 201–202 of Moore's article) is a certain physical object, and so its accordance with the above-mentioned semantic rule can be established only empirically. Similarly, in reference to the same language, the proposition "A dog is a dog", which we will call 'D', is syntactically valid, and even tautological according to "established" usage. For "correct" English contains the syntactical rule "If *a* is any entity, then *a* is *a*". Yet the proposition "D is syntactically valid" can be validated only empirically since the sentence-event D (which is printed as part of this sentence) is a physical object and its accordance with the above-mentioned syntactical rule can be established only empirically. Or (*b*) the reference-language is just ordinary English everyday-language, in which case I can not see how *any* rule could be established and therefore how *any* sentence could be tautologous. I believe it is plain that applying any terms like 'tautologous', 'self-contradictory', etc., involves the use of certain explicitly stated or implicitly assumed rules.

6. Two pages further (p. 204), Moore argues that to make a certain assertion is "absurd for the same reason for which it is absurd to say such a thing as

"I believe he has gone out, but he has not" is absurd.[11] This, though absurd, is not self-contradictory; for it may quite well be true. But it is absurd, because, by saying "he has not gone out" we *imply* that we do *not* believe that he has gone out, though we neither assert this, nor does it follow from anything we do assert. That we *imply* it means only, I think, something which results from the fact that people, in general, do not make a positive assertion, unless they do not believe that the opposite is true: people, in general, would not assert positively "he has not gone out", if they believed that he had gone out. And it results from this general truth that a hearer who hears me say "he has not gone out", will, in general, assume that I don't believe that he has gone out, although I have neither asserted that I don't nor does it follow, from what I have asserted, that I don't. Since people will, in general, assume this, I may be said to *imply* it by saying "he has not gone out", since the effect of my saying so will, in general, be to make people believe it, and since I know quite well that my saying it will have this effect.

The sense of 'imply', which is discussed in the quoted passage (let us call this sense '*pragmatic*') "far from being mysterious"[12] — here I wholeheartedly share Moore's opinion — seems to me to be of the utmost

---

[11] The last two words of this sentence, namely 'is absurd', must of course be cancelled, to make sense.
[12] *Cf.* Moore's "A Reply to my Critics", *The Philosophy of G. E. Moore*, The Library of Living Philosophers, vol. iv (1942), p. 542.

importance in any linguistic behaviour-situation, so I intend to clarify it myself, as Moore's explanations seem to me to be unsatisfactory and confused, in the quoted passage as well as in the other place known to me.[13]

Let us assume that the following two *pragmatic* laws are highly confirmed:

(a) If, during a discussion, one of the participants starts to shout, he is excited.

(b) If, during a discussion, one of the participants starts to use abusive language, he is excited.

Now, let us imagine a marital dispute, during which Mary says to her husband "Henry, please, don't get excited", to which Henry responds by shouting "I am not excited" or by saying quietly "I am not excited, damn you". In both cases, Mary, we all, and even Henry himself (after having calmed down), will be fully justified in inferring that he *is* excited.

I am afraid that for exact evaluation of the situation here involved, no less rigorous terminology than, say, that of Carnap's *Syntax* will do. So let us start:

In the following three definitions only, 'implies'[14] will be used as expressing approximately that relation between sentences which, as a relation between either sentences or propositions, is called 'entails' by Moore, 'strictly implies' by Lewis, 'L-implies' by Carnap, 'logically implies' by other logicians.

(1) We shall say that s_1 implies s_2 relative to a sentence-class a_1 (shortly, s_1 a_1-*implies* s_2), if, and only if, $a_1 \cup \{s_1\}$ implies s_2.

(2) We shall say that s_1 *induces* s_2 if, and only if, there exists a highly confirmed a_1 such that s_1 a_1-implies s_2.

(3) We shall say that s_1 *Pr-induces* s_2 if, and only if, there exists a highly confirmed a_2 of pragmatic laws (where a law is called 'pragmatic', when it refers to users of language, roughly stated), such that s_1 a_2-implies s_2.[15]

Let s_3 be 'Henry is excited', s_4 be 'Henry shouts $\sim s_3$',[16] s_5 be

---

[13] *Op. cit.*, pp. 542–543.

[14] In accordance with Quine's usage in *Mathematical Logic*, 1940, §5.

[15] I hope to publish shortly a more detailed and exact study of the concepts here involved.

[16] I have replaced 'I am not excited' by 'Henry is not excited' to avoid the pitfalls connected with the use of "egocentric" (Russell) or "indicator" (Dr. Nelson Goodman) words, like 'I', 'this', etc. The '$\sim$' in '$\sim s_3$' is *autonymous*. To avoid this usage I could have made use, *e.g.*, of Quine's *corner*-notation.

'Henry says $\sim \mathfrak{s}_3 \frown$ 'damn you' ' (where '$\frown$' designates *concatenation*[17] of expressions), α_2 be the class of the two above-mentioned pragmatic laws. Then, according to (3), we get: $\mathfrak{s}_4$ Pr-induces $\mathfrak{s}_3$ and $\mathfrak{s}_5$ Pr-induces $\mathfrak{s}_3$.

Since I believe that 'Pr-induces', as here defined, explicates fairly well that sense of 'implies' which is intended by Moore in this connexion, I shall return to use 'implies' and 'entails' in Moore's sense. It is important to notice that 'implies', though referring to a *pragmatic* class of sentences, is still a *strictly logical* relation, just as is 'entails', upon which it is based.

The interesting situation that Henry's shouting $\sim \mathfrak{s}_3$ *implies* $\mathfrak{s}_3$ may be specified by judging Henry's behaviour as *absurd*, since his *shouting* a certain expression implies the *contradictory* of that sentence. Similarly, by saying $\sim \mathfrak{s}_3 \frown$ 'damn you', Henry *implies* $\mathfrak{s}_3$, and we may again specify this related situation by judging Henry's behaviour as *absurd*, since his saying a certain sentence implies the contradictory of (part of) it. (By the way, we should not have called his behaviour 'absurd', if by saying (not *asserting*) $\sim \mathfrak{s}_3$ with a certain twinkling of the eyes he had been supposed to imply that the proposition he intended to *assert* was the contradictory of that which he *said*.) These cases are remarkably different, since, in the first case, the implication is based wholly upon the *mode of saying* and not at all upon what is said, so that we should have implied that Henry is excited even if he had *shouted* "I am going now to the pub", whereas our implication in the second case is based upon *what* he said (though not upon that part which is contradicted by implication). In both cases, assuming that the imagined disputes have actually taken place, we should also infer that since $\mathfrak{s}_4$ and $\mathfrak{s}_5$ are true, therefore $\sim \mathfrak{s}_3$ is false.

We are now ready to return to the example given by Moore in the quoted passage. Let 'P_6' and $\mathfrak{s}_6$ be 'Bill has gone out', $\mathfrak{s}_7$ be 'Dick believes $\mathfrak{s}_6$, but $\sim P_6$',[18] $\mathfrak{s}_8$ be 'Dick says $\mathfrak{s}_7$', $\mathfrak{s}_9$ be 'If X is human and X says $\mathfrak{s}$, then X does not believe $\sim \mathfrak{s}$'. On Moore's assumption that $\mathfrak{s}_9$ is a (generally) highly confirmed pragmatic law, we get: $\mathfrak{s}_8$ implies 'Dick does not believe $\sim \mathfrak{s}_7$'. Let 'P_7' be the designatum of $\mathfrak{s}_7$; then, according to Moore, we may re-formulate the last sentence as: $\mathfrak{s}_8$ implies 'Dick does not believe that P_7'. Since 'P_7' is a conjunction of two propositions ('but' may, in this case, be safely replaced by 'and'),

---

[17] For this use of the *arch*, *cf*. Quine, *Mathematical Logic*, §53.

[18] Of course *not*: 'Dick believes $\mathfrak{s}_6$, but $\sim \mathfrak{s}_6$', which would be complete nonsense. I make use of Carnap's proposal (*Syntax*, p. 248) to interpret 'Dick believes P_6' as 'Dick believes $\mathfrak{s}_6$'. The argument is not altered thereby.

we get: s_8 implies 'Dick does not believe that Dick believes s_6 or Dick does not believe s_6', which may be simplified to: s_8 implies 'Dick does not believe s_6'. Our final result is therefore: 'Dick says 'Dick believes s_6, but $\sim P_6$'' implies 'Dick does not believe s_6'. We are therefore entitled to judge Dick's behaviour as *absurd*, since his asserting a certain sentence implies the *contradictory* of (part of) it. And we may infer that since s_8 is true, 'Dick does not believe s_6' is true, i.e. (according to the semantic truth definition) Dick does not believe s_6.

I admit that the preceding section was rather complicated, but I do not believe that Moore's confused and confusing argument could have been explicated more simply. As one example of the inherent confusion let us investigate the second sentence of the quoted passage: "This, though absurd, is not self-contradictory; for it may quite well be true". 'This' seems to be short for 'to say such a thing as "I believe he has gone out, but he has not",' since 'absurd' is used by Moore (correctly, I believe) to characterise a linguistic behaviour rather than a sentence; 'it', on the other hand, must refer to the sentence "I believe he has gone out, but he has not", since 'true' characterises sentences (or propositions) but not behaviour. Though this interpretation now seems to me evident, it took me rather a long time to assure myself of the necessity to assume that Moore has been grammatically careless. But what about 'self-contradictory'? This term should refer to the behaviour; otherwise the grammatical (or perhaps logical) blunder involved would exceed by far what may be excused by carelessness. But, on the other hand, Moore has never used this term, at least in this article, for that purpose, and several times (e.g. p. 203 and p. 205) he has used it for characterising a proposition. I am really at a loss, but I prefer to interpret Moore's intention in the second sense, though I believe that, generally, 'self-contradictory' may be used in the first sense too. I am led, therefore, to assume that what Moore intended to say was: "To say such a thing as "I believe he has gone out, but he has not" is absurd, though the proposition "I believe he has gone out, but he has not" is not self-contradictory, as it might quite well be true". This proposition is true — if by "it may quite well be true" is meant no more than that it is a *synthetic* (factual) proposition, and therefore not necessarily false, though, as things are, it is false. And it is not only true but even important. For it shows that a certain linguistic behaviour, viz. asserting a proposition, may be *absurd* not only when the asserted proposition is self-contradictory or absurd (in which case the epithet 'absurd' is transferred from the proposition to the act of asserting it), but also when it only *implies* its contradictory. ('An absurd proposition' is synonymous with 'a self-contradictory proposition', as is 'absurdum' in "reductio ad absurdum".)

After this digression, let us return to Moore's argument in the quoted passage, in its restated version. Is it sound? I am not sure, for two reasons: (*a*) I doubt whether $\mathfrak{S}_9$ is highly confirmed, though I should not doubt that $\mathfrak{S}_{10}$, namely, 'if X is human and X says $\mathfrak{S}$, then X believes $\mathfrak{S}$', is (generally) highly confirmed. $\mathfrak{S}_9$ does not follow from $\mathfrak{S}_{10}$, nor is $\mathfrak{S}_9$ even Pr-induced by $\mathfrak{S}_{10}$. 'A believes $\mathfrak{S}$' does not imply (in Quine's sense) 'A does not believe $\sim \mathfrak{S}$', and I do not even think that 'A believes $\mathfrak{S}$' Pr-induces 'A does not believe $\sim \mathfrak{S}$', since I am not sure that a certain positive psychological attitude always involves (empirically) a certain negative attitude. (*b*) I am not sure that we are entitled to simplify 'Dick does not believe that Dick believes $\mathfrak{S}_6$ or Dick does not believe $\mathfrak{S}_6$' into 'Dick does not believe $\mathfrak{S}_6$'.

I was myself astonished to see what complicated structures resulted from my restatement of Moore's argument but one never can tell what confused and inexact formulations may lead to when submitted to a certain tentative clarification. Anyhow, I do not think it is worthwhile to investigate further into the psychological soundness of the argument, since Moore's intention in using it was merely to show that we may sometimes, by asserting a certain proposition, *imply* its contradictory, and this fact has been sufficiently illustrated by my examples at the beginning of this paragraph.

As a conclusion of this criticism, I should like to summarise its positive results:

(1) There is an important *pragmatic* sense of 'implies', namely what we called 'Pr-induces', which is different from the other important senses of this term. This hitherto rather neglected sense should prove of decisive value in discussing, not only ethical problems,[19] but any problem involving linguistic behaviour, or even — after a certain extension of its applicability — sign behaviour generally. It is possible and even probable that, by asserting certain sentences, which are 'meaningless' according to some empiricist criterion of 'meaning' (e.g., sentences of a metaphysical or aesthetic nature), one may nevertheless *imply* sentences which are perfectly meaningful, according to the same criterion, and are perhaps even true and highly important.[20]

---

[19] *Cf.* Moore's *Reply*, pp. 540–543.

[20] To provide just one example of an application of this thesis, *cf.* the recent discussion between Mr. Morris Weitz and Mr. Raymond Hoekstra in *Philosophy*

(2) There is an important *pragmatic* sense of 'absurd', in which it refers to a certain linguistic behaviour, where asserting a proposition *implies* its contradictory.

7. I asked several language-teachers to give me their opinion about Moore's statement (p. 211) that to translate the French sentence "*Le soleil est plus grand que la lune*" into the English sentence "The moon is smaller than the sun" (to be called 'E') would be definitely incorrect. None of them assented, but most of them were ready to consent to my proposal that though such a translation would by no means be *definitely* incorrect (I assume that 'definitely', as used by Moore in this context, means 'in *every* sense of this word'), and on the contrary quite correct, according to the semantic rules of the "sum" of the "correct" English and French everyday-languages, it would be *inferior* to the *literal* translation into "The sun is larger than the moon" (to be called 'E_1'), since a literal translation is, *ceteris paribus*, preferable to a non-literal one. I, personally, should hesitate to call such a translation even 'pragmatically incorrect'.

8. I find it extremely difficult to imagine the reasons which led Moore to state (p. 211) (1) that "it would be definitely incorrect to say "The proposition '*Le soleil est plus grand que la lune*' both entails and is entailed by the proposition 'The sun is larger than the moon'", or to say that "we have here *two* propositions which are logically equivalent"; (2) at the same time to doubt (pp. 210–211) "whether it is incorrect to say that the proposition 'The sun is larger than the moon' is *one* proposition, and the proposition "the moon is smaller than the sun" is *another* proposition"; and finally, (3) to assert "And yet I do not think we can say that the sentence "The sun is larger than the moon" brings before the mind any ideas which are not brought before it by the sentence "The moon is smaller than the sun", nor yet that the latter brings before the mind any ideas which are not brought before it by the former". I interpret the last assertion to mean that the propositions E and E_1 are, in addition to being semantically equivalent, also pragmatically equivalent. I can therefore by no means see what should prevent the sentences E and E_1 from expressing the *same* proposition, in *every* "correct" usage of the word 'same'.

I now proceed to my final remark. I believe I am entitled to infer from

and Phenomenological Research, vol. v, 3, March 1945, about an article by the former "Does Art tell the Truth?", published in vol. iii, 3, March, 1943, of the same Journal. How about "Artists (normally) do not *assert* true sentences, but sometimes, by uttering false or even "meaningless" sentences, *imply* true sentences"?

Moore's assertion (p. 212) "I must, therefore, confess that I am unable to point out where the fallacy lies in these arguments..." that he is quite aware of the fact that *his* system of rules governing the "correct" use of English is *inconsistent*. This point is rather trivial, since the inconsistency of "correct" everyday-language has been elaborated often enough — Russell's "Theory of Description", e.g. was partly intended to correct some of the inconsistencies of "correct" English and may "be plausibly interpreted as a contribution to the reform of common syntax",[21] but I do not think that either Moore or most of the other adherents of Contemporary British Analytic Philosophy are ready to draw the consequences from this fact. *The reform of common syntax* (and of common semantics and pragmatics) *cannot be accomplished by direct logical analysis alone*. This task should be approached by construction of consistent language-systems, by elaborating a "pure semiotic", which will supply the necessary terminology, etc.: in short, by the methods of *logical empiricism*. Now, I do not deny the value of analysing (in a much more general sense of this word than Moore's) and reforming everyday-language; on the contrary, these tasks are of the utmost importance, since everyday-language — "Universal-jargon", to use Neurath's term — is ultimately the only medium for constructing, interpreting, and comparing artificial language-systems, and therefore (and for many other reasons) absolutely indispensable. But Moore's method of approaching these tasks is just as Sisyphian as a physicist's who should start to "analyse" the facts of free fall, without constructing or imagining artificial ("ideal") conditions (vacuum, etc.), in the manner of Galilei.

The direct analysis of these [incredibly complicated word-languages], which has been prevalent hitherto, must inevitably fail, just as a physicist would be frustrated were he from the outset to attempt to relate his laws to natural things — trees, stones, and so on. In the first place, the physicist relates his laws to the simplest of constructed forms; to a thin straight lever, to a simple pendulum, to punctiform masses, etc. Then, with the help of the laws related to these constructed forms, he is later in a position to analyse into suitable elements the complicated behaviour of real bodies, and thus to control them. One more comparison: the complicated configurations of mountain chains, rivers, frontiers, and the like are most easily represented and investigated by the help of geographical co-ordinates — or, in other words, by constructed lines not given in nature. In the same way, the syntactical property of a particular word-language, such as English, or of particular classes of word-languages, or of a particular sub-language of a word-language, is best represented and

---

[21] *Cf.* Max Black "Russell's Philosophy of Language", *The Philosophy of Bertrand Russell*, The Library of Living Philosophers, vol. v (1944), p. 242.

investigated by comparison with a constructed language which serves as a system of reference.[22]

It is as an illustration of this thesis that my article was written.

I hope I have "implied" that the whole idea of the existence of a unique "correct" English everyday-language is illusory, and that even if, by some miracle, one of the various sets of "correct" linguistic rules should be recognised as *the* "correct" one, there would still be no good reasons to assume this set to be consistent, and very good ones to assume it to be inconsistent.

I further hope I have shown that many of Moore's mistakes could have been avoided and many of his puzzles easily solved by the recognition of the multi-dimensional character of language and by the use of the most elementary tools of "pure semiotic", e.g. by the use of 'syntactical', 'semantic', 'pragmatic' in expressions like 'syntactically valid', 'semantically equivalent', 'pragmatic law'.

The direct analytical approach seems to me a deplorable waste of time and energy, and if I should succeed in persuading some of its capable adherents to try more promising approaches, writing this article will have been no waste of energy on my part.

---

[22] R. Carnap, *Syntax*, p. 8.

THE REVIVAL OF "THE LIAR"

§1. In a recent article,[1] Professor Alexander Koyré tries to revive the discussion around the semantic antinomies from the point of view of traditional logic. But it does not seem to me that his attempt to defend classical logic and to show the futility of Russell's Theory of Types and the Tarski-Carnap hierarchy of languages and metalanguages has been successful. On the contrary, without adding anything new to the discussion, he makes several blunders which tend to diminish the value of his contribution even as a recapitulation of old arguments.

Let us first remark that Koyré limits his discussion to two representatives of what are now known as "semantic antinomies", viz., to several forms of "the Liar" and to Berry's paradox of the least integer not nameable (in English) in fewer than nineteen syllables. Even if we were to assume that Koyré had succeeded in proving the harmlessness of the other known semantic antinomies, it is still difficult to see how the so-called "logical antinomies", such as that centering around the class of all classes which are not members of themselves, will be outlawed. Even if Koyré's claim to have shown the unnecessariness of the hierarchy of languages should prove to be valid, I still cannot see how "the labyrinth of the theory of types" will be avoided by his arguments.

It is rather strange not to find, in a modern discussion of semantic antinomies, any mention and discussion of the relevant works of Gödel,[2] Tarski,[3] and Carnap,[4] and I could not help feeling the small likelihood of a successful approach to this subject based on a complete disregard of these standard contributions. And a careful study of Koyré's arguments convinced me *a posteriori* that my attitude was justified.

I shall confine my criticism to what Koyré has to say about the anti-

---

[1] "The Liar," *Philosophy and Phenomenological Research*, VI, 3 (1946), pp. 344–362.

[2] Über formal unentscheidbare Sätze der Principia Mathematica und verwandter Systeme. I," *Monatshefte für Mathematik und Physik*, XXXVIII (1931), pp. 173–198. Cf. also B. Rosser's "An Informal Exposition of Proofs of Gödel's Theorem and Church's Theorem," *The Journal of Symbolic Logic*, IV (1939), pp. 53–60, and J. Findlay's "Gödelian Sentences: A Non-numerical Approach," *Mind N.S.*, LI (1942), pp. 259–265. Findlay's article, however, is not completely exact.

[3] "Der Wahrheitsbegriff in den formalisierten Sprachen," *Studia Philosophica*, I (1935), pp. 261–405, especially §1 and pp. 400–405.

[4] "Die Antinomien und die Unvollständigkeit der Mathematik," *Monatshefte für Mathematik und Physik*, XLI (1934), pp. 263–284, reprinted in English translation in *The Logical Syntax of Language* (London–New York, 1937), §§60a–d.

nomy of "the Liar," and shall not deal with his remarks either on an article by Professor Ushenko[5] or on Berry's paradox.

§2. We shall pass quickly over the first formulation of "the Liar" which Koyré calls 'Epimenides'. This formulation, as cited by Koyré in the head of his article, is so obviously *not* an antinomy that I find it hard to understand why he should have dedicated two whole pages to it.

Let us quote the first passage in full:

> The Cretan, Epimenides, said "All Cretans are Liars." But Epimenides is a Cretan, therefore *he* is a Liar and, consequently, his assertion is false. *Ergo*, Cretans are *not* liars — and this implies that Epimenides did not lie but spoke truly. Accordingly . . .[6]

Now, I believe that very elementary logic is sufficient to see that the sentence opening with 'Ergo' is a gross and simple *non sequitur*. From the falsehood of Epimenides' assertion it plainly follows only that not all Cretans are liars, which implies nothing whatsoever about Epimenides himself.

Before I pass to the second formulation, I must deal with two remarks made by Koyré which, though not directly connected with our subject, may have some interest for themselves.

The first remark is the following:

> The proposition, "Epimenides the Cretan said,[7] 'All Cretans are liars'," considered in its entirety, is necessarily false; for, either the Cretans are not all (and always) liars, or it is false that Epimenides has said it. Or, again, if he did say it he could not be a Cretan.
>
> Thus, the composite proposition, "Epimenides etc." is false in that it contains incompatible members, subassertions that cannot be true together and at the same time.[8]

How a proposition which states that somebody says something can possibly be "necessarily false," I do not know. The fact that Koyré has failed to make the now famous distinction between use and mention of signs, in our case, between a sentence and its name, is an explanation of, but hardly an excuse for, the serious blunders contained in the quoted passage. The proposition "Epimenides, etc.," is not composite at all, it contains no subassertions, but only a *name* of a sentence. And this proposition is perhaps false, since the whole story is probably invented, but of

---

[5] "A New Epimenides," *Mind N.S.*, XLVI (1937), pp. 549–550.
[6] *Op. cit.*, p. 344.
[7] Koyré has 'says'.
[8] *Op. cit.*, p. 349.

course by no means "necessarily false." Incidentally, Koyré uses in his article five closely related notions, viz., 'proposition', 'assertion', 'statement', 'judgment', 'sentence', and it is not at all clear in which sense he intends to use these notoriously ambiguous terms. This is particularly disturbing with regard to 'proposition' which is apparently used sometimes in Carnap's sense (1) i.e., as synonymous with '(declarative) sentence', sometimes in Carnap's sense (2) i.e., as 'that which is designated (or expressed, according to some usages) by a sentence'.[9] (In what follows, I shall use 'sentence' only, whenever I am not dealing with quotations.)

But it is possible that Koyré intended to say something different. Perhaps he wanted to state that the sentence "All Cretans are liars," *when uttered by Epimenides the Cretan*, is necessarily false. That this interpretation might conform to his intentions, is corroborated by what he says further on:

> To Epimenides the assertion, "All Cretans, etc." is forbidden. He cannot make it. In his mouth it suffers a perversion, it becomes a *contre-sense*, a self-contradiction. However, this case is not unique. If someone said, "The boat that I travelled on was lost with all hands," we could and should doubt either the truth of the assertion or the truthfulness of the speaker or both. . . . It is curious and even strange, perhaps (but not incomprehensible or contradictory), and it has not been sufficiently noticed, that some propositions may not be uttered by everybody, that certain verbs may not be used in the first person. It is not permissible, for example, truly to say, "I am silent," "I am absent," or "I am dead."

Be the interpretation of the former quotation whatever it may, the new quotation by itself contains many queer sentences which it will be difficult to defend. Why should it be forbidden to Epimenides to utter his assertion? Why can he not make this assertion? Even if this assertion were self-contradictory, perverse and a countersense, none of the consequences drawn by Koyré would be justified. But, perhaps, Koyré uses the phrases 'is forbidden' and 'cannot make' in a new sense, according to which, whenever a sentence is contradictory, it "is forbidden" to utter it, and one "cannot make" the corresponding assertion. In this case, his mode of expression is very misleading, to say the least. The awkwardness of the way Koyré chose to express his intentions is particularly obvious in the last quoted sentence. "It is not permissible, for example, truly to say, 'I am silent', 'I am absent', or 'I am dead' " is surely a queer way of saying "The sentence 'I am silent', etc., is self-contradictory."

---

[9] Cf. R. Carnap, *Introduction to Semantics* (1942), p. 235.

We are now coming to a much more important point: Is this last sentence, in its new formulation, true? Though it has some plausibility, on a first view, I think that, on reflection, we shall soon see that it cannot be so. Every expression-event[10] "I am silent," if it is to be a sentence at all, must be equipollent with ". . . is silent," where the blank is filled by a certain proper name or a definite description. Let us deal with the event of the utterance of this expression by a certain John. It is then equipollent with "John is silent," and this sentence is certainly not self-contradictory, *even when uttered by John himself*.[11] An analogous situation has been described by Moore[12] in saying that it is *absurd* (but *not* self-contradictory!) to make an assertion when by making this assertion we *imply* (in a certain peculiar sense of this word) its contradictory. Since I discussed this interesting situation at some length elsewhere,[13] we may now pass to the second formulation of "the Liar" dealt with by Koyré, and named by him 'I am lying'.

§3. Let us assume that somebody is saying "The sentence that I am now uttering is false." It is easy to see that if this phrase is recognized as a genuine sentence we shall get a genuine antinomy, i.e., when true, it is false, and when false — true. Koyré tries to show — as many others before him — that classical logic is sufficient to show that this phrase is not a sentence but meaningless.

The arguments brought forward boil down to the following dilemma, if I have rightly understood him: (1) Either the words 'the sentence' appearing in the above-mentioned phrase do not refer to this phrase itself, then the phrase is a genuine sentence, but a false one, because there is no object corresponding to the definite description appearing in it; but no paradox arises, because in this case we are not entitled to infer "The sentence that I am now uttering is true." (2) Or these words do refer to the phrase in which they appear, then this phrase is meaningless, since it is self-evident that a sentence cannot be its own subject.

We need deal only with the second horn of the dilemma. The categorical statement that a sentence cannot be its own subject is justified

---

[10] For an explanation of this useful term, see *op. cit.* in previous note, §3.

[11] It is possible that the use of an egocentric (Russell) or indicator (Nelson Goodman) word like 'I', with its special peculiarities, is partly responsible for the many confusions. Cf. also *The Logical Syntax of Language*, p. 168.

[12] "Russell's 'Theory of Descriptions'," *The Philosophy of Bertrand Russell*, The Library of Living Philosophers, Vol. V (1944), p. 204.

[13] "Analysis of 'Correct' Language," *Mind, N.S.*, LV (1946), pp. 328–340 [reprinted here as Ch. 19].

by its being *self-evident*. Now, this justification is surely a poor one; self-evidence in such delicate situations has so often proved to be unreliable that it can hardly count as a sufficient reason against the opinion of other logicians to whom this statement, far from being self-evident, is plainly false.

Koyré himself cites a counter-argument to which I shall give a slightly different form. The second sentence in this section contains nine words. By counting the fullstops in this section and the words between the first and second fullstop in this section we find that the phrase between the first and the second fullstop in this section is doubtlessly a genuine English sentence and, incidentally, even a true one. And it is plain that the expression heading this sentence, viz., 'the second sentence in this section' refers to exactly this sentence itself. Koyré's only reason against this consequence is: "These propositions are not about themselves, but about their verbal contents or their verbal forms."[14] The moment we replace 'propositions' by 'sentences', this counter-argument breaks down.

§4. The confusion arising from the disregard of the distinction between use and mention of signs, and the therewith connected careless use of quotation marks, leads Koyré to make very strange notes on the form given to "the Liar" by Professor Łukasiewicz. The confusion starts in the first quoted passage (the quotation is not from Łukasiewicz himself, but from an article by Grelling[15]), viz.:

Let the letter Q be an abbreviation for the phrase: 'the proposition occupying the twelfth line of this page.'

Łukasiewicz himself has, of course, 'Q' instead of 'Q',[16] so that the original reading is: "Let the letter 'Q', etc."

Let us restate the first sentences of the form given by Łukasiewicz to "the Liar," using the unambiguous 'sentence' instead of 'proposition' and a more suitable phrase instead of 'the sentence occupying the twelfth line of this[17] page'.

[14] *Op. cit.*, p. 354. 'these propositions' refers to another example as well.

[15] "The Logical Paradoxes," *Mind N.S.*, XLV (1936), pp. 481–486.

[16] Or perhaps some other letter. According to the account given by Tarski, *op. cit.*, pp. 270–271, Łukasiewicz used "c". It turned out to be highly unfortunate that Grelling, for some reason unknown to me, omitted the quotes around 'Q', after the word 'letter'. (At another occasion, p. 484, he has the quotes!) This autonymous use of 'Q' as a sign of itself did not lead Grelling into any troubles, but its dangers for a man less versed in modern formal logic are well exemplified in our case.

[17] 'this' in this sentence refers to Grelling's article where Q occupies indeed the twelfth line. In Koyré's article, another sentence-event of the sentence-design Q

Let the letter 'Q' be an abbreviation for the expression 'the second sentence of the third paragraph (of §4 of this article)'. Q is a false sentence. Q is identical with the second sentence of this paragraph, viz., with 'Q is a false sentence'. (The reader will now be able to continue the construction of the antinomy by himself.) What does Koyré find wrong with this "elegant form"[18] of "the Liar"? He thinks that the third sentence of this paragraph is

quite false. Q is not identical with the second sentence of this paragraph, and Q is not a sentence. Q is an abbreviation for an expression forming only the subject of the second sentence of this section. Q does not stand for "The second sentence of the third section is a false sentence" but only stands for "The second sentence of the third section." In other words, Q *does not* mean "Q is a false sentence." Therefore Q cannot be identical with the expression written between the first and the second fullstop of this section. Or, vice versa, if it is, then the expression written between these fullstops is not "The second sentence of the third paragraph is a false sentence" but only "The second sentence of the third paragraph." Which expression is not a sentence at all. It is therefore impossible to operate with it as if it were one. The paradox — if only we are careful enough not to change the meanings of our symbols — does not arise. If, on the other hand, we substitute for the original meaning of Q the "meaning" "Q is false," we have no right to identify it with Q. Finally if we start from the identification of Q and "Q is false," i.e., Q and non-Q, we must not wonder that we come to contradictions. And we have no right to incriminate the rules of classical logic.[19]

Perhaps it will not be superfluous, as a preparation for the discussion of the quoted passage, to point out some facts with regard to the use and mention of signs. It is deplorable that many otherwise good and acute thinkers should continue to fall easy prey to the intricacies of this subject.

If somebody introduces an expression as an abbreviation for another expression, say 'Bill' for 'William', then these two expressions are synonymous and their designata identical; in our example, 'Bill' is synonymous with 'William' and Bill is identical with William. But Bill is not an abbreviation either of William or of 'William', or synonymous with either of them.[20]

---

occupies the seventh line. We have here another example of the pitfalls connected with the use of indicator-words, this time of 'this'.

[18] The ironical quotes around 'elegant form' are Koyré's.

[19] *Op. cit.*, p. 356.

[20] This sentence violates, of course, the rule of types (in its rather doubtful application to ordinary language), but it is added anyhow for persuasive purposes. Cf. *The Logical Syntax of Language*, pp. 297–298.

With these simple facts in mind, let us turn to the last quotation. We shall examine the first six sentences following 'quite false'. Both components of the first sentence, viz., "Q is not identical with the second sentence of the third paragraph, and Q is not a sentence" are false: Since 'Q' is, by definition, an abbreviation for 'the second sentence of the third paragraph', Q *is* identical with the second sentence of the third paragraph and, hence, a sentence. If we replace in the cited sentence 'Q' by ''Q'', we shall get a true but completely trivial sentence; nobody, and certainly not Łukasiewicz, intended to say that the letter 'Q' is identical with a sentence. The second sentence, viz., "Q is an abbreviation for an expression forming only the subject of the second sentence of the third section," is likewise false, since Q is *not* an abbreviation of any expression whatever. Replacement of 'Q' by ''Q'' will yield once again a true and completely innocuous sentence, following immediately from the definition of 'Q'. The third sentence, viz., "Q does not stand for 'The second sentence of the third paragraph is a false sentence' but only stands for 'the second sentence of the third paragraph'," is false for the same reasons; Q *does* stand for — 'stands for' is apparently intended to be synonymous with 'is synonymous with' — 'the second sentence of the third section is a false sentence' and does not stand for any name of any expression whatsoever. If we replace in this sentence 'Q' by ''Q'' and drop 'only', we shall get a true sentence. 'Only' has to be dropped, because nobody ever tried to contest this sentence and to assert that 'Q' stands for 'the second sentence of the third paragraph is a false sentence'. The fourth sentence is correct, if 'mean' is used as synonymous with 'designate'. Q indeed does not designate "Q is a false sentence," but just because, in complete contradiction to the fifth sentence, Q *is* identical with the expression written between the first and the second fullstop of the third paragraph. The sixth sentence is particularly curious. The second half of it is plainly false: If Q is identical with the expression written between the first and second fullstop of the third paragraph, then Q is *not* — 'is not' is apparently used as synonymous with 'is not identical with' — 'the second sentence of the third paragraph'. But the first half is true indeed, though for entirely different reasons than Koyré's: Q is indeed not identical with 'the second sentence of the third paragraph is a false sentence', as everybody can find out by inspection; Q is only identical with an expression synonymous with 'the second sentence of the third paragraph is a false sentence', viz., with 'Q is a false sentence'.

The following schemata will enable the reader to find his way more easily through the labyrinthic situation: (For the sake of brevity, the expression 'of the third paragraph' will be omitted; the symbol '=' will be used as an identity sign, the expressions 'is synonymous with', 'is an abbreviation for', 'designates', will be abbreviated by 'syn', 'abbr', 'des', respectively.)

Q is a false sentence = the second sentence is a false sentence.
Q = the expression written between the first and the second fullstop.
   = the second sentence.
   = 'Q is a false sentence'.
Q syn 'the second sentence is a false sentence'.
'Q' syn 'the second sentence'.
'Q' abbr 'the second sentence'.
Q des (the proposition that) Q is a false sentence.
'Q' des (the sentence) 'Q is a false sentence'.

The following theorems, stated in terms of the theory of relations, may be of some further help:

syn is a reflexive, symmetric, and transitive relation between expressions.
abbr is an irreflexive, asymmetric, and transitive relation between expressions.
abbr is included in syn.
Relative multiplication by = leaves a relation unchanged.
The relative product of abbr by syn is included in syn.

I believe that this tiresome examination (perhaps quite useful as an exercise in the handling of expressions and quotes) of the first six sentences of the cited passage will do. If only we are careful enough not to confuse the use of signs with their mention, expressions with their syntactical designations, the antinomy of "the Liar" *will* arise, so long as we stick to the customary rules of classical logic.

This examination has been so tiresome, partly because Professor Koyré preferred not to make full use of the introduced abbreviation in his discussion. He explicitly characterizes the use of 'Q' as an "abbreviation" for a certain expression as "not only useless but even worse than useless."[21] I admit that excessive use of abbreviations may *sometimes* lead to pedagogical difficulties, but certainly it should not do so in our case. Had we only made full use of the proposed abbreviation, our discussion would have been much more concise and shorter. The con-

---

[21] *Op. cit.*, p. 355.

fusion which has arisen is most emphatically not an effect of the use of the letter 'Q' instead of 'the second sentence of the third section' (it would perhaps be an interesting exercise for the reader to restate Łukasiewicz's form of "the Liar," its refutation by Koyré and our criticism of this refutation without making any use of abbreviations[22]), but — as far as I can see — simply an outcome of the failure to distinguish between 'Q' and 'Q'.

§5. I should like to add that the problem of the antinomies is still far from having been solved to our complete satisfaction. But any reasonable attempt to find such a solution must start from the recognition of the sad fact that no language may be "universal" on pain of being inconsistent.[23] What restrictions must be imposed on the formalized counterparts of ordinary languages, this is a question which is still on debate. And it seems that the answer will not be unique, that many entirely different methods of restrictions will be employed, each with its own merits and limitations. But it is quite sure that each of the proposed solutions will have to be based on most careful semiotical studies and will require a certain amount of technical skill for handling complex logical situations. It is very improbable that Husserl's distinction between countersense and non-sense,[24] i.e., in modern terms, between contradictory sentences and word-sequences which are not built in accordance with the rules of formation of the language in discussion, important as it was fifty years ago, though now a commonplace, will be sufficient by itself to avoid these careful studies; I hope to have shown that Koyré, at least, has failed to prove that under the rules of formation of classical logic the word-sequence "I am uttering now a false sentence" is nonsensical. How this commonplace distinction, which is indispensable not only for the theory of types but for all modern logic, will lead us to "a resolute abandonment of the extensionalist interpretation of logic" I am utterly unable to see, for the time being (though I see many other reasons for the investigation of non-extensional language-systems), and must content myself therefore with looking forward to Koyré's announced publication to this effect.

[22] The possibility of formulating "the Liar" without any recourse to abbreviations and artificial symbols disposes of Perelman's remark in his "Réponse à MM. Grelling et Beth," *Mind N.S.*, XLVI (1937), pp. 278–279, to the effect that the source of the antinomy is the faulty definition of 'Q', and that its solution should, therefore, be given as an exercise for beginners.
[23] Cf. Tarski, *op. cit.*, p. 278, and Grelling, *op. cit.*, p. 486.
[24] *Logische Untersuchungen*, Vol. I, pp. 152 ff.

NEW LIGHT ON THE LIAR

Ten years ago, I published a discussion note[1] in which I criticized a certain attempt at solving the antinomy of "The Liar" without departing from the point of view of traditional logic. Though I still believe that my criticism there was basically correct, I no longer think that my own way of looking at the problem at that time is the only proper and fruitful one. I hope that my change of mind will be of some general interest.

My motive for writing this paper was supplied by an article written by John G. Kemeny for the 1957 edition of the *Encyclopaedia Britannica*.[2] It is perhaps not quite up to customary academic standards to write a paper for a technical journal in reaction to an Encyclopedia article, but in this case I hope my breach of custom will be forgiven. Kemeny's article is outstanding in its amazingly successful fusion of precision, clarity and readability and is in my opinion fully entitled to the claim of presenting an authoritative up-to-date description of (logical) Semantics.

There is only one point in which I find fault with Kemeny's presentation: his treatment of the Liar paradox and the consequences he draws from it. The view he presents is probably quite typical for many modern logicians, and I myself adopted it ten years ago. Let me quote:

The next sentence is true. The previous sentence is false.
If you consider either one of the foregoing sentences, you note that it is a perfectly simple and clear sentence of the English language. And yet the two sentences together constitute a paradox; they are a version of the ancient paradox of the liar. A (declarative) sentence must be either true or false, and cannot — of course — be both. Let us suppose that the first sentence is false. That means that the second sentence is not true. But to say that "The previous sentence is false" is not true is equivalent to the assertion that the previous sentence is not false. This itself is not a paradox; from the assumption that the first sentence is false we have derived a contradiction which shows only that the assumption was wrong. Hence *the first sentence is not false*. That implies that it is true which means that the second sentence is true. But if "The previous sentence is false" is true, then *the first sentence is false*. We have now derived two contradictory results using only the rules of logic.

After presenting in an equally clear and precise fashion Grelling's antinomy, the author concludes:

[1] "The Revival of 'The Liar'," *Philosophy and Phenomenological Research*, Vol. VIII, 1947, pp. 245–253 [reprinted here as Ch. 20].
[2] "Semantics as a Branch of Logic", *Enc. Brit.* (1957) Vol. **20**, p. 313.

The above paradoxes show that English allows the derivation of contradictory conclusions by means of the rules of logic, i.e. that English is inconsistent. Since it can be shown that in an inconsistent system anything at all, true or false, can be proved, we have to conclude that ordinary English is a language not suitable for logical arguments. And it is not the case that some simple trick will remove this inconsistency.

It is ironic that Kemeny tries to show that ordinary English is a language not suitable for logical arguments by offering us a fine specimen of a logical argument presented in ordinary English. (But I would not like my *argumentum ad hominem* to be taken too seriously.)

Now, though Kemeny's argument seems to be perfectly valid, is it really sound? Is it really the case that "a (declarative) sentence of ordinary language must be either true or false"? What about 'It is raining' or 'I am hungry', to mention only the most simple and obvious counter-examples? With regard to these sentences *qua* types it is nothing short of ridiculous to regard them as being either true or false. But what about these sentences *qua* tokens? (Kemeny has clearly sentence-tokens in mind: only of a certain *token* of the sentence 'The next sentence is true' does it make sense to ask for its truth-value.) On another occasion,[3] I have tried to show how misleading it is to regard even tokens of sentences whose reference is context-dependent as being true or false (though I would now want to put my argument in different terms). But instead of repeating the argument, it should suffice to point out how silly it sounds to ask for the truth-value of a declarative sentence (-token) like 'I want you to close the door' or 'I hereby declare the meeting open'.

All this is of course commonplace in Oxford for many years. Truth and falsity, according to the view prevalent there, apply directly only to *statements* and not to (declarative) sentences. And a statement can, but need not necessarily, be made by uttering a declarative sentence; it is made quite often by uttering a non-declarative sentence or even a non-sentential expression, and occasionally by nodding or through some other non-linguistic device. (Nor, of course, are all declarative sentences uttered in order to make statements.) It would be pedantic to disqualify *all* usages of the form '—— is true', where the blank is filled by some sentence or by the words 'the next sentence' or the like; but such usage, according to the view presented just now, is always derivative and can be definitely misleading; and any philosophical generalization to the

---

[3] "Indexical Expressions", *Mind*. Vol. LXIII, 1954, pp. 359–378 [reprinted here as Ch. 5].

effect that all declarative sentences must be either true or false is most definitely wrong.

But could not the version of the Liar paradox chosen by Kemeny be reformulated in statement terminology? Let us try. Assume that John is uttering in an appropriate voice the following two sentences one after the other: "The statement I am going to make by uttering the next sentence is true. The statement I made just now by uttering the previous sentence is false." It should be clear that on the assumption that John, by uttering these two sentences, made two statements a paradox immediately arises, if we grant that *a statement must be either true or false*. But we are perfectly free to conclude that, despite appearances, no statements were made by uttering these sentences. Indeed, this conclusion is reasonable on reflection, quite independently of the argument through paradox. I for one would have judged so, after some consideration, even if John had said 'true' in the second sentence, instead of 'false'. (All this has, of course, been said *in essence* many times before, but I believe that the specific terminology used here is of decisive importance.)

Whether a given sequence of English words constitutes a sentence or not, is a question that — after certain qualifications and refinements — should be answerable on the basis of a list of formation rules which English grammarians should in principle be able to produce. There are even good reasons for thinking that the answer could be given by a mechanical procedure. (To use, for once, highly technical terminology, the term 'sentence in English' should be "definite" in Carnap's terminology of the *Logical Syntax*, or the set of English sentences "generally recursive" in the customary post-Gödelian terminology.) But there is no reason to expect that the same should hold for 'statement'. It is, on the contrary, quite obvious that no general procedure could exist for determining whether a statement has been made. Examining the sentence used is certainly never quite enough, though occasionally not much more might be required. But for present purposes it is, fortunately, not necessary to go into the extremely difficult problem of determining what a statement is.

My "solution" of the Liar paradox — and it is easy to see that it applies also to the other known versions of it — should by no means be regarded as a defence of traditional logic. It is rather an attack against whoever, traditionalist or modernist, misdescribed the uses of ordinary language by stating, or implying, that declarative sentences must be either true or false (myself of years ago included). Nor does the proposed change of attitude to the concept of truth in ordinary languages commit us to any change of view about the concept of truth in systematized languages. There, a semantic truth concept is fully appropriate and the problem, how to safeguard these languages against the semantic paradoxes, is a serious one. But in the case of ordinary languages, the semantic truth conception loses its point, once we decide to regard truth as a property[4] of statements rather than of sentences. Paraphrasing Tarski[5] himself, we may say that *the attempt to set up a semantical conception of the term 'true sentence', applicable to ordinary languages, is misguided.* Tarski's famous criterion for the adequacy of a definition of truth for ordinary languages becomes, in our terminology, something like (T′) A-statement-(to-the-effect-)that-*p* is true if, and only if, *p*. (It is by no means the case that all usages of 'true', even if referring to statements, conform to this criterion, in spite of its utterly trivial appearance. There is, for instance, a quite common usage, not only in philosophical but also in ordinary discourse, under which a statement-that-*p* is regarded as true (-for-N) if the assumption-that-*p* is, in some sense, useful (-for-N), even if not-*p*.)

Truth as applying to statements should not be confused with truth as applying to propositions[6] — where 'proposition' is meant as synonymous with 'what is expressed by a declarative sentence'; on the contrary, my misgivings about treating truth as a property of sentences (of ordinary language) apply, *mutatis mutandis*, also to treating it as a property of propositions. (Statements are "made", but neither sentences nor propositions are "made".)

It is, of course, much simpler to manipulate sentences in logical arguments than the incomparably more elusive and less definite statements. It is indeed quite often perfectly safe to deal not with certain statements but with the sentences that are usually uttered when one wants to make these statements. In scientific matters especially it does little harm and a lot of good to work with sentences and assign them truth-values, so long as it is kept in mind that this is a matter of convenience only and that one must be prepared to return to statements as soon as trouble arises. But this procedure is suicidal when working with context-dependent sentences. Applying logic to context-independent sentences of ordinary

---

[4] I am aware of the objections raised against this term, but do not think that they are relevant in this context.

[5] "Concept of Truth in Formalized Languages", in *Logic, Semantics, Metamathematics*, 1956, p. 164.

[6] This conception was once called the "absolute" one by R. Carnap. See *Introduction to Semantics*, 1946, p. 90.

language has been on the whole fairly successful; applying logic to context-dependent sentences by treating them as entities that are either true or false must occasionally lead to spectacular failures, as we can now say by hindsight. But the proper conclusion from these failures is not that ordinary language is inconsistent, but that when the application of the rules of logic to ordinary language sentences leads to paradox, one has to fall back on statements. In the case of the Liar at any rate, the paradox disappears; and this holds not only for those versions of the paradox that work with context-dependent sentences, like Kemeny's, but also for such versions as Stroll's[7] where the sentences involved are context-independent, as the reader is invited to check by himself.

Even if it could be shown that ordinary language is inconsistent, for reasons other than the occurrence of the Liar paradox, much could be said — much more than was said by Stroll — against Kemeny's claim to infer from this the unsuitability of ordinary language as a medium of logical arguments. But I have reasons to suspect that Kemeny and other recent authors who have expressed themselves on this issue in a similar vein (like R. M. Martin[8]) do not really want their claim to be taken both literally and seriously, but rather as an indirect and persuasive appeal for doing philosophy with the assistance of (partly) formalized language systems. And as this is something to which I consent wholeheartedly, I feel that further discussion might conceivably do more harm than good and tend to perpetuate a mainly, if not purely, verbal issue.

---

[7] Avrum Stroll, "Is Everyday Language Inconsistent?" *Mind*, Vol. LXIII, 1954, pp. 219–225, especially pp. 224–225.

[8] See "Some Comments on Truth and Designation", ANALYSIS, Vol. X, 1950, p. 65, and "On 'Analytic'", *Philosophical Studies*, Vol. III, 1952, p. 44.

A PREREQUISITE FOR
RATIONAL PHILOSOPHICAL DISCUSSION

Communication between philosophers has been deteriorating during the last decades. Logical empiricists and British linguistic philosophers have been branding large parts of the output of their speculative colleagues as 'nonsense' and 'literally unintelligible'. Speculative metaphysicians, after having recovered from the first shock, either just disregard these declarations, or else declare, on their part, that the standards of intelligibility employed by the critics are arbitrary.

The breakdown of communication is not always as radical as the situation just described might lead one to believe. An analytic philosopher (let us use this term to cover both logical empiricists and linguistic philosophers) might often try to suggest one or more reinterpretations of his colleague's original formulations, thereby making them intelligible to himself. (This, of course, indicates that he does 'understand' the original formulation; thereby his behaviour is not made absurd since this kind of understanding is clearly different from the one he professes not to have.) Unfortunately, this conciliatory action seldom does much good. The reinterpretations have a tendency to become either flagrant truisms or flagrant falsities. Even in case they do neither, more often than not the speculative philosopher will reject them as completely missing the point of his intentions, perhaps adding that this failure could have been foreseen, since there is no reason why his deep insights should be expressible in the analytic philosopher's shallow and arbitrarily restricted language.

One might have expected that another development would arrest and reverse this trend of deteriorating communication. I refer to the well-known fact that the standards of intelligibility of the late twenties and early thirties — 'whatever can be said at all, can be said in ordinary (thing-, observational) language' — have been undergoing a process of continuous liberalization, the history of which has been told many times. In one of the latest attempts at explicating the empiricist's standard of intelligibility[1]), a discourse is regarded as intelligible, not only if it is formulated wholly in observational language, but also if it is formulated

---

[1] R. Carnap, The methodological character of theoretical concepts, The Foundations of Science and the Concepts of Psychology and Psychoanalysis, Minnesota Studies in the Philosophy of Science, vol. I, pp. 38–76, University of Minnesota Press, Minneapolis, 1956.

in theoretical or mixed language, if only the theoretical terms occurring in it are connected via theoretical postulates and rules of correspondence with the observational terms. True enough, the degree of intelligibility of such discourse is deemed to be inferior to that of a purely observational one. However, thereby such discourse is not disqualified nor is one entitled to draw the consequence that it is somehow less important or scientific than fully intelligible observational discourse. Clearly, a treatise in theoretical physics, psychology or linguistics is not the worse off because of the fact that its theoretical terms are only partially and indirectly interpretable.

It is nevertheless rather doubtful whether this liberalization will bring about a reunion in philosophy. Though the analytic philosopher may be willing to regard the specifically metaphysical terms used by his colleague as theoretical terms of which he is quite ready not to require more than partial and indirect interpretation in observational terms, he will continue to ask his colleague to supply him this interpretation, at least in sufficient outline. But the speculative philosopher will quite often refuse to do this, just as he refused to comply with the earlier demand to supply full and direct interpretation by operational definitions. He might even point out that just as the empiricist will now agree that his earlier demands were unjustified, so he will come to realize in due time that his present demands are still unduly restrictive.

This may indeed turn out to be the case. Most analytic philosophers are today aware that the whole conception of an observational language is rather vague, that the line of demarcation between observational and theoretical terms is blurred, elastic and even to a considerable degree arbitrary, and will therefore be rather careful with their use of the epithets 'meaningless', 'nonsensical', or 'unintelligible'. But they will continue refusing to exert themselves overly in order to supply for their own benefit all those theoretical postulates and rules of correspondence, or at least a sufficiently large outline of these, which they regard as necessary in principle for ensuring a modicum of intelligibility. If an analytic philosopher finds that a certain philosophical text is *underinterpreted*, he may or may not attempt to suggest to the reader of this text one or more ways of supplementing the missing links, but if the author refuses to follow suit, the analytic philosopher will still know no more rational reaction than to count himself out. The possibility that he himself twenty years hence, or the next generation of analytic philosophers, might conceivably liberalize the standards of intelligibility still further and then rejoin the metaphysical game, will be more or less cheerfully acknowledged but will not influence the present breakdown of communication.

Is this then the end of the conversation? I am not convinced it must be so. Though I myself, for instance, as an analytic philosopher see no way of joining many metaphysical discussions because of the hopelessness of remedying their state of underinterpretedness, I am ready to explain why I regard the language of these discussions as underinterpreted, what are my present standards of intelligibility, why I believe that a discussion that does not comply with them holds little or no promise of being fruitful, etc. And I am ready to listen, and listen attentively, if my colleague will challenge my evaluation, criticize my standards of intelligibility and try to persuade me that the language of this or that speculative philosopher, or of all speculative philosophers, is one which it is worthwhile to adopt, at least for certain purposes. *But I am ready to listen and argue with him only if the (meta-) language, in which he explains to me his reasons for challenging my standards, itself complies with these standards.*

This may sound preposterous, but I don't see how it can be helped. My insistence is due to the fact that the situation is objectively asymmetrical. One cannot expect that the analytic philosopher, while endeavouring to persuade by rational means his speculative colleague of the cognitive poverty of his ways of philosophizing, should himself use speculative discourse for this purpose. This type of discourse is unintelligible to him in any capacity, including that of a metadiscourse. This does not mean that he is unable to manipulate intelligently such discourse for other purposes, should the occasion require it. On the other hand, no similar scruples could prevent the speculative philosopher from using scientific (observational plus theoretical) metalanguage to impress his analytic colleague with the importance of using metaphysical object-language.

Here then, it seems, the final *conditio sine qua non* of continued philosophical discussion has been reached. Those *speculative philosophers* who are interested in having analytic philosophers discuss their theses couched in metaphysical language *must use a scientific metalanguage as their rational tool of persuasion*. (I shall not discuss here, for obvious reasons, the possible use of extra-rational tools.) The analytic philosopher who is interested in having speculative philosophers stop formulating their theses the way they do need do nothing beyond stretching his standards of intelligibility to the limit and offering constant reinterpretations in scientific language of the original metaphysical formulations. This includes occasionally reformulating these theses as proposals, comments, exhortations, etc. As I am using the term 'scientific language' now, such languages contain not only declarative sentences but also question sentences, etc.

I am under no illusions as to the effects of my proposal. Even if speculative philosophers should accept it in principle, there is little likelihood that agreement could be reached as to the extent of the *index verborum prohibitorum* for the common philosophical metalanguage. Differences will arise as to which terms of ordinary language are entitled to be considered directly intelligible. As to the theoretical terms, it is only with regard to rigorously constructed language systems that it is precisely, though not necessarily effectively, determined whether they are or are not empirically significant (relative to the given observational language and after a certain criterion of significance has been adopted). Since nobody, and certainly not myself, seriously requires that a theoretical term of ordinary language should be admitted into philosophical metadiscourse only after this discourse has been completely formalized, it cannot be assumed that agreement would be reached on the admissibility of all candidates, in anticipation of future formalization. It is notorious that no such agreement has been reached as to the status of, say, certain psychoanalytical terms, and this among methodologists who would all of them be regarded as adherents of analytic philosophy. Similar disagreements exist as to the character of such terms of theoretical semantics as 'class', 'proposition' and the like, which some analytic philosophers simply claim not to understand. Add to this that a given term may well be doubtless intelligible, perhaps even straight observational, in some of its uses (meanings) but of doubtful status in other uses (meanings), and this even in the discourse of one and the same author — think of what theologians call 'analogical use', for instance, — and the very great difficulties of agreeing upon a common metalanguage in which to discuss the relative merits of the various object-languages used by philosophers should be clear. Nevertheless, I think that an agreement in principle to use for this purpose a language of about the same structure the analytic philosophers believe that the object-language of science has, should have its beneficial impact. One can only wish that prestige considerations ('having to talk the other fellow's language') will not blind the speculative philosophers in this context. I see no rational reason why they should refuse apriori to use a scientific metalanguage in order to justify their conviction that the scientific object-language is not adequate for certain philosophical purposes. Should they contend, however, that for intrinsic reasons such a metalanguage is not up to its purpose, then this would now indeed mean either the end of the conversation, or else the whole issue will just be pushed one step higher the hierarchy of philosophical metalanguages. The simple argument that a scientific metalanguage is unsuitable for the phiosopher's use for the *same* reason for which a scientific object-language is unsuitable for this purpose would surely be a rather weak one, as can be shown by innumerable analogies. One can and does show in ordinary non-symbolic (meta-)-language that ordinary non-symbolic (object-)language is unsuitable for algebraic purposes. Any contention that a discussion of the relative merits of various proposed notational systems for chemistry should be held in a metalanguage in which these notations are not only mentioned (which they clearly must be) but also used would meet with very strong initial disbelief. Though philosophy is neither chemistry nor algebra, this by itself is not a sufficient reason for rejecting the analogy. My plea is necessarily of a general and vague nature. No recipe follows from what I said. Any single word which the analytical philosopher professes not to understand (sufficiently) in an initial stage of a discussion can be made (sufficiently) intelligible by supplementing a few suitable sentences (though there constantly lurks the danger of *obscurum per obscurius* in such situations). However, as to those notorious types of metadiscourse which analytic philosophers tend to regard as definitely underinterpreted *in toto*, it might be simpler to omit them altogether rather than to try giving a sketch of the theory behind them, which would at the best tend to become a very complex and time-consuming affair. But clearly no hard and fast rules of thumb can be expected. Goodwill helps. But unfortunately, though necessary, it is not sufficient.

NEOREALISM vs. NEOPOSITIVISM
A Neo-Pseudo Issue

That theories are necessary to explain *phenomena* (or 'save' them, as the Greek philosophers used to say) became clear to many thinkers from the very infancy of science. In these theories we find expressions which denote entities of a special type whose mode of existence is radically different, at least *prima facie*, from that of the entities encountered in everyday life, such as tables, chairs, trees and stones, special entities that cannot be seen, heard or perceived by any of the senses. These theories also contain expressions and functions of a special type whose application to the ordinary and the special entities cannot be verified by our senses. An illustration that readily occurs to us is the ancient theory of atoms which goes back to the 5th century B.C. (I shall not here treat the much discussed connection between the assumed existence of invisible entities required for scientific explanation and the existence of entities required for purposes of magic or theology, such as gods, devils and ghosts, entities which are *in general* invisible, but which reveal themselves on appropriate occasions to the initiated. Nor shall I treat the entire question of the growth of scientific explanations from a magico-theological background.) The question of the exact nature of the existence of the particular type of entities, properties, relations and functions required by scientific theories has never ceased to interest philosophers. The problem is often formulated in terms of 'reality' (or its counterpart in Greek, Latin, Arabic and other languages) and thus it was often asked whether atoms are more real or less real than trees, or 'every bit as real' as trees, yet different from them in some other respect which cannot be clarified by the term 'reality'. It would lead us too far afield to discuss the long history of what is known today as 'the problem of the ontical status of the theoretical entities'. I shall only mention that in the first quarter of this century the *Realismusstreit*, the battle of realism, broke out anew in the philosophical circles of Germany and other countries. In 1927 an attempt was made by Rudolf Carnap[1] to put an end to this controversy by showing that the discussion between the idealists (or

---

[1] In the book *Scheinprobleme in der Philosophie* which, however, appeared only in 1928. In 1961, Felix Meiner in Hamburg published a second edition of this book, bound in one volume with the second edition of another book by Carnap, *Der logische Aufbau der Welt*, the first edition of which also appeared separately in 1928; cf. the new introduction to the second edition.

positivists) and realists was devoid of cognitive (or scientific) meaning. It must be admitted that Carnap and many of his followers were rather naive to believe that they had succeeded in laying the ghost of the *Realismusstreit*. It is, nevertheless, disconcerting to witness the revival of this venerable controversy in our days, except for some minor changes in the terminology, in such unexpected quarters as the Minnesota Center for the Philosophy of Science. The controversy is unexpected, despite the surprising confession of the head of the Center, Herbert Feigl, that he had always been a realist at heart, except for his brief lapse in the late twenties when, under the influence of Schlick and Carnap in the Vienna Circle, his genuine belief was repressed and temporarily relegated to his subconscious whence it emerged after his emigration to the United States.[2]

I shall try to show that the new controversy between neorealism and instrumentalism (as neopositivism is sometimes called) is as devoid of scientific and methodological interest as the old one and that the ontological question whether *theoretical entities* (as we shall henceforth call the above-mentioned entities, properties, relations and special functions) are 'every bit as real' as tables and chairs or whether they are endowed with a lesser degree of 'physical reality' by being only 'computational devices', is a pseudo-question as were its forebearers forty years ago when 'fictitiousness' was used in place of 'computational device'. (The third possibility, namely that theoretical entities are more real than everyday entities, has not been discussed in those circles in whose views I am interested.)

Ernest Nagel has dedicated an entire chapter of his excellent book *The Structure of Science*[3] to similar statements, although somewhat less radically formulated. The controversy between the realists and the instrumentalists is described by Nagel as 'a conflict over preferred modes of speech' and he concludes 'that the question as to which is the "correct position" has only terminological interest'.[4] Many scholars, however, do not accept Nagel's evaluation and cannot be persuaded that the question has been disposed of. Thus, Grover Maxwell, a member of the Minnesota Center and one of the editors of the Minnesota Studies in the Philosophy of Science published by this institution, presented, in an

---

[2] Herbert Feigl, 'The Power of Positivistic Thinking', *Proceedings and Addresses of the American Philosophical Assoc.*, 1962/1963, pp. 21–41.

[3] Ernest Nagel, *The Structure of Science — Problems in the Logic of Scientific Explanation*, Routledge & Kegan Paul, London 1961.

[4] *Ibid.*, Ch. 6.

article that appeared in 1962 in the third volume of this series,[5] 'new constructive arguments for a radical realistic interpretation' of scientific theories. He published this article even though he continued to believe 'that the key to the solution of all serious problems in ontology is to be found in the classical paper by Carnap, "Empiricism, Semantics and Ontology",'[6] which in my innocence I believed had conclusively demonstrated that traditional questions of ontology are devoid of all theoretical significance. Maxwell's questions concerning the ontic status of the theoretical entities are what Carnap calls in this paper 'external existence questions' whose ontic character is pseudo in contradistinction to 'internal existence questions' which mean what they say. One who asks whether there are prime numbers between 1,000,000 and 1,000,100 is concerned with a genuine problem, but one who asks whether natural numbers exist at all, seems rather to be nursing a grudge against the traditional theory of numbers in general. One who desires to know whether Abominable Snowmen exist in the Himalayas is asking an internal existence question and means what he says. He who asks whether human beings in general exist (excluding or including himself) or whether physical entities or the external world really exist, is at loggerheads with standard anthropology, with traditional physics or with tradition altogether and his question is, in all likelihood, only meant to serve as a prolegomenon to the presentation of some novel theory.

I dwell upon Maxwell's article not so much because of its assumed importance but because it is the clearest presentation of the neorealistic point of view that has come to my attention in recent years. Hence, my remarks are concerned exclusively with the opposition from the realist right to Nagel's position. I should have liked to criticize the views of the opposition from the instrumentalist left in this matter but refrain from doing so because of the limited time at my disposal. In spite of this omission, it will be clear from my remarks that my criticims of the neorealistic attitude is not made from an instrumentalistic position. I have, indeed, little sympathy with 'the intrumentalist views of outstanding physicists such as Bohr and Heisenberg' and I cannot seriously believe

---

[5] Grover Maxwell, 'The Ontological Status of Theoretical Entities', *Scientific Explanation, Space and Time* (edited by H. Feigl & G. Maxwell), Minnesota Studies in the Philosophy of Science, III, University of Minnesota Press, Minneapolis 1962, pp. 3–27.

[6] *Ibid.*, p. 22. This article by Carnap, first published in 1950, has since been republished many times and has also been incorporated into the second edition of his book, *Meaning and Necessity*, University of Chicago Press, Chicago 1959.

'that the entities referred to by scientific theories are only convenient fictions, or that talk about such entities is translatable without remainder into talk about sense contents or everyday physical objects, or that such talk should be regarded as belonging to a mere calculating device and, thus, without cognitive content.'[7] On the contrary, I am convinced that these formulations are utterly confusing, an opinion which, I feel certain, is at present also shared by Carnap and Nagel. It is, therefore, all the more surprising that Maxwell should associate the name of Nagel with that of Bohr and Heisenberg in the first paragraph of his article in order to justify his decision to deal anew with the problem, apparently adopting the celebrated principle that 'whoever is not with me is against me'.

What precisely is the fault that Maxwell finds in Nagel's formulation? I read Maxwell's article several times hoping to find an answer to this question but I am still not sure that I have fully understood the contents of what is ostensibly the clearest of the neorealistic articles. An indication of Maxwell's intentions can perhaps be gleaned from the very title of his article, 'The Ontological Status of Theoretical Entities', which appears like a caricature, whether conscious or not, of the title of Carnap's article in the first volume of the Minnesota Studies called 'The Methodological Character of Theoretical Concepts'.[8] It seems that Maxwell was dissatisfied with Carnap's clarification of the methodological character of theoretical terms for the following two reasons. In the first place, according to Maxwell, Carnap's ontological asceticism fails to explain *why* certain theories 'work' whereas the simple ontological assumption that the entities referred to by these theories actually exist does provide such an explanation.

I could hardly believe that Maxwell would present such a threadbare argument, which he sets forth in all seriousness, twice in the course of his article.[9] Since the *only* valid reason for believing in the real existence of certain theoretical entities is, to use Maxwell's language, the fact that the theories referring to them are well-substantiated or 'work' (two expressions treated by Maxwell as synonymous) it is obviously arguing in a circle to look upon the existence of these entities as an explanation

---

[7] *Ibid.*, p. 3.

[8] Rudolf Carnap, 'The Methodological Character of Theoretical Concepts', *The Foundations of Science and the Concepts of Psychology and Psychoanalysis* (edited by H. Feigl & M. Scriven), Minnesota Studies in the Philosophy of Science, I, University of Minnesota Press, Minneapolis 1956, pp. 38–76.

[9] *Ibid.*, pp. 20 and 22.

for the fact that the theories 'work' as well as they do. I find it difficult to persuade myself that Maxwell was unaware of such an obvious flaw in his argument and that he is not hiding something up his sleeve. It is apparent from many passages in Maxwell's paper that he succumbed to the seductions of the *material mode of speech*, so brilliantly outlined by Carnap some thirty years ago.[10]

Maxwell's second reason is to be taken more seriously and I am prepared to accept it with reservations. Carnap's view of the methodological character of theoretical concepts is based on the existence of a dichotomy between *observational* and *theoretical*. As many thinkers before him, Maxwell doubts the validity of this dichotomy. It is, of course, legitimate to doubt the validity of any dichotomous polarization in a given conceptual continuum even though it can in many cases be justified, however difficult it may prove to be. It is not difficult, for example, to point out that there are goals for which it is worthwhile polarizing the concept of cleverness — in itself a multi-dimensional continuum — into the qualitative dichotomy Clever–Stupid. There are innumerable other goals for which it is preferable to work with the comparative concept More-Clever-Than, and finally, there are objectives to attain which it is necessary to deal with the quantitative concept Degree-Of-Cleverness (or Intelligence Quotient, as the psychologists call one of its measures). I agree with Maxwell that the dichotomy Observational–Theoretical is of little use, although for reasons other than those given by him and which in no way support his conclusions.

It seems to me that the dichotomy Observational–Theoretical is the result of confusing *two* different though somewhat related dichotomies — namely, the dichotomy between what I call the *observable* and the *unobservable* and the dichotomy between the *theoretical* and the *nontheoretical* (*atheoretical* or *pretheoretical*). The first dichotomy does not seem to me to be of any particular relevance for the types of meaning of the various concepts and here, as I intimated before, lies the area of my agreement with Maxwell. I fail to see the importance of distinguishing between an object that is visible to the naked eye and one tath reveals itself only under the microscope, a distinction made by some authors in an effort to find a line of demarcation between the observable and the unobservable. What, then, shall we say of eyeglasses, magnifying glasses, electronic microscopes, etc.? The distinction between a theoretical

---

[10] Rudolf Carnap, *The Logical Syntax of Language*, Kegan Paul, Trench, Trubner & Co., London 1937, § 78 ('Confusion in philosophy caused by the material mode of speech'). The German edition of the book appeared as early as 1934.

term that has a distinct meaning only within the framework of a definite theory, presented explicitly, implicitly or only in outline, and a non-theoretical term whose meaning is clear and independent of theory, seems to me to be valid and fruitful, although this dichotomy is nothing but a slice in a continuum. (In an earlier article[11] I used the term 'immediately intelligible' instead of 'non-theoretical', but this gave rise to so many semantic difficulties that I decided to change the term.) This dichotomy makes for more instructive and edifying formulations in the methodology of science than can be obtained with the help of the corresponding comparative or quantitative concepts. It is precisely this dichotomy, non-theoretical *vs.* theoretical, which such authors as Carnap, Hempel,[12] Braithwaite[13] and others must have had in mind even though, for definite historical reasons, they used the *Observational* vs. *Theoretical* terminology, and thereby prepared the way for the fusion (and confusion) with the sterile dichotomy between the *Observable* and *Unobservable*.

All such terms as 'observable' and 'unobservable', 'theoretical' and 'non-theoretical', are clearly theoretical terms (although Maxwell seems rather surprised at this fact[14]). I shall doubtlessly be asked what exactly I understand by the term 'non-theoretical', since the explanation I gave a moment ago will be found unsatisfactory in that it fails to provide a criterion by which to determine whether a given term is non-theoretical or not. An interesting dialectic movement, however, has been created here. Merely to ask a question of the type: 'What precisely do you mean by a certain term?' may almost by itself serve as a criterion for the theoretical nature of this term. Indeed, I would even go further and clarify the meaning of the term 'non-theoretical' by pointing out that it is meaningless to ask questions of this type regarding such a term, since it is immediately intelligible. I do not say that *whenever* it makes sense to ask 'What exactly do you mean by that term?' we have before us a theoretical expression, since the expression in question may be ambiguous and yet non-theoretical in all its different meanings. In this

---

[11] Yehoshua Bar-Hillel, 'A Prerequisite for Rational Philosophical Discussion', *Synthese*, 12, 1960, pp. 328–332 [reprinted here as Ch. 22].

[12] Carl G. Hempel, 'The Theoretician's Dilemma — A Study in the Logic of Theory Construction', *Concepts, Theories and the Mind–Body Problem* (edited by H. Feigl, M. Scriven & G. Maxwell), Minnesota Studies in the Philosophy of Science, II, 1958, pp. 37–98.

[13] Richard B. Braithwaite, *Scientific Explanation — A Study in the Function of Theory, Probability and Law in Science*, Cambridge University Press, Cambridge 1953.

[14] *Ibid.*, p. 2.

case the question should not be interpreted as meaning: 'In the framework of which theory are we to understand the expression you just used?' but simply: 'Which of the many ordinary and non-theoretical senses of your expression are you using at this particular moment?'

This observation might serve as an additional clarification of the term 'non-theoretical', although it does not completely answer the question as to the meaning of the methodological terms under discussion. Such an answer would necessitate setting forth the entire theory to which these terms belong. It would be uncharitable to expect me to present my total methodological theory at this time, particularly since I am not in possession of such a complete theory. As in almost all discussions on theoretical matters, we shall probably fail to agree as to the exact nature of the subject we are discussing at this very moment. To reduce the area of such disagreement I shall repeat the above clarification more precisely: *An expression is non-theoretical for a given speech community if it is understood by all members of this community to such a degree that there is no point in asking questions as to its meaning*. (It would be a commendable exercise to refine this definition further and thus make it less vulnerable to ambiguous expressions with two or more non-theoretical meanings. It should also be borne in mind that in natural languages the same expression can be at the same time theoretical and non-theoretical, that is, some *tokens* of the same expression-*type* are theoretical, whereas other tokens are non-theoretical, usually depending on the context. We all recall what we were told at school by our physics teacher about terms such as 'force' or 'work'.)

For a theory to be intelligible to the members of a given speech community, then, its terms must be either immediately intelligible or reducible to such terms, using 'reducible' in the strict meaning given to it by Carnap[15] and others. It is precisely this reduction which renders these terms significant, however incomplete and indirect it may turn out to be. I cannot imagine any other way which would convince me that I know what other people are talking about or even what I myself am talking about.

In accordance with our analysis, the degree of observability of a term does not directly determine the kind of *meaning* it has, although there can be no doubt that this degree is of paramount importance — and here I am in complete agreement with Maxwell — in whatever concerns *evidence* and *confirmation*. The morganatic marriage of the concepts

---

[15] For instance, in the article mentioned in note 8.

Meaningful and Confirmable in the third decade of this century will deteriorate still further as a consequence of this analysis, but few will have cause to regret this development.

The term 'table' and 'omega-minus particle' differ, then, with respect to their kind of intelligibility: the intelligibility of 'table' is direct, complete and free of theory, whereas the intelligibility of the term 'omega-minus particle' is indirect, incomplete and laden by theory. He who would attempt to express this methodological difference as a difference in the ontic status of the entities denoted by these expressions by claiming, for instance, that tables are more real than omega-minus particles, spreads confusion, while he who says that omega-minus particles are as real as tables, is no less culpable, since such a formulation obliterates the decisive distinction between theory-dependent and theory-independent expressions. To say that the entity phlogiston was as real as iron in 1780 when the phlogiston theory was considered to be well established, and that it gradually became less real in the following years when this theory had lost its prestige sounds like a sorry jest.

How is the realistic philosopher to describe a situation in which two different but equally cogent theories contain the same term 'electron'? Should he say: 'Electrons were just as real as tables, and electrons were just as real as tables', or perhaps: 'Electrons (in the sense of theory A) were just as real as tables, and electrons (in the sense of theory B) were etc.'; and should he add that: 'Electrons (in the sense of theory C) were slightly less real than tables', since theory C was at that time not as well confirmed as the other theories? Is it not simpler to renounce the realistic mode of speech altogether and describe the facts as they are by simply stating that at such and such a time there existed two equally well-substantiated theories of electrons and a third theory not as well confirmed?

The realistic mode of speech, as already noted above, is not only unable to provide us with a non-circular explanation for the fact that certain theories 'work', but it also serves as an inexhaustible source for pseudo-problems. This mode of speech is superfluous from a methodological point of view and must therefore be eliminated from methodological discussions. It could be shown, if time permitted, that a similar critique applies *mutatis mutandis* to the instrumentalistic mode of speech. I therefore believe that Nagel's characterization of the controversy between the neorealists and the instrumentalists as a 'disagreement in preferred modes of speech' was far too mild. In my opinion both preferred modes of speech should be eliminated from methodological discussions. I trust that I have succeeded in proving the thesis I had set forth at the outset, namely, that the controversy between metaphysical neorealism and metaphysical neopositivism is as futile as the old quarrels between realism and idealism.

Two remarks should be made by way of conclusion. First, I believe that my argument would not suffer even if the qualitative dichotomy Theoretical *vs.* Non-theoretical should turn out to be of no methodological importance. In that case we would be obliged to say that the word 'table' is highly non-theoretical and that its intelligibility is direct and complete, whereas the term 'omega-minus particle' is very highly theoretical and its intelligibility extremely indirect and incomplete. From this point I could have continued my counter-argument without any essential change in the formulation I preferred to use.

Secondly, it is quite possible that there should be a difference in the degree of enthusiam evinced by a researcher — whether he believes that a certain theory, which he himself was perhaps the first one to formulate, is an integral part of eternal absolute Truth, whether he looks upon it as a device which produces certain observation sentences when it is fed other observation sentences, or whether he entertains other feelings towards it which cannot be formulated in either of these two ways. It seems that these attitudes of the researchers have not been satisfactorily analysed, for which the psychologists, rather than the philosophers and methodologists, are to be held responsible. In the absence of authoritative findings, the prevalent view seems to be that the first attitude makes for greater sense of dedication and perseverance on the part of the researcher who would hence be more likely to achieve success so that such an attitude is to be encouraged in the interest of science and humanity. There may indeed have been cases in which a less fanatical belief in the truth of a certain theory ended in failure and obstinate perseverance resulted in success. I am quite certain, however, that there were just as many cases in which the researchers failed to develop adequate theories precisely because of their blind faith and the consequent lack of self-criticism. In the absence of reliable findings, I myself am inclined to believe that, on the whole, the harm done to research by the realistic beliefs of the researchers outweighed their benefits, but this opinion may well be the result of subjective impressions and personal temperament rather than an objective evaluation which, as I mentioned before, is non-existent. Be that as it may, I trust that I have made it plain that any inference from the usefulness of having certain beliefs to the truth of these beliefs, in the manner of William James, is fallacious. Even if it pays to be a neorealist — an hypothesis I am not as yet prepared to accept — and even if such reputable scholars as Maxwell are convinced that only neorealistic beliefs will provide explanations for facts that will otherwise remain inexplicable, all this does not invalidate our conclusion that from a philosophical and methodological point of view neorealism (just as instrumentalism) is an indefensible attitude, even in Nagel's disguise of a preferred mode of speech.

DO NATURAL LANGUAGES CONTAIN PARADOXES?

0. *Introduction*

It seems to be reasonably clear what it is for a *theory* to contain a paradox, viz., that from the axioms of this theory two contradictory (or at least contrary) theorems can be derived. One has also spoken of a *notion*, or *concept*, being paradoxical, approximately in the sense that the theory "of" that notion led to paradoxical results. When Bolzano and others were discussing the "Paradoxes of the Infinite",[1] they had in mind such facts as that, in the theory of infinite classes of numbers, one and the same class could have both as many members as some other class and more members than it. This seems, for instance, to be the case with regard to the classes $N = \{1, 2, 3,...\}$ and $E = \{2, 4, 6, ...\}$, since N seems to have more members than E, every member of E being a member of N but not vice versa, while N also has as many members as E, as can be shown by the existence of a one-to-one correspondence between those two classes:

$$1, 2, 3, ..., n, ...$$
$$\updownarrow \updownarrow \updownarrow \quad \updownarrow$$
$$2, 4, 6, ..., 2n, ...$$

However, the relations "having-as-many-members-as" and "having-more-members-than" seem to exclude each other.

Sometimes, a theory is charged with being paradoxical when one of its theorems seems to stand in opposition to some commonsensical truism. Einstein's Special Theory of Relativity has been said to yield the Twin Paradox, since it seems that, as a result of this theory, someone who winds up a long journey at speeds close to those of the speed of light returns younger than his twin brother who stayed home in the meantime, while commonsense would say "once twins, always twins", and nothing could change the fact that they are of the same age.

A theory — and, derivatively, a notion — that leads to a "real" paradox, i.e., to a contradiction that cannot be explained away, is *inconsistent*. Since inconsistent theories have obvious defects, methodologists of science have always taken great pains to try to prove the absolute con-

---

[1] Bolzano's book on this topic, *Paradoxien des Unendlichen*, appeared posthumously in 1851. An English translation appeared in 1950.

sistency of certain theories or — since such proofs were often either very difficult or even impossible — at least their consistency relative to some other theories; for many purposes, even to know that theory A is no more paradoxical than theory B is of considerable importance.

1. *Recent History*

The famous paradox of *The Liar* (whose oldest version goes back to the fifth century B.C.) can perhaps best be exhibited as follows: Someone says, on a certain occasion, "What I am saying right now is false", and nothing else. The reader, who has never before been through the motions, is cordially invited to make it clear to himself that what the man was saying was true if and only if it was false and therefore that it was both true and false. This paradox has been interpreted as showing that the notion of truth (and falsity) is paradoxical, or that the theory of truth, as embedded in our ordinary language, is paradoxical and therefore inconsistent.

I am not quite sure at what time philosophers and logicians started talking about *languages* being inconsistent and containing paradoxes. It stands to reason that this probably happened at about the same time when uninterpreted calculi began to be called 'languages', i.e., some thirty-five years ago. And again I presume that in the beginning it was to such constructed, formal language-systems that the terms 'consistent' and 'inconsistent' were applied, and only at some later stage was this usage extended to natural languages. The picture behind this usage was, again presumably, that each language, even an utterly uninterpreted calculus, had to contain at least a logic, i.e., a set of rules, known as rules of inference (proof, transformation, deduction, derivation), which would allow us to deduce (or, perhaps, "to deduce") certain sentences (or "sentences") — the conclusions — from other sentences — the premises. Those sentences that turned out to be "deducible from the null-set of premises" — by fiat or by whatever other way — were then the logical truths of that language. When a certain sentence and its negation (or "negation") turned out to belong both to the set of logical truths — as could be shown to happen on occasion for certain such "languages" — these languages were thereby shown to be inconsistent, since they contained logical paradoxes. (In this description, I am glossing over very many details that would deserve discussion in a more thorough treatment. Such discussions, however, are readily available in the literature and would be too technical for our present purposes.)

Sometimes, an interpreted language-system that was irreproachable as to its logic turned out to be paradoxical when it was considered to contain its own syntax and semantics, e.g., a "theory of truth" or "theory of designation", or something of the kind, applying to itself. If such a system could have been shown, for instance, to allow for the formation of an expression that turned out to be a sentence, under the syntactical rules of that language, and whose interpretation, under the semantic rules, was that this very same sentence is false, then a rigorous version of The Liar paradox would have arisen in that language, proving its inconsistency.

It was only natural that logicians should at that stage have started asking themselves the question whether natural languages, too, were not inconsistent, in particular whether semantic paradoxes of The Liar type could not be derived in them. (Of course, The Liar was originally derived through the use of a natural language, namely, classical Greek, but at that time the paradox was not blamed on the language and it did not occur to anybody to draw from this derivation the conclusion that Greek was inconsistent.) I am not sure who exactly it was who had the (somewhat doubtful) privilege of having asked this question for the first time. From the remarks of Tarski [14: 155–157; 15: 371][2] it is not quite clear to what degree the responsibility lies with St. Leśniewski, who began to lecture on these issues at the University of Warsaw in 1919, rather than with his colleagues, J. Łukasiewicz and T. Kotarbiński. The year 1919 seems, at any rate, to be the earliest date at which this question was raised by the Warsaw-Lwów school of philosophers and logicians. I am not aware of any earlier treatment that can be viewed as more than a vague anticipation of the problem.

I do not know what were the exact answers given by Leśniewski, Łukasiewicz and Kotarbiński to this question of whether natural languages contain semantic paradoxes, if it indeed was put in this form at all. (Incidentally, the terms used, in Polish or German, in this connection were not, in general, the literal translations of "natural language", but rather terms that were later translated into English as "everyday language", "the language of everyday speech" and "ordinary language". Moreover, usually the singular was used, almost creating the impression that when talking about our everyday affairs in English, Polish or German we were using different dialects of the same "language of everyday speech". The lack of linguistic sophistication shown by this attitude is amazing.

---

[2] Read: Item no. 14 in the Bibliography, pp. 155–157 and item no. 15, p. 371. Similarly for other such references in brackets.

None of the authors found it necessary to quote a single linguist. But this is a topic that should be elaborated on some other occasion.) Western philosophers who took up this question referred to Tarski [14; 15] in this connection, who started working on the concept of truth in everyday and formalized languages in 1929.

2. *The Claims for the Inconsistency of Natural Languages*

Now, Tarski himself had a definite tendency to answer our question in the positive, but was rather guarded about it. In the Introduction to [14] we find him saying that "with respect to this [colloquial] language, not only does the definition of truth seem to be impossible, but even the consistent use of this concept in conformity with the laws of logic" [14: 153]. A few pages later [14: 162] he claims that "Our discussions so far entitle us in any case to say that *the attempt to construct a correct semantical definition of the expression 'true sentence' meets with very real difficulties*". After showing that "the attempt to set up a structural definition of the term 'true sentence'—applicable to colloquial language—is confronted with insuperable difficulties" [14: 164],[3] he comes to the conclusion that "there is no satisfactory way of solving our problem" and continues to give "important arguments of a general nature" to this effect. I shall quote the next two paragraphs in full.

A characteristic feature of colloquial language (in contrast to various scientific languages) is its universality. It would not be in harmony with the spirit of this language if in some other language a word occurred which could not be translated into it; it could be claimed that "if we can speak meaningfully about anything at all, we can also speak about it in colloquial language". If we are to maintain this universality of everyday language in connexion with semantical investigations, we must, to be consistent, admit into the language, in addition to its sentences and other expressions, also the names of these sentences and expressions, and sentences containing these names, as well as such semantic expressions as "true sentence", "name", "denote", etc. But it is presumably just this universality of everyday language which is the primary source of all semantical antinomies, like the antinomies of the liar or of hetero-

---

[3] That such a thinker as Tarski should have spent so much time on speculating about the possibility of coming up with a structural definition of 'true sentence' for natural languages, is nothing short of amazing, even taking into consideration the fact that almost forty years have since passed. And it is almost incomprehensible that he should have regarded such a task as only "almost hopeless" and given as reasons for this evaluation the "openness" of natural languages — for a discussion of this issue, cf. [6: 56] — and the indefiniteness of the notion of sentence rather than that whether it is true that John is hungry at a certain time depends on certain physiological facts and not only on the structure of the sentences invoked.

logical words. These antinomies seem to provide a proof that every language which is universal in the above sense, and for which the normal laws of logic hold, must be inconsistent. This applies especially to the formulation of the antinomy of the liar which I have given on pages 157 and 158, and which contains no quotation-function with variable argument. If we analyse this antinomy in the above formulation we reach the conviction that no consistent language can exist for which the usual laws of logic hold and which at the same time satisfies the following conditions: (I) for any sentence which occurs in the language a definite name of this sentence also belongs to the language; (II) every expression formed from (2) [i.e., from "*x is a true sentence if and only if p*"] by replacing the symbol "p" by any sentence of the language and the symbol "x" by a name of this sentence is to be regarded as a true sentence of this language; (III) . . .

If these observations are correct, then *the very possibility of a consistent use of the expression "true sentence" which is in harmony with the laws of logic and the spirit of everyday language seems to be very questionable, and consequently the same doubt attaches to the possibility of constructing a correct definition of this expression.*

In [15: 347], Tarski states the following:

The problem of the definition of truth obtains a precise meaning and can be solved in a rigorous way only for those languages whose structure has been exactly specified. For other languages — thus, for all natural, "spoken" languages — the meaning of the problem is more or less vague, and its solution can have only an approximate character. Roughly speaking, the approximation consists in replacing a natural language (or a portion of it in which we are interested) by one whose structure is exactly specified, and which diverges from the given language "as little as possible".

He winds up the discussion — to the degree that it concerns us — with the following passage which shall be quoted in full (with only two inconsequential sentences omitted):

If we now analyse the assumptions which lead to the antinomy of the liar we notice the following:

(I) We have implicitly assumed that the language in which the antinomy is constructed contains, in addition to its expressions, also the names of these expressions, as well as semantic terms such as the term "*true*" referring to sentences of this language; we have also assumed that all sentences which determine the adequate usage of this term can be asserted in the language. A language with these properties will be called "*semantically closed*".

(II) We have assumed that in this language the ordinary laws of logic hold . . .

. . . the assumptions (I) and (II) prove essential. Since every language which satisfies both of these assumptions is inconsistent we must reject at least one of them.

It would be superfluous to stress here the consequences of rejecting the assumption (II), that is, of changing our logic (supposing this were possible) even in its more elementary and fundamental parts. We thus consider only the possibility of rejecting the assumption (I). Accordingly, we decide *not to use any language which is semantically closed* in the sense given.

This restriction would of course be unacceptable for those who, for reasons which are not clear to me, believe that there is only one "genuine" language (or, at least, that all "genuine" languages are mutually translatable). However, this restriction does not affect the needs or interests of science in any essential way. The languages (either the formalized languages or — what is more frequently the case — the portions of everyday language) which are used in scientific discourse do not have to be semantically closed. This is obvious in case linguistic phenomena and, in particular, semantic notions do not enter in any way into the subject-matter of a science; for in such a case the language of this science does not have to be provided with any semantic terms at all. However, we shall see in the next section how semantically closed languages can be dispensed with even in those scientific discussions in which semantic notions are essentially involved.

The problem arises as to the position of everyday language with regard to this point. At first blush it would seem that this language satisfies both assumptions (I) and (II), and that therefore it must be inconsistent. But actually the case is not so simple. Our everyday language is certainly not one with an exactly specified structure. We do not know precisely which expressions are sentences, and we know even to a smaller degree which sentences are to be taken as assertible. Thus the problem of consistency has no exact meaning with respect to this language. We may at best only risk the guess that a language whose structure has been exactly specified and which resembles our everyday language as closely as possible would be inconsistent.

In spite of Tarski's clear *caveats*, he has been quoted many times as having shown the inconsistency of natural languages. One otherwise very careful writer has it [10: 65]:

Now it is clear from the work of Tarski that the language of everyday speech is "semantically closed" and hence inconsistent.

True enough, a couple of years later, the same author has a more cautious formulation [1: 44]: "... it seems very likely that natural language is inconsistent". Six years later, he has become still more cautious. After presenting once more the arguments for the inconsistency of natural languages, he continues [12: 21].

It is not essential here to take sides one way or another concerning the consistency of natural language. One cannot settle this issue definitively perhaps until much more is known about the precise syntactical and semantical structure involved ...

All precautions and provisos are thrown to the winds by another author in an article written for the *Encyclopaedia Britannica*. After having derived a Liar type paradox, he goes on [9: 313]:

> The above paradoxes show ... that English is inconsistent. Since it can be shown that in an inconsistent system anything at all, true and false, can be proven, we shall have to conclude that ordinary English is a language not suitable for logical arguments.

(I cannot help repeating a comment I have already made once before [3] on this quotation, namely, that the whole article aimed — among other things — at showing that English is not a language suitable for logical arguments is an outstanding specimen of a series of logical arguments presented in impeccable English.)

Stroll [13], interestingly enough, is ready to grant that Everyday Language is inconsistent but wants to dispute the conclusion which Martin, Kemeny and others draw from this fact, viz., that if one wants to do philosophy in a clear-minded way, one has to use concepts explicated in formalized languages. I shall not discuss his contribution since I shall insist that there is no good reason at all to grant the inconsistency of natural languages.

3. *The Counterclaims*

More specifically, I make the following three claims:

(1) The question of whether natural languages contain semantic paradoxes (or any paradoxes, for that matter) should not be treated as a question of empirical fact. It can be decided in the negative a priori, though only at a considerable price.

(2) Since such a decision can be made, it should be made.

(3) The price, though high, is tolerable and, more importantly, one that has to be paid in any case, for independent reasons.

Let me elaborate.

There are, of course, very good reasons for regarding natural languages as being "semantically closed" and even as being (potentially) universal, though a good amount of care has to be taken in the interpretation of these expressions. But there are no good reasons for regarding these properties as responsible for the occurrence of semantic paradoxes in natural languages other than that this is indeed the case for almost all constructed language-systems investigated so far. As a matter of fact, the analogy breaks down at the very first step. Though "a (declarative) sentence must be either true or false" in such language-systems, it is simply false — ridiculously false, I am tempted to say — to assume that this should hold also for natural languages. Leaving aside all those innumerably many sentences which might be too vague, obscure, indefinite, etc. to have the epithets 'true' and 'false' applied to them *simpli-*

citer, there are many other classes of declarative sentences to whose members truth-values are not applicable. This point has been argued so many times during the last two decades that I shall briefly mention only two such classes here. The one consists of all those sentences whose standard use is performative (and not constative) such as all sentences starting with "I hereby . . .", e.g., "I hereby declare the meeting open", or "I hereby solemnly promise to serve my country to the best of my abilities", for which it would be ridiculous to ask for their truth-value. The other is the vast class of indexical sentences whose very reference is context-dependent — think of "I am hungry" or "It will be raining here tomorrow" — so that, depending on the context, some tokens of these sentence-types are true and others false (all this according to a mode of speech which I shall shortly urge to abandon altogether), making it again pointless to ask for the truth-values of the sentences (-types) as such [1].

But rather than polemicize against the conception that it is sentences which are the (primary) carriers of truth-value in natural languages — mainly because this polemic has already been carried out many times before in the last years — let me only mention an alternative conception which seems to me to be in an incomparably better position to account for our linguistic intuitions and which, almost as an afterthought, does away with the very possibility of regarding natural languages as paradoxical.

The alternative conception consists in drawing a sharp distinction between

declarative sentences	and	statements
interrogative sentences	and	questions
imperative sentences	and	commands
.	.	.
.	.	.
.	.	.

and, where necessary, between

uttering[4] a declarative sentence	and	making a statement
uttering an interrogative sentence	and	asking a question
uttering an imperative sentence	and	giving a command
.	.	.
.	.	.
.	.	.

---

[4] I am using, throughout this paper, the word 'utter' and its derivatives to stand for any type of linguistic performance, not necessarily through the use of the vocal cords. Writing, typing, printing, Morse, semaphor, etc. are included in uttering.

Declaratives, interrogatives, etc. are linguistic entities, whether, *qua* tokens, concrete and occupying a certain position in (space and) time, or, *qua* types, abstract. Statements, questions, etc. are non-linguistic entities, and the type-token distinction makes no sense for them.

Statements are often, but not always, made by uttering declarative sentences, and declarative sentences are often, but not always, uttered in order to make statements. However, a sentence uttered by A in order to make a certain statement may be understood by B to make a different statement or even as having been uttered for a different purpose altogether. Finally, A, by uttering a certain sentence, may have intended to make a statement but may not have succeeded in doing so. (Somebody may perform certain acts with the intention of catching a lion but not succeed; if his intention is to catch a unicorn, he cannot succeed.[5])

Truth and falsity should be regarded as primarily properties of statements and only derivatively as properties of certain sentences, namely, of those (declarative) sentences of some formalized language or of standardized (or "sterilized", as I often say in front of my students) natural languages which, by convention or otherwise, can be taken as rendering these statements in a many-to-one fashion. To illustrate (though much more will have to be said on some other occasion to make the very many issues invoked here totally clear): If John Doe utters, on February 16, 1966, at 1:30 PM (in a certain situation which shall not be further specified here), a token of the English sentence "I am hungry", he will be taken, by those who hear him utter this sentence, to have made a certain statement (and to have claimed that this statement is true). (That he may be taken to have perhaps also performed certain other linguistic acts, is immaterial for our considerations at present.) When asked to specify the statement made, this request can be fulfilled in many different ways. If this specification is carried out by saying, e.g., "The statement made was that John Doe be hungry on February 16, 1966, at 1:30 PM" (with an appropriate explanation for the peculiarities of "standardized" English of this particular brand, containing, among other features, no tensed verbs), then the sentence used after 'that', namely, "John Doe be hungry on February 16, 1963, at 1:30 PM" can be taken to be itself either true or false, since, by convention, such declarative sentences will be used to make the appropriate statement. Analogous conventions will hold, *mutatis mutandis*, for standardized interrogatives and questions, standardized imperatives and commands,

---

[5] To all this, cf. [2; 3; 5].

etc. (Let me repeat that I am not unaware of the innumerably many problems lurking about here. But it is just impossible to treat them all at a time in restricted space.) If the specification is performed by saying, "The statement made was the one always made by a proper utterance of the sentence 'H (jd, $t_{160219661330}$)' in the constructed language-system L_{792}" then it would be foolish not to talk, for the sake of simplicity, about the truth and falsity of the *sentence* "H (jd, t...)", in addition to the truth and falsity of the *statement*.

Notice that the transition from statements to sentences is absolutely necessary for certain purposes such as the application of formal logic, say, for talking about the validity of certain arguments. Statements have, of course, no form. It is only sentences — and other linguistic entities —, whether in natural or constructed languages, which possess form. Sentences, but not statements, may have subject-predicate form, be atomic, molecular, quantified, etc. The same statement can be made by sentences of very many forms, perhaps even of any form.

When a declarative sentence in some natural language is uttered, it always makes sense to inquire whether the utterer intended thereby to make a statement, whether a statement was indeed made, and which, if any, statement was understood by a specific listener to have been made on this occasion.

When someone enters a room in which there are two blackboards and sees written on one of them "2 + 2 = 5" and on the other "The sentence written on the other blackboard is false" he may — and under many circumstances almost automatically will — understand what is written on the second blackboard as making the statement that the statement made by uttering "2 + 2 = 5" — in general, or under certain circumstances — is false. Of course, it is quite possible that at the time the second sentence was being written on the second blackboard some quite different sentence was visible on the first blackboard, etc.

Now, when someone enters a room with only one blackboard and sees there written "The sentence written on this blackboard is false" and nothing else, he will in all likelihood assume that some other sentence, previously visible on this blackboard, has been erased in the meantime. If assured that this is not what has happened but that somebody else, a few minutes ago, entered the room and wrote that sentence on the otherwise utterly blank blackboard, he will — outside of a logic class — wait for some explanation and not worry, unless forced to do so. He may, of course, somehow come to believe that a statement was intended to be made by the utterance on the blackboard and, if asked which statement, might perhaps answer, "The statement that the statement made by the utterance written on the blackboard is false" (if he is sufficiently sophisticated to use this mode of speech) or something to this effect. When further pressed for some more specification, he might resent the pressure and insist that there is no need to comply with the request just as there is no need to comply with the request to be more specific when one utters "The first statement made by Julius Caesar on his 45th birthday was false." But just as one is entitled to doubt whether Caesar, on his 45th birthday, made any statement at all (for all we know, he might have slept through this whole day after a rather heavy drinking celebration the night before), so it is of course perfectly legitimate to doubt whether the man who wrote that utterance on the blackboard really intended to make a statement or — if one has outside information about the reality of this intention — whether he succeeded in doing so. Whereas in the case of Caesar, we might either already have, or in due time come to have, sufficient information to decide that in all likelihood Caesar made a lot of statements on that ominous day, it turns out, strangely and interestingly enough, that in the blackboard case the situation is different. Not only is it impossible, in principle under the given circumstances, to become more specific about the statement made by the utterance on the blackboard, but the assumption that a statement was made at all leads to contradiction, with the result that we can tell a priori that if a statement was intended to be made, this intention ended in failure.

Some people might find it disturbing that, in the blackboard story, there was no more direct way to determine that no statement was made by the utterance in question, other than by deriving a contradiction from the contrary assumption. Imagine, they might say (and have said on occasion) that in that utterance 'false' were replaced by 'true' and we would be out of luck and could never decide whether a statement has really been made on that occasion or not.

However, I would insist that recognizing the essentially non-recursive character of the notion of statement in natural languages. i.e., the non-existence of a mechanical procedure for deciding whether, given an utterance, a statement was made by it, is just another part of the price that has to be paid for keeping our natural languages consistent.

I can now be very short with my third claim. Even if there were no threat of paradoxes, the distinctions between sentence and statement, as well as the other distinctions drawn above — and, doubtless, many more — would have to be made anyway in order to get along best with the facts of life. It is somewhat sad that one has had to wait for the British "ordinary language" philosophers to drive this point forcefully home, but I have yet to find a linguist who would disagree, once this issue is clearly explained to him. Let me repeat, for the last time, that realizing the existence and importance of these distinctions is only the first step towards realizing the existence of innumerably many problems, many of which could not even have been posed before with sufficient succinctness.

As to the non-recursiveness of the notion of statement, the only really disturbing fact about it is that so many people still find it disturbing. Statement is, of course, a highly theoretical notion [7] in the field of pragmatics (or psycho-linguistics) of natural languages. Only very little methodological sophistication is required to realize that no decision procedure should be expected to exist for such a notion. I presume that the main reason for the prevalence of the belief to the contrary is that, due to a very long tradition, which has of course also found its expression in the ordinary use of these terms, 'statement' and 'declarative sentence' are still somehow regarded to be synonyms. As to the notion of 'sentence' in general and of 'declarative sentence' in particular, many linguists feel today [8], contrary to a feeling widespread a few years ago [4], that these notions, for natural languages, could (or perhaps, rather, should) turn out to be recursive in words,[6] so that in principle at least the question whether a given sequence of words in some natural language is a sentence should allow for a mechanical decision procedure. Tarski's previously mentioned remarks to the contrary might perhaps better be explained as referring to the notion of "uttering a sentence". For this notion, indeed, being again a pragmatic one, one should not expect a decision procedure to exist. Whether someone in making a sequence of vocal noises has or has not uttered a well-formed (grammatical) sentence is not mechanically decidable since there exists no mechanical procedure for determining which exactly was the sequence of words realized by his utterance.

4. *Summary*

In summary, let me state that I first tried to trace the origin of this curious formulation "inconsistency of natural languages" which, if I am not mistaken, has always been used only by philosophers but never

---

[6] Roughly speaking, for concept A to be recursive in concept B means that, on the assumption that there exists a decision procedure for B-hood, there also exists a decision procedure for A-hood.

by any linguist of repute. I then tried to point out how the philosopher's argument for his claim that natural languages contain semantic paradoxes and are therefore inconsistent can be met — or rather left without any basis — by making, among others, a clear distinction between sentences and statements, realizing that it is to statements that, primarily, truth-values have to be assigned and that the supposedly paradoxical situations can be shown to evaporate by realizing that in those situations no statements had been made at all, so that the question of truth and falsity does not arise to begin with. As a result of this view, but also for independent reasons, it turns out that the notions of "statement", "making a statement" and "uttering a sentence" are non-recursive so that no mechanical decision procedure exists for their application. This result, though perhaps surprising and distressing for those logicians and linguists who still keep believing in reductionist behaviourism and operationalism, is in full concordance with more advanced methodological views. "Inconsistency — no, undecidability — si!"

REFERENCES

[1] BAR-HILLEL, Y.: Indexical expressions. Mind 63, 359 (1954) [reprinted here as Ch. 5].
[2] — : Three remarks on linguistic fundamentals. Word 13, 323 (1957) [reprinted here as Ch. 28].
[3] — : New light on the 'Liar'. Analysis 18, 1 (1957) [reprinted here as Ch. 21].
[4] — : Decision procedures for structure in natural languages. Logique et Analyse 2, 19 (1959) [reprinted here as Ch. 29].
[5] — : Remarks on Carnap's Logical Syntax of Language. The Philosophy of Rudolf Carnap (P. A. SCHILPP, ed.). The Library of Living Philosophers, vol. IX. La Salle, Illinois: Open Court 1963, p. 519 [reprinted here as Ch. 11].
[6] — : Language and Information. Reading, Mass.: Addison-Wesley 1964.
[7] CARNAP, R.: The methodological character of theoretical concepts. Minnesota Studies in the Philosophy of Science. Vol. I. University of Minnesota Press 1956, p. 38.
[8] CHOMSKY, N.: Aspects of the Theory of Syntax. Cambridge, Mass.: M.I.T. Press 1965.
[9] KEMENY, J. G.: Semantics as a branch of logic. Encyclopedia Britannica 20, 313 (1957).
[10] MARTIN, R. M.: Some comments on truth and designation. Analysis 10, 65 (1950).
[11] — : On 'Analytic'. Philosophical Studies 3, 44 (1952).
[12] — : Truth and Denotation. University of Chicago Press 1958.
[13] STROLL, A.: Is everyday language inconsistent? Mind 63, 219 (1954).
[14] TARSKI, A.: The concept of truth in formalized languages. Chapter VIII of Logic, Semantics, Metamathematics. Oxford: Clarendon Press 1956. (The German original appeared in Studia Philosophica 1 (1936).)
[15] — : The semantic conception of truth. Philosophy and Phenomenological Research. 4, 341 (1944).

METHODOLOGY OF LINGUISTICS

CYBERNETICS AND LINGUISTICS

This is not a scholarly essay. There will be no footnotes and only few references to the rich literature covering the topic of the essay. I hope someone else will in due time take upon himself to deal with the subject of the impact of cybernetics on linguistics with all the scholarship and objectivity it deserves. I intend to represent here a highly subjective picture of the encounter of someone, who is neither a cybernetician nor a linguist, with these fields at the time when, and the place where, they smashed into each other in an explosion of fireworks and almost unlimited hopes, and who continued to watch this encounter after the excitement was over, the fire extinguished, the great hopes subdued and a relatively impartial attitude could again be taken.

The tale to be told will be "highly subjective" in the sense that it will be told from the point of view of one onlooker and partial participant, but it will try to be objective in the sense of self-critical. No attempt will be made to play down the fact that I myself was led into confusion by the strong surrounding currents and was responsible to a degree for increasing this confusion and leading others into blind alleys from which some never returned.

The justification for telling this tale is not only historical — as such it is probably premature and too one-sided — but mainly that it is my strong impression that many of my colleagues are still nursing false hopes and wasting much of their ingenuity and time barking up the wrong tree.

My interests in the workings of language are old and deeprooted. While still in high school, I was intrigued by the formal aspects of grammar and by problems of translation. In the autumn of 1935, at the beginning of my second year of studies at the Hebrew University of Jerusalem, I happened to get hold of the first three volumes of *Erkenntnis*, edited by Carnap and Reichenbach, the two most prominent members of the Vienna Circle and the Berlin Group, respectively, and the spiritual leaders of logical positivism at the time. For two weeks I devoured these volumes, hardly doing anything else beyond the absolute necessities. The effect of this "reading period" was nothing short of a revelation. Never before had I come across such an unrelenting strife toward clarity and testability in matters philosophical as in the articles of Carnap in these volumes; never before had I seen such a powerful denunciation of metaphysical obscurantism combined with a thorough understanding and analysis of its seductive appeal as in the contributions of Carnap, Neurath, Schlick and Reichenbach published there.

The year after, in 1936/37, Professor Abraham A. Fraenkel conducted a seminar on Carnap's *Logische Syntax der Sprache*. For the next couple of years, I was seldom seen without a copy of this book under my arm. My fellow-students dubbed it "Bar-Hillel's Bible". It was doubtless the most influential book I read in my life, and a good part of my work is directly or indirectly related to it. Never since has my interest in language abated for a minute.

It was while working in 1938 on my Master's Thesis on *The Antinomies of Logic* that I came across Ajdukiewicz's article "Die syntaktische Konnexität" which was later to become a major factor in my work on logical and algebraic linguistics. In 1938, however, my knowledge of linguistics was precisely nil, so that I did not realize the importance of this article for that field. Neither, I gather, did Ajdukiewicz himself fully grasp its linguistic potential at the time.

In the following years, while teaching mathematics at various high schools in Jerusalem, I began working on my Ph.D. Thesis. The first blue-covered booklets of the *International Encyclopedia of Unified Science*, and the contributions there by Carnap, Morris and Bloomfield, kept the fire of my interest in language burning. I had already written a few dozen pages on the pragmatics of adult learning of a totally new language — a subject that used to fascinate Carnap and which he had treated, though for illustrative purposes only, in *Foundations of Logic and Mathematics*, and which was later taken up by W. V. Quine in his discussion of "jungle linguistics" in *Word and Object* — when the Africa Corps of Field Marshal Rommel came, in 1942, uncomfortably close to the gates of Palestine.

When I returned, in 1946, after four years of service to teaching high school and to my thesis, much of what I had planned to say in it had been said in the meantime by other people. The chapters of Moore and Black in *The Philosophy of Bertrand Russell* gave my thoughts a new turn. The question of the amount of philosophical insight one can obtain from direct analysis of natural language and ordinary speech, with common sense and linguistic sensitivity serving as the main tools of investigation, in comparison with what can be done by indirect approach through logically rigorous constructed language systems, the approach favoured by Carnap and the "logical (re-)constructionists" in general, came to the fore and remained since then in the centre of my interest. Strange to say, at that time it never seriously occurred to me that there could be a third approach, namely the one attacking natural languages and ordinary speech with the best methods of theoretical and statistical linguistics, respectively. But then both these disciplines were still in a rather poor state in the late forties.

Some of Black's remarks on Russell's Theory of Logical Types made me go back to what Carnap had to say in *Der logische Aufbau der Welt* on the topic of *Sphärenvermengung* (a type of philosophically important fallacy which was twenty years later rediscovered by Ryle as "category mistake", apparently without any awareness of Carnap's prior profound investigations) and of the relations Syntactically Related and Isogenous, to his treatment of syntactic categories published between these books, and to Ajdukiewicz's discussion of syntactic connexity based on a theory of semantic categories adapted from Leśniewski. Leśniewski in his turn had departed from Husserl's *Bedeutungskategorien* which could be partly traced back to ideas of Aristotle. This whole topic of "syntactic categories" fascinated me to such a degree that I decided to write my Thesis on a *Theory of Syntactic Categories* (in Hebrew). A greatly revised version of the second chapter of this Thesis, together with some additional philosophical discussions, was later, in 1950, published as "On syntactical categories", in the *Journal of Symbolic Logic*.

I am afraid that my linguistic views of that time, though probably not more naïve than those of any other contemporary philosopher or logician, were still deplorably naïve. I thought that by going over large texts in any given unknown language, segmented into sentences and words, not only should it be possible to arrive at a categorization of the word sequences occurring in the text, which is trivial, but that this procedure would also yield a grammar of the whole language, whose adequacy would increase with the length of the text and in some cases converge to "the" grammar of the language. But worse, I was then — and still for some years to come — under the illusion, shared with all logicians and most linguists who cared to think on that issue, that all sentences of natural languages are "parsible", i.e. can be split up, according to definite rules, into two or more consecutive and contiguous immediate constituents, each of which, unless already itself a final element (a word, or a similar unit), is again segmentable into its immediate constituents until the final nested segmentation is obtained, and that by this procedure the whole syntactic structure of these sentences is exhaustively determined.

To put my linguistic view of 1950 in terms which have become fashionable since the epoch-making appearance of Noam Chomsky's *Syntactic*

Structures in 1957, I believed then both that natural languages are adequately representable by *context-free phrase-structure grammars* and that there exist approximative and self-correcting discovery procedures for these grammars. I am afraid that both these prejudices were strengthened by talking with Zellig Harris during his visit to Palestine in 1947 and by reading in manuscript some chapters of his classic *Methods in Structural Linguistics*, whose first edition was to appear only three years later. If I have the facts straight, around 1948 Harris began his investigations into what he called *discourse analysis* which led him later to the development of *transformational grammars* that transcend the framework of phrase-structure grammars in general, including their *context-sensitive* type, and thereby present a clear departure from *immediate constituent* type grammars, which at that time dominated linguistic thinking in the United States and many other countries.

Of all these developments I was to learn only after I came to the United States in 1950. In the meantime, however, the talks with Harris shattered my linguistic naïveté and convinced me that the neglect of linguistics, so perspicuous in the works of such authors as Carnap, Ajdukiewicz and Tarski in the field of logical syntax and semantics, as Wittgenstein, Ryle and Austin in so-called linguistic philosophy, and as Morris (though to a lesser degree) in semiotics, could not but lead to distorted and partly irrelevant results in philosophy of language. Even Reichenbach's famous Chapter VII, entitled "Analysis of conversational language", of his *Elements of Symbolic Logic*, presenting in its more than one hundred pages the by far most extensive treatment of the grammar of natural languages from the standpoint of a modern symbolic logician, owes its not inconsiderable shortcomings mostly to linguistic innocence — the only linguist of stature quoted in it being Jespersen. I think that the only work by a modern professional linguist I had studied in some depth before the talks with Harris, was Bloomfield's little contribution to the *Encyclopedia of Unified Science*, published in 1939. This booklet showed a surprising convergence between the ways of thinking of at least certain circles of American linguists and those of, say, Carnap, and I made a mental note to pursue this issue further sometime. But only in 1951 did I find the time to do so.

A fellowship from the Hebrew University had enabled me to go to Chicago to spend the winter term of 1950/51 with Carnap. It was then that Carnap, in connection with certain ideas he intended to incorporate in the second volume of his *Logical Foundations of Probability*, called my attention to Information Theory, in the sense of Statistical Theory of Communication, as discussed in the two classics, *Cybernetics* by Wiener and *The Mathematical Theory of Communication* by Shannon and Weaver, that had appeared during the two preceding years, and indicated that some of the formulations developed in these new fields should be transferred to a rigorous treatment of *semantic information*. I don't quite remember in what form Wiener's revolutionary ideas had come to my attention in 1949 while I was still in Jerusalem. I might have seen the book *Cybernetics* itself, more likely it was some review of it.

The ideas of cybernetics fitted in rather well with my general utter distrust of metaphysics and speculative philosophy, which has never wavered, and with my increasing interest in the use of mechanical methods in logic and linguistics. I have already mentioned that at the time I still believed in the possibility of finding a mechanical discovery procedure for grammars, given long enough corpora, and I had already heard from Harris that he considered using the newly developed electronic computers for just this purpose. I myself had always regarded it of great importance, for testing the validity of a certain consideration, to perform the *Gedankenexperiment* of telling a machine how to carry out this consideration, and I was enchanted by the idea that some such experiments could now be performed in the flesh rather than only in the spirit. As a matter of fact, one of the persons, after Carnap, I wanted to meet most in the States was Wiener. With this aim in mind, I left Chicago for Cambridge, Massachusetts, in March, 1951. My fellowship money was touching bottom, and I was badly in need of a paying job. Carnap had advised me to contact Walter Pitts, who was a former student of his and had a few years before collaborated with Warren McCulloch in writing a rather obscure but still extremely influential article that paved the way for the Theory of Automata and thereby for what was to become one of the major parts of Cybernetics. Pitts had joined the Massachusetts Institute of Technology (MIT) in order to write his Thesis with Wiener (a task which remained unfinished till this very day). He introduced me to Jerome Wiesner who was then Associate Director of the renowned Research Laboratory of Electronic (RLE) (and became later Director of the Office of Science and Technology to the President of the United States). Wiesner offered me on the spot a research associateship with RLE, thereby starting an association that has never since been severed.

To my dismay, starting research at RLE failed to establish contact with Wiener who had been strongly connected with this Laboratory for many years. Unfortunately for me, Wiener had just shortly before my arrival severed his contacts with the RLE, because, if I remember correctly, McCulloch had been invited to join it, and Wiener did not see eye-to-eye with McCulloch. Wiener refused to see me, a member of RLE, for many months, and it was only after a year or so that we met over a chess board at the MIT Faculty Club. Quickly, friendly relations were established, but by then my interests and research work had switched to fields in which Wiener was less interested. Talking to Wiener or listening to his lectures and discussions, something I did thereafter on many occasions, was always extremely stimulating. But I was unable to follow most of his technical stuff, because of an insufficient knowledge of mathematics, and a good amount of his less technical discussions, in particular those centering around information and its measures, left me unconvinced.

In spite of the fact that Wiener himself did not participate in the activities going on at RLE, his impact was felt everywhere, as was Shannon's, who was a graduate of MIT, and was later to join RLE but at that time was doing his research rather with the Bell Telephone Company. There was an ubiquitous and overwhelming feeling around the Laboratory that with the new insights of cybernetics and the newly developed techniques of information theory the final breakthrough towards a full understanding of the complexities of communication "in the animal and the machine" had been achieved. Linguists and psychologists, philosophers and sociologists alike hailed the entrance of the electrical engineer and the probability mathematician *into the* communication field as the forebodings of the millennium. Roman Jakobson and Joshua Whatmough, linguists from Harvard University, only a couple of miles away from MIT and closely collaborating with RLE scholars, George Miller, J. R. Licklider and Alex Bavelas, psychologists from Harvard and MIT, and a host of other people were only too eager to rub shoulders with Robert Fano and C. Y. Lee, electrical engineers and mathematicians at RLE, to meet with them at luncheon meetings and innumerable other occasions, and to exhilarate each other with the feeling that another obstinate secret has finally been unveiled. Few linguists in Greater Boston at that time dared not use freely "message" and "code", "information" and "bits" in their shop talk, and nobody was "in" if he did not master, or at least professed to master, a good amount of probability theory and statistics. Everybody who was somebody in the field would sooner or later show up at MIT, and many, like Dennis Gabor and Colin Cherry from Great Britain, stayed there for longer periods and joined in the fun. All of us were enormously impressed by Shannon's well known experiments in what he called "approximations to ordinary English" and were convinced that speech, in English or any other language, was a Markov process. From this to the conviction that the English language, i.e. the set of all English sentences, can be generated by a Markov source, was only a small step, and I am not sure that we noticed at the time that this was a step at all. Everyone was certain that the only thing missing for a complete understanding of the communication process through natural language was reliable statistics on the relative frequencies of digrams, trigrams, etc., and it was deplored that getting these statistics would be such a costly affair. All over Greater Boston, and in due time all over the United States, students were put to work to amass such statistics.

The favourite game was measuring, or estimating, redundancy of speech. Everyone knew of course that *mttng th vwl lttrs n nglsh wrtng hrdl mprd th ndrstndng f sch sntncs*, if this was done in the fashion just exhibited, and, as a matter of fact, there are systems of stenography based on this. It was obvious that this should be much more difficult for omission of consonant letters. *i eee o iae oay uey uieiie*. But strangely enough, when I asked Carol Chomsky — Noam Chomsky's wife — who at that time was also working at the RLE on phonetic problems, to pronounce the vowel sequence of a Hebrew sentence (Carol knew Hebrew very well and had been teaching it in summer camps), she came up with *ai oee a aie*, and I responded without a minute's thought with *ani joševet al hakise* ("I am sitting (fem.) on the chair"). This was right, and we felt elated. (My correct guess was, of course, based upon my subconscious assumption that Carol, on a moment's notice, would probably be coming up with a relatively familiar sentence, one she would have used at an early stage in her teaching career.)

At the time, we felt that such findings not only provided us with better insight into human *speech* and *communication* (which I still believe to have indeed been the case, though to a far lesser degree than we had then assumed) but also into *language* itself. In this we were dead wrong. But it took some time before this began to dawn upon us, and some still haven't yet learned the lesson. It is sad to see how many linguists, in particular in Soviet Russia, are still hampered by the illusion that their grammatical problems will be solved by more and better statistical investigations into speech or texts, whereas it should be perfectly clear by now that such investigations can at their best only provide (not too decisive) tests for linguistic theories (in the broad sense of "theory" which includes rules of interpretation).

There can be no doubt that the decisive influence in this direction of drawing a much clearer distinction than had ever been drawn before between speech and language, with language being considered a *theoretical construct* and grammar a *theory of language*, came from Chomsky. At the time, i.e. in 1951–53, he was still a Junior Fellow in Philosophy at Harvard University but was often around MIT where, as already mentioned, his wife was working. He was then still very much under the influence of his two major teachers from the University of Pennsylvania, the linguist Harris and the philosopher Nelson Goodman, and tended to exhibit their radical operationalist nominalism. Slowly but surely, this influence began to wear off, and within a few years, the operationalist approach, still in general vogue in 1952 in Cambridge, with such scientists as Percy Bridgman, C. F. Skinner and Roman Jakobson serving as its spokesmen, became greatly liberalized. Though every science, linguistics included, must remain firmly rooted in experience, this rooting was no longer taken in the literal sense favoured by the operationalists. Though Chomsky himself still has certain reservations with regard to the views of such people as Carnap, Carl G. Hempel, or Richard Braithwaite on the status of scientific theories and theoretical entities, I am convinced that he does accept these views in their essence and that this acceptance has aided him in turning linguistics into a theoretical science, on a par in this respect with other theoretical sciences such as theoretical physics or genetics. In a terminology which he later developed together with George Miller, he regards it to be the task of the (theoretical) linguist to develop a *theory of linguistic competence*, whereas *linguistic performance*, in speech and writing, was left for the communication scientist (including the applied linguist) to study. This study is, of course, based, among other things, on theories of linguistic competence, just as these theories get their inspiration and motivation from the observation of linguistic performance and are, in the final count, tested by it. But these obvious interrelationships, exactly analogous to those between (theoretical) physics and applied physics, should not blind anybody to make light of their essential methodological differences.

Cybernetics has turned out to be as irrelevant to the study of language as it has turned out to be of decisive relevance, amounting to almost revolutionary changes of outlook, to the study of speech. The enthusiasts of Cybernetics better accept this evaluation lest they continue to damage their own cause. There is no room for probability and statistics (beyond trivialities) in the study of language. That a certain linguistic structure is seldom used by the members of a given speech community should definitely be noted down when the speech behaviour of this community is to be exhaustively described but it has no place in the description of the language of this community (though this fact may also be used, under appropriate circumstances, to induce a different description from the one originally envisaged, or for the establishment of two simultaneous different descriptions, resulting in the splitting of the language into dialects, etc.). Whether cybernetics will be of help in solving the monumental problem of understanding how children become, at the age of five or so, competent in the use of their native language, i.e. master (subconsciously) the theory of their language, remains to be seen. I am not aware so far of any great insights, or any particularly interesting models, that have come from the cybernetic direction. On the contrary, thinking in terms of machine models has so far done more harm than good. People began speculating about how a computer, having been told that such and such word sequences are English sentences and such and other word sequences are non-sentences, would learn to construct an adequate grammar of English, totally missing the point that the only mechanism which is able of performing such a feat so far, viz. the human brain, can do so only because of its being innately structured in a peculiar way, of which we have hardly more than the slightest of inklings so that we are utterly unable either to model it or to stimulate it by appropriate programming.

The actual impact of cybernetics (even when taken in a very wide sense so as to include all of the statistical theory of communication) on theoretical linguistics seems, then, to have been close to nil, in spite of what some linguists are apt to feel and say. This does not preclude that these linguists might have felt motivated to embark on certain investigations because of the impact of cybernetic ideas, but then the impact was of the nature of that of rotten apples on Schiller's poetry. If you look at the work of Harris or Chomsky, cybernetics might never have existed.

However, I was ready to grant that cybernetics, in particular in the form of the statistical theory of communication, did have a great influence on the development of descriptive and applied linguistics, in particular on the statistical aspects. But even this impact should not be exaggerated and generalized. Let me illustrate this through the early history of *machine translation* (MT).

My own appointment at RLE was mainly for the study of the application of computers to linguistic work, and in particular to MT. I mentioned already my motivation for this endeavour, and I would hesitate to call it "cybernetic" in any serious sense of the word. Like so many other people, I was then intrigued by the problem of making computers work toward the solution of non-numerical problems, and I picked the translation problem, because of my independent interests in the "mechanisms" of language and in the existence of "mechanical" decision procedures for sentencehood and syntactic structure in general.

As a matter of fact, Wiener's reaction to Warren Weaver's famous memorandum of 1949, which was probably the major factor in putting MT research under way, was definitely negative, as I learned from secondary sources at the time and later on from him personally. (Wiener never changed his view on this point, though he considered it, later on, around 1957, at least worthwhile to investigate into MT with the help of machines with learning abilities.) This did not deter me then, but on the other hand I am not aware that cybernetic considerations ever seriously determined my thinking or that of my colleagues who were working on the same problem. We became increasingly aware of the capacities of a digital computer as a symbol-manipulator, and it was this, together with certain rather naïve views of language, which set us to work, rather than a cybernetic worldview.

True enough, during the first conference on MT, which I organized at MIT in June 1952, I did use, according to the stenographic notes, the phrase "if a human being can do it, a suitably programmed computer can do it too" more than a dozen times, but the actual impact of this cybernetic credo was close to nil, and it certainly was more an expression of willingness to work toward a certain goal than an exhibition of a deep philosophical insight. It did nothing toward the solution of the real problem which was, of course, how to "suitably" programme a computer for translation work.

My own partial success in presenting an outline of a quasi-arithmetical description of syntactic structure which could serve as a basis for mechanization of syntactic analysis had nothing to do with my cybernetic inklings. It resulted from a development of certain ideas of Adjukiewicz's from a new point of view which I had not realized thirteen years before, when I first became acquainted with them. And when the inadequacy of this approach became clear, this was due not to better cybernetic insights but to certain completely independent developments in theoretical linguistics.

The only point where cybernetic ideas could have had a real impact on MT was the utilization of the learning capacities of a suitably programmed computer for this purpose. I myself paid many times lip-service to this possibility, from my first days of interest in the field until around 1961. But I did very little along this line beyond lunch talk, nor, for that matter, did anybody else. But when I became fully convinced that not only was high quality fully automatic translation a practical impossibility but that even the outlook for an economically sound man-machine partnership in translation, based on fixed algorithms, was rather dim, I finally felt myself compelled to think through the issue of MT as based on computers with learning abilities. And again, cybernetics was of no help. I realized that human ability to translate at all and to learn to translate still better in time and with experience is based upon a type of innate organization for which there is nothing at present to indicate that we shall, in the foreseeable future, come to know it to a degree sufficient for either modeling or programmed simulation. I don't see at all that cybernetic ideas of self-organization will be of any help here, since the degree of initial organization apparently required as a start for arriving, through additional self-organization, at a level adequate for high-quality translation is far beyond our present skills at modeling or programming. In more philosophical terms, it seems that we humans, in order to acquire that particular first-order disposition called competence in a given language, make use of an innate second-order disposition whose anatomical and physiological aspects are utterly unknown to us. We better admit that with such an abysmal lack of knowledge — for which I see no point in blaming anybody or any particular development — even cybernetic magic will not pull rabbits out of the hat.

Let me finish this article with two remarks, referring to the future rather than to prehistory. First, I continue to believe that thinking in terms of writing programmes for computers will remain a good check on one's theorizing, in linguistics as in any other science, by forcing it into a framework whose rigidity, though it may appear to many to be a Procrustes' bed, has highly attractive and remunerative features. Computational linguistics, then, pulls into approximately the same direction as formalization and the employment of the hypothetico-deductive method, though for different reasons and in a less direct way. I am not aware of any significant achievement in theoretical linguistics that was obtained through the use of computers. I am aware of very few significant achievements in applied linguistics that were obtained through the use of computers and could not have been obtained more cheaply and quickly by more conventional methods. Though computers may in the future play a more important role in testing linguistic theories and hypotheses than they have done so far, this will only be achieved if the science-fictional claims often made on their behalf will be toned down and people will seriously begin to think of how optimally to make use of the intrinsic properties of symbol-manipulating mechanisms.

Second, it may be hoped that structural linguistics will be allowed to sever its enforced ties with cybernetics and mechanization in People's Democracies just as it is about to do in Western Europe and the United States. Theoretical linguistics, in its various variants including the combinatorial and algebraic ones, should have already sufficiently proved its mettle to deserve full-fledged academic standing and research support without being obliged to promise payment in terms of aiding in the immediate mechanization of various linguistic data processing endeavours. Too close a tie with cybernetic ways of thinking will only hamper the complete shedding of its operationalist fedders, remnants of which are still noticeable in the otherwise rather advanced type of thinking of such Russian linguists as S. K. Shaumyan and I. I. Revzin. Computational linguistics will earn its place in the sun as a respectable technology only if it will stop trying to wag theoretical linguistics and be satisfied in being wagged by it.

The shot-gun marriage of Cybernetics and Linguistics should be dissolved by mutual consent, though there is no reason why they should not remain, after the divorce, "good friends" ever after. Let them continue to join forces in the study of linguistic performance in speech (and communication, in general), but let the study of linguistic competence in language be given into the exclusive custody of Linguistics, with cybernetics entitled to visit this offspring and follow its growth only during one afternoon each month. It will be to the best of all concerned.

REFERENCES

ADJUKIEWICZ, K.: Die syntaktische Konnexität, *Studia Philosophica*, vol. 1 (1935), pp. 1–27.

BAR-HILLEL, Y.: *Language and Information*: Selected Essays, Addison-Wesley Publishing Company, Reading, Mass., USA; Jerusalem Academic Press, Jerusalem, Israel, 1964.

BLACK, M.: Russell's philosophy of language, *The Philosophy of Bertrand Russell* (P. A. Schilpp, ed.), Tudor Publishing Company, New York 1951, pp. 227–255.

BLOOMFIELD, L.: Linguistic Aspects of Science, *International Encyclopedia of Unified Science*, vol. 1, no. 4, University of Chicago Press, 1939.

CARNAP, R.: *Der logische Aufbau der Welt*. 2nd edition, Felix Meiner, Hamburg 1961.

CARNAP, R.: *Die logische Syntax der Sprache*, Springer-Verlag, Vienna 1934.

CHOMSKY, N.: *Syntactic Structures*, Mouton & Co., The Hague 1957 (2nd printing, 1962).

HARRIS, S. Z.: *Methods in Structural Linguistics*, University of Chicago Press, 1951.
LEŚNIEWSKI, ST.: Grundzüge eines neuen Systems der Grundlagen der Mathematik, *Fundamenta Mathematica*, vol. 14 (1921), pp. 1–81.
MILLER, G. A. and CHOMSKY, N.: Finitary models of language users, *Handbook of Mathematic Psychology*, vol. 2 (Bush, Galanter and Luce, eds.), John Wiley and Sons, New York 1963.
MOORE, G. E.: Russell's "theory of descriptions", *The Philosophy of Bertrand Russell* (P. A. Schilpp, ed.), Tudor Publishing Company, New York 1951, pp. 175–225.
QUINE, W. V. O.: *Word and Object*, Technology Press of the Massachusetts Institute of Technology and John Wiley and Sons, New York 1960.
REVZIN, I. I.: *Modeli yazyke*, Publishing House of the Academy of Sciences USSR, Moskva 1962.
SHAUMYAN, S. K.: Operational definitions and their use in phonology, *Primeneniye logiki v nauke i tekhnike*, Moskva 1960.
SHANNON, C. E. and WEAVER, W.: *The Mathematical Theory of Communication*, University of Illinois Press, 1949.
WIENER, N.: *Cybernetics*, 2nd edition, The M.I.T. Press and John Wiley and Sons, New York 1961.

ON RECURSIVE DEFINITIONS
IN EMPIRICAL SCIENCES

Recursive definitions are important not only in the formal sciences, like logic and mathematics, but also in many empirical sciences. This has often been overlooked and sometimes even outrightly denied.[1] I think that the lack of explicit recognition of the important role recursive definitions play in empirical sciences, a neglect of which scientists and methodologists are equally culpable, has been a constant source of misunderstandings and futile disputes.

I shall try to substantiate my claim by exhibition of an example. It is not necessary, for our purposes, to give a detailed explanation of the general notion of recursive definitions. It will suffice to recall that the concept of sum is introduced into the Peano system of arithmetic,[2] built upon the primitive notions of the number 1 and the immediate-successor function,$'$, (together with auxiliary signs like parentheses) by such a recursive definition, taking in this case the form of a pair of equations, viz.:

(1) $\quad a + 1 = a'$
(2) $\quad a + n' = (a + n)'$

What makes these definitions so specifically different from other better known kinds is not so much the occurrence of more than one definition sentence, — this property is shared with certain types of partial definitions — as the occurrence of the sign to be defined, in our case the '+' sign, on *both* sides of the identity sign in a definition sentence. This might look to untrained eyes as if the "new" sign were being defined with the help of an expression that contains just this sign, hence that the whole procedure is flagrantly circular. And circular definitions are illegitimate, as everybody knows who has ever taken a course in logic. But what is the reason for this banishment? I believe that the customary ground is that any attempt to eliminate the term introduced by a circular definition will lead to an infinite regress and would hence defeat itself. And it is generally regarded as being an essential characteristic of a definition

---

[1] Carl G. Hempel, in Fundamentals of Concept Formation in Empirical Science, *International Encyclopedia of Unified Science*, Vol. II, No. 7, University of Chicago Press, 1952, p. 11, note 11, says that "recursive definitions which play an important role in logic and mathematics... are not used in empirical science".

[2] Strictly speaking, I should say "into one of the Peano systems of arithmetic".

that any new term introduced by it should be eliminable in any context whatsoever.

Now, it can easily be seen that all occurrences of the '+' sign between two numerical expressions without variables are eliminable, even constructively so, in the sense that another expression can be exhibited denoting the same number. Let me show this in a specific example. Let the expression from which the '+' sign has to be eliminated be

$$4 + 3$$

Let us assume that the numerals have been introduced by the customary explicit definitions

(3) $2 = 1'$
(4) $3 = 2'$
(5) $4 = 3'$

The elimination proceeds now as follows:

$$\begin{aligned} 4 + 3 &= 4 + 2' & (4) \\ &= (4 + 2)' & (2) \\ &= (4 + 1')' & (3) \\ &= (4 + 1)'' & (2)^3 \\ &= 4''' & (1) \end{aligned}$$

(If elimination of all defined sign were required, we could wind up with $1''''''$, on the basis of (5), and (4), and (3).) In our case, the attempt at elimination did not result in an infinite regress. The dreaded circle turned out not to be a vicious one. Strictly speaking, it is not a circle at all but a harmless terminating spiral.

Has it, then, been shown that recursive definitions are plain definitions with no specific problems? Not at all. Though the '+' sign is eliminable in all contexts of the aforementioned form, it is not so, at least not in any such obvious fashion, in other contexts. 'a + b' is a simple example of such a context. If we stick to eliminability in all contexts as a necessary condition for being a definition, then recursive definitions are not definitions, and one should better use another term for them. But does this mean that they are not a perfectly legitimate means of concept formation? Certainly not. The fruitfulness, and in a sense even indispensability, of this means, whatever the name we are going to give it, in arithmetic and other formal sciences cannot be doubted. To be

---

[3] The notation has been simplified through omission of certain parentheses.

sure, there are some problems connected with their use, and it may turn out to be more practicable to look upon "recursive definitions" not as sentences introducing a "new" term but as "meaning postulates"[4] which determine the meaning of the additional primitive term, with which they deal, fully in some contexts and partially in others. And the problem of eliminating, in a somewhat weaker sense, this term in *all sentential* contexts is a major, and extremely interesting, one to which much thought is given in recent mathematical logic.[5]

But it has not been so far realized, to repeat what I stated at the beginning, that recursive definitions play an equally important role in empirical sciences. It is true that certain definitions which would turn out to be recursive in a proper formalization of a given scientific system have not been recognized as such even by their originators. As a result of this failure, they have often been mistaken for genuinely circular definitions. And it has happened that a scientist, introducing a new and obviously important concept into his field by what is really a recursive definition, failed to realize this and was thereby led to denounce logic for condemning the introduction of a good term as circular. And it is, of course, even more frequent to see one scientist denounce another scientist's introduction of a new term as being circular when it is in reality only recursive. It is sometimes tragicomic to observe the helplessness of the accused who is convinced of the legitimacy of his procedure but is unable to make this clear to his opponent or, for that matter, even to himself.

Instead of touching superficially on the various places where recursive definitions arise in different empirical sciences, let me treat with some detail one example in one specific scientific field. For a change, to break with the tradition of most logicians in using physics as their primary field of application, I shall take as this field Linguistics. If one is to introduce into English as metalanguage for the description of the grammar of French as object-language the term "sentence", not as a primitive term, to be specified by axioms, but by definition, it is inevitable (waiving the discussion of the exact nature of this inevitability) to use in the definiens the term "sentence" itself, if the definition is to be adequate. Each such definition must have, using customary, non-symbolic formulation, something like the following form:

---

[4] See Rudolf Carnap, "Meaning Postulates", *Philosophical Studies*, Vol. III, No. 5, 1952, pp. 65–73.

[5] See, e.g., S. C. Kleene, *Introduction to Metamathematics*, New York, 1952.

x will be called a *sentence* (in French) if (and only if) x is a sequence of a nominal[6] and a (intransitive) verbal,[6] or a sequence of a nominal, a (transitive) verbal, and a nominal, or . . ., or a sequence of a sentence, the word "et", and a sentence, or . . .

How else could we deduce the theorem, whose validity is certainly a necessary condition for the adequacy of the definition of "sentence", that the result of joining *any* two French sentences by "et" is itself a sentence? I can well imagine how a linguist, who is not well versed in mathematical logic, might start cursing logic in view of the inevitability of using "sentence" in defining "sentence".

But it should now be clear to us that the mentioned definition is recursive in disguise. To bring this into the open, let us replace it by a pair of definition sentences:

x is a *sentence*$_1$ (a *simple sentence*) = $_{df}$ x is a sequence of a nominal and a (intransitive) verbal or a sequence of a nominal, a (transitive) verbal, and a nominal, or . . .,

x is a *sentence*$_{n+1}$ (a *compound sentence* of the n + 1 — th order) = $_{df}$ x is a sequence of a sentence$_p$, the word "et", and a sentence$_m$, where either p or m (or both) are equal to n and none is greater than n, or . . .

Sometimes the situation is even more opaque. There may be cases where it seems inevitable to define some term A with the help of B and B with the help of A. It is, for instance, not implausible that not only will the term "nominal" have to be used in the definition of "sentence" (in French) — if such a term occurs at all in a specific inventory of grammatical terms —, but also that the term "nominal" will have to be defined using "sentence". We might well have, for instance, the following definitions simultaneously:

x will be called a *sentence* if (and only if) x is a sequence of a nominal and . . ., or . . .,

x will be called a *nominal* if (and only if) x is a proper name, or . . ., or x is a sequence of the word "que" and a sentence, or . . .

However, nobody will now fail to realize that these definitions do not form a set of viciously circular definitions but that they are rather a

---

[6] Where a nominal is, approximately, a word sequence that functions syntactically similarly to a proper name, and a verbal is, approximately, a word sequence that together with one or more nominals forms a sentence, but is defined, of course, in our illustration, without recourse to "sentence".

pair of *simultaneous recursive definitions*, the like of which are well known to the mathematical logician. Notice how simple it is to check, in a completely mechanical way, that

Paul croit que Jean est malade,

for instance, is a proper French sentence. After some trial and error, we (or for that matter, a machine given this task) would arrive at the result that this sequence is a sentence provided that

que Jean est malade

is a nominal, which could be so if only

Jean est malade

were a sentence, which in its turn would be so if *Jean* were a nominal and *est malade* a verbal, which then turns out to be so indeed, *Jean* through appearing in the list of proper names, *est malade* through a longer check involving the definition of verbal which we skipped here. The fact that we had to move from "sentence" to "nominal", then back to "sentence", and finally once more to "nominal" did not vitiate the process since we arrived at a stage where no further recursion was necessary and a matching with certain lists, for instance that of proper names, settled the question. (In order not to be involved in sophisticated linguistic arguments, the description of the actual procedure has been highly simplified, but I hope that the omitted complications are of no relevance to our present problem.)

Let us notice, as we should expect by now, that the term "sentence" is not eliminable from all its contexts, relative to a certain formalization of French grammar which contains the formalized counterparts of the aforementioned definitions. The sentence "All French sentences contain at least one noun" would be a relevant example.

We have already seen that it hardly matters whether one decides to call recursive definitions "definitions" or not. They are introduction sentences of a type different from that exhibited by the more customary explicit definitions. Recursive definitions share with the so-called conditional definitions and other types of partial "definitions" the property that the definienda are not always eliminable. Their function in concept formation is, therefore, coupled in the same curious way — which has been discussed at length by Hempel[7] — with their function in theory formation. However, this is a difficult topic which cannot be discussed here.

[7] *Loc. cit.*, p. 28.

Let me finally remark that I believe that recursive definitions may also turn out to be the formal counterpart of at least a portion of the doctrine of "definition by successive approximations" which has played an important role in the methodology of physics in the Twenties and Thirties.[8] The analogy between the successive approximations and the successive steps of regression is probably more than formal. However, also this discussion must be left for some other occasion.

In conclusion, let me say that, in view of the role played by recursive definitions in concept formation in empirical sciences, it is the task of the methodologists to dedicate time and effort to the evaluation of their precise impact in different fields of inquiry and the task of the scientists to become acquainted with the recent investigations on recursive definitions to a degree, at least, that would free them from the misconceptions that have so frequently been connected with their occurrence in disguise.

---

[8] See, e.g., Victor F. Lenzen, Procedures of Empirical Science, *International Encyclopedia of Unified Science*, Vol. I, No. 5, University of Chicago Press, 1938, pp. 41 ff.

SOME LINGUISTIC PROBLEMS CONNECTED WITH MACHINE TRANSLATION

During my recent work on machine translation,[1] I have come across many problems of a linguistic nature that should be of general methodological interest. Some of these problems have never been treated extensively before. Others that have been discussed previously appear now in a different and rather interesting light.

The task of instructing a machine how to translate from one language it does not and will not understand into another language it does not and will not understand presents a real challenge for structural linguists, in that their thesis that language can be exhaustively described in non-referential terms undergoes here an *experimentum crucis*. If, in a translation programme, some step has to be taken which directly or indirectly depends upon the machine's ability to understand the text on which it operates, then the machine will simply be unable to make this step, and the whole operation will come to a full stop. (I have in mind present day machines that do not possess a semantic organ. The situation might change in the not too distant future.)

I intend to deal with four specific problems, of which the only obvious common feature is the decisive role which they play in machine translation. The problems are, in the order in which they will be treated:

1. Operational Syntax
2. Intertranslatability of natural languages
3. Idioms
4. Universal syntactic categories

1. *Operational Syntax*

One of the decisive steps in certain methods of machine translation is the determination of the syntactic structure of any given sentence in the *source-language* (i.e., the language from which we translate) to a required degree of explicitness. Since thinking in terms of machines might perhaps be difficult for the reader, let him imagine an utterly moronic student without the slightest knowledge of either the source-language or the *target-language*, i.e., the language into which the given text is to be translated, and with an extremely restricted understanding

---

[1] YEHOSHUA BAR-HILLEL, "The Present State of Research on Mechanical Translation," *American Documentation*, 2, 229–236, 1953 [reprinted in LI as Ch. 10].

of his own native language, but with the following abilities which are rather remarkable for a human being with such a constitution: he is able to identify the letter shapes of the source-language, he has an unfailing and unlimited memory, and he is extremely fast in carrying out those instructions which are formulated in that small language fragment he understands. I shall not go into the detailed specification of these instructions. Let me mention only the two most important operations he is able to carry out: *matching* the given text or any part of it with any of a number of lists presented to him, and *counting*.

Though it might appear as if these operations were quite restricted in their range, it can be shown that they, together with some of the other minor ones which I have not mentioned, would suffice to give our moronic student a full understanding of the grammar of any source-language as it should be presented by a structural linguist. He would be able, for instance, to derive from any noun-stem its plural genitive (coded for him as, say, derivation number 11), from any verb-stem its simple past singular second person, etc., and to synthesize sentences fulfilling all kinds of conditions. But — and this is the decisive point — he would be unable to take even one step when presented with a sentence in the source-language and asked to tell its structure. Briefly, though somewhat vaguely, we might say: the structural linguist provides, in general, a description from which the linguistic forms of the treated language can be synthesized, but he does not provide a method by which any given sentence, presented as a sequence of certain discrete elements, can be analysed into its constituents and their syntactic function determined.

An analogy might help to bring out the difference between the customary synthetic syntax and that type of syntax which is required for our present purposes, for which *analytic syntax* would have been a good name, were it not already in use for a different concept. A student of chemistry who has, either in his mind or on his shelves, a complete description of all chemical substances, as well as a thorough description of all known methods of synthesizing or otherwise producing them, would be at a complete loss when presented with the task of determining the composition of an unknown mixture of substances. What should he do first? And what then? If he is very clever, he might be able to deduce from his extensive synthetic knowledge one sequence of operations that would yield a solution of his problem. But it would probably take him many years to do this and he could hardly be sure, at the end, that his solution is a relatively effective one. Now, this is not the way in which students of chemistry are taught to proceed. Before they are admitted to the laboratory, they have to take a special course in Analytic Chemistry, during which they learn nothing essentially new about the properties of the substances or their synthesis, but learn a set of instructions which, when carried out in proper order and with proper care, will enable them to analyse any given mixture of substances.

Our fictitious student of linguistics will be incomparably duller than the average student of chemistry but, on the other hand, incomparably quicker in performing those specific basic operations to which he is accustomed. The main difference between the set of instructions for the chemist and the linguist will therefore lie in the necessity of formulating the linguist's instructions in terms of these basic operations only, though perhaps iterated hundreds of thousands of times, in a very definite order that might depend, and usually will depend, on the outcome of prior operations.

Just as the chemist has to be provided with an Analytic Chemistry, so the linguist has to be provided with an *Operational Syntax*. He must be told what to do first, as well as what to do as the n-th step depending on the outcomes of the preceding n – 1 steps (preferably, of the (n – 1)th step only). To my knowledge, no sufficiently complete operational syntax of any language has thus far been produced, mainly because the importance of such a syntax has not been recognized. Though this importance is highlighted by machine translation, it extends far beyond the reaches of this specific application. The preparation of an operational syntax for any or all languages is, in my opinion, a task which should prove highly rewarding even for the most theoretically minded linguist.

Without any attempt at being complete, let me stress that Pollard[2] and Oswald-Fletcher[3] have obtained many valuable results towards an achievement of our aim. One essential step toward such an operational syntax has been described in a recent article of mine.[4]

2. *Intertranslatability of Natural Languages**

---

[2] C. V. POLLARD, "A Key to Rapid Translation of German," University of Texas, 1947.

[3] VICTOR A. OSWALD, JR., AND STUART L. FLETCHER, JR., "Proposals for the Mechanical Resolution of German Syntax Patterns," *Modern Language Forum*, 36, 1–24, 1951.

[4] YEHOSHUA BAR-HILLEL, "A Quasi-Arithmetical Notation for Syntactic Description," *Language*, 29, 47–58, 1953; [reprinted in LI as Ch. 5].

* [This section has been omitted since it has been reprinted in LI as Ch. 4.]

3. *Idioms*

Among the obvious difficulties that arise when considering machine translation is the treatment of idioms. Somehow one can envisage how a machine could proceed in a kind of word-by-word translation but it is exactly this type of translation which collapses when confronted with an idiom which by definition, to wit, definition 3 of Webster's Collegiate Dictionary, 1951, is "an expression in the usage of a language, that is peculiar to itself either in grammatical construction or in having a meaning which cannot be derived as a whole from the conjoined meanings of its elements (as, *the more the merrier, a picture of the king's, to make friends with him*)."

However, as soon as one starts thinking about the situation, many things that seemed to be clear on first thought become more and more obscure. Any structural linguist would immediately be put on his guard by the fact that in this definition the word "meaning" occurs, and even twice. What exactly is meant by "conjoined meanings of its elements"? How does one determine that, to utilize one of the examples mentioned in Webster, the meaning of the phrase "to make friends with him" is not derivable as a whole from the conjoined meanings of the elements of this phrase? And what are these elements? Words? Morphemes? And where does the order of the elements come into the picture?

I could continue and question every single word of this definition, but this would hardly be very fruitful. I shall, therefore, shift my approach. Notice first that the problem with which I started was the treatment of expressions that are idiomatic with respect to translation into some other language, whereas Webster's definition applies to expressions that are idiomatic with respect to the very same language to which they belong. For a reason that will become clearer later, I shall deal, to begin with, only with idioms of the first kind, for which I shall use the term *bilingual idioms*. Now what would one consider a bilingual idiom in an unknown source language? I think that it boils down to the following: a sequence of elements in a source language, whatever these elements may be, is an idiom when none of the sequences of elements in the target language which are correlated to the original sequence through a given set of rules (including among others also a bilingual dictionary) is a satisfactory translation of the original sequence. If this is so, and I hardly see any good reason to doubt the adequacy of our reconstruction, then, strictly speaking, one must talk about an expression of a source language being an idiom with respect to a target language and a set of translation rules.

This double relativization seems to me of great importance, and I am not sure that it is always taken into due account.

But now the importance of idioms for machine translation becomes glaring. From the meaning of the term "idiom" itself, with respect to a target language and a set of translation rules, it follows that no idiom can be satisfactorily translated into this target language by a machine that follows these rules. Therefore, the only method of mechanically translating idioms is — not to have idioms at all. When people are raising the idiom objection to machine translation, they have in mind some dictionary and a certain set of rules which they accept as standards. Now, it may well be that, relative to this dictionary and to this set of rules, no satisfactory translation of certain expressions will be forthcoming, dooming these expressions to the state of idioms. But the remedy is obvious: we have only to change the old set of rules, usually simply by adding some more rules, so that satisfactory translations will be forthcoming if one works with the new set. Which rules to change will still be an interesting question, the solution of which may decide the practical feasibility of a whole translation procedure. There are at least three different methods of eliminating idioms, each of which is theoretically self-sufficient. Practically, however, and relative to the achievement of certain aims, an optimal procedure will probably make use of all three of them, and perhaps of others too.

a. According to the first method, the only change would be the enlargement of the list of correlates in the target language to some of the entries in the source language. Assume, for instance, that in some German-English dictionary the German word "es" has as its English correlates the words "it," "he," "she," and that to the German "gibt" the English "gives" is correlated. (Whether the last correlation is direct as a result of an intermediate use of certain grammatical rules is unimportant for our purposes.) If somebody who does not know German were presented with the task of translating the German sentence "Es gibt einen Unterschied" into English, he would wind up, after due consultation of the dictionary and the relevant grammatical rules, with "it (he, she) gives a (one) difference (distinction)." Most readers who do not know German will find it difficult to decide, from this data, what the proper translation of the original sentence is. As soon as they will be told that a correct translation into English is "there is a difference," they will probably decide that the German sentence is idiomatic in some sense, perhaps even that its idiomatic character is due solely to its first two words "es gibt", since the translation of the last two words remains unchanged. With respect to the given dictionary, "es gibt" would be a German idiom relative to English. (It should be clear that, even more strictly speaking, a relativization with respect to the receiver of the sentence is indicated. What is unsatisfactory for A might well be satisfactory for B.) To "deidiomize" "es gibt", one has only to add to the English correlates of "es" the word "there" and to those of "gibt" also "is (are)," and "there is" would immediately appear as one of the possible translations of "es gibt"!

This proposal sounds preposterous. But why does it? How can we counter the argument that this is an extremely reasonable procedure that fulfills its function well and does no harm, since none of the formerly legitimate translations is overthrown by it? Well, the only reasonable answer I can see is that this procedure fulfills its function too well. In addition to the welcome combination "there is" many other gratuitous combinations will be introduced, the elimination of which through consideration of context might be at least troublesome, sometimes perhaps impossible. To have to cope with "she is a doll" as one of the possible translations of "sie gibt eine Puppe," even if this translation would be excluded through the context in which the German sentence is embedded, seems too high a price to pay for the elimination of one idiomatic expression. If I am not mistaken, "es gibt" (and its variants like "gibt es") is the only phrase that might encourage us to have "is" as a correlate of "gibt." Were there more of such phrases, say a hundred, then it would probably be worthwhile to have "is" as a correlate. Where to draw the line is a question of expedience which I am in no position to answer.

b. A second solution for the same difficulty looks even more promising. Just supplement the ordinary word- or stem-dictionary by a special phrase-dictionary whose entries will be exactly those phrases of which a word-by-word translation would turn out to be unsatisfactory. For our case, the phrase dictionary would contain "es gibt" as one of its entries with "there is (are)" as the correlates of this entry. Notice that sometimes certain grammatical rules will have to be applied before the phrase dictionary will be invoked. One such rule will have to deal with the translation of question sentences like "Gibt es einen Unterschied?" Notice also that the fact that "es gibt" would appear in the phrase dictionary does by no means imply that *all* tokens of this phrase will have to be translated by "there is (are)." In general, this will only be an *additional* possible translation. "Es gibt" in "Es [das Mädchen] gibt mir einen Kuss" will certainly not be rendered by "there is." In some cases, however, the so-called *literal* translation may never be to the point. The instruction for the machine (as well as for the dull student) will be to hunt first for the possible occurrence of idioms in the given sentence, and the phrase dictionary will have to indicate whether the correlate to some phrase is the only possible translation or whether "literal" translations should also be considered.

This second method is, of course, theoretically completely foolproof. The only practical drawback is the size of the phrase dictionary. I do not know how many entries we can afford to have in it. It would certainly be very unwise to have in the regular English-German dictionary for the entry "fair" only, say, "schön" and "nett" as correlates, so that "fair play" would have to be treated as an idiom and would appear such in the companion phrase dictionary. This is because "fair play" is not the only combination where "fair" cannot be satisfactorily rendered by either "schön" or "nett."

As a matter of fact, a variant of this method of dealing with idioms is quite customary in many large-scale dictionaries. For machine translation, certain changes in arrangement would be indicated.

c. The third method is logically nothing but another variant of the second one. This variant shows, however, enough interesting features of its own to deserve special treatment. According to this method, no changes would be introduced into the standard dictionaries, nor would a special phrase dictionary have to be compiled. Instead, the reader of the translation would be told that certain target language phrases should, or perhaps only might, be replaced by other phrases. The rough translation of "es gibt" would still be "it (he, she) gives" but the English reader would be instructed to replace, or at least to consider a possible replacement of, "it (he, she) gives" by "there is (are)." The main difference of this method as against the second one is, of course, the fact that, according to the third method, elimination of idioms is handled on a monolingual basis.

To sum up, it appears that the treatment of bilingual idioms poses no grave theoretical problems. In a given practical case, however, the question how to combine optimally the three mentioned methods, as well as others that might come into one's mind, is a serious one. The task of answering this question should prove to be highly interesting.

Now we are ready to explicate what a monolingual idiom is. A phrase in a given language is regarded as a monolingual idiom, with respect to a given monolingual dictionary and a set of grammatical rules for this language, if none of the phrases resulting from replacing any or all of its constituents by their correlates, according to the dictionary and set of rules, is synonymous with the original phrase to a sufficient degree (to be determined by some authority).

I am fully aware that this last statement needs much refinement. In many monolingual English dictionaries, "pal" appears as a correlate of "friend." Assume that "to make pals with him" were synonymous with "to make friends with him." I think that in such a case, we would tend to regard both phrases as idioms, instead of, in accordance with our statement, regarding none of them as such. It would not be difficult to provide the refinement necessary to cope with this situation and similar ones, but there is no need to go into this now.

4. *Universal Syntactic Categories*

My remarks on the problem whether there exist universal syntactic categories, i.e. categories fruitfully applicable to all languages, will be much more tentative than my remarks on the three other problems treated above. I regard this problem as one that is not to be settled completely by empirical observation. I do not think that the question "Are there universal syntactic categories?" is similar to the question "Are there dogs with tails longer than two yards?" I would consider it as being rather of the kind "Is our universe Euclidean?" Whereas the second question should be answerable, in principle and waiving certain methodological complications, by a simple "yes" or "no," it is different with the third question. Here we have a curious mixture of a question of a purely empirical nature with one of worthwhileness. There is always an undertone of "Is it worthwhile to apply Euclidean geometry in physics and what would be the price to be paid for using this convenient geometry?" in such a question, at least for sophisticated physicists.

Similarly, there is for me in the question of the existence of universal syntactic categories the very noticeable undertone, "Is it worthwhile to impose certain syntactic categories upon all languages and what would be the price to be paid for this?" That it would be an advantage, for many purposes, to have a common set of linguistic categories need hardly be stressed. But would not this advantage be counterbalanced by the disadvantages which might enter as a consequence of the establishment of a universal category-system?

My attitude toward this question is tentatively as follows: it seems to me that the syntactic category *sentence* can be imposed universally upon all languages without any methodological loss. This does not mean that I am able to give a universally suitable definition of this term. It also seems to me that all languages contain proper names or at least expressions which could be considered as proper names under some slight pressure. It seems therefore to be innocuous to assume that all languages contain expressions which form sentences with proper names. These three categories are the only ones I would impose upon all languages, without hesitation, since the price to be paid for this procedure appears to be negligible.

But I think that more can be said. There is an infinitely ramified category scheme which can be imposed upon all languages in the sense that no language need be described with the help of any category outside this scheme. Following the lead of the Polish logicians Leśniewski and Ajdukiewicz,[5] we can assume that in each language there is a finite number of *basic categories*, among them at least the universal categories of sentence and proper name, but perhaps also others, universal or specific. In addition, we have a finite or infinite number of operator categories, the members of which form, with the members of the basic categories or with the members of other operator categories, expressions belonging to any of these categories. This sounds complicated, but I believe that it cannot be helped. There is no reason to expect that the establishment of a universal category scheme for all languages will be simple.[6]

---

[5] Kasimir Adjukiewicz, "Die syntaktische Konnexität," *Studia Philosophica*, 1, 1–27, Lwów, 1935.

[6] See my article referred to in note 4.

THREE METHODOLOGICAL REMARKS ON
FUNDAMENTALS OF LANGUAGE

Though the booklet *Fundamentals of Language* by Roman Jakobson and Morris Halle[1] does not contain much material that is new relative to earlier publications by these authors, the fact that this booklet is more or less self-sustaining makes a critical examination of some of its major methodological points a relatively simple and rewarding task.

For the following discussion, I selected three theses; I shall examine them not in the order in which they appear in the booklet but rather in the order of increasing importance (as I see it, not necessarily as the authors would judge them).

1. The authors present a new version, couched in their "code" terminology, of the old thesis of the primacy of speech over writing. I shall not deal here with the history of this thesis nor try to disentangle the different, sometimes radically different, interpretations given to it by various linguists, but concentrate on the formulations given on pp. 16–17 of the *Fundamentals*.

The authors start with the factual statements, "In contradistinction to the universal phenomenon of speech, phonetic or phonemic writing is an occasional, accessory code that normally implies the ability of its users to translate it into its underlying sound code, while the reverse ability, to transpose speech into letters, is a secondary and much less common faculty. Only after having mastered speech does one graduate to reading and writing." (I believe that these statements will only stand under an extremely liberal and benevolent interpretation of the word 'normally', but, for my present purposes, I need not, fortunately, enter into a discussion of these statements at all.) Then they go on to make the following methodological statements: "There is a cardinal difference between phonemes and graphic units. Each letter carries a specific denotation — in a phonemic orthography, it usually denotes one of the phonemes or a certain limited series of phonemes, whereas phonemes denote nothing but mere *otherness* (cf. 2.3). Graphic signs that serve to interpret phonemes or other linguistic units stand for these units, as the logician would say."

It seems to me that the mode of expression chosen here by the authors is in many respects unfortunate and misleading. The terms 'denote' and

[1] R. Jakobson and M. Halle, *Fundamentals of Language* (Janua Linguarum Nr. 1), Mouton & Co. 'S-Gravenhage 1956.

'denotation' occurring here as well as on pp. 10–11, to which the authors refer in the last-quoted passage, are used with such a high degree of ambiguity and vagueness, and with such a high degree of deviation from both ordinary and logico-semiotical usage, that the understanding of the sentences in which they appear is highly impeded. The phrase, "phonemes denote nothing but mere *otherness*," if you take away from it its metaphysical flavour and the associations with some of the worst formulations of Ch. S. Peirce and F. de Saussure, seems to mean no more than what would be expressed in ordinary language by something like "Phonemes do not denote and their functioning is purely differential," with some elaboration needed to clarify the matter of 'differential functioning'. But when the authors contrast the denotation of a phoneme with the denotation of a letter, their usage, "[a letter] usually denotes one of the phonemes," carries the misuse of 'denote' beyond possible justification. A letter does not denote anything, not even in the most stretched sense of 'denote' — in general, of course, because within certain symbolic formulae letters very definitely do denote something; but the authors clearly do not refer to this exceptional usage. Between a letter in a phonemic orthography and a certain phoneme there exists, of course, by definition, a certain relationship, but it is not that of denoting. The status of a letter, in a graphic system, is *analogous* to that of a phoneme, in a phonemic system. They are counterparts in their respective systems. This seems to a logician so obvious that he is often at a loss to understand all those distinguished linguists who claim otherwise. The explanation that the linguists are confusing here historical with logical primacy, the asymmetricity of the relation 'precedes-in-time' with the asymmetricity of 'denotes', is not always sufficient, certainly not in the present case. Could it be that the authors here fell prey to the fallacy, well-known to logicians, of "the confusion of use and mention of signs"? Could it be that because something that looks like a letter is often used to denote a phoneme — the phoneme /k/ being customarily denoted by '/k/' — that their misleading formulation arose? (Notice that nothing is denoted either by the letter 'k' or by the phoneme /k/, whereas the letter 'k' is denoted, for instance, by "k", though so-called autonymous denotations[2] are also often used by linguists, with certain confusions occasionally arising.

[2] I.e., a situation where a sign is denoted by itself, or rather where a sign-type is denoted by one of its sign-tokens. Cf., e.g., R. Carnap, *Logical Syntax of Language*, London-New York 1937, § 42, A. Tarski, *Introduction to Logic*, New York 1946 (2nd ed.) § 18, or W. V. O. Quine, *Mathematical Logic*, New York 1940, § 4.

At the end of the passage, the authors try to strengthen their point by invoking a musical analogy: "One could neither state that musical form is manifested in two variables — notes and sounds — nor that linguistic form is manifested in two equipollent substances — graphic and phonic. And just as musical form cannot be abstracted from the sound matter it organizes, so form in phonemics is to be studied in relation to the sound matter which the linguistic code selects, readjusts, dissects, and classifies along its own lines. Like musical scales, phonemic patterning is an intervention in nature, an artifact imposing logical rules upon the sound continuum." This analogy is interesting but totally wrong. The sound *re* is not analogous either to a phoneme or to a letter, not even to a morpheme, but rather to what a morpheme denotes. This sound can be denoted by a certain geometrical pattern of lines and ellipses just as it can be denoted by (the written letter-sequence) 're' or (the spoken sound) [re]. In music, the denotata of the various possible denotational systems *are* sounds — with *other* sounds, in some of the systems, denoting them; but in linguistics, phonemes and letters have no denotata, whereas the denotata of morphemes and graphemes are, in general, non-linguistic entities — 'dog' and /dog/ both denote dogs (though they also fulfill other functions).

The word 'logical' in the last sentence of the quoted passage is irksome. In order to interpret the function of this word in the phrase 'an artifact imposing logical rules upon the sound continuum', as well as in many other phrases used by Professor Jakobson in prior publications, I replace it by — zero. Could I be mistaken?

2. On the whole, there can be no good arguments against trying to reduce the set of phonemes of any language (or all languages) to a smaller set of other entities. And there are many good reasons for using such more basic units, call them 'features'. The specific treatment, however, which this reduction receives in *Fundamentals* leaves me still not quite convinced, and the claim for exclusiveness and uniqueness of the presented analysis seems to me totally unjustified. But a detailed criticism, though certainly a most worthwhile enterprise, is beyond the frame of these remarks. I intend to comment here on one aspect only of the whole problem, which has some special methodological interest, viz. to the claim of the authors that the distinction they make between distinctive and redundant features is an absolute and intrinsic one. I do not think that this claim is anywhere explicitly formulated in the *Fundamentals* but it is everywhere implicitly involved.

If ten people gather in a room containing six chairs, four people are "redundant", in the sense that even if the seating capacity of the room is fully exploited — assuming that only one person can sit in one chair at a time — four people will remain unseated. So far, it makes no sense to say that John, Bill, Mary and Ann are redundant whereas the other six are not. Only by introducing additional considerations and conventions can an assignment of the redundancy to certain four people be justified. One might, for instance, take the time of arrival into consideration or invoke a "family hold back" principle or take age into account. None of these assignments, however, can make any claim to exclusiveness or naturalness.

When the articulation of a certain sound S in a language L can be characterized by its possession of the features A, B, C, D, and E — no "different" sound (-type or -design) possessing the same features, and it turns out that wherever a sound in L possesses feature D it also possesses feature E, and vice versa, and that whenever a sound in L, if produced under certain circumstances or in a certain environment, possesses feature B, it also possesses feature C, and vice versa, it makes sense to say that the *feature set* [A, B, C, D, E] characterizing S is redundant to a certain degree under any conditions and in any environment, and to an even stronger degree under certain specific conditions or in certain specific environments. So far, it makes no sense to single out the feature D, rather than E, as being an absolutely redundant feature, or to single out B, rather than C, as being a conditionally redundant feature. Such a singling out is extraneous to the situation, though there might be certain purposes for which a conventional assignment of redundancy to some of the features, instead of to the whole set, might be a worthwhile procedure. But it must be clear that for different purposes different assignments are appropriate, and that for some purposes no such assignment might turn out to be helpful.

If in French, the phonemes /b/ and /p/ share so many features but differ (only) in that /b/, under normal conditions, is implemented by a lenis and voiced sound, whereas /p/ is implemented by a fortis and voiceless sound, there being no phoneme whose implementation, under normal conditions, shares the common features of /b/ and /p/ with them but is either lenis and voiced or fortis and voiceless, then the feature sets [—, —, —, —, lenis, voiceless] and [—, —, —, —, fortis, voiced] are redundant (the dashes indicating the common features). But so far, there can be no justification for the claim that the lenis/fortis opposition (to change now somewhat the terminology, in accordance with the author's none too consistent usage) is distinctive, whereas the voiceless/

voiced opposition is redundant. If the authors still make just this claim, they seem to justify it by considerations of simplicity and elegance of characterization. Characterizing /b/ by [—, —, —, —, lenis] is certainly simpler, more elegant and more economical than characterizing it by [—, —, —, —, lenis, voiceless]. (The assignment of distinctiveness to the lenis feature rather than to the voiceless feature is due to still other considerations that need not be discussed here). But this gain is a spurious one. The statement that the implementation of /b/ by a normal French speaker under normal conditions is voiced, rather than voiceless or indifferent with respect to these features, has still to be made somewhere. Simplicity is a virtue of a whole system. An increase of simplicity in one part of a system, if accompanied by a decrease in the remainder, is of doubtful value. But the situation in our particular case is even worse. The authors are obliged to state that under abnormal conditions, such as energetic shouting, or whispering, the distinctive function of the distinctive features may be taken over by the (normally) redundant features (pp. 9–10). Here the spurious elegance surely backfires. No such statement has to be made at all for a characterization of phonemes by redundant feature sets. From a comparison with the other feature sets one can read off immediately whether the disappearance ("neutralization") of certain features under certain conditions will or will not lead to a loss of unique identification of the phoneme involved.[3]

The taking over of the distinctive function by a (normally) redundant feature should by no means be understood as a psychological observation, as if the listener, under normal conditions, were to take account only of the distinctive features, whereas he attends to the redundant features only under abnormal conditions. This interpretation is explicitly repudiated by the authors. To use a certain well-known slogan, they do not claim that the distinctive features have a greater psychological reality than the redundant ones.

Altogether, I believe that there remain no good reasons for the distinction between distinctive and redundant among the features. I believe that all the valuable points incorporated in this terminology can be made as simply, or even more simply, by the 'redundant feature set' terminology which avoids, in addition, the less desirable points of the 'distinctive-redundant feature' terminology.

[3] I believe that C. F. Hockett intends to make a similar, if not identical, point in his criticism of the "determining-determined"-terminology; see his *A Manual of Phonology* (Indiana University Publications in Anthropology and Linguistics, Memoir 11), Baltimore 1955, especially pp. 172–175.

For those who are not yet convinced of the pointlessness of the "economy" introduced by the distinctive-redundant division, let me give an analogy from elementary geometry. A rectangle is customarily defined as a quadrangle whose four angles are right angles. One might accuse this definition — and some mathematicians did so — of redundancy: it would suffice to require in the definiens that at least three angles should be right; for Euclidean geometry the rightness of the fourth angle can then be proved. Though this might be a useful thing to do for certain axiomatic purposes, it is regarded as pointless by most mathematicians. The gain in "economy" is offset first by a certain loss of intuitiveness — which has its pedagogical values, to say the least — and second by the fact that the statement that every rectangle has four right angles, an immediate consequence of the ordinary definition, has now to be laboriously proved. On the other hand, of course, under the ordinary definition a theorem has to be proved to the effect that any quadrangle with at least three right angles has exactly four right angles. Incidentally, such a theorem seldom occurs in ordinary textbooks, because of its relative unimportance. (The reader will find no difficulty in pointing out the weaknesses of the analogy, but my argument does not depend only on its strength.)

3. The authors dedicate much space to the discussion of the relationship between phonological entities and sound. They distinguish between what they call an *inner*, immanent approach adopted, for instance, by Bloomfield and themselves, and various *outer* approaches. Unfortunately, the mode of expression they use to explain the inner approach is rather metaphorical; locutions like "the distinctive features are present in the sound waves," or "the inner approach locates the distinctive features and their bundles within the speech sounds, be it on their motor, acoustical or auditory level" are certainly not to be taken literally. And they are of little help to someone who, for methodological reasons, is interested in the relationship between phonemes, features and sounds. They even look slightly inconsistent — sound waves have no motor level — though this can easily be remedied.

I shall not go into a discussion of the authors' presentation of the various outer approaches and the validity of their criticisms. None of the views presented, including the authors' own one, is completely convincing, especially because of their heavy reliance on metaphors and the subsequent lack of clarity and precision. Nevertheless, almost all views presented seem to contain some grain of truth, and their mutual inconsistency seems occasionally to be due more to unfortunate modes of expression than to the fact that all except at most one must be wrong.

It is at this point that a certain methodological insight, recently obtained — or, to be more precise, recently clearly formulated — might be of help, both in eliminating inessential differences and in bringing into focus the essential ones. The terminology, in which this insight will be formulated here, is in part already quite customary among psychologists, with the remainder coined in the investigation of Professor Rudolf Carnap on the methodological character of theoretical concepts,[4] in which this insight has found its concise formulation.

Let me give a rough outline of the main ideas of this investigation, insofar as they are of relevance to our present problem. Many methodologists of science, though not all, distinguish between two parts in the language of science, the *observational* part, on the one hand, and the *theoretical* part, on the other. (The actual terms are, of course, sometimes quite different.) A logician might prefer to speak about two languages of science instead of two parts of the one language. I shall use here an intermediate way of expression and talk of the two *sublanguages* of science, the observational and the theoretical one. This distinction is mostly drawn with respect to physics, for certain well-known historical reasons, but is now occasionally applied to psychology. I intend to show that a similar distinction should prove to be of great methodological usefulness also for linguistics.

The observational sublanguage of physics contains such terms as 'warm', 'loud', 'red', 'warmer than', 'louder than', 'brighter than', referring to observable properties and relations. The theoretical sublanguage of physics, on the other hand, contains such terms as 'atom', 'spin' and 'electromagnetic field'. According to some conceptions, the observational sublanguage contains also such simple quantity terms as 'temperature' and 'weight'. Each sublanguage contains, of course, also all those terms that are explicitly definable on the basis of the primitive descriptive terms of this sublanguage (in addition to the logical terms). This last statement will later be expanded.

Since the terms of the observational sublanguage are ordinary words and phrases (say, of English) or their one-to-one symbolic counterparts, and their combination into sentences follows the rules of ordinary syntax

---

[4] R. Carnap, "The methodological character of theoretical concepts" in: Feigl and Scriven (eds.), *The Foundations of Science and the Concepts of Psychology and Psychoanalysis* (Minnesota Studies in the Philosophy of Science, vol. I), Univ. of Minnesota Press, 1956.

(or, again, their simple symbolic counterparts), no problems arise as to the interpretation of the sentences of this sublanguage.

The situation is different with regard to the theoretical sublanguage. Unfortunately, it is impossible, without presupposing a considerable amount of knowledge in modern logic, to describe in detail the logical structure of this sublanguage. A certain loss of precision in the following discussion is the inevitable result. It is hoped, however, that this loss will not seriously impair the value of this discussion.

The theoretical sublanguage will contain a number of primitive descriptive constants, in addition to its logical vocabulary, as well as the terms defined on their basis. Instead of 'theoretical terms', the expressions 'theoretical constructs' and 'hypothetical constructs' are often used. A theory, formulated in this sublanguage, consists of a finite number of *postulates* containing, in addition to logical terms, only the theoretical terms. Finally, *correspondence rules* are given, which connect the theoretical terms with the terms of the observational sublanguage.

The theory by itself, without the correspondence rules, is an *uninterpreted calculus*. Its terms and sentences are so far without meaning, and the theoretical language, so far, is useless as a means of communication. With the adjunction of the correspondence rules, the theoretical terms become interpreted, the theoretical sentences meaningful, the whole theoretical language a means of communication. However,— and here comes the decisive new insight — these correspondence rules connect in general only *some* of the theoretical terms with the observational terms, providing them with a direct though still in general incomplete interpretation, whereas the remainder of the theoretical terms receive their interpretation only indirectly and still more incompletely by their being connected with the first terms through the postulates. Let me stress at this point that, without going into a detailed description of the form of the correspondence rules, these rules should by no means be considered as definitions, not even as disguised ones; such a shapeless conception of definitions would, in our case, result in much harm to an understanding of the situation.

I promised before to elaborate on the status of terms definable on the basis of the primitive descriptive terms of the observational sublanguage. The situation is quite complicated, due to the fact that one may be more or less liberal with regard to the structure of the definitions admitted for this purpose. The strictest approach would admit only explicit definitions of an extensional form (i.e. a form that does not involve either logical or causal modalities). Less strict approaches would also admit the introduction of non-primitive terms either by means of explicit definitions in a non-extensional form, i.e. using modal terms such as 'possible' and 'necessary' or subjunctive conditionals, or by means of certain kinds of conditional definitions, so-called reduction sentences. The most important kind of terms introduced by definitions of the latter types are the so-called *disposition terms* like 'elastic' or 'brittle'; such terms, if their introductory phrase makes no use of theoretical terms, will be called *pure disposition terms*.

I already mentioned that not all philosophers of science subscribe to the double-sublanguage view. Operationists, like the physicist Bridgman and the psychologist Skinner, would claim that the language of science need not contain anything besides terms that are either logical or else observable predicates or pure disposition terms; no scientific term needs to be considered as a theoretical term. Carnap, like many other scientists and philosophers, regards this view as too narrow and as not easily reconcilable with current scientific practice.

I am afraid that the outline given here was none too convincing. The interested reader will be well advised to read Carnap's article in extenso as well as a careful and detailed paper by C. G. Hempel on the same topic, in the second volume of the Minnesota Studies in the Philosophy of Science. As to psychology in particular, the paper by MacCorquodale and Meehl[5] should be consulted, whose distinction between *intervening variables* and *theoretical constructs* seems to coincide, more or less, with that between pure disposition terms and theoretical terms, though the observation language to which the authors refer contains also certain quantitative terms.

It must therefore come rather naturally to try to apply this whole view, or rather this whole gamut of views, to the present status of linguistics. I do not think that this has been done before.

It seems, if one is somewhat bold in the interpretation of the various metaphors that mar the authors' discussion of the "inner" and "outer" approaches on pp. 8–17, that this distinction mirrors once more the distinction between the pure-disposition-term view (or the one-language view) and the theoretical-term view (or the double-sublanguage view). The authors, following Bloomfield, insist on defining phoneme (and distinctive feature) on the basis of the observable properties of speech

---

[5] K. MacCorquodale and P. E. Meehl, "Hypothetical Constructs and Intervening Variables," *Psychological Review* 55 (1948), reprinted in Feigl and Brodbeck, *Readings in Philosophy of Science*, New York 1953, pp. 596–611.

sounds, though these observable properties have again to be interpreted in a liberal way and to include properties whose establishment involves certain measurements. The adherents of the various variants of the outer view, on the other hand, seem to regard the terms 'phoneme' etc., as theoretical terms, whose connection with "concrete sounds" is only indirect and incomplete.

So far, this is, of course, all very vague and perhaps unconvincing. Only a very detailed study could conclusively prove the fruitfulness of showing that the recent methodological quarrels within linguistics fall into a pattern well-known from other sciences. Such a study will not be easy: the ways in which linguists are used to formulate their methodological attitudes is often very idiosyncratic and metaphorical, and a constant danger of misinterpretation lurks behind any attempt to put their formulations into a unified terminological framework.

The following scattered remarks will therefore be of a programmatic and sketchy nature.

a. I already once[6] had the opportunity of calling attention to the fact that insufficient knowledge of recent developments in logic and methodology often causes linguists anxieties over the seemingly unbridgeable disagreements on such issues as the definitions of the most basic concepts. Let me intimate, as an illustration, that the difficulties in coming to agreement on the definition of phoneme might not be due to the ineptitude of the (fellow-)linguist but rather to the fact that such a definition cannot be given, at least not in the form of an explicit definition using observational predicates only. It might perhaps be more appropriate to treat 'phoneme' as a primitive theoretical term, connected by postulates with other theoretical terms like 'feature', 'environment', 'immediately preceding' etc., and connected with the observational terms like 'speech sound', 'phone', 'velum', directly or indirectly, by certain correspondence rules. Instead of being bewildered by the failure of arriving at a generally acceptable definition of the basic terms of linguistics and by the accompanying weird controversies, linguists could now perhaps come to an agreement on the underlying postulates and on the worthwhileness of transferring their disagreement to the exact form of the correspondence rules to be adopted. The old schoolbook recipe of 'define your terms' has now to be recognized as misleading

---

[6] Y. Bar-Hillel, "On Recursive Definitions in Empirical Sciences", *Proceedings of the XIth International Congress of Philosophy*, volume V, 1953, pp. 160–165 [reprinted here as Ch. 26].

and unjustified, especially when the terms involved are theoretical ones. The new recipe, 'list your postulates and correspondence rules', is less attractive as a slogan but more efficient.

I believe that the double-sublanguage view is already implicit, for instance, in the "fictionalist" view of Twaddell, criticized by the authors on pp. 13–14. It is understandable that scientists who have not quite mastered the methodological niceties of the double-sublanguage approach to their discipline will be worried about the ontic status of their theoretical concepts and, misled by the fact that these concepts are not defined in terms of observable predicates, tend to assign them a kind of second-quality reality, often dubbed as "fictional." This again will irk other scientists who will interpret the fictional character of these theoretical constructs as being "arbitrary," "having no necessary correlate in concrete experience" and who will feel that the objective value of this discipline is thereby endangered. A clear understanding of the workings of the two sublanguages of science should completely eliminate these quibbles.

b. I hope that I am not using too much force when I interpret the "algebraic" approach of Hjelmslev as an attempt to stress the theoretical character of the basic linguistic notions. That the "expression plane" of language can be studied without any recourse to phonetic premises — as the authors formulate Hjelmslev's thesis — may mean nothing more than that the postulational theory of the linguistic structure of a certain language can be usefully studied as such, without having to invoke at every stage the correspondence rules, a thesis to which I think one cannot but consent. Without the correspondence rules, however, the theory remains an uninterpreted calculus and is, therefore, in a certain important sense, not a linguistic theory at all. I venture to interpret the authors' criticism of Hjelmslev's approach as accusing it of playing down the role of these rules, on the one hand, which might be correct, and as a critique of the double-sublanguage view in general, on the other, which seems to me unsubstantiated.

I hope to have made it clear that I am not interested in cheap peace-making or in an uncritical eclecticism but that it is my firm belief that many of the currently raging methodological controversies in linguistics are due to misunderstandings that are based, in their turn, on an insufficient utilization of the tools that modern general methodology is able to put at the disposal of the scientists. I am, of course, quite aware that an important role in these controversies is also played by all kinds of overt or hidden metaphysical beliefs cherished by the participants in these controversies. I hope that a unified terminology will also help to assess the exact role played by these beliefs, and hence perhaps help to overcome their detrimental effects.

It is my impression that the double-sublanguage view will also solve another puzzle (at least it was a puzzle to me). I refer now to the relation between utterance and sentence. The customary view which regards a sentence as a kind of utterance not only runs into seemingly insuperable difficulties in determining the specific nature of this kind but left me, at least, dissatisfied in principle. I had always the feeling that linguists *treat* these two terms as being on two entirely different levels, whereas they *talk* about them as belonging to the same level. I am quite convinced now, and I think that not too much deliberation is required in order to come to this conviction, that 'sentence' is best treated as a theoretical term — as used by linguists, not necessarily as used in ordinary life — whereas 'utterance' is rather an observational term. What connects 'sentence' with 'utterance' is not a definition but rather a set of correspondence rules.

Let me stress again that my last remarks were sketchy and occasionally rather dogmatic. A more systematic and better documented treatment will perhaps be undertaken at some other occasion.

DECISION PROCEDURES FOR STRUCTURE IN NATURAL LANGUAGES

The rules of formation of a logistic system are by definition[1] such that the notion of formula, well-formed formula or sentence, determined by these rules, is effectively decidable. However, I am not convinced that the arguments brought forth by Church[2] to the effect that sentencehood *has* to be an effectively decidable notion for *any* system that may be used for communication purposes are conclusive. I therefore regard it to be a serious problem whether the syntactic structure of a natural language such as English can always be adequately described by a set of formation rules that guarantee the decidability of the notion of sentence or, for that matter, of any syntactic structures such as nominal phrases etc. Inasmuch as there exist good reasons for doubting whether the answer to this problem is affirmative, the prospects for completely automatic, high-quality machine translation from one natural language into another natural language look dimmer than many workers in the field of machine translation would like to think. This since not even one necessary, though by no means sufficient, condition for this process, namely the mechanical determination of the syntactic structure of any given sentence in the source language, could possibly be completely fulfilled. Though applicability to machine translation is often in the back of my thinking on the description of the syntax of natural languages, I shall refer here no longer to this application, having dealt with it elsewhere at some length.[3]

The seriousness of our problem has apparently not been sufficiently recognized so far because many linguists explicitly, and most, if not all of them, as well as most logicians, implicitly believed that the syntactic structure of natural languages is adequately describable by an *immediate constituent model*, or a *phrase structure model* according to the term recently introduced by Chomsky.[4] It is indeed true that if

---

[1] See, e.g., A. CHURCH, *Introduction to mathematical logic* I, Princeton, 1956, p. 51. There exist, however, less demanding conceptions.

[2] *Ibid.*, p. 53.

[3] In *Some linguistic obstacles to machine translation*, forthcoming in the Proceedings of the Second International Congress of Cybernetics, held in Namur, September 1958 [reprinted here as Ch. 27].

[4] See N. CHOMSKY, *Three models for the description of language*, IRE Transactions on Information Theory, Vol. IT-2, No. 3 (1956) and *Syntactic Structures*, 's-Gravenhage, 1957.

natural languages were adequately describable in terms of such a model, there would exist a decision procedure for structure, as I have shown in effect, though not with full rigour, in a paper published some five years ago.[5]

Before I proceed to present some arguments for the fact that the phrase structure model is not fully adequate, let me spend some time in presenting again, in briefer and I hope improved form, an informal outline of this proof. The basic idea behind the immediate constituent model is that every sentence can be regarded as a result of the operation of one continuous part of it upon the remainder such that those constituent parts which in general are not sentences themselves, but rather phrases, are themselves again the product of the operation of some continuous part upon the remainder, etc., until one arrives at the final constituents, say words or morphemes. To illustrate:

Young John slept soundly

would be regarded as the result of the operation of *slept soundly* upon *young John*; *slept soundly* in its turn would be considered the result of the operation of *soundly* upon *slept* and *young John* the result of the operation of *young* upon *John*. All this so far is nothing but reformulation in somewhat unfamiliar terms of the procedure well known from school days as parsing. As linguists put it, *young John* and *slept soundly* are the immediate constituents of the sentence under discussion, *young* and *John* the immediate constituents of the first immediate constituent of the sentence, *slept* and *soundly* the immediate constituents of the second immediate constituent. *young*, *John*, *slept* and *soundly* are the final constituents of the given sentence.

Another basic feature of the model is that all operator constituents must be contiguous with their argument constituents. Both these features are exemplified in our illustration, but this of course is by no means a proof that this model can be carried through all of language. On the contrary, linguists have realized that occasionally discontinuous constituents have to be taken into account, but they seem to have believed that these were exceptions which did not seriously affect the validity of the model with which they were used to work.

In most language systems invented by logicians, the two mentioned features were automatically incorporated into their respective rules of

---

[5] *A quasi-arithmetical notation for syntactic description*, Language 29: 47–58 (1953) [reprinted in LI as Ch. 5].

formation. The problems arising in connection with discontinuous expressions were, to my knowledge, never explicitly discussed by logicians.

According to the immediate constituent model, every word — and we shall for our purposes consider words to be the basic syntactic elements — of a natural language belongs to one or more syntactic categories. Among these categories some will be *pure argument categories*, by which term I denote a category whose members always serve as arguments and never as operators, as well as *operator categories* whose members may operate upon other words though they may perhaps also be operated upon by other operator expressions. *John*, for instance, in as much as it belongs to the syntactic category of *nominals*, is always an argument and never an operator. *Slept*, inasmuch as it belongs to the category of *intransitive verbals*, may operate upon a nominal such as *John* to form the sentence *John slept*, but may also be operated upon by the adverbial *soundly* to form the intransitive verbal expression *slept soundly*. A word may belong to more than one category not only because it may be regarded as homonymous — as would be the case with regard to *sleep*, which clearly belongs to the category of nominals as well as to the category of intransitive verbals — but also because, for instance, many adverbials operate upon intransitive verbals as well as upon transitive verbals: *soundly*, for example, in the sentence

Belgium soundly defeated the Netherlands

(in the last soccer game, of course) operates upon the transitive verbal *defeated*, forming the transitive verbal expression *soundly defeated*, and has therefore a different kind of argument as well as a different kind of value than has *soundly* when operating upon *slept*.

In order to exhibit the decision procedure or constituent structure let us denote, following Leśniewski and Adjukiewicz,[6] the category of nominals by "*n*" and the category of declarative sentences by "*s*". (Since I am engaged in presenting an outline only, I shall not here go into the very difficult question to what degree these two argument categories would have to be refined and expanded in order to get even the beginnings of a reasonably working model.) Operator categories will be denoted by symbols that will indicate both the categories of their arguments and the category of the resulting expression. In addition, since arguments may be positioned either at the immediate left or at the

---

[6] See K. ADJUKIEWICZ, *Die syntaktische Konnexität*, Studia Philosophica, 1:1–27 (1935-36); cf. A. A. FRAENKEL and Y. BAR-HILLEL, *Foundations of set theory*, Amsterdam, 1958, pp. 169–170.

immediate right of their operator, these positions too will have to be indicated in the symbolism. Therefore, I shall, for instance, denote the category of *slept* by "$n\backslash s$" — read: n sub s — and the category of *young* by "n/n" — read: n super n[7] —, where the direction of the slash indicates in an obvious fashion whether the argument is to the left or to the right. *And*, for instance, *qua* sentence connective will be assigned to the category $s\backslash s/s$, since in this function it is a word that out of a sentence to its immediate left and a sentence to its immediate right forms a sentence. *Soundly* will belong to the categories $(n\backslash s)\backslash(n\backslash s)$ — to be abbreviated in a self-explanatory way as $n\backslash s\backslash\backslash n\backslash s$ — and $n\backslash s/n /\!/ n\backslash s/n$ — as well as to a few other categories.

Assume now that we have a complete category list of all English words, i.e. a list which gives all the categories to which every English word may belong. In order to arrive by a completely mechanical procedure at the constituent structure of any given English sentence, one would only have to copy from the category list the category symbols for all the words in this sentence, write them down in columns and go to work on them according to the following rule: *Replace a sequence of three symbols having, respectively, the form* α, $\alpha\backslash\beta/\gamma$ *and* γ, *with* β. This rule comprises as limiting cases the following two subrules: (1) Replace the sequence of symbols of the form α and $\alpha\backslash\beta$ by β. (2) Replace the sequence of symbols of the form β/γ and γ by β.

Instead of going into a detailed but rather obvious description of the decision procedure, let us illustrate through a somewhat more elaborate example. Assume that the word sequence to be tested for sentencehood as well as for its constituent structure is

Paul thought that John slept soundly.

Assume further that copying from the category list yields the following result:

$$\begin{array}{cccccc}
\textit{Paul} & \textit{thought} & \textit{that} & \textit{John} & \textit{slept} & \textit{soundly} \\
n & n & n & n & n\backslash s & n\backslash s\backslash\backslash n\backslash s \\
 & n\backslash s & n/n & & & n\backslash s/n /\!/ n\backslash s/n \\
 & n\backslash s/n & n/s & & & \cdot \\
 & n\backslash s/s & & & & \cdot \\
 & \cdot & & & & \\
 & \cdot & & & &
\end{array}$$

---

[7] In the paper mentioned in note 3 I used a less convenient symbolism. The present symbolism is due to J. LAMBEK, *The mathematics of sentence structure*, American Mathematical Monthly 65:154 (1958).

(the three dots indicating that the complete list would probably contain further entries which shall, however, be here disregarded for the sake of simplification). The reader will do well to envisage contexts in which *thought* and *that* will belong to each of the given categories. He might as well try to find out to which categories *thought* would belong in such contexts as *John had thought of* ..., ... *thought processes*, and ... *thought provoking* ... .

Now, taking into account only the categories explicitly indicated we have twenty-four initial symbol sequences to which we will apply our rule. Starting for instance with

$$n \quad n \quad n \quad n \quad n\backslash s \quad n\backslash s\backslash\backslash n\backslash s$$

we see that sub-rule (1) can be applied for the fourth and fifth symbols, yielding *s*. The resulting sequence is now

$$n \quad n \quad n \quad s \quad n\backslash s\backslash\backslash n\backslash s,$$

which obviously cannot be further operated upon. The same sub-rule operating upon the fifth and sixth symbols yields $n\backslash s$, hence the sequence

$$n \quad n \quad n \quad n \quad n\backslash s,$$

which has once more to be operated upon by the same sub-rule, yielding

$$n \quad n \quad n \quad s,$$

which cannot be processed any further.

Performing these operations upon all the twenty-four initial symbol sequences through all possible continuations, we would find that there exist exactly three *derivations* as we shall call columns of symbol sequences each of which (with the exception of the first, of course) results from the preceding line by one application of the rule — whose final line, or *exponent*, consists of a single symbol which in all cases is "*s*".

Here are the derivations:

$$
\begin{array}{llllll}
n & n\backslash s/n & n/s & n & n\backslash s & n\backslash s\backslash\backslash n\backslash s \\
& & & & \multicolumn{2}{c}{\underline{\hspace{2em}}} \\
n & n\backslash s/n & n/s & n & \multicolumn{2}{c}{n\backslash s} \\
& & & \multicolumn{2}{c}{\underline{\hspace{2em}}} & \\
n & n\backslash s/n & n/s & s & & \\
& & \multicolumn{2}{c}{\underline{\hspace{2em}}} & & \\
n & n\backslash s/n & \multicolumn{2}{c}{n} & & \\
\multicolumn{3}{c}{\underline{\hspace{4em}}} & & & \\
\multicolumn{2}{c}{s} & & & &
\end{array}
$$

$$
\begin{array}{cccccc}
n & n\backslash s/s & n/n & n & n\backslash s & n\backslash s\backslash\backslash n\backslash s \\
 & & & & \multicolumn{2}{c}{\underline{\qquad\qquad}} \\
 & & & & \multicolumn{2}{c}{n\backslash s}
\end{array}
$$

$$
\begin{array}{cccccc}
n & n\backslash s/s & n/n & n & n\backslash s & \\
 & & \multicolumn{2}{c}{\underline{\qquad}} & & \\
 & & \multicolumn{2}{c}{n} & &
\end{array}
$$

$$
\begin{array}{cccccc}
n & n\backslash s/s & & n & & n\backslash s \\
 & & & \multicolumn{3}{c}{\underline{\qquad\qquad\qquad}} \\
 & & & \multicolumn{3}{c}{s}
\end{array}
$$

$$
\begin{array}{cc}
n & n\backslash s/s \\
\multicolumn{2}{c}{\underline{\qquad\qquad\qquad\qquad\qquad\qquad}} \\
\multicolumn{2}{c}{s}
\end{array}
$$

$$
\begin{array}{cccccc}
n & n\backslash s/s & n/n & n & n\backslash s & n\backslash s\backslash\backslash n\backslash s \\
n & n\backslash s/s & n/n & n & n\backslash s & n\backslash s\backslash\backslash n\backslash s \\
 & & & & \multicolumn{2}{c}{\underline{n\backslash s}} \\
n & n\backslash s/s & & n & & n\backslash s \\
 & & & \multicolumn{3}{c}{\underline{n\backslash s}} \\
n & n\backslash s/s & & & s & \\
\multicolumn{2}{c}{\underline{\qquad\qquad s \qquad\qquad}}
\end{array}
$$

The last two derivations being equivalent, in a rather obvious sense of the word, we have only two essentially different derivations before us, indicating, probably to the surprise of many readers — and to my own surprise some six years ago when I came across this situation simulating a machine processing of this illustration —, that the sentence under discussion is *syntactically ambiguous* or *constructionally homonymous*. The reader will do well to read out aloud this sentence according to its two essentially different constituent structures which in this case make the sentence also semantically ambiguous as such, though one constituent structure is much less likely to be used than the other.

I hope that this illustration is sufficient to show that under the essential and, as we shall see, highly problematic assumption that a complete and completely adequate category list is available, there exists indeed a wholly mechanical procedure to determine whether a given word sequence is a declarative sentence under one of its constituent structures as well as what all of its constituent structures are.

For certain purposes it is worthwhile to look upon our derivation procedure upside down, i.e. to deal with *expansion* rather than with derivation. The expansion corresponding to the first derivation exhibited above of our sample sentence would look like the following tree:

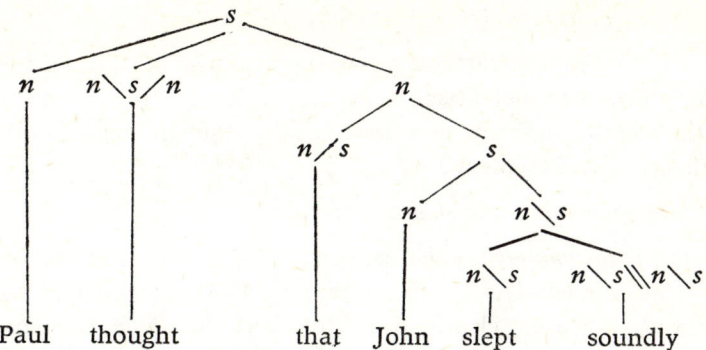

(Two derivations, by the way, are equivalent if they correspond to the same tree.)

How well, then, does the immediate constituent model work? Apparently quite well for relatively short sentences such as those discussed so far, but even there not too well. The number of categories to which the English words will have to be assigned to make the category list reasonably adequate will occasionally have to be rather large, and the categories themselves rather complex. In addition, it is quite clear that not only will one have to work with highly complex refinements of the categories mentioned so far in order to take care, for example, of the fact that *John sleeps* is a sentence but not *John sleep*, but that one will also have to refine the sentence category and distinguish between declarative sentences, imperative sentences, yes-or-no question sentences, *wh*-question sentences, etc., these various types not being reducible to each other under our model. These refinements may result in such piling up of category symbols assigned to the words occurring in a given sentence that the number of derivations would easily run into the trillions, hence be beyond the practical capacity of even the fastest electronic computers. For instance, if the average number of categories of the twenty words of a given English sentence is four, we will have up to 4^{20} initial lines and a still higher number of derivations. This means, then, that the indicated method of mechanically resolving the syntactic structure of any given English sentence would certainly be impractical as such. However, were it the case that this is still a theoretically adequate method, one could think of certain refinements which would reduce the required number of operations by many degrees of order. Unfortunately, however, the actual situation seems to be much worse. It is not only a matter of practicality, but it seems that the whole model is just not good enough. Already six years ago I was worried by sentences such as

>   *John, unfortunately, slept soundly*

which, so it appears at least, cannot be handled by a model incorporating the two above-mentioned basic features. Notice that there is no trouble with the slightly different and semantically, though perhaps not stylistically, equivalent sentence

>   *Unfortunately, John slept soundly.*

Assigning *unfortunately* to the category s/s — a wholly natural and intuitive assignment — we arrive at an adequate syntactic analysis. This assignment, however, clearly does not work for *John, unfortunately, slept soundly* as the reader will easily verify for himself. It is of course possible that some other less natural category assignment to *unfortunately*, perhaps combined with some ingenious treatment of the commas (which so far have been completely disregarded in the immediate constituent model), would do the trick. It seems, however, unlikely that such an assignment could be made in a fashion which would not be almost entirely *ad hoc*. And this would not only be aesthetically and methodologically repugnant, but also in all likelihood have unpleasant repercussions inasmuch as word sequences which intuitively would not be regarded as grammatical sentences would have derivations with an exponent s.

A similar situation, but even simpler since no commas are involved, arises with regard to the word sequence

>   *He looked it up.*

Regarding *he* and *it* as belonging to the categories n — leaving aside once more the clearly required refinements —, *looked* as belonging to the category $n\backslash s/n$, as seems natural, it looks highly implausible that any category assignment of *up* which would not be woefully *ad hoc* would insure the sentencehood of the given word sequence. Assigning *up*, for instance, to the category $s\backslash s$ would obviously result in a derivation with an exponent s, but this unnatural saving of the phenomena would immediately retaliate with the unwanted imposition of sentencehood to such sequences as

>   *He went home up.*

(For further examples of the breakdown of the phrase structure model see Chomsky's *Syntactic Structures*,[8] to which I owe much of the present argument.)

---

[8] See above, note 4.

Every English speaker, I presume, feels that in our sentence

He gave it up

gave and *up* belong somehow together. Indeed, there is no trouble with such a sequence as

He gave up this idea,

as the reader will easily verify for himself if only *up* is assigned in a completely intuitive fashion to the category $n\backslash s/n\backslash\backslash n\backslash s/n$. This being so, assigning *up* to a different category, whatever it may be, in the sentence

He gave it up

looks now even more artificial than before.

These simple facts indicate, though it cannot be said that they prove in the strong sense used in mathematics, that the immediate constituent model is not an adequate one as such, but has to be supplemented in one way or another.

Let me finish this discussion by presenting a very brief outline of one such supplementation, referring the reader for a fuller discussion to Chomsky's mentioned book and other publications of his.[9] The new model, called the *transformational model*, assumes that sentences are generated not only by the procedure we called above expansion, but also, in addition, by so-called *transformations*. One such transformation, for instance, would transform the so-called *terminal string* of the following expansion

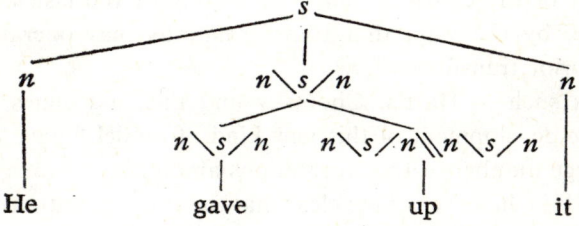

i.e. *He gave up it*, which is, of course, not an English sentence, into *He gave it up* by a certain *obligatory* transformation. This transformation rule, which states in effect that in certain environments certain word

---

[9] Viz., to those mentioned above in note 4, as well as, for instance, to a forthcoming paper, *A transformational approach to syntax.*

sequences have to be turned around, is clearly beyond the reach of an immediate constituent model. On the other hand, this way of looking at how the sentence *He gave it up* was generated has a rather natural appearance, and might well correspond, at least in spirit, to the way old-fashioned, traditional grammar has dealt with the situation.

Other transformations transform two terminal strings into one sentence. One of these, for instance, would operate upon the sequence of the two terminal strings (which are in this special case sentences in their own right)

Paul thought that. John slept soundly.

and turn this sequence into the sentence

Paul thought that John slept soundly.

This very same transformation operates upon the sequence

Paul thought that. That John slept soundly.

and transforms it into

Paul thought that that John slept soundly.

Yet another transformation to the effect that under certain determined conditions *that* may be omitted, hence an *optional* transformation, would transform this last sentence into

Paul thought that John slept soundly.

This way of looking at the situation results now in a natural and adequate explanation of the constructional homonymy of the last sentence. We also realize, by the way, that transformations may operate upon the results of prior transformations.

Linguists such as Harris, Chomsky and their associates who are at work at the development of this new kind of model[10] have already unveiled a large number of transformations amounting to many hundreds, in English. It is, however, quite clear that the transformations introduced so far are not yet sufficient to account for all intuitively possible English sentences. It is at this state that the question mentioned at the beginning of this paper arises — *whether there exists a decision procedure for*

---

[10] In addition to Chomsky's publications, see Z. HARRIS, *Cooccurrence and transformations in linguistic structure*, Language 33:328–340 (1957) and the excellent review of Chomsky's *Syntactic structures* by R. L. Lees in Language 33:375–408 (1957).

structure in English, or in other natural languages for that matter, since it is unlikely that the natural languages should differ among themselves in this respect. Obviously the answer to our question will depend upon the exact nature of the transformations. Only when we will have a better and more extensive understanding of the kind of transformations at work, will we be in a position to fruitfully attack our problem. At this moment one could only speculate about this answer, and it is doubtful whether such speculations would be worthwhile. In any case, even the possibility that for a certain set of formation rules in English the notion of English sentence would not be a decidable (or general recursive) one seems exciting enough to warrant an increase in interest in our problem among mathematical logicians, who by training are in many respects in a better position to attack it than are linguists. Chomsky has already been able to show that there exist highly interesting connections between the theory of linguistic models and such theories as the theory of automata, recursive function theory (perhaps especially conspicuous in the form of the theory of algorithms) and the theory of Post canonical systems. This multiple relationship indicates that we have, in all probability, in the theory of language models an interesting new field in which cross-fertilization of mathematical logic and structural linguistics should lead to important results.

ON A MISAPPREHENSION OF THE STATUS OF THEORIES IN LINGUISTICS

Professor Hall's recent paper[1] is not the first one in which theories are confused with fictions. To look on theories as fictions, i.e., as useful hypotheses known to be false — a characterization Hall accepts from Vaihinger who raised this view to the status of a whole philosophy, the famous *Philosophy of As If* — has been customary among methodologists at all times, but does not make this conception less of a confusion. As Nagel[2] states, "It does not follow, however, that... theories are 'fictions' ...." Had Chomsky, the main linguist under attack by Hall for adhering to fictions, been an instrumentalist (which he definitely is not), he would have claimed that theories have no truth-values at all, hence cannot be known to be false, hence cannot be fictions. Being the realist he is, he has insisted many times that he regards the theories he propounds as true, although, error being human, he might be wrong in doing so.[3]

What Hall does not understand is that the way in which a formal calculus is interpreted to form a theory — in our case, a linguistic theory — is much more complex than is taught in high school and was taught until recently in colleges. As a matter of fact, theoretical terms seldom obtain a full and complete interpretation at all. The relationship between such theoretical linguistic terms as "sentence" or "morpheme" (in a given theory) and observations of linguistic behaviour is not that of a fictional entity to real entities. And the relation between the English sentence *I am hungry* and its innumerable possible realizations in speech, writing, etc. — the various "utterances" of this sentence — is anything but simple.[4] Invoking "fictions" can but befuddle an issue which, though

---

[1] Robert A. Hall, Jr., 'Fact and Fiction in Grammatical Analysis', *Foundations of Language* 1 (1965) 337–45.

[2] Ernest Nagel, *The Structure of Science*, London 1961, p. 134.

[3] I have reservations about both fashionable methodological views, but according to my own anti-ontologizing view, Hall's strictures will fare even worse; see 'Neo-realism vs. Neopositivism: A Neo-Pseudo Issue', *Proceedings of the Israel Academy of Sciences and Humanities*, vol. II, no. 3, 29–37, Jerusalem 1964 [reprinted here as Ch. 23].

[4] More on this relation in my paper mentioned in footnote 3. Cf. also my paper, 'Three Remarks on Linguistic Fundamentals', *Word* 13 (1957) 323–35. [reprinted here as Ch. 28].

complicated, is in principle well understood today. Chomsky, of course, never used the term "fiction" in this connection himself.

Let me now deal in some detail with Hall's four specific objections.

a. *Synchronicity*

This whole section (pp. 337–8) is pointless, since there exists no intrinsic connection whatsoever between transformational rules and "processes in time". Interestingly enough, Hall makes no reference to the literature in the discussion of this "fiction". That transformational grammars may turn out to be useful for the treatment of linguistic change is an interesting recent development, not anticipated in the earlier stages of transformational grammars, but has again nothing to do with whatever Hall may have in mind. As a matter of fact, he does not mention these recent developments.

The analogy Hall draws between the relationship of theories to observations and that of maps and guide-books to a terrain is of very restricted validity. Hall's remark (p. 341), "the publisher of a map of Hamburg, Germany, states that some change in the city's street- and transportation-systems, which are represented 'as if' unchanging on his map, takes place on the average once every two days", is misleading on two counts. First, I am quite sure that the relative clause, "which are represented 'as if' unchanging on his map", is neither a quotation nor even a paraphrase of whatever the publisher stated. Second, taken as an interpretation volunteered by Hall, it is indefensibly biassed. The publisher clearly intended to say no more than that his map, though accurate for a certain date (perhaps left unspecified), should not be taken to reflect with complete accuracy the situation at the time of its use. He presumably issued his warning because many people have a tendency to overlook the time-restricted validity of maps, a tendency which can be partially explained by the fact that some maps, such as so-called physical maps, have indeed a long-range validity. (In addition, there is a certain propaganda value in the statement since it indicates the dynamic development of Hamburg — but let us not go into these chamber-of-commerce aspects.) A map in itself says absolutely nothing about statics or dynamics. Some publishers of maps may be more conscientious than others in drawing attention to their time-restricted validity, but there is nothing 'as-if' about maps as such.

b. *Unidirectionality*

In the passage dealing with the fiction of unidirectionality, the term "fiction" takes, unnoticed by Hall, a meaning different from his original one. He is now talking about "the fiction that description is to proceed, if not exclusively, at least primarily in one direction" (339), from the "top" (syntax) "downwards" (to phonology). Since this fiction is now a certain methodological rule (and no longer a hypothesis), it is clearly senseless to argue about its truth or falsity. Whether this methodological rule is good or bad, useful or misleading, is of course another question that need not concern us here.

Regardless of the validity of Hall's paraphrase of Chomsky's alleged statement that "the human ability to acquire language must be explained by a theory of universal general grammar" (p. 341), I utterly fail to see the connection between this "unwarranted aprioristic statement" and the fiction of unidirectionality. When transformationalists postulate "that certain aspects of mental activity will forever remain unobservable" (p. 342), this is nothing more than a somewhat unfortunate expression in the customary material mode of speech[5] of what in the formal mode of speech would be formulated as "certain mental terms are theoretical, hence not observational (relative to some given theory)" which is a truism. Hall's misunderstanding points to the dangers inherent in the material mode of speech, so persuasively argued by Carnap and others. The move from "permanent unobservability" to "(hence) unaccountability" is Hall's own responsibility (or irresponsibility). Transformationalists have innumerably many times tried to show how their theories can be accounted for, i.e., can be empirically tested. Impossibility of direct, complete interpretation is not unaccountability!

c. *Binary choice*

Hall's claim, "That every step in a process of description must be framed in terms of an 'either-or' alternative is a fiction which is quite useful for certain types of work, especially with machines that operate on this very principle" contains yet another misuse (339) of his own "fiction". Whatever "*must* be" cannot possibly be a fiction. Machines — I guess that Hall has computers in mind — do not always work on the

---

[5] For a treatment of the material mode of speech and the dangers inherent in its use, see Rudolf Carnap, *The Logical Syntax of Language*, London 1937, 308–12, and my paper, 'Carnap's Logical Syntax of Language', *The Philosophy of Rudolf Carnap*, La Salle, Ill., 1963, 519–43, especially section II [reprinted here as Ch. 11].

principle of "either-or" alternatives. They may work on any finite number of alternatives, if digital, or even with a continuous set of alternatives, if analogue. This is a fact that even a linguist should know nowadays. It is also of some interest that Hall finds it necessary to bring up once more the red herring of the close relation between transformational grammar and machine translation. There appears to be a belief in some quarters that if such a relation could be shown to hold, this would provide a powerful argument *ad hominem* against transformationalists, implying perhaps their moral depravity or opportunism. Just for the fun of it, let me corroborate once more that Chomsky's account of this relationship in his own thinking is correct. When I was at MIT during the years 1951–53, working, among other things, also on machine translation,[6] Chomsky showed little interest in this topic. (He was, at that time, a Junior Fellow at Harvard and working on what was to become his Thesis.) When I came back to MIT in the fall of 1955, I officially belonged to a group headed by Victor H. Yngve working on machine translation and related topics in applied linguistics, and so did Chomsky, I think half-time. But let me assure whoever needs this assurance that though I did indeed spend most of my time on applied problems (incidentally, more on mechanization of information retrieval than on machine translation and much more on a critique of these fields than on their development), Chomsky himself was engaged in his own purely theoretical research which was to culminate in the publication of *Syntactic Structures*.

Still under the heading of 'Binary Choice', Hall states: "A further fiction, arising out of obligatory binary choice, has aroused considerable discussion because of its rather obviously fictional nature: that of 'ungrammaticality', the assumption that the end-out-put [sic!] of a transformational process must be either wholly acceptable or wholly unacceptable" (p. 339). This whole subject has already been discussed *ad nauseam* and I see no point in going on. Nobody has worked as much on *degrees of grammaticality* as Chomsky himself.[7] I remember discussing this topic with him in 1952 or 1953. Of course we both knew then what Hall still does not know today, namely, that there exists a large literature on the development of scientific concept formation from

[6] I have told the story at some length in the 'Introduction' to my book *Language and Information*, Reading, Mass., 1964. [Cf. also Ch. 25, here.]

[7] In a review of *The Structure of Language* (J. A. Fodor and J. J. Katz, eds.), Englewood Cliffs, New Jersey, 1964 [reprinted here as Ch. 14]. I have to say more about this topic as such.

the qualitative through the comparative to the quantitative stage, and within the qualitative stage from binary to *n*-ary families of predicates. We both knew that the "grammatical-ungrammatical" dichotomy would have to be replaced, in due time, by more refined conceptual frameworks, though we also knew that even when such a refinement would be forthcoming the simple-minded dichotomy might still remain useful for many purposes.[8]

That dichotomism, as everything else, can be misused is a banality. That it has been so misused in linguistics would be a less trivial observation, but Hall presents little evidence for its truth. In particular, I find it difficult to understand the psychological connections Hall sees between dichotomism and normativism. When "ungrammatical" is understood as the theoretical term it is in Chomsky's framework, it should be clear that no normativist implications could possibly follow from its use. What connection could there be between being a transformationalist and supposing that *than* is only a conjunction and never a preposition (p. 342)? It is certainly true and even important that by not treating *than* as a preposition we would save a rule, but whether this rule can be saved without paying an exorbitant price is an empirical question that no transformationalist I know would want to prejudge.

d. *Writing 'versus' Speech*

Hall's treatment of his fourth "fiction" borders on farce, and the herring is getting redder. He uses again the term "fiction" — contrary to his own definition — for a methodological rule, this time for the rule that "language is to be formulated primarily in terms of writing rather than speech" (p. 340). Hall claims that transformationalists adhere to this rule at least in practice (though on occasion they pay lip-service to the contrary rule). Now, in one sense of this very curious phrase "to formulate language", Hall's claim is of course entirely wrong. All transformational grammars contain morphophonemic rules. Halle has devoted a whole book to *The Sound Pattern of Russian*, and Chomsky and Halle have long ago announced the publication of another book to be called *The Sound Pattern of English* (though I hope they will change the title[9]).

---

[8] For the best presentation of this topic, see Rudolf Carnap, *Logical Foundations of Probability*, Chicago 1950, sections 4 and 5.

[9] [They didn't, and the book was published in 1968 by Harper & Row, New York–Evanston–London.]

By treating language theoretically, no "absolute separation between speech and language" (p. 340) is set up. On the contrary, an interpreted theory provides the unified treatment of language and speech Hall is looking for, and all theories envisaged by transformationalists are of course interpreted, at least in principle, since they are supposed to be theories of (or behind) linguistic behaviour. True enough, this type of unified treatment allows also — when it is carried through with a sufficient amount of precision — for separate treatment of the calculus *qua* algebraic system and thereby allows for the employment of the powerful techniques of algebraic linguistics. The situation is exactly like that prevailing, for instance, in physics. By establishing theoretical physics, it became possible to use the powerful techniques of differential equations, group theory, and probability theory, and of other mathematical calculi. A characterization of this development as a return to "Neo-Platonism and the 'idealistic' dualism" would be greeted with a certain smile.

In this mood, it is difficult to be alarmed by the sinister implications Hall sees in the use of the word "re-write" in the verbal formulation of transformations. Let me assure Professor Hall that this custom is very harmless and is based upon the simple fact that, whenever systems of rules are discussed, it is necessary in practice to write them down to lighten the burden of memorization and to simplify back reference. The arrow used in generative rules, whose customary reading as "rewrite" disturbs Hall so much, is a metalinguistic symbol, and I hope he would agree that, in metalinguistic discussions at least, the "reactionary" view of the superiority of writing and printing over speaking is empirically correct. I know of no intimation by transformationalists that sentences are first produced in one's brain by writing certain symbols on (or in?) one's neurons and then rewriting them there, prior to their utterance of the last line. The question, "What are the neurophysiological counterparts of a linguistic rule and of the application of such a rule?" is still an open one.

There is no doubt that one of the dangers in theorizing mentioned by Hall (though his term is "fictions") is indeed a serious one. People do get enamored of calculi and on occasion start "skating around on the surface ice and cutting fancy figures for their own sake" (p. 345). As a matter of fact, I myself have recently[10] used the same kind of argument in accusing logicians of having gotten so enamored of their formal calculi as to have forgotten to investigate to a sufficient depth

---

[10] In a paper, 'The Logicians' Betrayal' [in Hebrew], *Iyyun* 14 (1964) 120–25.

the question of the applicability of their calculi to argumentation in natural languages. Some recent papers in algebraic linguistics indeed exhibit no obvious applicability to natural languages. Let me then interpret Hall as admonishing his fellow linguists to pay sufficient attention to the rules of interpretation of the theories they construct and not to get lost in the treatment of the calculi exclusively. To this admonition — if it is already needed in linguistics — I am ready to give my wholehearted support.

DICTIONARIES AND MEANING RULES

Such is the force of a precise treatment of a field previously treated in a vague and non-committal way that people who value precision will sometimes accept the terminology and some of the basic tenets of a theory even if they are critical of the theory as a whole.

Since Katz and Fodor in their 1963 paper introduced a new dimension of precision together with a lot of ingenuity into the treatment of linguistic semantics, i.e., descriptive semantics of natural languages, many linguists have tended to accept their conception that the semantic rules of a given natural language can be expressed in terms of a 'dictionary' (plus 'projection rules', which we shall leave aside here), even though they have been critical of other aspects of their approach. As a matter of fact, sometimes they were even dissatisfied with the concept of 'dictionary' as such, but rather than draw the conclusion that perhaps there is no good reason why semantic rules should be forced into this particular straitjacket, they preferred to propose changes in the details of the original Katz-Fodor conception of dictionaries but keeping this conception intact.

I have elsewhere[1] claimed that the Katz-Fodor conception cannot be saved even in principle, unless one just sticks — for reasons stated in the first paragraph — to the term 'dictionary' but exempts it of any specific content, i.e., just turns it into an, at best, superfluous and, at worst, quite misleading synonym for 'semantic rule' (or 'meaning rule'). Let me illustrate this.

In a very interesting recent article, Professor J. F. Staal (1967) is easily able to show that the Katz-Fodor conception of a dictionary is not in a position to account for the fact that, say,

(1) *John precedes Mary*

and

(2) *Mary follows John*

---

[1] 'Universal Semantics and Logic; a critique of some recent theories of semantics', the first of a series of two Forum lectures delivered during the 1966 Linguistic Institute at UCLA; published as the first half of "Universal Semantics and Philosophy of Language", *Substance and Structure of Language* (J. Puhvel, ed.), University of California Press, Berkeley and Los Angeles, 1969, pp. 1–21 [reprinted here as Ch. 15].

are paraphrases of each other, as are

(3) *John sells books to Peter*

and

(4) *Peter buys books from John.*

Now, for any logician (and certainly for one acquainted with Carnap's (1955) notion of 'meaning postulate') it would come natural to explain these paraphrastic relations by saying that English contains, among others, something like the following two meaning rules:

(5) For all X and Y, X precedes Y $\leftrightarrow$ Y follows X,
(6) For all X, Y, and Z, X sells Y to Z $\leftrightarrow$ Z buys Y from X,

or, in a more technical but also more concise mode of speech customary in the logic of relations:

(7) follows is the converse of precedes,[2]
(8) buys from is the 1–3 converse of sells to.

The magic appeal of 'dictionaries' is, however, so strong that Staal regards such treatment as *ad hoc* (twice, on p. 69 and on p. 70) and insists that their effect has to be taken care of by some enlargement of the dictionary, for instance in the form

(9) (*sell*, [+ V, + —— $NP_2 \frown$ to $\frown NP_3$ {*buy from*}]).

(Staal's paper has, in formula (35) — which is our (9) —, NP in lieu of NP_2, but this is doubtless a printing error.) Whether the semantic indicatory symbols in curly brackets, newly introduced by Staal, will be able to do the trick, remains to be seen, but at best they will have the same effect as the meaning rules given above, and are at least as *ad hoc* as these. But I fail to see the whole point of this approach. Something has to be stated somewhere that will have the effect of making (1) and (2) paraphrases of each other; such are the idiosyncrasies of the English verbs *precede* and *follow*. The only question is whether there exists one simplest method of making the required statement. Staal

---

[2] The meaning of this rule, which of course is not formulated as such in grammatical English, is that the relation follows, i.e., the relation denoted by the English verb *follows*, is the converse of the relation precedes, and not that the verbs are converses of each other, though, if one wishes so, one can introduce this mode of speech by definition and say, thereafter, that two phrases (of English, or of any other language) are converses of each other if they denote converse relations.

seems to believe that his curly bracket indicatory symbols are somehow simpler than the converse-relation form, though he gives no argument to support his view. The '*ad hoc*' remark seems to stand in lieu of such argument but is really no more than an indication of the lack of an argument.

Now, Lyons (1963, 72) says in dealing with *converse terms*: "The lexical substitution of *buy* for *sell*, etc., can be thought of as associated with a set of automatic syntactical transformation rules, which carry the sentence containing *buy* over into the *corresponding* sentence containing *sell*." Staal, having quoted this sentence, continues (1967, 69): "But he does not say how this is done." But I am sure that Lyons' only reason for not saying it is that it is so obvious to anyone with a minimum of logical training, namely: in one of the forms I presented above, or any other form essentially equivalent to them, such as

(10) *buys from* = $\text{Cnv}_{1,3}$ (*sells to*).

It is, however, possible that Lyons' somewhat unfortunate term 'automatic syntactical transformation rule' disturbed and misled Staal. There is nothing particularly 'syntactical' about these rules. On the contrary, I definitely prefer the term 'meaning rule' for them, since they say something about the meanings of the phrases with which they deal. Staal may have, correctly, felt this, but being under the magic spell of the 'dictionary' conception drew the automatic conclusion that therefore these rules belong with the dictionary.

That *equals* denotes in English a symmetrical relation, i.e., that

(11) for all X and Y, X equals Y $\leftrightarrow$ Y equals X,

has to be stated somewhere in an adequate linguistic description of English, and though I have (for the time being) no particular objection to doing this in the form

(12) (*equal*, [+V, +——NP{*}]),

I see nothing wrong with stating it as in (11) or, preferably, as

(13) equal is symmetrical,

or as

(12) Sym (equal),

or even, having defined *symmetrical phrases* as phrases denoting symmetrical relations, as

(13) sym (*equal*).

In this particular case, there will, of course, also be no objection to putting this statement into the 'dictionary' so that the dictionary entry for *equal* will be

(14) (*equal*, [..., sym, ...]).

The properties of Sym — alone, and in combination with other relations such as Trans(itive), Refl(exive), Con(nex), etc. — will be treated in Universal Semantics (or Logic) once for all, since they are language-independent. Just to illustrate, one such statement of Universal Semantics will be

(15) (Sym $\cap$ Trans) $\in$ Refl

(read: any symmetrical and transitive relation is also reflexive).

In general, however, the dictionary format for semantic rules will be a Procrustes bed. It follows from the meanings of *father of* and *older than* that

(16) for all X and Y, X is father of Y → X is older than Y.

One simple way of taking care of this semantic fact is to include it among the meaning rules, or preferably its symbolic counterpart

(17) (biological) father of $\in$ older than.

Any attempt to do this in the dictionary format will, in my view, be *ad hoc* and clumsy, at the best. Notice that from (17),

(18) (biological) mother of $\in$ older than,

(19) Trans(older than),

and

(20) grandfather of = father of/(father of or mother of)

or, preferably,

(21) grandfather of = father of/(father of $\cup$ mother of),

we shall deduce that

(22) grandfather of $\in$ older than

and therefore will not have to put this down as a meaning rule.

Not enough attention seems to have been paid so far to the fact that for Katz a dictionary is neither an intralinguistic nor an interlinguistic affair, but a device to represent each of the senses of a term from a natural language "in the form of a theoretical construction, called a 'reading', that is composed not of words from that language, but of symbols expressing language-independent constructs, called 'semantic markers' drawn from the theoretical vocabulary of empirical linguistics" (1967, 41). While lexical definitions, and listings of intra- or interlinguistic (quasi-)synonyms is quite all right, in Katz' opinion, for ordinary reference dictionaries, they do no more than tell us that certain expressions have (approximately) the same meaning but not what this meaning is. This aim of theoretical semantics can only be achieved by theoretical definitions as explained in the quoted text.

Without wanting to enter here into a discussion of this hyper-Leibnizian conception of a world of uniquely determined language-independent constructs in terms of which the senses of every expression in every natural language are to be determined, let me only say that the *theoretical meaning rules* — I hope I do no injustice to Katz in creating this term — will not be exclusively statable in form of *theoretical dictionary definitions* (not even when supplemented by *theoretical projection rules*). This much, I am sure, will be granted by Katz himself. But it seems that the only additional rules he has been ready to consider so far are the *redundancy rules* (and perhaps also *metalinguistic rules*). But this will still not do (again on condition that 'redundancy' retains the meaning intended by Katz). Though

(23)   human $\subset$ animate

can be regarded as a redundancy rule, and perhaps also, though only with a lot of stretching, (15), neither (12) nor (17) should be included, without creating utter confusion. To regard all laws of relational logic, for instance, as either redundancy rules or metalinguistic rules would only mean continuing playing the word magic game.

Let me summarize: I have claimed elsewhere that the thesis that meaning rules can be exhaustively and usefully presented in form of dictionary entries plus projection rules is false. Here, I tried to show that this thesis remains false, even if the notion of dictionary is broadened, along proposals made by Staal, and even if the set of rules is enlarged to contain also redundancy rules and metalinguistic rules. There still remain a number of semantic statements that cannot be usefully put into any of these forms. Nor is there any particular rational reason for wanting to do so. And my claim holds not only for 'normal' intra- or interlinguistic dictionaries but also for 'theoretical' dictionaries.[3]

Traditional dictionaries are useful, both for practical and for theoretical purposes. Katz-type theoretical dictionaries may be useful for certain theoretical purposes. They are so, because some meaning rules can be conveniently put into a dictionary format. But there is a large number of other meaning rules for which this format is not adequate. So why not present them in a different format? That thereby Katz' theory of analyticity will be clearly exhibited as what it is, namely as a very small improvement over Kant's theory and therefore as being about equally inadequate, unpleasant as this result may be for Katz himself who has a different evaluation of his contribution, is just a minor bonus.

REFERENCES

Carnap, R.: 1955, 'Meaning and Synonymy in Natural Languages', *Philosophical Studies* 6, 33–47. (Reprinted in R. Carnap, *Meaning and Necessity: A Study in Semantics and Modal Logic*, 2nd, enlarged edition, Chicago, 1956.)
Katz, J. J.: 1966, *The Philosophy of Language*, New York.
Katz, J. J.: 1967, 'Some Remarks on Quine on Analyticity', *Journal of Philosophy* 64, 36–52.
Katz, J. J. and Fodor, J. A.: 1963, 'The Structure of a Semantic Theory', *Language* 39, 170–210. (Reprinted, with minor revisions, in *Structure of Language: Readings in the Philosophy of Language*, ed. by Jerry A. Fodor and Jerrold J. Katz, Englewood Cliffs, N.J., 1964, pp. 479–518.)
Lyons, J.: 1963, *Structural Semantics: An Analysis of Part of the Vocabulary of Plato*, Oxford.
Staal, J. F.: 1967, 'Some Semantic Relations between Sentoids', *Foundations of Language* 3, 66–88.

Postscriptum:

After completion of the manuscript, Katz's still more recent paper, 'Recent Issues in Semantic Theory', *Foundations of Language* 3 (1967), 124–94, came to my attention. I had seen earlier a preprinted version of

---

[3] Katz's entry for 'Neg' (1966, 201) is, of course, anything but a dictionary entry, or a redundancy rule, or etc., nor does it in any intelligible sense provide for a 'reading' of Neg. It is just a nice old — though very complicated — meaning rule. But even in a still later publication, Katz (1967, 46, n. 5), continues to speak about "introducing adequate readings for 'and', 'or', 'all', 'some', etc.", though already with some hesitations. But I cannot envisage that anything short of an axiom system of propositional logic, or the appropriate truth tables (with their required background), will suffice to establish the truth-functional sense of 'and' — and this format of meaning rules is again a far cry from dictionaries, etc.

it and, still before that, discussed some of the points of my recent paper with Katz himself, Chomsky, and others. There is nothing in this new paper that would want to make me change my view on the exaggerated evaluation of the role of dictionaries in the semantic component. On pp. 171–3, Katz deals explicitly with the *sell-buy* problem discussed above. But Katz's 'solution' indicates very clearly the clumsiness of any attempt to put an appropriate meaning rule, such as our (10), in dictionary format. At the very best, the result of such a straitjacketing is a very inefficient and inelegant duplication of semantic representation. What Katz is essentially doing there is to put a clumsily formulated meaning rule under some 'dictionary entry'.

A NEGLECTED RECENT TREND IN LOGIC

In a recent article,[1] Professor Rescher gave us an illuminating short synopsis of recent trends and developments in logic, together with a useful multiple classification ("map") of logical topics and a concise bibliography of philosophical logic. I am sure that this synopsis will prove of great value for all those who will plan changes in extant curricula in the teaching of logic at university level.

But just for this reason, it is mandatory to call attention to a curious oversight in Rescher's presentation, an oversight that leads him to a partially wrong evaluation of the situation followed by wrong "inescapable" conclusions as to future developments.

After having correctly pointed out that for more than a century the major developments of logic have had a doubly mathematical character, inasmuch as logic obtained an algebraic (and more recently, a number-theoretical, "recursive") look while simultaneously serving as the foundational science for mathematics, he indicates that in recent years, logicians have got interested in a variety of topics of primarily philosophical interest. He envisages a rift developing between mathematical logic and philosophical logic, which he deplores, but regards as close to inevitable. On the other hand, he is greatly gratified by this development of philosophical logic and regards it as an assurance that the threat of logic cutting itself off from philosophy and setting itself up as an autonomous science in its own right has been successfully thwarted.

It is here, I believe, that Rescher goes astray. At no place, either in his synopsis or in his map, does Rescher show any awareness of the fact that logic might perhaps also have something to do with evaluation of the validity of argumentation in natural languages (and whatever other topics are connected with this one). His item B3a (logical analysis of "ordinary usage", falling into Logical Pragmatics which is part of Metalogic) may have something to do with what I have in mind, though it more likely refers to certain (Wittgensteinian ?) philosophical views. I would have thought that the development of methods of evaluating arguments in natural languges should have been the prime topic of logic, of which all the others should have been regarded at most as secondary, and sometimes even "stray", developments. And though I

[1] Nicholas Rescher, Recent developments and trends in logic, *Logique et Analyse*, vol. 9, no. 35–36 (December 1966), pp. 269–279.

would not want to insist on this extreme view too strongly, the total neglect shown by Rescher (and let it be said in all fairness, by the large majority of both mathematical and philosophical logicians) is an indication of an interesting and, in my view, definitely pathological development among professional mathematicians and philosophers in this respect.

Rescher could, of course, counter by claiming that argumentation in natural languages is a topic for whose treatment linguists rather than logicians should be responsible and be held responsible. I don't want to be very dogmatic about this claim which turns on a problem of division of labour. The sad fact, doubtless well known to Rescher, is, however, that linguists have not shown any enthusiasm in taking upon themselves this burden. If possible, they have dealt with argumentation in natural languages even less than the logicians. (Rhetoricians — when this profession was still flourishing — did deal with it, but more from the angle of pragmatic persuasiveness than of logical — or analytic — validity.[2])

Since I have dealt with this *Streit der Fakultäten* in reverse elsewhere,[3] let me not go into any further historical details here. Somebody, some profession, will have to take up this vital and so deplorably neglected field of human activity, and I don't care whether those who do so belong to the Linguistics or Philosophy departments, or even — in view of the enormous importance of the subject — to an independent Logic department, which will be exactly the kind of development which Rescher believes has been avoided in the last minute through the turn of logicians to topics of philosophical interest.

And this is not pure speculation. I would not be surprised to learn that the number of people presently engaged in the "logic of natural languages" (not the "logical analysis of ordinary usage") is not much smaller than the number of people working in philosophical logic. True enough, they usually do not belong to well-established departments in institutions of higher education; more likely, they will be found in industrial research laboratories connected in some way or other with

---

[2] Nor has the New Rhetoric of Professor Ch. Perelman and his associates changed the picture decisively. It is still amazing that this school should not even be mentioned by Rescher in his "map" — the closest is B3b: rhetorical analysis (Aristotelian "topics") — and this in a paper published in a journal appearing under the auspices of the Belgian school of logic.

[3] In a review of J. A. Fodor and J. J. Katz, (eds.), *The Structure of Language*, 1964, *Language*, vol. 43, pp. 226–550 (1967) [reprinted here as Ch. 14]; and "Universal semantics and philosophy of language", *Substance and Structure of Language* (J. Puhvel, ed.), pp. 1–21 [reprinted here as Ch. 15].

computers. These are people who worry about how computers could "process" data fed to them in natural languages, how they could answer questions posed to them in natural languages (or something close to them), how computers could determine whether a certain legal statute formulated in some natural (without quotes!) language is relevant to a lawsuit, with the case presented in the same natural language, etc.

It is close to tragic that these people can get no, or at most only very little, help from either logicians or linguists (and they might not even have heard of rhetoricians). Many of them become amateur linguists and logicians themselves, sometimes doing commendable work, more often, though, wasting their time and that of the computers put at their disposal through the generosity, and vital interest, of their sponsors. "Logic of natural languages" is one of the most cherished and discussed topics at Computer Conferences, but the discussants will seldom learn something useful from attending Philosophy or Linguistics Congresses, not even from talks given there about "Logic and Language".

The plight of these people is finally beginning to make an impression, perhaps because there is money behind them. But be the driving force whatever it is, I suggest that professional logicians and linguists pay heed to the demands. Validity of arguments in natural languages is far too important a topic to be left to amateurs. If the price to be paid for the professionalization of the treatment will be setting up Logic as an autonomous department, I would not mind. I do not think that this will particularly jeopardize those people who would like to apply Logic to Mathematics or to Philosophy. Let us by all means have Natural (Language) Logicians and Computer (Language) Logicians in addition to Mathematical Logicians and Philosophical Logicians. Only thereby will a serious misdevelopment in the history of science be corrected.

It is only fair to say that it is not only computer people who have recently realized the need for a serious logic of natural languages. And it should not be difficult to supplement Rescher's concise bibliography with a few items in this direction. Let me mention just three:

(1) J. LYONS, *Structural Semantics*, Oxford: Basil Blackwell, 1963.
(2) N. CHOMSKY, *Aspects of the Theory of Syntax*, Cambridge: M.I.T. Press, 1965.
(3) J. J. KATZ, *The Philosophy of Language*, New York: Harper & Row, 1966.

THE OUTLOOK FOR COMPUTATIONAL SEMANTICS

Let me first apologize for the utterly inadequate title of my talk. At the time when I submitted the title, I thought I would be able to get a full conception of computational semantics sufficient for a talk about the outlook for the whole field. In the meantime something happened to me that, had I been wise enough, I should have predicted would happen; namely, that the more I got involved and the more I was thinking about it, the more the field as a totality started to recede, and the more countless details began to come up front, and I came to realize how pointless it would be to attempt to predict the future of a whole new field in twenty or twenty-five minutes. So I am afraid I will have to do something much less than what my title might have promised to you, and perhaps it is much better so.

Let me start, appropriately, with a couple of semantic remarks to the phrase "Conputational Semantics" occurring in the title. I can predict, almost with certainty, that this combination of two very fashionable terms, "semantics" and "computational", will soon become itself so fashionable that it will be jumped upon from various sides and will quickly become as ambiguous, maybe more so, as each of these terms is separately. Particularly I think at least three meanings of this term are already in the offing (and may have already showed up in last night's informal discussion).

The one meaning is "semantics of computer languages". I think this is a highly interesting field. I have dealt with it on other occasions, but for lack of time shall not do so today.

A second meaning which the term already has or will have is that of using computers as an aid for producing semantic theories of natural languages. Here again I wish I had more time and could argue my view at length. Since I do not have this much time, let me state quite dogmatically that I do not think, contrary to what other people are already attempting to, that computers could possibly be of any serious help for the mentioned aim, i.e. that they could not do much beyond supplying statistics and concordances and things like that.

Let me then turn to the third meaning, which I believe is still the most frequent one; namely, of using computers for analysing the semantic structure of sentences, in some natural language, English or Russian or what have you, in such a way that the output of this analysis will in some way or other more clearly, more precisely, or more overtly, exhibit the semantic structure or structures of these sentences.

The first questions that have to be answered are "Why do so altogether?" "Who is interested in this job?" "Why should we want to input an English sentence and output something that will exhibit the semantic structure of this sentence more clearly than it was to begin with?"

Well, it seems that one aim of this job is translation. It now seems that for the purpose of computer-aided translation the semantic structure of the sentences to be translated has to be exhibited. Without such exhibition of structure it is not very likely that an adequate computer-aided translation will be forthcoming.

Another use of semantic analysis is information processing. It seems to be almost generally agreed at the moment that with natural language input as such, without preliminary semantic processing — for which I shall use here the term "standardization", and have been using, following Quine, on other occasions, the term "regimentation," — one cannot, certainly not at the moment, maybe not even in the foreseeable future, do much about processing this input for the innumerably many purposes for which this input could be brought to use. But in order to arrive at that standardization, it seems that going over the meaning or meanings of the input is of particular importance.

Something else. A minor side effect of computational semantics would be to exhibit hidden ambiguities, and on occasion a computer might do this better than human beings. This has been often put to a psychological test, and one has found that human beings, when in appropriate conditions, very often understand a given utterance in one particular way, which is indeed one of its meanings, but is only *one* of its many meanings, even within the whole context.

Just recently Martin Joos told me that on a certain occasion he uttered a request which half of the people around understood in one way and half in another way, while nobody was aware that his request was ambiguous. In such special cases, an appropriately programmed computer could more easily come up and say, "Well, there are the two meanings. Now pick whatever is appropriate."

One can also envisage that one could want to have a computer test for consistency or any of the many other logical relationships between the input statements. However, I hope that you are all aware of the fact that for medical diagnosis, for jurisprudential purposes, and presumably even for straightforward scientific purposes, so long as the input is given in some natural language and not in some formalized language, these tests cannot be performed by purely syntactical means. The inconsistencies, if there are any, will in general only turn up through what is called meaning analysis or semantic analysis. Obviously, if semantic analysis of natural language texts could be done with the help of computers, it would be a major achievement.

In the rest of my lecture — which so far was pure description — I intend to make only two points. In the discussion, if we have time, other things might be brought up.

My first point is the following: It is my belief that the extant semantic theories of natural languages, including those that were proposed during the last two years or so, are woefully inadequate and that something very central has been missed.

Just for the sake of illustration let me refer to the Katz-Fodor theory since this theory is presumably best known to the participants of our meeting. But what I am saying now should apply to any other semantic theory.

The major cause of the inadequacy of the Katz-Fodor theory lies in its conception of a semantic theory as being composed of a dictionary and projection rules. The dictionaries that they have in mind differ from standard dictionaries but not to a degree that will affect my remarks.

You might want to find out for yourselves why dictionaries should have obtained such a prominent role in the thinking of the people in the field. But whatever the reasons, I have a strong conviction that to state the *meaning rules*, or *semantic rules*, or whatever other term one is going to use in the future for this purpose, in the form of dictionary plus projection rules is just not adequate at all. The meaning relationships that have to be described in these rules cannot be described in those two forms alone.

I would not want to say for a minute that these are not also forms in which to render the meaning relationships. Of course they are. I don't want to abolish them. But they are not enough.

The clearest discussion of meaning relationships, though originally related mostly to formalized languages, are due to Rudolf Carnap. His term for what we have come to call "meaning rules" is "meaning postulates", again because he is thinking mostly in terms of constructed languages, so that for him those rules are postulates, whereas for us they are empirical findings.

The meaning rules, the rules that describe the meanings of terms and phrases of natural languages, cannot be handled by dictionaries alone.

They are unable, in principle, by their very form, to take care of all the complex meaning relationships.

Let me present only a trivial example at the moment. There are infinitely many others. By virtue of the meaning of the English expression "is warmer than", if A is warmer than B and B is warmer than C, then A is warmer than C. This is not a fact of logic but of English semantics. Anybody who understands the meaning of "is warmer than" must agree that the relation denoted by this expression is transitive, to use the logical lingo.

Now, of course, nothing of this kind could possibly be treated by a dictionary. Where will you find in a dictionary of either classical or the Katz-Fodor type an entry for "is warmer than"? You have an entry for "warm", of course. But this entry could not possibly take care of the transitivity of "warmer than". Nor can the projection rules account for this extremely simple fact and innumerable others.

The meaning rules that in combination will create a semantic theory will have many different forms — I don't know how many. One might want to classify these rules and see how many of them can be handled by something like a dictionary. It is, in general, advantageous to replace algorithms by table look-up. I therefore hope that, even in the future, dictionaries will be able to carry a good amount of the load involved. But they will not be able to carry the whole load.

This brings up the second point. Due again to certain highly interesting historical developments which I shall not try to sketch here, linguistics has become divorced from logic for most contemporary linguists, in particular for most American linguists.

The result is extremely unfortunate. This divorce between logic and linguistics is intolerable. It is inherently a wrong view.

As an illustration, let me come back to what I said a few minutes ago. Most linguists, presumably most of the linguists sitting here, would say that it is not the business of linguistics to state that the relation "is warmer than" is transitive. (They might not even understand this mode of speaking.) Without using this "logical" terminology, they might insist that it is not the business of linguistics to interfere with whether one is entitled to deduce from the facts that A is warmer than B and B is warmer than C that A is warmer than C.

But this looks to me utterly wrong. Obviously it is *only up to the linguist* to tell, to explain, to exhibit, to clarify the meaning of "warmer than" — and uncountably many other phrases in English — in order to enable anybody to deduce from these two premises the conclusion.

A logician as such, of course, will not take this task upon himself, because the straight logician will say that his profession has nothing to do with the English language. What is happening in the English language is not his business. What is his business is to state that if a particular relation is transitive, then such and such. "If A stands in the relation R to B, and B stands in the relation R to C and R is transitive, then A stands in the relation R to C." But whether the expression "warmer than" is transitive, what can he, *qua* logician, say to that? He is not, *qua* logician, an expert in the English language. Let me repeat: It is the business of the English *linguists*, and of them alone, to provide the information that entitles anybody to draw the mentioned conclusion.

In general, I would say that there has been, in connection with this dictionary business, an incredible overestimate of the role of synonymy and paraphrasability in all linguistics, but strangely enough in particular in modern linguistics. The terms "synonymy" and "paraphrasability" — as well as some of their variants — have become the most basic terms for modern semanticists. This is again historically understandable to a degree, but still essentially a very strange development because, as a little logic and perhaps even a little common sense will tell you, from such symmetrical relationships — and both of these terms denote symmetrical relationships — it is either impossible or, in any case, very hard to define certain asymmetrical relationships which definitely are of extremely great importance in semantical thinking. Such notions like "hyponymy", or "meaning inclusion" — the property expression 'A' is hyponymous to 'B' if and only if anything that has the property A also has the property B but not vice versa — clearly cannot be defined by synonymy, though it is clearly possible to define synonymy by hyponymy.

But the fact that linguists think that paraphrasability and synonymy is their business, while hyponymy is not and belongs to logic, because it lies at the basis of inference and drawing conclusions, is a strange development which has been quite fatal to modern linguistics, and particularly to modern semantics.

As one conclusion from these considerations, I think that light can be shed on the question of the borderline between semantics and syntax, a question which has already been discussed and will probably come up many times more during our present meeting. I presume you know that the M.I.T. School has been changing its mind every few months on this quite confusing question.

As soon as we understand that dictionary-type rules or rules of paraphrase are *only part* of the totality of semantic rules, then the question of the status of "Misery loves company", to illustrate by one of the standard examples, whether this sentence is syntactically acceptable, but semantically somehow not quite at the top of the ladder of meaningfulness, can be seen in a new light.

When we are asking ourselves, what is the meaning of "Misery loves company", we cannot turn to dictionaries and projection rules to find the answer. It is not inconceivable that the actual meaning rules for expressions of the form "A loves B" would be such as to assign a certain meaning to such expressions in case A is human, but leave it without any specific meaning when A is non-human.

That the meaning of "A loves B" is in this particular case not established by those rules should, however, not be understood to imply that the expression is meaningless. It only means that this expression is *so far without meaning*; that the existing meaning rules just are not sufficient to give this expression any specific meaning. This is quite different from saying that *it is meaningless*, because if it is so far without meaning, we can add new rules to the meaning rules of this particular language at that particular stage, without changing any of the old meaning rules, something that couldn't happen for dictionary-type meaning rules.

We should realize that there is nothing wrong with having in a language expressions whose meaning is, at a certain stage or even at any stage, not completely determined, which will be intelligible in some contexts but meaning-indeterminate (rather than void-of-meaning) in others.

It might turn out to be that with regard to certain expressions, particularly with regard to the so-called *theoretical expressions*, any attempt of expressing their meaning by a single entry in a dictionary is in principle utterly wrong. We already know that theoretical expressions get their meaning in an entirely different way. Their meaning is theory-dependent and can only be determined by taking into account the whole set of postulates of that particular theory. But the issue is too complicated and technical for us to discuss it here. My final conclusion is that inasmuch as semantics is concerned, we have been living in a fool's paradise until this date. We knew that semantics is difficult. But we kept fooling ourselves to believe that we knew at least the type of semantic rules that would be employed, so that our only problem was to get sufficient empirical information to be able to state all our semantic findings in the form of a dictionary plus projection rules.

We must now realize that this was an illusion. We will have to live up to the fact that semantic rules in general will be of many additional types. It seems to me that for the time being we should let them have every form that seems appropriate for a problem at hand and that only much later should we start again and see whether these innumerably many ways of forming semantic rules can be reduced to a more manageable subset. Some of them will turn out to be rules of paraphrasability and projection. Others, of course, will not. Only when this is accomplished — and I would not dare estimate today how much time this will take — will it become feasible to develop computational semantics, in the third meaning of this expression, i.e. to determine with the help of a computer the meaning or meanings of any given natural language text. If this estimate will be regarded, as presumably it will be, as another expression of my by now well-known "pessimism", I am afraid it can't be helped. My own way of putting it has always been that I have had the misfortune of arriving at realistic evaluations quicker than most other workers in the fields tended to do, so that it has been my unfortunate privilege to insist from time to time that other people's thinking is marred by a good amount of wishful thinking. As I see it, I am not pessimistic, I am realistic.

REVIEW OF JOHN LYONS'
*INTRODUCTION TO THEORETICAL LINGUISTICS**

This is the best book of its kind to appear during the last decade and the first, to my knowledge, to carry the long overdue adjective 'theoretical' in its title. My high opinion is shared by many of my colleagues in various countries to whom I had a chance to talk on this matter. Many of us have been using it as a main or auxiliary textbook in a number of courses, and I assigned it as a prerequisite for my course on Philosophy of Language.

There would be no point in spelling out its many assets. Let me therefore make the convenient — and, for review articles, not very customary — assumption that the reader of this review has already read the book itself or will at least do so before a second reading of the review. But before I turn to my initial comments, in the hope that some of them at least will be accepted by the author and implemented in the second edition, which I am sure will not be long in coming — this hope being based upon some correspondence with the author —, I think I must mention the author's treatment of semantics in the last two chapters. Chapter 9, in particular, is in my view the best of the many excellent chapters, and quite superior to the treatment by J. J. Katz, for instance, with which it obviously invites comparison.

The indebtedness of the book to Chomsky's teachings is too obvious to need stressing. But it is also obvious that Lyons by no means bought Chomsky in bulk and does not hesitate to express his misgivings on what he regards, often correctly, to be weak points in Chomsky's conceptions.

My comments will be made by topics, in the order of their appearance in the book.

I. SENTENCES AND UTTERANCES

In honour of the journal for which this review is written, I shall start with a 'semiotic' point, more particularly, with one that has interested me for quite some time (beginning with "Three remarks on linguistic fundamentals"**, *Word*, 13 (1957), 223–235, continuing with "Do natural languages contain paradoxes?"**, *Studium Generale*, 19 (1966) 391–397, a Review of *The Structure of Language*** (J. A. Fodor and J. J. Katz,

---

* Cambridge University Press, 1968, pp. x + 519.
** [Reprinted here as Ch. 28, 24, and 14 respectively.]

eds.) in *Language*, 43 (1967) 526–550, and finally, in one of the Linguistic Forum talks I presented before the 1966 Linguistic Institute of the Linguistic Society of America at the University of California, Los Angeles, and published in the Proceedings, *Substance and Structure of Language* (Jaan Puhvel, ed., 1969, pp. 1–21)*, and whose continued insufficient appreciation by almost all linguists (and logicians, and general philosophers, and philosophers of language, for that matter) seems to me responsible for many unnecessary mistakes and unwanted polemics.

May I start with quoting myself (from one of the Forum talks, *ibid.*, p. 16):

> Who does not know that one has to distinguish between a SENTENCE, qua abstract linguistic entity, and an UTTERANCE of it, qua concrete physical product of some linguistic act, or even between a sentence and the set of all its actual and potential utterances? (One does not have to make this distinction by using these terms, of course; anything will do, so long as it is realized that one has to deal here with two entities which are different under any name.) But are you really sure that you know how to avoid the trap of regarding (as has been done quite often in the past) this distinction as being of the well-known type-token kind or of the class-member kind? And are you really sure that you will know how to make this distinction when making it is crucial? I could give you hundreds of quotations, including recent ones from leading linguists, where it is obvious that the distinction was not made in places where it hurts.

Now, Lyons is one of the few linguists who insists that "a distinction must be made between 'utterances' and 'sentences'" (p. 52) and that "this distinction... is fundamental in most modern linguistic theory", being a distinction between units of *langue* vs. instances of *parole*. Nevertheless (and for no good reasons I could discern — none are explicitly given), he thinks that he "can develop certain preliminary notions without invoking" this distinction and therefore decides to "use the terms 'sentence' and 'utterance' more or less synonymously" throughout chapters 2–4. I can only deplore this decision (which, predictably, carries beyond these two chapters) which made him join the list of the many leading linguists who neglected to make this distinction — in their case, mostly through ignorance — in places where it hurts. May I express the hope that the author will make the (admittedly not inconsiderable) effort of enforcing a consistent terminology in the second edition?

* [Reprinted here as Ch. 15].

I shall give just one explicit illustration of the effects of this deliberate negligence (though further illustrations will be contained implicitly in some of the later comments). The author is at great pains to insist, after a careful and balanced discussion of the hackneyed opposition between *langue* and *parole*, that "it is therefore the *langue*, the language-system, which the linguist describes." Along the same line, he urges us to recognize "that linguistic theory, at the present time at least, is not, and cannot be, concerned [I have allowed myself to correct an obvious misplacement of a comma] with the production and understanding of utterances in their actual situation of use (except for . . .) but with the structure of sentences considered in abstraction from the situation in which actual utterances occur" (p. 98). [This view mirrors Chomsky's, as expressed, for instance, in footnote 16 on p. 127 of his 1961 paper "On the notion 'rule of grammar'", as reprinted in the Fodor-Katz *Readings*; in my Review, mentioned above, I voiced my misgivings on this view and stressed the point that it would be harmful to wait for a full development of the theory of competence before one starts serious work on a theory of performance — to use the more modern counterparts of *langue* and *parole* —, a position which I now hold in still greater strength, regardless of whether the scientist dealing with the theory of linguistic performance is going to be called a linguist, a psycholinguist, a sociolinguist, an ethnolinguist, or what have you.] Some forty pages later, the formulation has undergone a considerable and, in my view, unfortunate twist. There (p. 139) the author says that "it is the linguist's task therefore in describing a language to establish rules capable of accounting for the indefinitely large set of potential utterances which constitute the language. Any linguistic description that has this capacity of describing actual utterances as members of a larger class of potential utterances, is said to be *generative*". It is possible that the contradiction is only a superficial one — as a matter of fact, I am convinced that this is indeed the actual situation — into which the author has been forced by having committed himself to saying, a few lines before, that "it is the class of potential utterances which we must identify as the sentences of the language." This identification is disastrous and wholly unnecessary (*pace* Occam's razor) and probably not even meant seriously. Utterances, whether actual or potential, are best treated as belonging to a level different from that of sentences. This difference is obvious with respect to single utterances which as physical four-dimensional entities are clearly *toto coelo* distant from such non-physical, 'abstract' entities as sentences. However, even the tendency, most noticeable in the early Fifties, to identify sentences with certain classes of utterances, though less offensive since classes are at least themselves non-physical and abstract, even if their members are physical, concrete entities, should be combatted. Usually, these classes are construed as equivalence classes over some equivalence relation between utterances. But either the appropriate equivalence relation is defined to be that relation which obtains between two utterances if and only if they are utterances of the same sentence (or some other kindred linguistic entity), turning the identification into an at best useless step, or else one looks for some physical equivalence relation of, say, acoustical nature, but then the identification will quickly turn out to be a false one, as has happened without exception in similar situations in the past. It is just one more illustration of the general tendency to misinterpret the status of a scientific theoretical entity and construe it as some class of observational entities.

Since Peircean terminology has become widespread in some linguistic quarters, it might not be superfluous to repeat here a warning I have given a few times before and to expand upon it. The Peircean type-token distinction is useful to a degree but has often been misused, even by Peirce himself. Two utterance-tokens are tokens of the same utterance-type if and only if — as just said — there obtains between them an equivalence relation of an acoustical, visual or some other perceptual nature. The first and the fourth word-token of the (printed) utterance-token of the English sentence the reader is just reading would be regarded by a Peircean as tokens of the same type, as the reader will quickly verify, and this in spite of differences in the first letter-tokens that should be visible to the naked eye and doubtless of still more differences in the physical shape of the tokens, were he to care to use a microscope, indicating that what makes these tokens equiform, tokens of the same type, is not some simple geometrical relationship. As a matter of fact, I have some doubts as to whether any tolerably clear and unequivocal explication of this relationship is at all possible. I am also not sure whether the type-token distinction is of much use outside the printing business, where many things — including payments — are often computed, so I am told, by the number of letter-tokens. This distinction has gotten its notoriety mainly because it has been confused with a different and incomparably more important distinction, namely that between some abstract linguistic entity, such as a word, and its equally abstract occurrences. The English sentence, into a printed utterance of which the reader has above been urged to look, is, among other things, also (representable as) an abstract sequence of abstract word-occurrences (it is not my fault that the word 'word' has to do such heavy and multiple duty) such that the first and fourth such occurrences are occurrences of the same (abstract) word. The fact that the first and the fourth tokens of that particular utterance of this sentence to which the attention of the reader has been drawn are tokens of the same word-type is not a logical consequence of the fact stated in the previous sentence but a consequence of particular orthographic and printing conventions, indicating the usefulness and appropriateness of these conventions, at least to a degree.

Look at the following formula displayed, for the convenience of the reader, on a special line:

$$a(b+c) = ab+ac$$

Of how many tokens does it consist? (Did the reader notice that my question was — on purpose — unclearly formulated? Only when 'tokens' are interpreted as short for 'single-symbol-tokens' did my question make good sense.) I guess that his answer was, perhaps after some hesitation and deliberation: twelve. What would his justification be, if challenged? How many different types are there? Seven? Not eight? What about the multiplication sign (which occurs three times in this formula)? He didn't see it? He wouldn't, qua publisher, want to pay the author of this formula for the three invisible and unprinted tokens of this sign? He is, of course, perfectly right in this refusal, but it only shows the necessity of clearly distinguishing between token and occurrence. The formula is a certain sequence of fifteen occurrences of eight symbols (the seven obvious ones plus the multiplication sign) some of which occur only once, others twice, and still others three times. The particular token of the formula the reader has just been looking into (and might want to look into again) contains only twelve symbol-tokens — unless, God forbid, the printer has introduced a last-minute mistake — since one of the symbols (the multiplication sign) has been tokened, in all its occurrences, by the 'empty' token. (But, of course, not all empty places are tokens of something or other.) Pedantic? Perhaps. Unnecessarily pedantic? I don't think so. If the reader can find a better and simpler way of formulating the situation, I shall be glad to hear of it, and so, I am sure, would Lyons.

It is tolerable (though still not devoid of difficulties) to define a (spoken) utterance with Harris as " 'any stretch of talk, by one person, before and after which there is silence on the part of that person' " (p. 172) but then one should not go on to say with Harris, as Lyons is unfortunately willing to do, that " 'the utterance is, in general, not identical with the "sentence" (as that word is commonly used), since a great many utterances in English, for example, consist of single words, phrases, "incomplete sentences", etc. Many utterances are composed of parts which are linguistically equivalent to whole utterances occurring elsewhere'." Utterances are not only not identical with sentences "in general", they are never so, and on principle. Whether we treat a certain utterance of *John's, if he gets there* as a complete utterance (of something or other, though certainly not of a sentence), or as an incomplete utterance of a sentence, or as both simultaneously — and there are still more ways of looking at the situation — is a highly interesting theoretical question which can only be posed after these distinctions are enforced. I don't think that Lyons' distinction between 'contextual completeness' and 'grammatical completeness' (pp. 174–5) does justice to this point.

II. Grammaticality

Lyons has some interesting things to say on that moot topic of 'acceptability', 'grammaticality', and the like. (I myself spent a few pages on this topic in my Review.) But on one occasion he states "as a general principle which governs all grammatical description ... the following fact: whether a certain combination of words is or is not grammatical is a question that can only be answered by reference to a particular system of rules which either generates it (and thus defines it to be grammatical) or fails to generate it (and thereby defines it to be ungrammatical)" (p. 153). He realizes, correctly, that most writers on the subject, including Chomsky, would reject this principle and rather claim that "the grammatical structure of any language is determinate and is known 'intuitively' (or 'tacitly') by native speakers" (p. 154).

Lyons seems to miss the point here and thereby to create an unnecessary confrontation. What Chomsky and other linguists have in mind is that whether a sequence of words is grammatical is, at the pretheoretical level of the explicandum, (trivially) independent of any particular system of rules, while it becomes (trivially) dependent on such systems, at the theoretical level of the explicatum. Linguists will then differ (as will ordinary people) when attempting to clarify the explicandum 'grammatical' and will differ on the adequacy of a proposed explication, but they will hardly differ on the question whether according to some given set of rules a particular sequence of words will be generated or not. How simple these things become when a few general points of recent methodology of science (in this case stemming from Carnap) are mastered.

III. Different Types of Sentences

Treating the traditional classification of sentences by function into the major types of statements, questions, exclamations and commands, Lyons again, I think, does not find the right (and simple) words to describe the actual situation. In lieu of his tortured treatment (pp. 178–9) it is possible to tell the story very simply: Simple English sentences can be classified (by structure, distribution, intonation pattern) as declarative, interrogative, imperative, and exclamatory. (I am not dealing here with the substance of the matter.) There are a very large number of linguistic acts that can be performed, such as making statements, asking questions, giving commands, making promises, proving, explaining, lecturing, sermonizing, cursing, lying, etc., and an equally large number of products of such acts, such as statements, questions, commands, promises, proofs, explanations, lectures, sermons, curses, lies, *etc.* (Some of these acts can also be performed without uttering anything but by nodding in appropriate circumstances, for instance.) Many, perhaps even most, statements (made by English speakers) are made by uttering declarative sentences, and by uttering declarative sentences one often, though by no means always, intends to make statements. Many, perhaps most, questions are asked by uttering interrogative sentences, and often — I really don't know how often — by uttering interrogatives one intends to ask questions. (The author is doubtless aware of all this but prefers, I think wrongly, to neglect this fact — *cf.*, *e.g.*, p. 441.)

This is the whole story. In the present case, it is not even necessary to develop a new technical terminology in order to deal adequately with the actual situation. That the traditional treatment is inadequate, goes without saying. That the remedy is so simple, is perhaps surprising. Let's hope Lyons will adopt it. (I treated the issue myself at some length in the *Studium Generale* paper, pointing out there some interesting philosophical implications.)

IV. Recursiveness

In order to generate infinitely many sentences with finitely many rules (which is obviously required when these are to represent a human's tacit mastery of the syntax of his language), some of these rules have to be recursive. But Lyons formulates this trivial point so as to open it unnecessarily to objections of the type made by Hockett (*The State of the Art*, 1968) and many others. Working with grammars that generate infinitely many sentences (and sentences with unbounded length) has nothing to do with the ability of a native speaker "to produce a sentence containing a noun-phrase the number of whose constituent, co-ordinated nouns exceeds any alleged 'upper limit' " (p. 221). Here Lyons himself must have fallen prey to the standard confusion between 'generate' and 'produce'. Speakers are, of course, unable to produce utterances of length greater than, say, 10^{20}, measured by whatever units; it is the grammar that generates, for any such sentence, a still larger and pretheoretically equally legitimate sentence. (That this should have happened even to Lyons is probably again due to his unfortunate decision not to distinguish everywhere between 'utterance' and 'sentence'.)

The reader would therefore also do best to just forget the first paragraph of the next page (p. 222). Introducing probability into the (uninterpreted) grammar to make it a more 'realistic' model for the production of utterances is probably the worst move that could be made for this purpose. (All similar attempts made in the past — and many were made in the good old days of machine translation — have failed miserably, and this should at least serve as a deterrent.) The appropriate place for probabilities is in the rules of correspondence (or interpretation, *etc.*) that connect linguistic theory with linguistic behaviour (language with speech, competence with performance).

Coming back to a topic already discussed above, let us again ask the question, Who, if not the linguistic theoretician, should occupy himself with these rules of correspondence? The answer is, of course, very simple: the linguistic theoretician in the wider sense, *i.e.*, the one who deals, in addition to the 'pure' theory with which his colleague, the 'pure' linguist, occupies himself exclusively, also with the 'applied' theory, *i.e.*, the pure theory plus the rules of interpretation. How simple! Just, distinguish between two (actual, not invented!) senses of 'linguistic theory' — which term has, unfortunately, still more confusing senses — and another pseudo-problem — or rather, as usual, another pseudo-formulation of a real problem — has vanished. And what is the real problem? Nothing more than one of division of labour. The 'applied' linguistic theoretician, be he a psycholinguist, a sociolinguist, an ethnolinguist, or what have you, needs a different type of training than his 'pure' colleague. I have already voiced above my misgivings over the conception of Chomsky and others that a more or less complete development of an adequate theory of competence is a prerequisite for the development of a theory of performance. That this could not be so can be seen simply from the fact that the very adequacy of a particular theory of competence can only be determined on the basis of performance, with or without theory. Whoever regards this 'dialectical' relationship (which is anything but viciously circular) as noteworthy is welcome to do so. I would warn him, though, not to fall into the trap that is waiting for him here.

V. Categorial Grammars

Since I myself had something to do with these grammars (and even coined the term so many years ago), let me stress categorically that Lyons' statement to the effect that "in a categorial system there are just two *fundamental* grammatical categories, sentence and noun" (p. 227) is not quite exact. Some of us tried to get along, for a time, with these two fundamental categories — and for the originators, the Polish logicians Leśniewski and Ajdukiewicz, it was indeed a kind of article of faith that there should be only these two — but when the fun of trying to express the syntactic functions of all words in terms of these fundamental syntactic categories had worn off, we were quite ready to experiment with additional fundamental categories, as well as to experiment with additional ways of combining them. I personally stopped my attempts when the phrase-structure grammars of Chomsky came along and so quickly attained their great popularity. For a time, I and my collaborators had our hands full with proving all kinds of equivalences between the various phrase-structure and categorial grammars. It might perhaps be useful to return to the treatment and further development of categorial grammars (without the restriction to two fundamental categories). (Incidentally, Lyons' remark on the lack of strong equivalence between categorial and rewrite systems (p. 231) is not correct, but is a minor point not worth discussion here.)

VI. The Elusive 'I'

The British philosopher, Gilbert Ryle, in his famous book, *The Concept of Mind* (1949), has a section heading "The systematic elusiveness of 'I'." How elusive 'I' is can be seen also from Lyons' treatment. Having stated, correctly (at least, as a first approximation), that "the pronoun *we* is to be interpreted as 'I, in addition to one or more persons'; and the other persons may or may not include the hearer" (p. 277) — obviously leaving aside the majestic plural — he continues: "In other words, *we* is not the 'plural of *I*'; rather it includes a reference to 'I' and is plural." It seems that some people (grammarians?) must have said that *we* is the plural of *I*, and it is perhaps quite all right for Lyons to stress his opposition to this stupidity; but who needs his continuation, "it includes a reference to 'I' "? I see no sense whatsoever in saying that *we* refers to 'I' nor that it refers to *I* and even less (if this were possible) that it "includes a reference" to such things. *Si tacuisses* . . .

But '*I*' is surely the most exciting of all the indexical expressions, and the lack of understanding of its operation has caused a lot of trouble not only for linguists but also, and even more so, for philosophers. It would be nice to have the issue clarified and clearly presented by some authoritative linguist. Lyons is the best candidate I know of for this job. Let's hope he will tackle it in the second edition and succeed in doing so.

VII. ANOMALY

Insufficient distinction between sentence and utterance is responsible for the statement (p. 461): "*John isn't married* is hardly less anomalous semantically than *The stone isn't married*, if the person referred to as *John* is not in fact 'marriageable' (by virtue of age and other criteria)." A much better though still not sufficiently precise formulation of the situation would be that the sentence, *The stone isn't married* is semantically anomalous, while the sentence, *John isn't married* is semantically in perfect order, but that its utterance in the circumstances described by Lyons is pragmatically anomalous (as it would be in innumerably many other circumstances). I made some more remarks on the issue of anomaly in my *Review*.

VIII. ATTENTION — LOGIC !

Though Lyons' mastery of modern logic is doubtless much greater than that of the average linguist, he does make an occasional mistake (which never disturbs the gist of his argument). Let me just point out three of these mistakes which can be easily corrected.

(a) A SYMMETRICAL relation is not one that "holds between *a* and *b* and between *b* and *a*" (p. 455) but one that holds between *b* and *a* whenever it holds between *a* and *b*.

(b) It is indeed characteristic of COMPLEMENTARY words such as *single* and *married*, or *male* and *female* that "the denial of the one implies the assertion of the other and the assertion of the one implies the denial of the other" (p. 461) (though a trained logician would doubtless find some more felicitous formulation for this situation). But the logical symbolization Lyons uses on this occasion, $\sim x \supset y$ and $y \supset \sim x$, is less than helpful. For the second formula read $x \supset \sim y$, which, though logically equivalent to Lyons' second formula, is clearly the only adequate symbolization, bad as it still is, since logicians are accustomed to use 'p' and 'q' as variables for sentences and not 'x' and 'y'; in addition, *male* is not a sentence but a predicate, and a constant and not a variable; finally, the best symbol to use here would have been the symbol for equivalence, rather than two implication signs.

(c) Since *buy* and *sell* are best treated as denoting three-place (and, for certain purposes, even four-place) relations, it is misleading to speak of them simply as converses of each other. If one treats, as the author does (p. 467), the sentential form NP_1 bought NP_3 *from* NP_2 as standard, it would be better to speak of them as 1–2 converses, as I proposed, for exactly these verbs, on another occasion.

Let me repeat that, in spite of a number of shortcomings, Lyons' book is the best Introduction to Theoretical Linguistics there is. Its second edition could and should be still better.

NOTES ON THE PUBLICATIONAL HISTORY OF THE DIFFERENT ESSAYS

CHAPTER 1. "Bolzano's Definition of Analytic Propositions" was submitted in 1948 for publication in *Theoria*. Due to failures in communication during the Israeli Independence War in 1948/49, the paper was resubmitted, in a slightly changed form, to *Methodos*, and finally published, almost simultaneously, in both journals, in *Theoria* 16.91–117, 1950, as well as in *Methodos* 2.32–55, 1950. A Hebrew translation appeared in *Iyyun* 2.34–62, 1950.

CHAPTER 2. "Comments on Logical Form" was originally published in *Philosophical Studies* 2.72–75, 1951.

CHAPTER 3. "Mr. Geach on Rigour in Semantics" was originally published in *Mind* 61.261–264, 1952.

CHAPTER 4. "Bolzano's Propositional Logic" was originally published in *Archiv für Mathematische Logik und Grundlagenforschung* 1.65–98, 1952.

CHAPTER 5. "Indexical Expressions" was originally published in *Mind* 63.359–379, 1954. Some of its points were later developed in Chapters 7, 10, 12, 16 and 17.

CHAPTER 6. "Husserl's Conception of a Purely Logical Grammar" was originally published in *Philosophy and Phenomenological Research* 17.362–369, 1957.

CHAPTER 7. "On Lalic Implication and the *Cogito*", was originally published in *Philosophical Studies* 11.21–25, 1960. One of its topics was later taken up again in Chapter 10.

CHAPTER 8. "On Mr. Sørensen's Analysis of 'To Be' and 'To Be True'" was originally published in *Analysis* 20. 93–96, 1960.

CHAPTER 9. "Critical Comments on the Introductory Papers on Logic, Language and Communication" was originally presented at a Symposium held at the Twelfth International Congress of Philosophy, Venezia-Padoa, 1958 and then published in the *Atti del XII Congresso Internazionale di Filosofia*, IV.9–17, 1960.

CHAPTER 10. "Can Indexical Sentences Stand in Logical Relations"? was originally published in *Philosophical Studies* 14. 87–90, 1963. It raised a further round of discussion to which I reacted in "More on Sentences, Statements, the *Cogito*, and the Liar", *Philosophical Studies* 19.55–57, 1968, not included in the present collection.

CHAPTER 11. "Remarks on Carnap's *Logical Syntax of Language*" was submitted for publication in 1954 but was published only in 1963 in *The Philosophy of Rudolf Carnap* (P. A. Schilpp, ed.), The Library of Living Philosophers, Vol. XI, Open Court, LaSalle, Illinois, pp. 519–543. In view of this delay, a postscript was added in January, 1962.

CHAPTER 12. "Et Tu, Diodorus Cronus?" was originally published in *Analysis* 26.54–56, 1965.

CHAPTER 13. "Imperative Inference" was originally published in *Analysis* 26.79–82, 1966.

CHAPTER 14. This Review of *The Structure of Language: Readings in the Philosophy of Language* was originally published in *Language* 43.526–550.

CHAPTER 15. "Universal Semantics and the Philosophy of Language: Quandaries and Prospects" is a slightly revised version of two Linguistic Forum Talks presented during the Linguistic Summer Institute that took place at UCLA in 1966; it was originally published in *Substance and Structure of Language* (Jaan Puhvel, ed.), University of California Press, Berkeley and Los Angeles, pp. 1–21, 1969.

CHAPTER 16. "Argumentation in Natural Languages" was originally presented at the Fourteenth International Congress of Philosophy, Vienna, 1968 and then published in the *Akten des XIV. Internationalen Kongresses für Philosophie*, Verlag Herder Wien, II.3–6, 1969. Both theses mentioned in the talk have been submitted in the meantime (in Hebrew). An English Summary of, and Introduction to, Mr. Kasher's thesis, "The Logical Status of Indexical Sentences", appeared as Scientific Report No. 9, Applied Logic Branch, The Hebrew University of Jerusalem, May 1970, an English Summary of Mr. Margalith's thesis, "The Cognitive Status of Metaphors", appeared as Scientific Report No. 8, *ibid.*, April 1970.

CHAPTER 17. "Argumentation in Pragmatic Languages" is the English translation of a talk originally presented in Hebrew before the Israel Academy of Sciences and Humanities in 1969; it will be published in Volume IV of the *Proceedings of the Israel Academy of Sciences and Humanities*, Jerusalem, Israel, by the end of 1970.

A greatly expanded version of this chapter, with the title "Communication and Argumentation in Pragmatic Languages", appeared in *Linguaggi nella Societa e nella Tecnica*, Edizioni di Comunita, Milano, pp. 269–284, 1970.

CHAPTER 18. This Review of Drange's *Type Crossings* was originally published in *Language* 46.449–454, 1970.

CHAPTER 19. "Analysis of 'Correct' Language" was originally published in *Mind* 55.328–340, 1946. Though I still subscribe to some of the points made there, I have changed my mind considerably on other points, as indicated in footnotes to other chapters in the present volume.

CHAPTER 20. "The Revival of 'The Liar'" was originally published in *Philosophy and Phenomenological Research* 8.25–253, 1947. The topic was taken up again, with considerable changes, in Chapters 21 and 24.

CHAPTER 21. "New Light on The Liar" was originally published in *Analysis* 18.1–16, 1957.

CHAPTER 22. "A Prerequisite for Rational Philosophical Discussion" was originally published in *Synthese* 12.328–332, 1960 and then reprinted in *The Linguistic Turn* (Richard Rorty, ed.), University of Chicago Press, pp. 356–359, 1967.

CHAPTER 23. "Neorealism *vs.* Neopositivism; A Neo-Pseudo-Issue" was originally published in the *Proceedings of the Israel Academy of Sciences and Humanities* II.29–37, 1964.

CHAPTER 24. "Do Natural Languages Contain Paradoxes?" was originally published in *Studium Generale* 19.391–397, 1966.

CHAPTER 25. "Cybernetics and Linguistics" was originally published (in Czech) as "Kybernetika a Lingvistika" in *Kybernetika ve Spolecenských Védách*, Nakladatelstvi Československa Akademie Ved, Praha, pp. 255–264, 1965; the version reprinted here is slightly revised from the one published in *Information und Kommunikation* (S. Moser, ed.), R. Oldenbourg, München-Wien, pp. 29–38, 1968. Parts of this essay were also used in the Introduction to my previous collection, *Language and Information*.

CHAPTER 26. "On Recursive Definitions in Empirical Sciences" was originally presented before the Eleventh International Congress of Philosophy, Brussels, 1953, and then published in the *Proceedings* 5.160–165, Brussels, 1953; A Russian translation was published in *Matematicheskaya Lingvistika*, Izdaeltsvo "Mir", Moskva, pp. 161–175, 1964.

CHAPTER 27. "Some Linguistic Problems Connected with Machine Translation" was originally published in *Philosophy of Science* 20.217–225; section 2 has been omitted here, since it has already been reprinted in a previous collection, Y. Bar-Hillel, *Language and Information*, Addison-Wesley, Reading, Mass., Chapter 4, pp. 56–58, 1964.

CHAPTER 28. "Three Methodological Remarks on *Fundamentals of Language*" was originally published in *Word* 13.323–335, 1957.

CHAPTER 29. "Decision Procedure for Structure in Natural Languages" was originally published in *Logique et Analyse* 2.19–29, 1959; a Russian translation was published in *Matematicheskaya Lingvistika*, Izdaeltsvo "Mir", Moskva, pp. 108–121, 1964.

CHAPTER 30. "On a Misapprehension of the Status of Theories in Linguistics" was originally published in *Foundations of Language* 2.394–399, 1966.

CHAPTER 31. "Dictionaries and Meaning Rules" was originally published in *Foundations of Language* 3.409–414, 1967.

CHAPTER 32. "A Neglected Recent Trend in Logic" was originally published in *Logique et Analyse* 10.235–238, 1967.

CHAPTER 33. "The Outlook for Computational Semantics" was originally published in the *Proceedings of the Conference on Computer-Related Semantic Analysis* I, Wayne State University, Detroit, Mich., pp. 1–14, 1966.

CHAPTER 34. This Review of Lyons' *Introduction to Theoretical Linguistics* was originally published in *Semiotica* 1.449–459 1969.

I would like to extend my thanks to the publishers and editors of the books and journals, in which the essays collected here were originally published, for their kind permission to reprint this material in the present collection.

INDEX OF NAMES

ADJUKIEWICZ, K. 290 291 292 298 300 316 331 372
ALEXANDER, P. 87
ÅQUIST, L. 146
ARISTOTLE 3 54 90 91 105 114 202 203 207 211 291
AUSTIN, J. L. 192 292
AYER, A. J. 103 108 109 110

BAVELAS, A. 294
BERGMAN, H. 33
BERKELEY, G. 101
BLACK, M. 242 290 291 300
BLOOMFIELD, L. 290 300 325
BOLZANO, B. 1 3–16 18 19–22 33–46 49–55 57 58 62–68 273 375
BRAITHWAITE, R. 158 268 296
BRÉAL, M. 119
BRIDGMAN, P. 296
BÜHLER, K. 119 199

CARNAP, R. 2–9 18 21 23 24 27 29–32 34 54 56 57 60 62–64 66–67 75–76 89 93–97 101 108–110 116–127 129 131–133 135–141 150–153 155 158–159 167 172–175 177 179–180 184 186 190 192–195 197–198 200 208 225 227 228 232–233 235 237 243–244 246 255–256 258 263–269 285 289–293 296 300 304 318 323 325 342 344 348 352 359 369 375
CASSIRER, E. 158
CASTAÑEDA, H. N. 98–99 112–114
CATON, CH. E. 179–180
CHAPPELL, U. C. 179 181
CHERRY, C. 294
CHISHOLM, R. 110
CHOMSKY, C. 295
CHOMSKY, N. 2 142 144 151 153 156–157 160–163 167–168 170 172 177–178 181 186 195 197 214 218 222 225 228 285 291 296–297 300–301 329 336–344 353 356 364 366 369 371
CHURCH, A. 4 105 108 109 151 173 179 181 329

COHEN, L. J. 87
CRUSIUS, C. A. 3
CURRY, H. B. 184 190

DESCARTES, R. 99
DIODORUS CRONUS 143–145 375
DRANGE, TH. 222–227 376
DUBISLAV, W. 7 33 43 68

EPICTETUS 220

FANO, R. 294
FEIGL, H. 264
FINDLAY, I. 244
FLETCHER, S. L. 310
FLEW, A. G. N. 125
FODOR, J. A. 150 153 175–177 181–185 191–192 218 225 228 347 352 359 360 366
FRAENKEL, A. A. 290 331
FREGE, G. 14 33–34 116 173 203 211 223 232

GABOR, D. 294
GEACH, P. T. 29 30–32 375
GÖDEL, K. 63 114 244
GOMBAY, A. 146–147
GOODMAN, N. 79 83 199 237 247 296
GRELLING, K. 248 252–253

HALL, R. A. 340–346
HALLE, M. 151 163 317 344
HARRIS, Z. 118 121 142 151 158–160 163–164 181 291 293 296–297 301 338 368
HEMPEL, C. G. 158 268 296 302 306 325
HILBERT, D. 63 114 119
HILL, A. A. 222
HINTIKKA, J. 195
HJELMSLEV, L. 327
HOCKETT, C. F. 182–183 321 370
HOEKSTRA, R. 240
HUSSERL, E. 1 14–15 34 89–97 189 199 222 252 291 375

JAKOBSON, R. 294 296 317 319
JOOS, M. 358

KANT, I. 3–7 22 177 211 352
KASHER, A. 204
KATZ, J. J. 150 153 167 170–173 175–
    187 190–195 197–199 201 218 225 228
    347 351–353 356 359–360 364 366
KEMENY, J. G. 181 253–255 257 279 285
KLEENE, S. C. 304
KLIMA, E. S. 151 163
KOTARBÍNSKI, T. 275
KOYRE, A. 244–252

LAMB, S. M. 182–183
LAMBEK, J. 332
LEE, C. Y. 294
LEES, R. L. 338
LEIBNIZ, G. 15 33
LENNEBERG, E. H. 151 178–179 181
LENZEN, V. F. 307
LEŚNIEWSKI, ST. 72 119 222 275 291 301
    316 331 372
LEWIS, C. I. 5 21 103
LEWY, C. 65
LICKLIDER, J. R. 294
LINSKY, L. 179 181
LOCKE, J. 3
ŁUKASIEWICZ, J. 248 252 275
LYONS, J. 183 349 352 356 364 368–374
    377

MAASS, J. G. E. 16 18–19
MACCORQUODALE, K. 325
MAIMON, S. 22
MARGALIT, A. 205
MARHENKE, P. 164
MARTIN, R. M. 30 257 279 285
MARTY, A. 89 96
MAXWELL, G. 264–269 272
MCGULLOCH, W. 293 294
MEEHL, P. E. 325
MEINONG, A. 5 34
MILLER, G. A. 90 294 296 301
MONTAGUE, R. 203–204 211 216
MOORE, G. E. 20 65 86 98 231–243 247
    290 301

MORRIS, CH. 11 135 208 290 292

NAGEL, E. 165 181 264–266 270 272 340
NEURATH, O. 290

O'CONNOR, D. J. 87
OSWALD, V. A. 310

PAP, A. 81–82
PEIRCE, CH. S. 79 82 199 208 318 367
PERELMAN, CH. 104–107 110 252 355
PITTS, W. 293
POLLARD, C. V. 310
POPPER, K. 11–12
POSTAL, P. M. 151 162 181 183
PUTNAM, H. 184 190

QUINE, W. V. O. 4 6 8–9 12 24 101 107–
    108 110 124 140 151 155–158 164 174–
    176 181 184 190 193 211 232 235 237
    238 290 301 318 358

REICHENBACH, H. 79 81 83 123–124 184
    190 199 289–290 292
RESCHER, N. 146–147 354–356
REVZIN, I. I. 300–301
ROBISON, J. 146–147
ROSSER, B. 244
RUSSELL, B. 5 20 25–26 30 34–35 63 79
    81–84 92 101–102 114 125 199 211
    223 231 242 244 247 291
RYLE, G. 71 86 101 123 125 129–131
    152 192 225 291–292 372

SAUSSURE, F. DE 318
SCHAECHTER, J. 166 181
SCHLICK, M. 264 290
SCHOLZ, H. 33 35 43 54
SHANNON, C. 293 294 301
SHAUMYAN, S. K. 300 301
SKINNER, C. F. 177–178 296 325
SMART, H. R. 7 33
SØRENSEN, H. S. 100–103 375
STAAL, J. F. 347 348 352
STEVENS, K. N. 151
STÖHR, A. 199
STRAWSON, P. F. 84–85 150 152 192 194

STROLL, A. 257 279 285

TARSKI, A. 33 43 63 72 114 232 234 244
   248 252 256 275–278 285 292 318
TWADDELL, F. N. 327

URMSON, J. O. 192
USHENKO, A. 245

WAISMANN, F. 200
WEAVER, W. 298 301
WEINREICH, U. 182–184 201

WEITZ, M. 240
WHATMOUGH, J. 294
WHORF, B. L. 158
WIENER, N. 293–294 298 301
WIESNER, J. 293
WILLIAMS, B. A. O. 146–147
WITTGENSTEIN, L. 66 114 125 192 200
   223 292

YNGVE, V. H. 161 181 343

ZIFF, P. 142 151 168–173